continued from front flap

reform campaign failed, the
forced contemporary politicians to clarify
their attitudes towards the issues which
would dominate politics in the new
century. Their acceptance of class politics
was reluctant, and emerged only in the
course of a decade of debate.

Alan Sykes is a Lecturer in Modern
History at the University of St. Andrews

TARIFF REFORM IN
BRITISH POLITICS
1903-1913

TARIFF REFORM IN BRITISH POLITICS
1903–1913

Alan Sykes

CLARENDON PRESS · OXFORD

1979

Oxford University Press, Walton Street, Oxford OX2 6DP

OXFORD LONDON GLASGOW
NEW YORK TORONTO MELBOURNE WELLINGTON
KUALA LUMPUR SINGAPORE JAKARTA HONG KONG TOKYO
DELHI BOMBAY CALCUTTA MADRAS KARACHI
NAIROBI DAR ES SALAAM CAPE TOWN

Published in the United States by
Oxford University Press, New York

© *Alan Sykes 1979*

British Library Cataloguing in Publication Data

Sykes, Alan
Tariff reform in British politics, 1903-1913.
1. Tariff—Great Britain—History 2. Political parties—Great
Britain—History—20th century 3. Great Britain—Politics and
government—1901-1910 4. Great Britain—Politics and government—1910-1936
I. Title
382.7'0941   HF2046   79-40384

ISBN 0-19-822483-4

*Printed in Great Britain by
Western Printing Services Ltd, Bristol*

For
'Tasha, Tom, and Claire

Acknowledgements

The initial research for this book was made possible by the generosity of the travel and study leave facilities of the University of Adelaide, and continued with the aid of the travel fund of the University of St. Andrews.

I am grateful to the following for allowing me to quote material from books which they publish or in which they control the copyright: Bell and Hyman (K. Young, *Balfour*); Basil Blackwell (G. Searle, *The Quest for National Efficiency*); C. and T. Publications Ltd. (Randolph Churchill, *Winston S. Churchill*); Cassell Ltd. (Sir Austen Chamberlain, *Politics from Inside*; Peter Fraser, *Joseph Chamberlain*; and Sir Charles Petrie, *Life and Letters of Sir Austen Chamberlain*); The Hamlyn Group (W. S. Churchill, *Lord Randolph Churchill*); Hutchinsons Publishing Group Ltd. (B. E. C. Dugdale, *Arthur James Balfour*; Sir Charles Petrie, *Walter Long and his Times*; and Mackail and Wyndham, *Life and Letters of George Wyndham*); Macmillan, London and Basingstoke (Julian Amery, *Joseph Chamberlain and the Tariff Reform Campaign*; J. L. Garvin, *Life of Joseph Chamberlain*; Lady Victoria Hicks Beach, *Life of Sir Michael Hicks Beach*; and Neal Blewett, *The Peers, the Parties and the People*); Penguin Books Ltd. (R. Taylor, *Lord Salisbury*); Routledge and Kegan Paul Ltd. (Viscount Chilston, *Chief Whip* and *W.H. Smith*). Cambridge University Press kindly gave permission for the use of brief extracts from articles by E. Bristow on the Liberty and Property Defence League and Neal Blewett on Unionist Factionalism, as well as of material from my own article on the Confederacy, all of which appeared in the *Historical Journal*. Excerpts from the two books by Randolph Churchill mentioned above are reprinted in the United States by permission of Houghton Mifflin Company. Dr. R. A. Rempel allowed me to quote from his book, *Unionists Divided*.

Manuscript collections nevertheless remained my principal source of information. For access to these I am grateful to the Librarian, the University of Birmingham; the Curators of the Bodleian Library, Oxford; the British Library Board; Cambridge University Library; Churchill College, Cambridge; Guildford Muniments Room; the

House of Lords Record Office; the Institute of Commonwealth Studies; the Trustees of the National Library of Scotland; the Librarian, the University of Newcastle; the Public Record Office; the Scottish Record Office; the Librarian, the University of Sheffield Library; Strathclyde Regional Archives, and the West Sussex County Record Office. I am deeply indebted to the archivists and staff of all these, not only for their warm welcome and well-informed advice so generously given, but for their willingness to reply to all the inquiries which subsequently followed my attempts to decipher my notes.

I am grateful also to the following for allowing me to quote from documents whose copyright they control: the Baron Ailwyn; the Rt. Hon. Julian Amery, M.P.; the Hon. Betty Askwith; the Executors of the third Viscount Astor; the Duke of Atholl; the Marquess of Bath; Baron Balfour of Burleigh; the Beaverbrook Foundation; the Earl of Birkenhead; the University of Birmingham; the Viscount Bledisloe; the British Library Board; the Bryce Trustees; the Hon. Mark Bonham Carter; the Earl of Cawdor; the Viscount Chaplin; the Viscount Chilston; Mr. Winston Churchill, M.P.; Mr. George Clive; the Hon. Miss Daphne Courthope; the Viscount Cowdray; the Earl of Crawford; the Viscount Croft; the Earl of Cromer; the Earl of Derby; the Duke of Devonshire; the Executors of the fifth Earl of Durham; the Earl of Elgin; Mrs. Hubert Elliot; the Baron Egremont; Mr. George Lane Fox; Lady Elizabeth Gass; Sir William Gladstone, Bt.; the Viscount Harcourt; the Baron Harlech; Vice-Admiral Sir Ian Hogg; Mr. Lionel Jebb; Professor Anne Lambton; the Marquess of Lansdowne; Mr. W. S. Hardcastle on behalf of the Trustees of the late Viscount Lee of Fareham; the Viscount Long; the Earl of Malmesbury; Mr. H. G. Matheson, M.A.; Major and Mrs. J. H. Maxse; the Earl of Midleton; the Baron Monkbretton; the National Farmers Union; the Trustees of the National Library of Scotland; the Warden and Fellows of New College, Oxford; the Duke of Northumberland; the Earl of Onslow; the Viscount Pentland; Sir Malcolm Perks, Bt.; Mr. George Pretyman; the Baron Rankeillour; Mr. I. D. M. Reid; the Viscount Ridley; the Hon. Mrs. Iris Robson; the Earl of Rosebery; the Duchess of Roxburghe; the Duke of Rutland; the Marquess of Salisbury; the Earl of Selborne; Mrs. Ursula Slaghek; the editor of the *Spectator*; Mrs. Gay Stafford; Strathclyde Regional Archives; Sir Richard Tatton-Sykes, Bt.; Mr. A. F. Thompson; the Earl of Wemyss and March; Sir Philip Williams, Bt.; the Marquess of Willingdon; the Baron Willoughby de

Broke. I have tried to contact the owners of all copyright material. I hope that anyone whose copyright has been inadvertently infringed will accept my most sincere apologies.

I have been greatly helped in the writing of this book by the patience and good-humour of my colleagues, both past and present. Professor Norman Gash and Dr. Ruddock Mackay both read versions of it, and saved me from several mistakes. Those that remain are of course my own. Jenny Tilby helped with the research from Australia; Lynn Meloy and Liz Usher did the typing; Marjorie Robertson helped clear up the mess left by yet further alterations. My good friends Peter Burns, Tom Jaine, and Ricky Paice gave hospitality to the impoverished and encouragement to the dejected. Above all, I have benefited on countless occasions from the wisdom and foresight of Hugh Stretton who more than anyone made this book possible. To him and to Pat my warmest thanks. Finally I would like to thank my wife, Siân, sometime research assistant and frequent distraction, whose unfailing optimism did much to keep this project alive.

ALAN SYKES

St. Andrews. July 1978

Contents

Abbreviations

A.C.P.	Austen Chamberlain Papers
B.P.	Balfour Papers
B.L.P.	Bonar Law Papers
C.B.P.	Campbell-Bannerman Papers
H.G.P.	Herbert Gladstone Papers
J.C.P.	Joseph Chamberlain Papers
M.P.	Maxse Papers
R.P.	Rosebery Papers
R.C.P.	Lord Robert Cecil Papers
S.P.	Strachey Papers

Introduction

Few controversies in Edwardian politics aroused the passions of contemporaries as much as the debate upon tariff reform. The policy which Joseph Chamberlain announced in 1903 challenged the established doctrine of free trade under which Britain had enjoyed unprecedented prosperity and power, and threatened with dissolution the party system which had emerged from the Home Rule crisis of 1886. Within a year Chamberlain had captured the extra-parliamentary organization of the Unionist party and won the sympathies of the majority of its members. By 1907 the policy was accepted as the official policy of the party, and in the general election of January 1910 it formed the main plank of the Unionist campaign. Yet by 1913 the tariff reform movement was in ruins and the controversy all but forgotten as the parties returned to dispute Home Rule with all the exclusive bitterness of the past. Britain remained committed to free trade, and the party system survived with scarcely an indication that it had come close to collapse. Superficially, the tariff reform campaign was an interlude in a period which derived its essential character not from imperialism and social reform but from Ireland.

The dramatic unity of the tariff reform movement has always attracted historians. But the essentially biographical approach of the great majority of the studies of the Edwardian Unionist party necessarily presents a fragmentary picture of the political environment of the campaign and of the evolution of tariff reform as a policy. Neither the initial success nor the ultimate failure of tariff reform can be comprehended except in terms of a policy which adapted to the dictates of changing priorities within a party structure subjected to pressures to which it could make no adequate response. The tariff reform policy upon which Balfour led the Unionist party into the general election of January 1910 was not the policy which Chamberlain had announced at Glasgow in October 1903, nor was the election centred upon free trade, protection, or the commercial unification of the Empire by means of preferential tariffs. Rather, it was the product of a purely domestic crisis, and the tariff reform of January 1910 was directed towards essentially domestic ends.

The successive reorientations of tariff reform were achieved without any apparent break of continuity. For although Chamberlain's primary purpose in campaigning for tariff reform in 1903 was to take advantage of the colonial desire for reciprocal preference within the Empire, he presented tariff reform to the British electorate as a policy of radical domestic reform which could reduce unemployment, increase wages, and raise revenue for much needed schemes of social welfare. In so doing he widened the debate between 'protection' and 'free trade' as alternative tariff policies, to embrace the whole question of collectivism and individualism in the domestic as well as the international sphere. He linked tariff reform to social reform as two sides of the same comprehensive collectivist approach to Britain's problems of declining trade, declining power, and social distress, and contrasted this in ideological terms with the equally consistent, but in his view outmoded, combination of free trade and individualism.

In reality, the issue was never that simple. Some free traders, Unionist and Liberal alike, accepted Chamberlain's logical rigour and opposed his policies root and branch simply because they were collectivist. But the main opposition to tariff reform came from the official Liberal party with policies which combined free trade and collectivist social reform. Essentially pragmatic, this development of Liberal policies in the Edwardian period could nevertheless find theoretical justification in the ideas of 'New Liberalism'. Moreover, the ideological debate could never be kept distinct from electoral tactics. The central problem confronting both parties after 1884 was the definition of their attitude to the newly enfranchised masses, and thus of the image of the party to be presented to the electorate as a whole. In presenting tariff reform as he did, Chamberlain made the debate the culmination of a continuing discussion within both parties upon the nature of Liberalism and Conservatism which had its origins in the struggles over parliamentary reform in the 1880s.

Until the announcement in December 1885 that Gladstone was prepared to co-operate with the Irish party upon Home Rule, both major parties were preoccupied with the question of reform and its consequences. Within both parties, moreover, the issue aroused differences of opinion which in the long run threatened their solidarity. As a radical Chamberlain welcomed the reform settlement of 1884 as 'the greatest revolution this country has undergone',[1] and looked forward to an era of rapid social change directed by the left wing of the Liberal party. The Radical Programme, which appeared in the *Fortnightly Review* between 1883 and 1885, contained controversial proposals for land, rating, and taxation reform which, as Chamberlain noted, sounded 'the death knell of the *laissez-faire* system'.[2] Chamberlain's campaign on behalf of this 'unauthorised programme' alarmed his contemporaries by its denunciation of the rights of property, and by the demand that property should pay a 'ransom' for its security in the form of higher taxation to finance social reform.

Chamberlain spoke against a background of rising criticism of property, especially landed property, which culminated in the land taxes of Lloyd George's budget of 1909 and the Liberal 'Land Campaign' of 1913. Henry George's *Progress and Poverty* was first published in Britain in 1881, and George visited Britain in 1882 and again in 1884 and 1885 to publicize his ideas.[3] His campaign for the taxation of land values was, because of his influence upon the Liberal party, the most important aspect of an attack mounted upon the landed interest not only by George but also by Alfred Russel Wallace's Land Nationalisation Society, H. M. Hyndman's socialist Democratic Federation, and several more moderate Liberal pressure groups. In the early 1880s the lead, for the extremists at least, came from Ireland, where the demand for Home Rule was inextricably linked to agrarian discontent and both were inseparable from violence. Henry George's first visit to Britain was as special correspondent for Patrick Ford's *Irish World*, and both he and Hyndman maintained close contacts with the Irish Land League. Both reformers and conservatives saw the land problem as one of wider application. Until Gladstone's adoption of Home Rule, taking account of Irish nationalism and raising the constitutional problem, the campaign for constructive social reform embraced Ireland within a general British context. The theories propounded by George, Wallace, and Hyndman were, according to their authors, applicable to the crofting counties of Scotland or the large cities of England as much as to Ireland. From the other side, the Duke of Somerset considered that 'Irish ideas have demoralised British statesmen', and with his fellow landowners feared the spread of those same ideas to England.[4]

But the lines of defence were not clearly drawn. Chamberlain's 'unauthorised campaign' had not, by 1885, driven the Whigs from the Liberal party. On the Conservative side, Salisbury negotiated a settlement of parliamentary reform that surprised Chamberlain by its radicalism, and accepted the Agricultural Holdings Bill of 1883 with the argument that 'Freedom of Contract is not on a level with the Ten Commandments.'[5] On the other hand, the reform settlement alarmed his rank-and-file supporters, whilst his easy compromise with principle brought him into conflict with the Earl of Wemyss and his Liberty and Property Defence League which opposed all collectivist reform simply because it was collectivist.[6] There were also limits to Salisbury's flexibility which separated him equally clearly from Lord Randolph Churchill and the 'Tory Democrats' at the other end of the Conservative spectrum. Tory Democracy always remained, in Churchill's hands, more a matter of style than of substance and he produced no programme to disturb Conservative repose as Chamberlain disrupted the Liberals. Apart from his campaign to increase the power and independence of the National Union in 1883–4, Churchill also maintained cordial relations with Salisbury and supported his leadership of the party.

But the tensions within the Conservative party upon social reform, which finally tore it apart in 1903, were nevertheless present before the realignment of parties in 1886, and could remain latent only so long as the party remained in opposition, free from defining its attitudes by legislation. They became apparent whenever Churchill attempted a forward move, as in 1885 when he proposed a liberalization of party policy in order to attract the support of the discontented Whigs. Salisbury's reply, that greater liberalization would be part of the bargain when it came,[7] reflected not only his own preference for waiting upon events, but the basic difference between his attitude and that held by Churchill and Chamberlain of seizing the initiative and anticipating developments to control their direction. In reality, Chamberlain's campaigns of 1883–5, although intended to stir the masses, were not designed to whip up class hatred. Chamberlain shared with his contemporaries the fear that the masses would only listen to appeals to their material interests in class terms, and that class conflict would be the result of parliamentary reform. It was a belief which remained with him throughout his political career, and which did much to influence the presentation of tariff reform in 1903. But in 1903, as in the 1880s, Chamberlain saw his policies of collectivist reform not as an attack upon property or individual liberty, but as a means of putting 'the rights of property on the only firm and defensible basis' by remedying abuses before popular discontent forced more extreme solutions.[8]

His campaigns fulfilled the expectations of both sides of politics. 'The central question' of parliamentary reform was still, as Wemyss had noted in 1866, 'one of property'.[9] Those who feared democracy did so because 'the bestowal upon any class of a voting power disproportionate to their stake in the country must infallibly give to that class a power . . . of using taxation as an instrument of plunder . . .'[10] In the long run the questions of property, collectivist legislation, and taxation were more fundamental to British political development than the question of Home Rule around which the formal structure of politics polarized in 1886. The intrusion of Home Rule distorted that development by aligning both the Whigs and Chamberlain alongside the Conservatives in defence of the Union, and depriving the Liberals of genuine radical leadership for almost a generation. But it did not eliminate the problem of determining attitudes to social reform. After 1886, neither party could afford to ignore the question of collectivism, if only for tactical reasons, but nor could they afford an open split upon the subject as long as the Union was at stake. The debate continued within the new groupings of 'Unionists' and 'Separatists', constantly threatening to tear them apart.

In this respect the tariff reform campaign returned political debate to a long-standing problem and opened not new, but long-standing divisions. The result was to make fully apparent the distortion caused by the crisis of 1886. For, implicit in Chamberlain's approach, was a distinction between 'Unionism' and 'Conservatism' that gave scant recognition to the traditional role of the Conservative party as the party of resistance to change. Rather, Chamberlain's propaganda in favour of tariff reform and social reform suggested an inversion of the traditional relationship of the Conservative and Liberal parties, with the former becoming the party of change in opposition to 'reactionary radicals'. Chamberlain's radical Unionism, and his avowed pursuit of labour support for the Unionist party, rested upon the same pre-emptive assumptions as his policies of 1883–5 and upon the myth of 'Tory Democracy' created by Churchill, a myth which still enjoyed considerable support within the Conservative party itself.

In consequence, tariff reform could draw upon several sources of support from within the Edwardian Unionist party. Tariff reform attracted not only committed imperialists and social reformers alienated from the Liberal party by its anti-imperialism and relatively backward social policies, but ordinary Conservatives, afraid of 'socialism' but devoid of any alternative policy which might attract support. They received periodic reminders of their danger from the riots which swept through the West End of London in 1886 to the emergence of the Labour party itself as an independent parliamentary force after the general election of 1906. The threat of socialism gave tariff reform a new lease of life after it had been all but discredited by the shattering defeat of the Unionists in the 1906 general election, and goes at least some of the way towards explaining Blake's 'baffling' question, 'the persistence of the party in a cause that was so politically disastrous'.[11] After 1906, tariff reform was advocated with conviction to a party without policies. It was not quite the same tariff reform, and it was certainly not directed towards the same end, but it was an essential attribute of tariff reform that it was a single policy to solve a multitude of problems, and that it could respond to changing circumstances by changes of emphasis. It was the prospective domestic application of tariff reform as distinct from its imperial application that ensured the continued hold of the policy over the Unionist party in the Edwardian period.

The real significance of tariff reform lies not in the policies, for they were never tested, but in the debate itself, as a debate not upon imperial but upon domestic affairs. As the individuals and factions of both parties threaded their way through the pitfalls of Edwardian politics, they made decisions which ultimately decided the attitudes of their respective parties towards 'democracy' and collectivist reform. The failure of tariff reform was the failure, not only of an attempt to unify the Empire and to prevent the economic and military decline of Britain by imperial preference, but the failure of radical Unionism itself. By 1913 it was clear that the Liberals would be the party of change and the Conservatives the party of resistance in social as well as constitutional questions. Those who disagreed, the 'moderates' of the Liberal League and the 'radicals' of the Tariff Reform League, withdrew from political life. This clarification of the parties' respective attitudes was a long time coming. But social reform was a problem which could not even be considered until the Irish question was, at least temporarily, out of the way. Salisbury's prediction that taxation would be 'the field upon which the contending classes of this generation will do battle'[12] was, in the long run, prescient. But he was at least a generation too early.

I

The Witches' Cauldron

When Chamberlain launched his campaign for tariff reform in 1903 he reopened rather than originated the discussion of Britain's fiscal system. The origins of the movement for tariff reform stretched back to the Imperial Federation League and the Fair Trade League of the 1880s.[1] In their pursuit of protection, or 'Fair Trade', the Fair Trade League had, by the middle of that decade, gained considerable support especially from the rank and file of the Conservative party where the protectionist inclinations of the landed interest remained strong. Lord Randolph Churchill campaigned upon Fair Trade in 1885 with some success, and at the National Union Conference at Oxford in 1887 the Fair Traders succeeded in passing a protectionist resolution. But at that time it was one which Salisbury, despite his sympathy with the movement, dared not act upon for to do so would be to smash the alliance with the Liberal Unionists, risk defeat at the next election, and endanger or destroy the Union.

The sudden and complete collapse of the Fair Trade campaign was a demonstration of how far political priorities had changed since 1885. In Parliament, if not in the country, all other questions suddenly became subordinate to that of Ireland. But the party structure that emerged from the crisis of 1886 was far from stable. The two sides were not political parties in the proper sense, with a general consensus of opinion over a wide range of issues, a single hierarchy, leadership, and organization, nor even, until 1895, governmental coalitions, but *ad hoc* alliances produced by a particular crisis. Nor could the Irish question contain the totality of British, or even Liberal, politics for a sustained period. Other questions, particularly those concerned with social reform and imperial security, existed or arose upon which the post-1886 coalitions had no clearly defined attitude, still less an agreed policy. Their long-term existence was in no way guaranteed as the difficulties of maintaining the alliances produced tensions on both sides, tensions which became entangled in and exacerbated existing internal disputes.

The Conservatives, although the beneficiaries of 1886 in that they became the party of government, felt these tensions most acutely at first. Their new Whig allies found co-operation straightforward enough, but Chamberlain and his radical Unionist followers were uncomfortable. The party to which Chamberlain was bound in uneasy alliance was still dominated, especially in its upper echelons, by those landed interests whom he had so recently denounced. To the Conservatives Chamberlain was a dangerous radical, the advocate of the doctrine of ransom. Even on Ireland, beyond the simple preservation of the Union there was little in common between the allies. In the new situation after 1886, however, the Conservatives could not afford to take advantage of Chamberlain's vulnerable position to destroy his influence. He was essential not only because of his undoubted abilities or the few votes he commanded in the House of Commons, vital as these were, but because of his reputation in the country.

English domestic politics after 1886, as before, were contained for both parties in the consequences of the extension of the franchise and the need to integrate the newly enfranchised working classes into the political system. Chamberlain could not deny his radical past, and despite his alliance with the Conservatives had no wish to do so. He continued to believe that an active programme of constructive reform was 'necessary in England and Ireland alike, and thus continued to agitate within the Unionist alliance for constructive measures. Only such a policy, moreover, would enable Chamberlain to maintain his hold over his Liberal Unionist followers in the constituencies who had not, by supporting the Union, abandoned their Liberalism. But the effect of Chamberlain's pressure within the Unionist alliance was to give considerable reinforcement to Churchill and the cause of Tory Democracy, intensifying the tensions which already existed within the Conservative party on domestic reform. Such points of contact made the working of the alliance in some respects easier, but they also made the potential disruption more serious.

The divisions were exacerbated also by the dichotomy between the reality of the Conservative party's situation in the late nineteenth century and the mythology that the party leaders, and in particular Disraeli, had created around it. The reality of the situation was that the party was becoming less and less the exclusive party of the land, and increasingly the party of property in general. This was true both in parliamentary and electoral terms but especially the latter. The urban and suburban middle classes, like the Whigs in Parliament, were becoming alarmed at the growing radicalism of the Liberal party under Gladstone's leadership, and the threat to property its attitudes appeared to contain. But as the Conservative party attracted propertied Liberals into its ranks, so also it absorbed their dislike of social reform which interfered with property rights and of the higher taxation which these reforms might entail. In many ways such tendencies did no more than reinforce already held prejudices, especially those concerning the rights of landowners. But this was not the image the Conservatives had of themselves, nor was it a face which appeared likely to win many elections in the new democracy. The mythology presented an alternative picture of the party as the party of social reform by state intervention, and played upon the legend of Disraeli, Young England, and the Factory Reform movement. The dichotomy between myth and reality, between positive and negative responses to democracy, constantly threatened to destroy the fragile structure that was the Unionist alliance, and the schism that resulted from Chamberlain's tariff reform movement in 1903 had its origins in these early basic differences.

The conflict was apparent from the first. Hartington's refusal to co-operate in a coalition government which excluded Chamberlain forced Salisbury to include Churchill in a purely Conservative administration. But far from discarding Tory Democracy in the face of his colleagues' suspicion, Churchill produced the fullest and most explicit statement of that doctrine at Dartford on 2 October 1886 and elaborated further at Bradford later in the month. He then faced, somewhat despairingly, the task of converting the cabinet to his views. 'I am afraid,' he wrote to Salisbury on 6 November, 'it is an idle schoolboy's dream to suppose that Tories can legislate . . . They can govern and make war and increase taxation and expenditure *à merveille* but legislation is not their province in a democratic constitution . . .'[2] What was lacking was not the ability but the will. Salisbury stated the alternative view of the role of the party, its composition and its future, with blunt clarity:

The Tory party is composed of very varying elements, and there is merely trouble and vexation of spirit in trying to make them work together. I think the 'classes and the dependents of class' are the strongest ingredients in our composition, but we have so to conduct our legislation that we shall give some satisfaction to both classes and masses. This is specially difficult with the classes—because all legislation is rather unwelcome to them as tending to disturb a state of things with which they are satisfied. It is evident, therefore, that we must work at less speed and at a lower temperature than our opponents.[3]

Compromise was impossible, and Churchill resigned in December. His resignation revealed the fundamental weakness in the negative Conservatives' position, their own conviction that they could not govern the country on a negative basis after the extension of the franchise. Beach thus feared that the government would be unable to carry on since Chamberlain and Churchill would unite to oppose it 'in all matters which formerly divided Radicals from Conservatives . . . The mere "patronage" of Hartington and Goschen would be no use against this. I confess to much doubt whether the country *can* be governed nowadays by persons holding opinions which you and I should call even moderately conservative.'[4] Again Hartington refused to come to the rescue and the Conservatives were forced back upon Beach's 'irreducible minimum' for continuing in office, the inclusion of Goschen as Chancellor of the Exchequer.

But the threat from the combined forces of Chamberlain and Churchill did not materialize. Chamberlain's immediate reaction to Churchill's resignation, 'The Government is doomed, and I suspect we may have to reform parties on a new basis',[5] was quickly followed by more sober second thoughts. Chamberlain was too much a party politician to remain for long outside the main organizations of political power despite his disruptive career. But confronted by what he regarded as a reassertion of reactionary Toryism he became increasingly restive, and after Churchill's resignation made overtures towards his former Liberal colleagues.

The Round Table Conference that resulted revealed, as Chamberlain apparently expected, that there was no way back to his former party. Nor did the threat of secession produce any results. During 1887 Salisbury made no concessions on policy and Chamberlain's position became impossible. He quarrelled with the government on its Irish Land Bill and its wish to outlaw the Irish National League, Liberal Unionist M.P.s revolted against the government's Irish policy, and Chamberlain's Liberal Unionist supporters in Birmingham condemned coercion. Chamberlain pursued with Churchill the possibility of a new 'central' or 'national' party which neither Hartington nor Rosebery was willing to lead, and by August had quarrelled with Churchill himself on Irish policy. Finally, the government came to the rescue of its distressed ally and whisked him away from politics to discuss fisheries in America. For Chamberlain and for radical Unionism there was no place in politics in the first years of the Unionist alliance.

Chamberlain returned to a situation that had changed and was still changing for the better. The Conservatives were not heedless of his warnings about the constituencies, reinforced as they were by by-election losses. The first major sign of the new progressive domestic policy was the change of heart which Henry Chaplin professed in introducing the Allotments Bill, a measure he had previously fought with determination. But the real breakthrough from Chamberlain's point of view was the public conversion of Salisbury, who seemed to have realized by January 1888 that something more than the bare minimum of concessions was needed to keep the alliance alive. Speaking at Liverpool he commented on the difficulties the collapse of the two-party system created for the government, and warned his supporters to expect a greater liberalization of policy in the future. From this point onwards a working compromise was achieved, although ripples from constituency disputes continued to disturb relations between the leaders for some years to come. By the end of the decade Chamberlain had moved from the defensive to the attack, no longer trying to wring sufficient concessions from the Conservatives to satisfy his radical supporters, but to make the Unionist party the spearhead of social reform and a serious competitor for the working-class vote.

Nevertheless, Chamberlain's position was only tenable because of the latitude allowed him to revive old Tory democratic legends as a basis on which to build his creed of radical, reforming Unionism. Chamberlain argued, with some justification, that the interest, at least of English electors, was social reform, a field in which the Unionists could campaign as, or more, effectively than the Liberals because of the traditional Conservative advocacy of state intervention in contrast to the Liberals' Cobdenite past.[6] In taking this line, however, Chamberlain threatened to resurrect the tensions which had brought about Churchill's resignation. Many members of the Conservative party did not see the new trends towards collectivism in the same optimistic light as Chamberlain, even if they did, theoretically, put both major parties on an equal footing of preparedness, and had no wish to see the Unionist party as the vanguard of radicalism. 'The extension of the suffrage has brought us face to face with the most grave possibilities', wrote W. H. Smith:

It has made the extreme Radicals masters of the Liberal party, and men support a policy now from which they would have shrunk with horror ten years ago . . . Men who are strictly honest in their transactions with their neighbours have come to regard Parliament as an instrument by which a transfer of rights and property may equitably be made from the few to the many . . .

It was a point of view with which Salisbury not unnaturally agreed. 'We are in a state of bloodless civil war. No common principles, no respect for common institutions or traditions, unite the various groups of politicians who are struggling for power. To loot somebody or something is the common object under a thick varnish of pious phrases.'[7]

But a common aversion to 'predatory socialism' brought Salisbury and Smith no closer to a solution of their problems. Chamberlain did not differ from them in the ultimate objective of preventing an onslaught on property rights, only on the best means of their defence, and the explanation he gave in 1894 for wishing to fight on a constructive programme of social reform held good for any election:

The intermediates—the men who hold the balance of elections—are disgusted and frightened . . . frightened at the projects of confiscation which are in the air and found expression at the Trade Union Congress the other day. If I am right, they want to be assured that the Unionists will take up the question of Social Reform in a Conservative spirit, and meet the unreasonable and dangerous proposals of the extremists with practical proposals of their own.[8]

The danger which both groups of Unionists, conservative and radical, faced was the emergence of class politics:

The working classes are not divided on party lines as absolutely as the middle and upper classes [wrote Chamberlain], and my experience is that very large numbers do not actually make up their minds till the time of election comes round and are then very much influenced by the issues presented to them at the moment . . . If Unionism or Conservatism gives them the promise of better results they will come over in large numbers and turn a small into a sweeping majority.[9]

His purpose in the short run was to win that shifting vote and thus the election, but in the long run it was to make this working-class support for Unionsim permanent, in effect integrating the working classes into the existing political structure by dividing them on existing party lines as other classes were divided. In so doing he would prevent the alternative line of development, the adaptation of parties to class feelings and the consequent realignment of politics to reflect class divisions. Salisbury's doubts remained both as to the merits of constructive proposals themselves and their acceptability to many long-standing Conservatives. 'I fear', he wrote to Balfour, 'that these social questions are destined to break up our party; but why incur the danger before the necessity has arrived—and while the party may still be useful to avert Home Rule.'[10] But it was not a convincing reply to Chamberlain's tactical arguments.

The Unionist party as it existed in 1895 was one which had its public image, as expressed in its policies, defined by Chamberlain more than by any other single politician. In the struggle on the party's attitude to 'democracy' since 1884, Churchill's resignation, however disastrous to his career, was not in the long run detrimental to Tory Democracy. The party was, as Chamberlain intended it to be, a 'national' party, appealing to the centre on a policy of safe practical reform. Ironically, this was not followed up by legislation after the 1895 victory. Chamberlain's decision to take office as Colonial Secretary, his increasing involvement in imperial federation, and the developing crisis in South Africa culminating in the war of 1899–1902, gave him little time to pursue his radical domestic interests. Domestic legislation after 1896 consisted of little more than measures in aid of the Church and clerical education, and rating relief for agriculture, all old Tory causes. Chamberlain found himself, to all appearances not unwillingly, making war and increasing expenditure '*à merveille*'.

The Unionists did not immediately have to pay the price which should, according to Chamberlain's arguments, have followed this neglect of domestic reform. Imperialism and the timing of the 1900 general election were largely responsible, but so too was the condition of the Liberal party. By 1887, large sections of the party were chafing against Gladstone's apparent obsession with Ireland and working to promote policies for English social reform. Amongst these one small group of younger Liberals, centred around Arthur Acland, maintained links with the Fabians and wished these policies to be collectivist in content.

This group, the embryo of the Liberal Imperialists, was supported by Rosebery and looked at first to Morley on the front bench for leadership. But as in the Unionist party, the debate upon the party's future social policies revealed a wide divergence of opinion between the individualist 'old radicals' and the new collectivists. Morley, their chosen leader, was typical of Gladstonian indifference to any new social departure. 'Do the mass of the electors (Ireland apart) want more than the transformed Tories are willing to give them?' he asked. 'The Tories are able to make the fear of Irish Home Rule an excuse for any amount of transformation. The election of '85 seems to show that the constituencies won't go very far or very fast. Ergo, I doubt whether the time is ripe for new party programmes.'[11] In the field of domestic politics, the Gladstonian leadership was as negative on the Liberal side as Salisbury on the Unionist, and, as always, Ireland blocked the way. Under these circumstances, the group turned slowly but increasingly towards Rosebery whose work in association with the Webbs as chairman of the L.C.C. made him appear the most likely successor to Chamberlain in the field of constructive radicalism and who, by birth, wealth, and brilliance, was the most rapidly rising star in the Liberal firmament.

In default of a lead from Gladstone the initiative passed to the rank and file. There, however, the collectivists had far less influence than the old leaders of traditional sectional radicalism, and the policies which emerged from the National Liberal Federation Conference at Newcastle in 1891, the 'Newcastle Programme', were an accumulation of old particularist grievances rather than a restatement of fundamental Liberal principles. As such the programme was the antithesis of all that the Liberal Imperialist group stood for. It was nevertheless easily accepted by Gladstone whose commitment to Ireland had never involved the scrapping of traditional causes, but only a reordering of priorities. For all its inadequacies, most of which only became apparent during the ministry itself, the Newcastle Programme was that upon which Gladstone took office in 1892. Nor were Rosebery and the Liberal Imperialists particularly vocal in their criticisms at this time, however much they condemned the programme later.

Nevertheless, dissension was the predominant characteristic of the unfortunate Liberal administration of 1892–5. Against the wishes of the majority of his cabinet, Gladstone insisted that Home Rule should have pride of place and the rest of the Newcastle Programme was temporarily shelved. Conflict also broke out immediately between Rosebery and Harcourt over the conduct of foreign and imperial affairs. By September 1892 Rosebery already thought of resignation, asking Gladstone whether it was 'worthwhile temporarily to bridge over a difference of policy so deep and so conscientious as that between Harcourt and myself'.[12] Harcourt and Rosebery quarrelled over Egypt in January 1893, and were again on opposite sides in December in the dispute in the cabinet over Spencer's naval estimates. Gladstone's resignation on these same estimates, and the intrigues for the succession which preceded it, brought the conflict to a peak and made harmonious co-operation between Harcourt and Rosebery impossible. In February 1894 Rosebery saw their disagreement in far wider terms than foreign policy, to encompass 'almost every other question'. This was brought out particularly by Harcourt's budget of 1894 which reopened the divisions within the party on social policy.

Rosebery strongly criticized Harcourt's proposals to 'woo the masses' by introducing higher direct taxation of the rich in the form of 'death duties', on the grounds that the masses had hitherto shown little enthusiasm for the Liberal party, and that Harcourt's policy would lead to class politics. Harcourt, in reply, condemned Rosebery's élitism which would leave the Liberal party 'appearing as the defenders of fiscal privileges and exemptions of the wealthy which are universally condemned'. Nor could he accept Rosebery's other criticisms of his policy. Rosebery's 'desire to avert the "cleavage of classes"' was 'natural, but . . . too late. "The horizontal division of parties" was certain to come as a consequence of household suffrage. The thin end of the wedge was inserted and the cleavage is expanding more and more every day.'[13] The question was central to the direction the party was to take in the future, to the support it would seek, and to the public identity it wished to present. Harcourt's readiness to accept class politics, his willingness to solve his revenue problems by higher direct taxation, and his anti-imperialism were based on a conception of Liberalism which differed fundamentally from Rosebery's. But neither Harcourt nor Rosebery gave much attention at the time to the crucial issues involved. Harcourt's injection of 'socialism' into Liberal fiscal policy foreshadowed 'new Liberalism' and the later 'socialism' of Lloyd George, but Harcourt himself made no attempt to link fiscal policy with social reorganization. In the 1895 general election he campaigned almost exclusively on the old radical issue of temperance. Similarly, Rosebery gave no indication of how to prevent the disaffection of the masses other than to deprive them of any political outlet by ignoring them. He too turned to an old radical cause in 1895, the House of Lords. Such a programme demonstrated no distinctive Roseberyite policy to contrast either with the Gladstonian past or with Harcourt's Liberalism. Rather, as Peter Stansky has commented, 'It postponed the decision as to what direction the party would take . . . it was the most conservative step forward the Liberal party could take'.[14]

The Liberals paid dearly for this failure to work out their social and imperial policies, not simply in electoral terms, but in the disintegration of their party and their coalition. To the despair of the Liberal Imperialists, Gladstone's suppression of the Newcastle Programme in favour of Home Rule in 1892 finally provoked the Fabians to advocate the separation of Labour from the Liberal party in their pamphlet 'To your tents Oh Israel' in November 1893. The Independent Labour Party sprang from other, deeper, causes of labour dissatisfaction, but the Fabians' action was symptomatic of the disillusionment of the collectivist left. Nor was the sacrifice rewarded. With Gladstone's resignation the alliance with the Irish crumbled. Rosebery's manifest lack of sympathy with Home Rule appeared in almost his first public statement as leader when he declared that Home Rule would not be conceded until 'England as the predominant partner' had accepted it. Attempts to pass this off as an electoral truism could not disguise the extent of Rosebery's admission. The Irish, like Labour, went their own way, and reverted to opportunism, revealing new sources of Liberal–Irish tension. By 1896, after the Irish had supported the Unionist Education Act, Wemyss Reid reported to Rosebery that all the M.P.s he met regarded Home Rule as dead.[15] The increasing importance of the South African crisis, Rosebery's desire to recreate Liberalism around an imperial policy which involved dropping Home Rule, and the extreme anti-imperialism of the Irish party all combined to widen the rift between the former allies until co-operation was rendered impossible.

In the closing months of his administration Rosebery laid increasing emphasis on the rejection of the past and the 'worn out and effete Newcastle programme'.[16] After the defeat of 1895 he was even more ready for new pastures. 'We have offended every interest by the Newcastle programme,' he wrote to Ripon, '. . . but there was a more general and deeply rooted cause—Mr. G.'s general programme since 1880.'[17] In 1895 Rosebery already viewed its attitude to foreign affairs and the Empire as the cardinal fault of Gladstonian Liberalism, and

Home Rule and the split of 1886 as symptoms of wider disagreements. But despite his approval of the 'purge' of the party effected by the 1895 defeat, he made little attempt to reconstruct the party afresh on the basis of Liberal Imperialism, still less on a Liberal Imperialism based on collectivist social policies. Instead, he seized the opportunity offered by Gladstone's intervention in politics to condemn the Armenian massacres in the autumn of 1896 to resign the leadership. His action, whether for personal reasons or as a tactical move to force the party to accept him back on his own terms, postponed the complete disruption of the Liberal party for the next two years.

The Liberals could not, however, avoid for ever a discussion of their political purpose. Under Harcourt's leadership they continued to seek refuge in opposition, allowing the initiative to come from the government. But events in South Africa forced the Liberals to face the fact that they had, in the absence of Gladstone, neither policies nor a leadership capable of formulating them. Controversy began in earnest in the autumn of 1898 with Rosebery's re-entry into the political arena. Kitchener's occupation of the Sudan and the confrontation with the French at Fashoda created a peculiarly difficult situation for the Liberal party, responsible as it was for the Grey declaration. Harcourt, who had disapproved of Grey's statement at the time, disapproved with equal intensity of Kitchener's expedition, but his initial response was to avoid the issue. Rosebery, however, speaking at Epsom on 12 October, identified the party completely with government policy, claiming it as 'the policy of the last government deliberately adopted and sustained by the present government...'.[18] Even before Rosebery's speech, Morley and Harcourt had considered their resignations from the front bench. Rosebery's renewed activity as the apostle of Liberal Imperialism forced them, as the leading spokesmen of the opposite, Little England, school of thought, to respond or withdraw. Like Rosebery they did both, withdrawing to fight the better from an independent position. The schism, when it came, was initiated deliberately by the Little England section of the party.[19] Morley's speech at Brechin on 17 January 1899 was the first shot in this campaign. In February, on Morley's motion condemning the attack on the Sudan, thirteen Liberals voted against their party and their new leader, Campbell-Bannerman, in support of the government.

The opening of the war in South Africa could not but intensify these divisions. From the Stanhope amendment in October 1899 to

those of Cawley and Dillon in January 1902, every attempt to criticize
the government demonstrated Liberal disunity. Campbell-Bannerman
was, in general, tolerant of these internal splits, and consciously tried
to pursue a central line during the war to placate Rosebery and, above
all, Asquith. But his real sympathies inclined him increasingly towards
the Little Englanders. After June 1901, when he denounced the government for using 'methods of barbarism' in its attempts to end the war,
the rift between him and the Liberal Imperialists was complete.

Henceforth the Liberal Imperialists found themselves opposed not
only to the Little Englanders but to the centre of their party and its
official leadership. Asquith came out openly as an imperialist opponent
of Campbell-Bannerman, inspired a dinner in his own honour as the
Liberal Imperialist response, and played a prominent part in the
organization of the Liberal Imperialist autumn campaign.[20] The
invitation of Liberal Unionists to the Asquith dinner indicated what
was meant by the restoration of the party to its pre-1886 condition.
Campbell-Bannerman managed to extract a unanimous vote of confidence at a meeting at the Reform Club on 9 July, but only in return
for promising the Liberal Imperialists 'full and unfettered liberty . . . to
express and act upon our honestly entertained convictions . . .'[21]

The effect of the Asquith dinner was considerably reduced by the
sudden intrusion of Rosebery who, on 17 July, published a letter
attacking the Reform Club compromise and urging an open split in
view of the 'irreconcilable division of opinions' within the party.[22] This
he reinforced by a speech to the City Liberal Club on 19 July, the very
day of the Asquith dinner, in which he demanded a complete break
with the policies the party had pursued since 1880. The end of the
Irish alliance and the commitment to Home Rule, and reunion with the
Liberal Unionists, the 'clean slate', were all ideas which Rosebery had
expressed, generally in private, since 1894–5. In his speech to the City
Liberals he finally gave the lead his followers demanded, and went
further than ever before. The proposal that the Liberal Unionists
should rejoin a remodelled imperialist Liberal party, together with the
hint that if the Liberal party did not reform 'some party will create
itself',[23] contained the threat of a Liberal Imperialist secession. Asquith
was more moderate, and reiterated his commitment to the Liberal
party. But in substance he agreed with Rosebery.

Rosebery, for once, was prepared both to lead and organize. He
persuaded the Imperial Liberal Council, set up by Sir Robert Perks in

April 1900, to become the Liberal (Imperial) League and to set up a fund of £10,000 to sponsor candidates of its own, and on 16 December, at Chesterfield, delivered his most important speech of the dispute. Announced well in advance and preceded by careful preparations, the speech was a great political occasion such as might precede the launching of a new party. On the immediate issue of the war Rosebery was conciliatory, in favour of a negotiated peace. But the bulk of his speech was devoted to a reassertion of his demand for a reconstructed Liberal party with a 'clean slate'. He was also determined to follow up the triumph he achieved by the event. In the preface to the printed edition of his speech he called for 'spadework' on behalf of the Chesterfield policy and began moves for the formation of a new organization for this purpose, the Liberal League. This was founded on 24 February and launched publicly two days later. In March, after considerable dispute, the L.I.L. agreed to dissolve and to recommend its members to join the new body.

The emphasis given to the 'clean slate' in the Chesterfield speech revealed the real nature of the divisions within the Liberal party. Liberal Imperialism was never exclusively, or even mainly, concerned with South Africa, even though events there provoked the final split. The primary interest of many of its most prominent supporters, including Asquith and Haldane, remained domestic issues, the neglect of which had led them initially to question the prominence Gladstone gave to Ireland. It was to domestic politics and to Ireland that the Liberal Imperialists returned the discussion during the autumn of 1901. Their approach too remained influenced by the Fabians and moderately collectivist. For some time prior to the Asquith dinner Haldane had been meeting the Webbs, and by early July he had decided with them 'to elaborate, if we can, a real programme of social reforms'.[24] Asquith, at his dinner, spoke mostly about social questions, the difference being that now collectivism was infused with imperialism. Asquith thus saw domestic reform 'not as a moral question . . . but as a question of social and imperial efficiency'.[25] Speaking at Liverpool on 14 February 1902, Rosebery widened the breach on Ireland, and made it abundantly clear that this and efficiency were the real subjects of the dispute, not the rights and wrongs of the war in South Africa. On 21 February, in reply to a challenge from Campbell-Bannerman to clarify his position *vis-à-vis* the Liberal party, Rosebery proclaimed his 'definite separation'.

The Chesterfield policy was an expression of a particular conception of the Liberal party and its function based upon the rejection of 'Mr. G.'s whole policy since 1880'. Gladstonian Home Rule was condemned as a particular aspect of the general Little Englander approach to overseas affairs and because, in practice, it handed the party over to the sectional extremists of the N.L.F. The party, in the eyes of the Liberal Imperialists, had failed because it appealed only to an association of self-interested minorities, had lost touch with the majority, and had ceased to be 'what . . . it has always been and must really be . . . the national party'.[26] The political role of the Liberal party as a 'national party', a party which 'looked at the interests of the community from the point of view of the community as a whole',[27] was mediatory, to contain all classes and thus prevent 'the ultimate division of parties into the Haves and the Have-nots'.[28] Liberal Imperialists' concern for social reform stemmed, as did Chamberlain's, from a desire to attach the newly enfranchised masses to the established political system. The corollary of their willingness to include working-class M.P.s in the Liberal party was hostility to independent Labour representation. They were, however, even more concerned at the defection of the middle classes to Unionism, and the apparent diminution of the threat from organized Labour in the 1890s gave the Liberal Imperialists a further push in a middle-class direction. Liberal Imperialism, following Rosebery's desire to reconstruct a 'new party which will embody all the elements which existed before 1886', meant, in effect, making the Liberal party once again palatable to the middle classes by restoring its imperial content.[29]

'Efficiency' provided the Liberal Imperialists with the conceptual means necessary to accomplish this object. It was explicitly collectivist, subordinating the individual to the state, but at the same time prepared to use the resources of the state to improve the efficiency of the individual. The Liberal Imperialists gave considerable prominence to the creation of a new positive Liberalism based on state intervention to replace the traditional Liberal concern for freedom from interference. They considered this part of the Liberal mission to have been accomplished and were not, in Fowler's words, 'prepared to go on munching the dry biscuit of an old political economy'.[30] In this respect also their analysis of the future trend of social reform resembled Chamberlain's. At the same time, however, the emphasis on reform for national rather than sectional or class purposes mitigated the otherwise discouraging impact of such collectivism on potential middle-class adherents. As a political cry efficiency was particularly effective in 1902 when recruiting for the war had demonstrated the unfitness of a large proportion of the population to carry arms, and the conduct of the war had exposed the unpreparedness of the armed services and the administration. The call for national efficiency echoed a mood of anxiety which had been growing throughout the 1890s and which reached its peak during the war. Initially these fears were largely economic, a continuation of the alarm raised by the Fair Trade League at Britain's apparent inability to meet the competition of her commercial rivals, particularly Germany and the U.S.A., in international and even home and colonial markets. To a lesser extent these fears were reflected also in the growing weight of evidence that even after a century of industrialization the country could still not provide a decent living for its people. Both economic and social 'inefficiency' had alarming implications for national security in an apparently hostile world. The failure of imperial Britain to defeat a handful of ill-trained farmers suggested that the inadequacy was all-embracing. Efficiency provided an all-embracing remedy, to make 'the condition of national fitness equal to the demands of our Empire—administrative, parliamentary, commercial, educational, physical, moral, naval and military fitness . . .'[31] The war brought all the strands of Britain's inadequacy together: 'In the rookeries and slums which still survive, an imperial race cannot be reared.'[32]

For all its apparent radicalism, however, efficiency as preached by the Liberal League was a conservative concept. In part this was a by-product of its concern for the middle classes and of the nature of League membership. The League did not consist of a dedicated group of collectivists set on thinking out a new positive creed for Liberalism but a cross-section of the Liberal party at large who had joined for widely differing reasons. The Webbs associated themselves with the League in the hope that it would prove the forerunner of that Fabian-inspired Liberal party that they and Haldane had aspired to since the late 1880s. On the other hand, Perks and his Nonconformist sympathizers supported Rosebery partly from a missionary interest in empire, and partly to free themselves from the Irish alliance. On social reform and state intervention Webb and Perks were almost polar opposites. Perks did indeed recognize the need for social reform but he drew a sharp distinction between the Methodist understanding of this and that of the Fabians:

I don't think that a communistic, as distinguished from an individualistic, social programme will attract the City voters.

I have always felt that one of the reasons why Toryism has got hold of the middle classes and the artisans is that as these classes have prospered and acquired their houses they have inclined to the Conservative party because they dread the doctrines which Sidney Webb thinks would prove so popular.[33]

Perks saw the League as an exclusive club. He disagreed with Rosebery's wish to use the £10,000 fund of the L.I.L. to sponsor candidates on the grounds that the League did not want such candidates: 'There are scores of wealthy young Liberals who will stand if you lead.'[34] The Liberal League, whose finances he handled, similarly bore the stamp of wealth: £5,300 of the League's funds came from just six wealthy men, and ordinary subscriptions were not accepted.[35] Weetman Pearson thus explained his promise of £1,000 to the League: 'Its existence is essential to the Liberal party if it is going to once more include in it the men of weight and substance who have been alientaed from it in recent years.'[36] With such backing the League had little room for manœuvre in pursuit of Fabianism.

But there was also an intellectual failure. The success of the Chesterfield policy as a solution to both national and Liberal ills depended upon its detailed application. Their past experience had given the Liberal Imperialists a deep distrust of programmes and they sought by the idea of efficiency to avoid details and commitments. But efficiency was in the last resort a programmatic concept. Webb, who dreamed of 'a dozen opposition planning committees',[37] was rapidly disillusioned by the lack of interest of the League leadership. On social questions to which they themselves directed attention, such as housing, the land, unemployment, the Liberal Imperialists proved disappointing apostles of a new Liberalism based on 'measures of construction'.[38] Haldane's policy of the municipal ownership of land to be let out to tenants,[39] as distinct from the Unionist policy of occupying ownership aided by state credit, and his desire for the 'systematic organisation of the means of employment'[40] did foreshadow later Liberal legislation, but they could not be called Liberal Imperialist policies. In other respects Liberal Imperialists appeared as, or more, conservative than their Little England rivals. They opposed the Trade Union demand for the reversal of the Taff Vale judgement, and on two questions to which they attached special importance, education and temperance, they sacrificed efficiency to political opportunism.[41]

By their failure to work out the details of their policy the Liberal Imperialists avoided both the complications of efficiency as a concept and the disruptive effects which such details might have had upon the League. Efficiency was never intended by most of its adherents to involve a fundamental restructuring of economic relationships either between classes at home or between the component parts of the Empire overseas. Rosebery defended the Chesterfield policy as a statement of moderate Liberalism and the formation of the League by the need to prevent the proscription of the wealthier moderate section of the party by the radicals. Even Perks, involved as he was with setting up a formal organization, was reluctant to leave the security of the party. 'I think', he told Rosebery, 'we should issue something to make it plain that we are, and mean to remain, Liberals . . .'[42] More significantly, Asquith rejected all thought of separation from official Liberalism.[43] Both publicly and privately Rosebery accepted this position. He could not have done otherwise without further support from outside the Liberal party.

This, however, was a possibility. Within the existing division of parties efficiency was a distinctly cross-party concept whether as Fabian collectivism or as moderate Liberalism. In the former aspect, the 'Co-efficients', an offshoot of the Fabian society which included both Liberals and Liberal Unionists, provided a cross-party think-tank to develop policies.[44] From within the League there were voices calling upon Rosebery to challenge Campbell-Bannerman for the leadership or else to form a new party altogether.[45] Rosebery's independent stance led to rumours of a ministry of all the talents formed from both major parties from the very beginning of the war. After the Chesterfield speech a new 'business-like' coalition, perhaps with Rosebery and Chamberlain as its strong men, was once again aired.[46] In their avowed aim of capturing the middle classes and the 'centre' the Liberal Imperialists sought much the same support for the Liberal party as Chamberlain sought for the Unionists. Rosebery himself, at the inaugural meeting of the Liberal League on 24 February 1902, noted 'that in fact there was little to separate him from the Liberal Unionists, more especially if they pursued a Liberal domestic policy'[47] as Chamberlain intended them to do. Moreover, Rosebery and Chamberlain spoke the same language on imperialism: both appealed to the same muted concept of racial superiority; both found in the Empire evidence of a 'Divine Mission'; both vaguely hinted at economic benefits to be gained from 'pegging out claims for the future'. But above all both the Liberal and Unionist imperialists thought of the Empire in terms of the white self-governing colonies and of the problems of empire as the problems of imperial federation. Both at times saw an impending crisis in imperial relations and the need for action before the Empire broke into fragments, although following the collapse of the Imperial Federation League Rosebery was more inclined to let sleeping dogs lie.[48] But when Chamberlain made his appeal for imperial unification by means of preferential tariffs in 1903 the ground had already been prepared by more than two decades of imperialist propaganda, much of it emanating from Liberal sources.

The possibility of a realignment of parties, which existed throughout the second half of the 1890s, was increased at the turn of the century by the friction which imperialism produced within the Unionist party. As Salisbury aged, so Chamberlain's pre-eminence within the Unionist cabinet grew, a tendency furthered by the concentration of politics around imperial issues. The only real resistance to Chamberlain came from Beach who, as Chancellor of the Exchequer, found himself obliged to finance 'forward' policies. By the end of the decade Beach thought that resources were becoming rapidly exhausted. Successive Chancellors, both Unionist and Liberal, had for some time found difficulty in raising the required revenue within the existing framework of taxation. As early as 1887 Goschen had emphasized that the basis of taxation was too narrow, a complaint he reiterated in 1889.[49] But the doctrine that indirect taxation should fall on only a few items of common consumption and that the income tax should be kept low as a wartime reserve precluded extension in any direction. Goschen in fact reduced the income tax in 1887 to aid manufacturers to overcome the depression. His subsequent transfer to the Admiralty revealed the real extent of the problem when Goschen the parsimonious Chancellor became, at the Admiralty, Goschen the spendthrift, the bane of his successor.[50]

Throughout his tenure of the Exchequer Beach pleaded for economy from the great spending departments and particularly from the War Office whose inefficiency he denounced in terms reminiscent of Rosebery, and from Chamberlain who, as the exponent of expense both at home and abroad, was the main target.[51] The budget of 1899, for Beach his last peacetime budget, showed matters reaching a crisis even before the cost of the South African war made the financial situation desperate. Beach anticipated a deficit of some £4 million:

But this is no temporary emergency—it is the result of continuous increase of expenditure, which will grow, rather than diminish, in future years. To suspend the Sinking Fund next year would be tantamount to suspending it altogether. The deficit, or at any rate the main bulk of it, must therefore in my opinion be met by increased taxation—and nothing but increased taxation will turn people's thoughts to some regard for economy and aid us in resisting the wild demands for expansion and expenditure everywhere . . .[52]

As so often in the past Beach found no support and he expected none in this instance. Already he thought in terms of resignation on the grounds of economy.[53]

Beach's policy of economy, involving opposition to old-age pensions at home as well as to expansion abroad,[54] threatened to undermine Chamberlain's whole conception of the Unionist party, its tactics and its base of support. The feud between them was thus bound to continue. Beach again contemplated resignation while preparing the budget of 1901,[55] but was placated by concessions. Nevertheless, he took the opportunity in introducing his budget to stress the general financial problem of rising expenditure and the need to broaden the basis of taxation, since no party was prepared to economize. In May he complained to Salisbury again of the cabinet's lack of co-operation and his own isolation, and yet again thought of resignation.[56] Over the summer his dissatisfaction increased as his opinions continued to be disregarded, and by September he decided that the time had come for an open confrontation.

The memorandum which Beach compiled on finance in September 1901 was prompted in the first instance by the inefficient conduct of the war which he felt, with some justification, was costing far more than it should because of mismanagement. But the crucial passages of the memorandum concerned not the immediate problem but the general trend of finances and the attitude of his colleagues:

I cannot anticipate that the revenue of 1902–3, including the war taxes, will do much more than meet the expenditure of the year . . . I see no hope, at any rate, of a sufficient surplus to take off even a penny of the income tax . . . This seems to me of the gravest importance if we examine the history of our expenditure during the past six years . . . There has been a total increase (in normal expenditure) of 40% . . .

I cannot conceive it possible that such a rate of increase in time of peace can long continue. It has been met, so far, by the great increase in our general revenue due to prosperity, by death duties and by taxation imposed for war purposes. The first two are now beginning to fail us. The third, even if wholly continued, cannot, in my judgement, be increased in peacetime. Heavier direct taxation would not then be borne; any attempt to increase the existing indirect taxes would be useless on a falling revenue, and the only possible new indirect taxes which would produce any important amount, without a complete return to a Protectionist policy, would be small duties on corn, or meat, or petroleum, on the political objections to which I need not dwell . . .

For these reasons it seems to me absolutely essential that a real check should be imposed on the continued increase of ordinary expenditure for which we have been responsible since 1895–6.[57]

Beach's concern was not simply economy for its own sake, and when challenged he gave further reasons. Seeing lightness of taxation as one of the main causes of Britain's past prosperity, he feared that, if expenditure and taxation continued to grow, 'wealth and comfort will be so diminished as to cause grave danger to our social system'.[58] Salisbury appreciated Beach's arguments but doubted the possibility of 'such a renovation of policy', not merely whilst the war continued, but even in peacetime afterwards. Rather he thought 'that whenever any thorough and honest effort is made to turn it into a practical policy, the Government will go to pieces'.[59] Chamberlain was predictably less sympathetic.[60]

The memorandum had no immediate effects. Expenditure did not decrease and the Chancellor in his last budget, in 1902, was forced into one of those politically disadvantageous expedients to which he had referred, the reimposition of a 1s. registration duty on imported corn. Shortly afterwards Salisbury's own resignation allowed Beach to escape from office as he had been vaguely trying to do for the previous two or three years. Balfour's attempts to persuade him to remain merely exposed the wide number of questions upon which Beach differed from his colleagues and particularly from Chamberlain.[61] In September, in a speech at Bristol, Beach made these differences public. He attacked the incompetent management of the recent war, demanded reductions in naval and military expenditure and reform in the administration of the army, and warned that the existing fiscal system could not bear continued expenditure on this scale.

Under the increasingly ineffective leadership of Salisbury who himself saw nothing but division and disaster in the future, the Unionist party was beginning to collapse under the strain of office and its own inertia.[62] In March 1902 Grey thought not only that the Liberal party was likely to split but that 'perhaps a corresponding split may come amongst the Conservatives and a large middle party come into being for a while'.[63] Beach's disaffection was but the tip of an iceberg of discontent at all levels of the party which Balfour's succession to the leadership in place of his uncle did nothing to alleviate. The idea of a Rosebery–Chamberlain coalition to breathe some vigour into the administration, which various of their admirers floated, was one possible outcome of such a split.

But so indefinite was the position of Rosebery and the Liberal League that a combination of Rosebery and Beach could also be entertained. Throughout the war Rosebery had maintained fairly close connections with one small group of Unionist dissidents, the 'Hooligans', or 'Hughligans', so-called after one of their leading members, Balfour's cousin, Lord Hugh Cecil. The Hooligans shared Rosebery's disgust with the inefficiency of the army and the War Office and were prepared to consider the creation of a 'middle party'. Winston Churchill, especially, toyed with the idea after Rosebery's speech to the City Liberal Club in July 1901, possibly as a response to feeling in his constituency, and the Chesterfield speech gave a new impulse to these ideas:

I see little glory in an Empire which can rule the waves and is unable to flush its sewers. The difficulty has been so far that the people who have looked abroad have paid no attention to domestic matters, and those who are centred on domestic matters regard the Empire merely as an encumbrance. What is wanted is a well-balanced policy . . . something that will coordinate development and expansion with the progress of social comfort and health . . . I shall watch the Chesterfield experiment with interest.[64]

Other Hooligans were both more Conservative and more cautious. Lord Hugh Cecil advised Churchill 'to keep both feet securely planted on Unionist terra firma until there is equally firm land, Middle or other, to step onto'.[65] But the idea of a middle party continued to appeal to Churchill's imagination. Again in the autumn of 1902 his interest was aroused by Beach's speech at Bristol, and he acted as intermediary for the reprinting of portions of the speech by the Liberal League. 'I should like to bring you and Beach together,' he wrote to Rosebery. 'There lies the chance of a central coalition . . . The one real difficulty I have to encounter is the suspicion that I am moved by mere restless ambition: and if some definite issue—such as Tariff—were to arise—the difficulty would disappear.'[66] But Rosebery and Churchill agreed that the autumn of 1902 was not the right time: 'perhaps not long hence, the psychological moment may come for a new departure, but it is not yet'.[67]

In one respect, however, the crucial moment had already passed. Because the Liberals reunited to oppose the Unionist Education Bill on Nonconformist lines rather than supporting it as an instalment of efficiency, the lines of division between Conservatives and Liberals were more clearly drawn in 1902 than they had been for some years, even if these lines were the traditional ones of Nonconformist and Anglican. But education, as an issue, could not restore stability to the two-party system of Unionists and Separatists created in 1886. Rather it revealed the one-issue nature of that alignment and the instability of the alliances then formed since the Irish supported the Unionists on education whilst Chamberlain and his Nonconformist supporters were alienated. Chamberlain himself opposed the Education Bill in the cabinet but for the sake of the alliance supported it in public. But his political base, which it had been the purpose of his 'liberal' domestic policies to preserve, had been destroyed. 'The Bill', he wrote to Balfour, 'has brought all the fighting Nonconformists into the field . . . Their representations and appeals to the old war cries have impressed large numbers of the middle and upper working classes who have hitherto supported the Unionist party without joining the Conservative organisation.' Moreover, Chamberlain felt that in the struggle with the Nonconformists the government would lose and that they would 'go on to what I believe is certain political destruction . . .'[68]

For tactical reasons Salisbury also opposed the bill that Balfour proposed in 1902, and suggested the postponement of the politically volatile question of primary education. The Tory back-benchers, however, would not permit concessions to Chamberlain on this measure. The progress of the bill from the first cabinet which met to discuss policy on 5 November 1901, until its final stages when Balfour at last recognized the danger and began to permit amendments and to speak more cautiously in public, witnessed the gradual erosion of Chamberlain's principal objections. The vital point was rate aid for the voluntary schools, on which the cabinet could do little to ease Chamberlain's position. Devonshire told him on 3 December that rate aid was inevitable since otherwise the Tory right would revolt. The core of the problem was financial, and provided Chamberlain with a clear demonstration of the political implications of the inelasticity of revenue and rising expenditure. For in this case Chamberlain could provide no alternative source of funds. He suggested to Morant that Exchequer grants would be less politically harmful since national taxation was not levied for specific purposes, but Morant considered this to be impossible because of the cost of the war. This was the revenue problem in a nutshell.

There were issues in the bill other than the immediate difficulties of party politics. Although in the short run the Education Act of 1902 was a triumph for the Anglican establishment, it was also, in the longer term, a reform based upon the extension of state responsibility. It was on these grounds that the bill gained the support of the Webbs and the 'efficiency' Liberals. Both Chamberlain and Salisbury realized this and to some extent based their respective attitudes to the bill upon it, demonstrating the divisive effects of collectivism. Chamberlain, confronted by a revolt of Nonconformists in his home base of Birmingham in 1902, warned that if he had to fight he would do so not on the sectarian aspects of the bill but on the interests of the children who had to be educated. Salisbury, in contrast, disliked the bill because it would destroy the voluntary principle behind education and ultimately lead to state control. It was precisely this sort of social reform, involving public responsibility for formerly voluntary services, that would prove expensive. But it was equally the sort of social reform that Chamberlain saw as the pattern for the future. The Education Act did not cause Chamberlain to take up tariff reform, as some of his critics later alleged. But as a result of it Chamberlain, like so many other leading political figures, was on the loose from the formal structure of politics, seeking a new departure. Unlike Rosebery he was less likely to wait for an opportunity than to create one.

Churchill's choice of tariffs as a potentially divisive issue which might lead to a realignment in politics was not taken out of the blue. Colonial pressure and commercial decline, as well as revenue difficulties, had focused attention on the possible need for a reconsideration of the fiscal system by 1902. In this the Liberal Imperialists had played their part. Their criticisms of British inefficiency were largely directed towards the government and the army, but they also directed attention to Britain's relatively poor commercial performance in support of their arguments. By demanding a reconsideration of Liberalism they cast doubts upon all traditional Liberal policies, not just Home Rule and Little Englandism. Chamberlain's denunciations of 'old shibboleths' echoed Rosebery; Fowler's denunciation of 'the dry biscuit of political economy' prefaced Chamberlain's attack on 'economic pedantry'. Liberal Imperialism and the Liberal League acted as powerful destabilizing forces throughout the Edwardian period. The vagueness of their ideas which made them appear attractive to collectivists, imperialists, and economists alike gave all dissident groups the impression that they would find in the Liberal Imperialists reinforcements for their own position. The existence of the Liberal League did more, in that it appeared as the possible nucleus of an entirely new party.

The 'Centre Party' was an abiding myth of Edwardian politics, partly because of the large number of national figures adrift from established political parties, partly because of the proliferation of dissident organizations. Both were expressions of the fluid political situation. In 1902 politicians and organizations were proposing, in their various ways, solutions to the problems of education, inefficient government, imperial federation, inelastic revenue, and social reform while still formally grouped into Unionists and Home Rulers. On the questions then at the forefront of politics neither of these formal groupings had a political identity. The course of events since 1886 had, on the contrary, shown them to be deeply divided and the alliances then formed to be utterly destroyed. Several lines of cleavage were involved. Unionists and Home Rulers remained divided by Home Rule to which, despite Rosebery's efforts, the official Liberal party was still pledged; Conservatives and Liberals were still divided by the preoccupations of traditional sectarian radicalism, such as education and temperance, issues upon which their respective allies, the Liberal Unionists and the Irish, favoured the other side; Conservatives and Liberals were divided amongst themselves on the attitude to be adopted towards social reform, the Empire, and the expenditure which these questions entailed. Under these circumstances, the choice between principle and party which individual politicians face in a party system became acute as they sympathized now with this party, now with that, on issues to which they attached equal importance. 'Politics and parties', Rosebery remarked to Churchill in October 1902, 'are at this moment in a witches' cauldron . . .'[69]

The Division of the Unionists[1]

The reimposition of the 1s. registration duty on corn in the budget of 1902 was intended as an expedient by a desperate Chancellor to find further sources of revenue in wartime. As a revenue duty it attracted little hostile comment, and despite Liberal protests that free trade was in danger and welcoming cries from Tory protectionists, there was nothing about the duty to cause serious disruption in the Unionist party. Only two Unionists, A. Cross and C. H. Seely, both future Unionist free traders, voted against the duty. But the significance of the duty was transformed by the interpretation put upon it by the Canadian premier, Sir Wilfrid Laurier, who linked it to the forthcoming Colonial Conference and saw in the duty 'a step . . . which would make it possible to obtain Preference for Canadian goods'. Challenged by Campbell-Bannerman about Laurier's interpretation, Balfour denied that the corn duty had any connection with either the Colonial Conference or preference. But Chamberlain left the question open. On 16 May, in a speech which Amery has called 'the prologue to the tariff reform campaign', he attacked rigid adherence to the doctrine of free trade, and linked the question of imperial preference to the dangers of foreign competition and the stagnation of British trade.[2]

The Colonial Conference itself met on 30 June, and the proceedings during July and August made it clear to Chamberlain that the only possible path towards closer imperial unity lay in commercial preference.[3] At the Conference, Chamberlain accepted the principle of preference and, as a result of further discussions with the Canadian minister of finance, W. S. Fielding, agreed to advocate the preferential remission of the corn duty in favour of Canada in the cabinet. But although it is clear from Chamberlain's speech of 16 May that many of the arguments by which tariff reform was ultimately to be advocated had already formed in his mind, in 1902 he had no clear idea either of the problems before him or of his own immediate tactics. In the

reconstruction of the cabinet following Salisbury's resignation, he
chose to remain at the Colonial Office rather than press his claims to the
Exchequer vacated by Beach, and thus allowed a confirmed free trader,
C. T. Ritchie, to become the dominant voice in economic matters just
as he was about to demand a major alteration in fiscal policy.[4] But, as
he later explained to Devonshire, Chamberlain was at that time thinking
solely in terms of the remission of revenue taxation and not of a fiscal
revolution.[5]

Chamberlain first raised the question of remitting the corn duty in
favour of Canada at the cabinet of 21 October 1902: 'There is a very
great deal to be said in favour of this proposal,' Balfour reported to the
King. 'But it raises very big questions indeed—colonial and fiscal . . .
On the whole Mr. Balfour leans towards it; but it behoves us to walk
warily.'[6] The discussion was postponed until November. But on 15
November Ritchie circulated a cabinet memorandum detailing his
objections, political and financial, to preference: 'I am told', he wrote,
'that the Corn Duty tells heavily against us in the constituencies.
Middleton tells me it is the one thing he is afraid of at an election . . .'[7]
Chamberlain disputed Middleton's judgement,[8] placing far greater
emphasis on the effects of the Education Act; Ritchie had, in fact, not
reported Middleton fully. Sandars informed Balfour that Middleton
'says that of course if the tax be the precursor of a general scheme of
fiscal reform in the direction of protection—well and good—it is
worth keeping'.[9] Attached to a scheme of imperial preference, capable
of a protectionist interpretation which would revitalize the Tories,
Ritchie's political arguments lost much of their force. But his real
objections were on fiscal grounds. Seeing preference as 'the imposition
of a charge on the taxpayers of the United Kingdom in order to benefit
our kith and kin beyond the sea', he saw the result only as 'an unknown
doubtful gain to certain British producers in return for an indubitable
loss inflicted upon British consumers'. At the same time he feared that
the government would be driven to an indefinite extension of preference as other colonies came forward with their 'specious proposals'.

Despite Ritchie's objections, Chamberlain secured a provisional
assent from the cabinet of 19 November for his proposals.[10] Nevertheless, Ritchie had reserved his position in his memorandum, asking
that no promise should be made to Canada 'which would bind us to
continue the imposition of a tax which circumstances between now and
the Budget might show it would be wise to abandon'. The question was

thus, in effect, still open when Chamberlain left to tour South Africa in the winter. During his absence Ritchie hardened his opposition to preference, and on 21 February circulated a further memorandum criticizing the proposals which had 'unfortunately' arisen on the grounds that colonial preference would result in a loss of revenue which would have to be made up by additional taxation at home: 'with a shilling income tax, and with bad times entailing want of employment, and perhaps an appreciably increased price of bread, there will be a violent reaction, resulting in sweeping and ill-considered reductions of our defensive expenditure'.[11] Shortly afterwards he pressed home his threat to resign if the 'previous decision' of the cabinet on preference was adhered to.[12] In the cabinet at the end of March, despite a majority in favour of the retention of the duty, Ritchie's view, backed by his threat to resign, prevailed. Balfour could not afford to lose his Chancellor so close to the time set for the announcement of the budget. Rather than see the tax retained but not used for preference, Chamberlain insisted that it was dropped altogether. On this occasion, however, following Ritchie's precedent, Chamberlain reserved the right to reopen the subject in the future.[13]

The result of raising the question of imperial preference in the cabinet was thus to reveal a serious split on the subject. Open conflict was avoided by postponing the decision but there had been no reconciliation or compromise, nor could there have been unless one or the other abandoned his fundamental beliefs, or unless the question lapsed into oblivion. Ritchie's memorandum of 15 November rested on free trade assumptions about British industrial competitiveness in international trade. Cheapness of food, labour, and materials, and consequently the cheapness of the finished product obtained by a system of free imports were for Ritchie essential if Britain's industrial position was to be maintained.[14] Taxation for preferential purposes would raise costs to British producers 'and must increase the difficulties already experienced by them in maintaining their hold on home and foreign markets . . .' But Chamberlain had already pointed to 'the presence of hostile tariffs, the presence of bounties, the presence of subsidies . . .' which in his view made the costs of production to a large extent irrelevant to the final selling price overseas.[15] Thus a stable home and imperial market, protected against subsidized foreign competition, was more important to the question of production and employment than cheap supplies of food and raw materials.

Ritchie and Chamberlain also disagreed fundamentally as to the value of the colonial market. Ritchie emphasized that:

foreign countries . . . now take more than twice as much of our exports as are sent to the Colonies: and a slight differentiation of duties might easily diminish the trade of the United Kingdom with foreign countries by a much larger amount than could be counter-balanced by any possible increase of trade with the Colonies whose markets this country already to a large extent commands.

But Chamberlain thought of eliminating dependence on foreign trade completely by developing the Empire into a completely self-sustaining economic unit.[16] In the final analysis Chamberlain saw foreign trade as irrelevant to the British economy:

whether your trade is prosperous at the present time, or whether it is not, its continuance depends essentially and mainly upon the continuance and even upon the increase of your trade with the Colonies. If that trade declines, if it does not increase, then I do not care what may be the truth as to the comparative figures dealing with our foreign trade, but I say there will not be sufficient employment for our population . . .[17]

Similar disagreement arose on the question of defence. Both ministers were concerned at the rising level of expenditure and its burden on the British taxpayer, and agreed that, whilst defence expenditure might be slightly reduced,[18] there should be no extreme reaction after the war. But whilst Ritchie dwelt on the dangers of maintaining wartime expenditure in peacetime as an argument for reducing taxation in a controlled fashion, Chamberlain sought to find new sources of revenue and manpower in the Empire. Ritchie's argument was weakest at this point, for his only alternative to an ill-considered reduction of defence expenditure was a well-considered reduction, both being based on purely domestic considerations, and in particular the reaction of the electorate. Yet, in the long run, the ultimate arbiter of British defence expenditure had to be the international situation if Britain was to maintain great-power status and even, in the international climate of the 1900s, her own security. Whatever the flaws in Chamberlain's tariff reform case he sought a positive escape from this dilemma. Ritchie saw Britain's problems, international and domestic, from an insular standpoint. 'I am as anxious as any of my colleagues can be', he wrote, 'to promote the idea of Imperial unity, but in so doing we must be careful not to lay ourselves open to the charge of endangering

British interests.' Chamberlain would not admit the distinction between British and imperial interests, for the interdependence of those interests was central to the whole idea of tariff reform. The net effect of these disagreements politically was that the cabinet was in reality already split by March 1903.

Ritchie announced the abolition of the corn duty on 23 April in terms which damned it utterly.[19] Apart from offending Balfour by its free trade dogmatism,[20] the speech produced an outcry from the Tory protectionists who viewed the corn duty as the first step on the road back to protection. The agitation which followed was headed by the old protectionist leader, Chaplin, and took the form of a farmers' revolt.[21] But other voices joined in the condemnation of Ritchie's action which demonstrated more clearly the strength of the opposition within the party. Beach, as the Chancellor who had imposed the duty, described its abolition as 'a great mistake',[22] and other Unionists who were shortly to join the Unionist free traders in opposition to Chamberlain's tariff reform proposals also wrote in support of Chaplin's deputation of protest which Balfour saw on 15 May.[23] The agitation against the repeal of the corn duty was not in itself of great importance. 'The real difficulty', Balfour commented, 'lies not in determining the policy to be pursued with regard to this year's Budget, but in determining the precise form in which a refusal to make any change should be couched.' It was typical of Balfour's concept of party leadership that he should attach such importance to verbal formulas as a means of resolving genuine conflicts of belief. It was typical also that he should find his formula in a policy of postponement, following the practice of reserving his own position into which the cabinet had already drifted. The formula agreed by the cabinet thus admitted 'the possibility of reviving the tax *if it were associated with some great change in our fiscal system* . . . such as the necessity of retaliating on foreign countries or of the expediency of a closer fiscal union with our Colonies . . .'[24] Whether this was or was not desirable, neither the cabinet nor Balfour had yet decided.

On the same day that Balfour addressed the deputation Chamberlain spoke at Birmingham. Chamberlain's reaction to the repeal of the corn duty was one of frustration, but he still had no clear idea of his future action, and did not yet cast himself in the role of missionary of empire. The Birmingham speech of 15 May 1903 was thus conceived and carefully prepared with strictly limited objectives. As Balfour later reminded Devonshire, Chamberlain 'proposed to say at Birmingham much the same as I proposed to say to the deputation, *only in a less definite manner*. The famous Birmingham speech embodies his practical endeavour to carry out this undertaking.'[25]

In the context of the prior disagreement within the cabinet, Balfour's uncommitted position, and his own uncertain purposes, Chamberlain's speech was a masterpiece of political tactics. Chamberlain outlined the position as he saw it—the enormous potential of the Empire beside which 'the smaller controversies upon which depend the fate of by-elections, and sometimes the fate of governments' faded into insignificance; the need of preference to unite that empire; the special circumstances of the moment, when the imperial sentiment generated by the South African war, the Canadian offer to increase the preference to British goods, and the resolutions of the Colonial Conference all created an exceptional opportunity for progress towards unity; yet at the same time the German threat to retaliate against Canada for granting preference, which stood as a danger that the Empire would 'fall apart into separate states' if no action was taken in its corporate defence. But, having presented this picture, Chamberlain went no further than to state that this was a problem which required consideration, and to confront his audience with the choice of maintaining a policy of free trade in all its doctrinaire rigidity or of recovering the freedom of negotiation and retaliation whenever British interests were threatened. 'I leave the matter in your hands. I desire that a discussion on this subject should be opened. The time has not yet come to settle it.'[26]

To anyone who knew Chamberlain's mind, and in particular his cabinet colleagues, Chamberlain's meaning was clear—the speech indicated that Chamberlain would not let sleeping dogs lie. But the tone of the speech was cautious and conditional, and the only definite proposal put forward was for a discussion. Chamberlain structured the discussion in terms favourable to preference. But the degree to which he had, in fact, raised the issue or advocated change was left within a penumbra of obscurity in which he could manœuvre in the weeks that followed. The obscurity was deliberate and the total effect was to leave Chamberlain no more committed to the advocacy of tariff reform than he had been at the beginning. The difference was that afterwards the whole country, and not just his cabinet colleagues, knew his views.

But the Birmingham speech differed from Balfour's reply to Chaplin's deputation in one significant respect—it was not, and was never intended to be, an isolated statement. Whilst Balfour attempted to close the subject for the foreseeable future, Chamberlain deliberately returned the issue to the forefront of political debate and widened the discussion to encompass the whole field of imperial and domestic fiscal policy. From the first Chamberlain spoke of a 'new programme' and of his intention to make tariff reform the main issue at the next general election.[27] Exactly what the 'new programme' would be, would depend on how events fell out in the forthcoming weeks. But having secured the two vital points of making the controversy public and room to manœuvre, Chamberlain's tactic was to maintain the pressure on the party, and particularly on Balfour, until the build-up of opposition forced him to halt. Four days after the speech Chamberlain wrote for publication a letter implying that higher wages would result from tariff reform,[28] and on 22 May in the Commons he linked tariff reform to old-age pensions, emphasizing that in tariff reform lay the solution to the revenue problem which had hitherto held up social reform.[29]

Even before this, however, Chamberlain's pressure had caused alarm and the inevitable opposition had begun to protest. According to Ritchie, Balfour had warned Chamberlain against making his statement on old-age pensions after Ritchie had threatened to repudiate 'his authority to make such a declaration on behalf of his colleagues', and Chamberlain had accordingly promised to 'absent himself from the House during the debate'. Chamberlain's intervention was thus, as Balfour commented, 'a distinct violation of an arrangement come to with me'.[30] Following this speech, Lord Hugh Cecil and Winston Churchill both wrote to Balfour expressing their opposition to Chamberlain's programme. These letters, both from members of the already disaffected Hooligan group, cannot be taken to indicate 'that Chamberlain had alarmed the Tory rank and file in the Commons'.[31] But together with Ritchie's threat to disavow Chamberlain publicly, they constituted a serious danger that the division of opinion in the party would break out into a public confrontation of opposed factions which Balfour wanted to avoid above all else. More significantly, on 29 May Devonshire expressed his own disquiet at the use Chamberlain intended to make of the Liberal Unionist Association to disseminate his propaganda. In so doing, the Duke was acting under pressure from other prominent Liberal Unionists, and if he did not at this stage condemn Chamberlain's policy outright, he gave notice that he felt 'extremely doubtful whether I can be a party to it, when it takes a more definite shape'.[32]

Balfour made his first public statement on the issues raised by the Birmingham speech on 28 May in a debate initiated by Lloyd George and Dilke. His speech was typically vague and non-committal, but that this was possible was largely due to the hypothetical nature of the Birmingham speech itself. Within the obscurity of Chamberlain's statements there was ample room for Balfour also to manœuvre, and he found no difficulty in aligning himself with Chamberlain's one positive proposal—the demand for a discussion. Balfour, in fact, went further and committed himself at least to a reassessment of Britain's traditional fiscal policy. He accepted Chamberlain's version of the problem as a problem of imperial policy which had been raised as a result of colonial initiative, and defended Chamberlain's duty to raise a discussion in view of the resolutions of the Colonial Conference. Similarly, he identified himself with Chamberlain's response to the German threat of retaliation against Canada and felt that preference 'is worth getting if you can get it without paying too heavily for it'.

Nor did Balfour reject food taxes out of hand, although he felt that such taxes would only be acceptable to the electorate as part of a larger policy:

But if, by means of a tax on food you can put the whole fiscal position and the whole Imperial position of this country on a different and better footing, is it so certain that the working classes would repudiate such a tax . . . I do not know . . . I asked a similar question about the Colonies—whether they would consent to . . . a modification of their tariff system? Again, I do not know.

Balfour thus took his stand on the Birmingham speech in favour of a discussion of fiscal policy untrammelled by the doctrines of the past. Only on two points was Balfour definite. He repudiated any taxation of raw material and he repudiated any allegations that the government had, or should have, an official policy on the subject.[33]

In this debate Chamberlain continued his pressure. His speech, like Balfour's, was vague and he still committed himself to no more than a discussion. But at the same time he was far more detailed than Balfour in outlining what the government might do if public opinion ripened sufficiently to grant a mandate for fiscal change. The next step would be to open negotiations with the colonies to work out the details of preference which, Chamberlain openly stated, would involve food duties. But in this speech Chamberlain also went on to consider, as he had not done at Birmingham, the domestic repercussions of his policy: higher wages, a large surplus revenue for social reform, incidental protection at least for agriculture, and protection for industry against dumping and 'unfair competition'.

This speech, which took Chamberlain away from imperial policy and dangerously close to the advocacy of domestic protection, marked the end of his room to manœuvre. In many ways it also achieved his main objective. For in speaking after Balfour had declared himself in general agreement with Chamberlain's views, yet developing the further implications of fiscal change, Chamberlain gave 'quite a different complexion to the Prime Minister's speech from that which it assumed when left to itself'.[34] After 28 May opposition reached a point where Balfour had no choice but to halt Chamberlain if his cabinet were not to break up beneath him. Lord Hugh Cecil and Winston Churchill had both spoken out during the debate against Chamberlain, and other free traders in the party were no longer prepared to remain silent. Ritchie complained to Balfour after the debate and followed this with a letter; Devonshire wrote to Ritchie 'to ask him what he was going to do', and voiced his concern in almost identical terms both to Lansdowne and to Balfour. Most dangerously from Balfour's point of view, Devonshire threatened to speak out rather than allow himself to be 'committed by silence'.[35] Devonshire's complaint was only the most important of many and Balfour had also received letters from 'Ritchie, G. Wyndham, Balfour of Burleigh and George Hamilton, all, in various degrees, expressing disquiet and anxiety'.

In face of this threat to raise their dissent publicly, and with so many of his cabinet ministers expressing discontent, Balfour had to make his own assessment of the position clear, which he did in a letter to Devonshire on 4 June. It was an assessment which, in its fundamentals, remained his attitude towards tariff reform for the whole period of the controversy. Pointing out that 'Chamberlain's views, both in their general outline and their particular details, commit no one but himself', Balfour saw no difficulty in the cabinet remaining together for the rest of the 'natural life' of the present Parliament:

Ritchie, I gather, dislikes Colonial Preference, 'simpliciter'. If a good fairy offered it to him tomorrow as a *fait accompli* he would reject it. I do not, as at present advised, share this view. If I could have it on my own terms I am disposed to think I should take it, though even then I should like to have more time for analysing its economic consequences before expressing a final decision. My hesitation, however, chiefly arises from doubts as to its practicability rather than its expediency. I question whether the people of *this* country will be sufficiently tolerant of the protective side of the scheme, or the people *of the Colonies* sufficiently tolerant of its Free Trade side, to permit them to accept the compromise in which it essentially consists.

But whatever be the merits of the question, whether looked at from the strictly economic or the political side, why should the fact that some of us differ and many of us hesitate, about it, break up, or tend to break up, the present Cabinet . . . I do not think we should anticipate such a misfortune . . . if we dissolved *now*, I, and I suspect many others of our colleagues, would be in the embarrassing, and indeed, somewhat ludicrous position, of having to say that on the point which divided us, we had not made up our *own* minds, and could not, therefore, pretend to give a decided lead to anyone else.

Balfour, therefore, suggested a temporary compromise, leaving preference as an open question, whilst the cabinet collected information and avoided further statements on the subject.[36] Above all, Balfour wanted to play for time to keep the discussion within the area of obscurity in which Chamberlain had originally placed it. In order to keep his cabinet together, he also attempted to shift the disagreement from the doctrinal dispute between free trade and protection to the practical question of whether food taxes would be acceptable to the electorate. His truce of silence was accepted in the cabinet of 9 June, and announced by Ritchie in the House of Commons. Ritchie nevertheless took the opportunity to make his own dissent clear. In the same debate Balfour announced his own opinion on the subject as one of 'no settled convictions'.[37]

Other members of the party, however, had settled their convictions at an earlier date and their actions were in no way affected by the cabinet truce. In the debate of 9 June, Chaplin, frustrated in his attempts to reverse the repeal of the corn duty by deputation to Balfour, furiously attacked Ritchie for his doctrinaire views,[38] and he was not without sympathizers. On 20 June some fifty members decided to support Chaplin's amendment condemning the repeal of the duty and on 22 June, when Chaplin moved the rejection of clause 1 of the budget, 32 Unionist M.P.s voted with him. An invitation signed by 109 Unionist M.P.s was issued to all Unionists to attend a meeting on 24 June 'for the purpose of furthering the views of the Prime Minister and Mr. Chamberlain upon the subject of Preferential Trade within the Empire', and some 130 attended the meeting.[39] Free trade opinion and organization developed along similar lines with the lead taken by Ritchie, Beach, and the Hooligans.[40]

Beach's original intention was to create no more than a movement of free trade opinion within the Unionist party which would 'make Joe's policy quite impossible',[41] but confronted with the apparent organization of the protectionists even Beach felt obliged to join in the formation of a more formal body. The leading free traders thus met on 25 June and invited all free trade Unionists to an inaugural meeting on 1 July, when a committee was set up to organize the Unionist Free Food League. The resolution carried at the meeting was hardly more combative than that of the protectionists a week earlier, and while condemning food taxation pledged support for the government's proposed inquiry.[42] On 21 July the tariff reformers responded with the formation of the Tariff Reform League, and whilst this body was initially of less importance than Chamberlain's Birmingham Tariff Committee,[43] the formation of rival organizations at the national level marked an important stage in the disintegration of the Unionist party. Neither was fettered by the truce of 9 June from which Chamberlain had specifically excluded literature, and the Birmingham Tariff Committee flooded the country with tariff reform propaganda.

At this point the movement for tariff reform began to merge, as it had always threatened to do, with the older agricultural protectionist opposition to the repeal of the corn duty. Moreover, Chamberlain's own policy evolved towards protection. Initially his scheme had been limited to a simple remission of the corn duty for preferential purposes, and even after Ritchie had announced the repeal of that duty, Chamberlain still thought in terms of revenue taxation remitted for colonial goods with the revenue to be spent on social reforms. But for preference, as he admitted on 28 May, such taxation had to fall on food. It was this, the threat of food taxation, which forced him to change his policy. As he subsequently explained to Devonshire:

If, as I originally hoped, the proposal that I made for discussion had been accepted on both sides, and had not been made a party question, we might have stood to what was my original idea and have treated the small taxation that will be necessary to give a preference to the Colonies as a Revenue tax, and have used the profits for the promotion of those social reforms which are certain to come in the future, and which ought, in my opinion to be provided for by indirect and not by an increase in direct taxation.

But the opposition thought the chance too good to be lost. They have raised the Free Food cry, and we must meet them on their own ground. I am, therefore, prepared to accept the responsibility of treating the change so far as preferential rates are concerned as a redistribution of taxation, and not as an imposition of increased burdens.[44]

Chamberlain announced this change on 24 June at the Constitutional Club. The meeting, at which both Balfour and Chamberlain were down to speak, was one which could not be dropped and was, therefore, excluded from the truce. Balfour on this occasion pointed out that preference did not depend on an increase in food taxation, but could be carried out 'without increasing the cost of living to the working classes of this country'. Chamberlain in reply took up the point, hypothetically at the time, but in a way which indicated the movement of his ideas:

I have suggested . . . that inasmuch as any alteration of our fiscal system must necessarily increase the sums received in the shape of indirect taxation, a portion of these sums, at any rate, should be applied in order to provide old age pensions for the poor . . . That is all I have done, but it has no part whatever in the question of a reform in our fiscal policy . . . When we have the money then will be the time to say what we shall do with it; and if the working classes refuse to take my advice, if they prefer this immediate advantage, why it stands to reason that if, for instance, they are called upon to pay 3d a week additional on the cost of their bread, they may be fully, entirely relieved by a reduction of a similar amount in the cost of their tea, their sugar, or even of their tobacco . . .[45]

By the time he wrote to Devonshire in August the plan of the compensatory reduction of taxes on other foodstuffs had become Chamberlain's policy. But he still had less than a system to propose, and the contradiction between the compensatory reduction of other food taxes and the provision of surplus revenue for social reform was one which Chamberlain never completely cleared from his mind. After his speech on 26 June, food duties would no longer provide increased revenue, and direct social reform would not, therefore, be the result of preference, although by promoting trade and by involving the colonies in imperial defence, closer imperial union might still provide solutions to British unemployment and high defence expenditure. But for direct social reform Chamberlain was forced to fall back on retaliatory duties against subsidized foreign competition and to 'square the Budget' by taking into account 'some tax on manufactured goods'.[46]

Chamberlain's change of course posed fundamental problems for a non-protective scheme of tariff reform. For if retaliation was fully

effective and reduction of their tariffs by foreign countries did permit
the maintenance of an 'absolutely free market', his scheme for preference might result in a net loss of revenue. Chamberlain did not
expect that it would, for neither he nor other tariff reformers believed
that home consumers would pay the whole of the duty. Competition
from the freely admitted colonial grain would, they thought, force
foreign suppliers to reduce their prices in order to retain a foothold in
the English market, a view which would be developed further into an
argument that, by securing a market for the colonies, colonial production of grain would be increased and its price actually reduced
because of the increased scale of production. But for political purposes
Chamberlain felt he had to confront the free traders on their own
ground, which meant accepting the free trade view that the consumer
would pay the whole of the duty. The result was to throw him back on
the compensatory reduction of other duties for preference, and upon
protection of manufactured goods to provide revenue for social reform
and also the reduction of agricultural rates. His references to social
reform projects consequently grew less frequent and more haphazard,
and increasingly the tariff reform case came to rest on the solution to
unemployment resulting from increased trade. 'Tariff Reform means
work for all' was not simply the most extravagant slogan of the Tariff
Reform League's propaganda machine, it was the only claim the
League could justifiably make.[47]

But the change in policy in the summer of 1903 indicated also what
was, and what was not, essential to Chamberlain in tariff reform.
Social reform and the production of revenue were ultimately profitable
incidentals. Chamberlain did not advocate tariff reform to provide
revenue for social reform or any other purpose; he advocated indirect
taxes to provide a basis for preference, and he advocated preference for
imperial union. If anything, he would have preferred to rest his case
upon 'sacrifice' rather than profit. When, impressed by the strength
of the 'dear food' cry, he thought preference might be endangered by
a rise in the cost of living attributed to taxes on food, he dropped
revenue taxes as a means of promoting preference and advocated
preferential tariffs in their own right.

The speeches of 26 June showed that Chamberlain's attitude was
still flexible, provided the essentials of preference could be maintained.
The real problem in the summer of 1903 was whether this flexibility
would be sufficient to enable him to reach some compromise with

Balfour, given that Chamberlain felt that food taxes were necessary
for preference, and that Balfour viewed them as impractical. In
principle, Balfour was closer to Chamberlain than to the free traders,
and there was nothing in his views which precluded the acceptance of
Chamberlain's policies. But the doubts which Balfour expressed to
Devonshire about the practicability of Chamberlain's scheme were of
vital importance. From Balfour's point of view, it was not worth
destroying a party for a policy so unlikely to achieve its objectives,
however worth while those objectives were in themselves. Balfour's
attitude was thus an amalgam of agreement in principle and doubt in
practice, which made him almost indifferent to the ideological war
between tariff reformers and free traders in the face of the overwhelming priority of the tactical considerations of party unity and electoral
exigencies.

The first problem Balfour faced in June 1903 was the disagreement
in his cabinet and within the parliamentary party. These were, in fact,
two facets of the same problem. With a parliamentary majority which
stood at 90 to 100 at the beginning of May and which was declining
with almost every by-election, a hostile vote by either the free traders
or the tariff reformers *en masse* would bring about the downfall of the
government, and involve going to the polls as a divided party. In the
cabinet, in the persons of Chamberlain and Devonshire, both factions
possessed leaders of national stature who could challenge Balfour's
own position in the event of total disruption. When the fiscal controversy broke out Balfour had been leader for less than a year, and had
not yet built up an unassailable position.

To offset this, the fact of being leader of the party and a Prime
Minister in office had certain advantages. The function of formulating
policy in a party so hierarchically organized as the Conservative party
belonged to the official party leader. Outright repudiation of Balfour
by either of the extreme factions would brand them as rebels and bring
to bear against them the weight of the party machine. Within the party
there were many, perhaps the majority, who shared Balfour's sympathy
with the ideal of imperial unity, but who also shared his doubts as to
the practicality of food taxation. Equally, the majority, even of the
committed members of the free trade and tariff reform factions, had
no desire to break up the party in rebellion against its official leader.
The situation in which Balfour drew up his official policy was thus one
of some complexity. Just as both factions wished to carry Balfour with

them and thus gain the sanction of official recognition for their views, so Balfour, if he wished to remain in office and lead a united party into the next election, had to carry at least the majority of both extreme factions with him. In terms of cabinet policies this involved satisfying both Chamberlain and Devonshire; in terms of policy it made the outright repudiation of either free trade or tariff reform impossible.

During the summer of 1903, in the relative calm created by the fiscal truce, Balfour turned his attention to defining his own attitude. By the end of July he had completed the first draft of a pamphlet, 'Economic Notes on Insular Free Trade', published in September, which set out his reasons for questioning the adequacy of the existing free trade system and which, with limitations, was to form the basis of his position on fiscal reform until 1907. In the pamphlet Balfour advocated 'fiscal freedom'—the complete liberty for the government of the day to make such commercial treaties as it thought fit, irrespective of any economic doctrine. Beyond this, his conclusions were left undefined. In sending a copy to Devonshire, however, Balfour added specific conditions not mentioned in the pamphlet itself:

1. No retaliatory duty should be threatened, or fiscal preference offered *with a view to protecting any industry in this country against legitimate competition* . . . *protection must not be its primary object.*
2. No such duty and no such preference should introduce any change into our fiscal system which would increase the average cost of living to the working-man.
3. I do not think that, as at present advised, we ought to attempt to carry out a retaliatory policy by the continental method of *starting with heavy duties against the world* and relaxing them in favour of those countries which give us privileges.[48]

This letter became the basis of a second paper, the 'Blue Paper', by Balfour,[49] and both documents were considered by the cabinet on 11 August. The 'Blue Paper' did not constitute an alternative policy in itself to that expressed in the pamphlet 'Economic Notes'. Rather, it was a commentary upon the pamphlet and delineated the limits within which Balfour visualized the use of the 'fiscal freedom' for which he argued. These did not necessarily go beyond limitations which Chamberlain was prepared to accept, and by making it clear that he still considered preference and food taxation a possible policy within the general policy of fiscal freedom, Balfour enabled Chamberlain to accept his proposed official line. At the same time, however, Balfour expected the policy to be unacceptable to the free traders and even to Devonshire.[50] If Balfour was forced to choose between Devonshire and Chamberlain, he would choose Chamberlain. This became increasingly clear during August as Balfour attempted to reconcile the Duke.

Devonshire's objections indicated that he did not equate his position to that of Ritchie, and was not altogether irreconcilable. Devonshire's concern was not with doctrine *per se*, but with the weakness he saw in the limitations which Balfour suggested.[51] This was to be a constant factor in the discussions between Balfour and Devonshire which followed during August. Devonshire would accept 'fiscal freedom' in principle, even though it was vague, if Balfour could guarantee that Chamberlain would not take advantage of that vagueness to interpret the policy in his own light, and thus commit the government not to the limited scheme proposed by Balfour, but to his own policy of protection and preference. Effectively this meant that, whilst the positions of Balfour and Devonshire and Balfour and Chamberlain were not irreconcilable, the positions of Devonshire and Chamberlain were. Balfour was faced with an insoluble dilemma. As long as he wished to keep Chamberlain in the cabinet he had to propose a formula within which Chamberlain could advocate his full policy, however it might develop; but if he wished to keep Devonshire in the cabinet, he had to propose a policy with limitations so tight that Chamberlain would be held rigidly to the government line, and no more.

At the following cabinet on 13 August, therefore, the issue was postponed until September because of the disagreement created by the policy outlined by Balfour. But as a result of the cabinet discussions Balfour had a clearer idea of the task before him and of the terms of both Chamberlain and Devonshire. In the intervening month Balfour set out to probe Devonshire's attitude further. Sandars met Dunville, the Duke's private secretary, and his report confirmed that the Duke might be reconciled: 'His ideas are not Ritchie's, who considers the mischief already done . . . But he honestly dreads the lengths to which acceptance of the proposed position may carry him . . . if by concordat you could set some bounds and limits to the present scheme, you would be in a fair way to reconcile the Duke, who wants to be reconciled.'[52] But this was just what Balfour could not do as long as he wished to keep in touch with Chamberlain. In the circumstances his strongest weapon was to move the discussion away from the narrow issue of tariff reform and on to the question of the place of tariff reform in the

Unionist programme, thus allowing him to emphasize the greater priority of other causes for which the party stood.

Accordingly, on 27 August, Balfour appealed to the Duke on general grounds that it was his duty as a man of the centre, a moderate, to remain within a moderate government:

a great many all-important interests, besides those immediately affected by our fiscal policy, are entrusted to the Unionist party, and . . . if that party be broken up, or seriously weakened by internal divisions, these interests must assuredly suffer . . . Our business is to prevent our divisions reaching a point which may convert them into a national disaster and may deprive the greatest interests of the country of the guardianship by which since 1886 they have been protected.[53]

On the same day that Balfour made this clear appeal to duty, with an oblique but no less clear reference to the dangers of Home Rule if the party broke up on the fiscal question, Devonshire sent Balfour another memorandum which indicated, or appeared to indicate, that he thought a compromise between himself and Chamberlain was possible. In so doing he defined, in so far as this was possible, his own indecisive position. Although highly sceptical of the outcome, Devonshire was prepared to accept both preference and retaliation as experiments, but 'I should like to see the new departure tried, if at all, in the most tentative and guarded manner'.

This, however, was not his main concern. As he saw it, a tentative approach to the question as he desired had already been rendered impossible by the headlong rush of Chamberlain and his followers into protection, and 'unless some very stringent limitations are imposed . . . the issue will become still more what it very nearly is already, viz: a controversy between Free Trade and Protection'. Devonshire therefore asked three times in this one memorandum for 'something in the nature of definite propositions placed before the Cabinet before the autumn agitation begins . . . to discover whether the differences between us are, or are not, fundamental'. To give these limitations teeth Devonshire proposed that the results of the government's inquiry should be embodied in parliamentary resolutions as a statement of official policy. At the same time the Duke was not optimistic. His covering letter stipulated that his suggestions should not be circulated 'until I have consulted our Free Trade colleagues in the Cabinet, as I am rather afraid that they may think that I have given away our position too much . . .'[54]

Balfour strongly objected to Devonshire aligning himself with a faction within the cabinet, but accepted the suggestion of resolutions 'which would clearly show the limits within which we were prepared to utilise that "freedom of fiscal negotiation" which I desire . . .',[55] and sent the proposed resolutions on 7 September with a covering note strongly condemning the free trade position as 'the one which will most quickly produce the most serious consequences. For, it will not merely break up the Unionist party: it will shatter each separate wing of the Unionist party, dividing Tory from Tory and Liberal from Liberal.' The resolutions, however, went no further than previous statements of policy, stating the theoretical desirability of retaliation and preference, and limitations which, apart from suggesting an absolute maximum on food taxes, had all been proposed before—the repudiation of the taxation of raw material, of protection, and of any increase in the working man's cost of living.[56] It was not enough to satisfy the Duke who still felt that, 'as in the case of the "Notes", Chamberlain would feel able to advocate under them the whole of his policy'.[57] The compromise between Chamberlain and Devonshire which Balfour had sought throughout the summer was at last seen to be impossible.

The difficulty was suddenly removed by Chamberlain's offer on 9 September to resign, an offer made with the explicit intention of enabling Balfour to retain Devonshire's support by temporarily removing 'the Preference part of our scheme' from the official party policy and concentrating upon retaliation. Chamberlain confessed that he had underestimated the strength of the 'superstition about the dear loaf', but found 'a very powerful and growing feeling in favour of retaliation'. If preference was thus 'jettisoned', Chamberlain felt obliged to leave the government, but he saw nothing in the situation which would preclude 'an absolutely loyal support of the Government afterwards'. The advantages, as Chamberlain urged them upon Balfour, were real enough. He would be free to advocate preference in the country without restraint; Balfour would be free of the personal bitterness which Chamberlain attracted, and 'would have, according to the hypothesis, a united Cabinet with a moderate policy which would secure a good deal of sympathy from a large proportion of those who now strenuously resist the imposition of a tax on food . . .' Chamberlain assumed that Balfour was favourable to his policy and would bring the government along after him as fast as he could. In so doing he trusted

Balfour, or his own genius for campaigning, perhaps more than was justifiable. But it was one of his main criticisms of Balfour's policy of retaliation that it was incomplete in itself and that 'however much you may limit the policy in the first instance, it would ultimately be extended and would include the preference that I desire . . .'[58] Both Chamberlain and Devonshire underestimated Balfour's ability to make bricks without straw and defend his 'half-way house' policy.

Chamberlain's offer to resign permitted Balfour in September to alter his tactical aims and thus the presentation of his own attitude. Assured of Chamberlain's support even if preference was not made part of the official programme, he was no longer obliged to attempt the reconciliation of Devonshire and Chamberlain. Instead, Balfour now sought to separate Devonshire from the other free trade ministers, and to ensure that the former remained when the latter resigned, by stressing to Devonshire alone the real significance of his doubts as to the practicality of preference in these new circumstances. The cabinet met on 14 September with Balfour's two policy documents, 'Economic Notes' and the 'Blue Paper', still as the basis for discussion. At the meeting, however, Balfour refused to elaborate on his attitude towards preference, and did not inform the meeting of Chamberlain's offer to resign, thus leaving the free traders to conclude that whilst 'the Prime Minister . . . was of opinion that the country was not yet prepared for a tax on food . . . he did not accompany that with any suggestion that preferential treatment was to be abandoned'.[59] Immediately afterwards, the free traders met to consider their position and decided to resign, but not until the cabinet meeting scheduled for the following day. Devonshire then went to see Balfour, where he received his first hint of Chamberlain's proposed resignation, after which, having consulted with Ritchie and Londonderry, he wrote for clarification of Balfour's attitude. At this stage Devonshire still shared with his free trade colleagues the belief that Chamberlain would be permitted to advocate preference and food duties within the official policy as a member of the government.

The free traders met again after the cabinet of 15 September, even though there had been no further discussion of fiscal reform, and agreed then to send in their resignations. An exception was made in the case of Devonshire, who was to see Balfour again before finally resigning. Devonshire accordingly met Balfour and received a stronger hint that Chamberlain 'would probably resign', with the request that he should not discuss this information with anyone else. Even after this, however, Devonshire was not satisfied and sent in his resignation, but with a covering letter allowing that his action might be based 'on a misapprehension of the circumstances'. Balfour's problems thus moved towards a solution. In informing Devonshire of Chamberlain's probable resignation, he sought time during which Ritchie, Balfour of Burleigh, and Lord George Hamilton would resign, whilst Devonshire was still uncommitted. By 16 September he was assured of their resignations and could thus tell Devonshire openly of Chamberlain's letter without the risk that other ministers, besides the Duke, would have the opportunity to reconsider. Having heard the text of Chamberlain's letter, and of Balfour's proposed reply stating that food duties were not 'at present within the bounds of practical politics', the Duke agreed to withdraw his resignation. Balfour could then, and only then, accept Chamberlain's resignation.[60]

Balfour's difficulty throughout the crisis had been the success with which the free traders had pushed the unwilling Duke into the position of free trade leader, and the constant consultations of this 'faction within the cabinet'. In view of the Duke's evident sense of obligation to his fellow free traders, Balfour was unable to reveal the situation brought about by Chamberlain's letter until he had secured their resignations, since the rejection of preference which the Duke required, would almost certainly have satisfied the other free traders as well. Not surprisingly, Balfour's behaviour during the crisis of 14–16 September led to considerable bitterness on the part of the free traders when the letters announcing Chamberlain's resignation were finally made public. The free traders concluded that he had agreed with Chamberlain a change of policy prior to the cabinet meeting of 14 September and had failed to inform them of this in order to bring about their resignations.

Balfour had indeed sought their resignations. But they were wrong in assuming that Balfour had changed his policy. His policy, in the long term, remained consistent—the 'fiscal freedom' advocated in 'Economic Notes'. Chamberlain's offer to resign allowed Balfour to elaborate more precisely the limits within which that 'fiscal freedom' would be officially used, to add that is, to the limitations already detailed in the 'Blue Paper' by the exclusion of preference. But the principle remained constant. As Balfour explained to the King on 15 September:

The root principle for which Mr. Balfour pleads is *liberty of fiscal negotiation* . . .

There are, however, two quite different shapes in which this 'freedom to negotiate' may be employed—one against Foreign Governments—the others in favour of our own Colonies. In dealing with Foreign Governments, we may threaten—and if need be employ—'retaliation'. In dealing with our own Colonies we can only offer 'Preference'. The second is perhaps the most important; *if*, that is, a really good bargain could be struck between the Mother Country and her children. But it is also far the most difficult. It is difficult because a bargain is always difficult: it is equally difficult because it is hard to see how *any* bargain could be contrived which the Colonies would accept, and *which would not involve some taxation of food in this country*.

In Mr. Balfour's opinion, there are ways in which such taxation *might* be imposed which would in no degree add to the cost of living of the Working Classes. But he is also of opinion that in the present state of Public feeling no such plan would get a fair hearing; to make it part of the Government Programme would be to break up the Party and to endanger the *other* half of the Policy—that which authorises retaliation—for which the country is better prepared. Mr. Balfour, therefore, as at present advised, intends to say that, though Colonial Preference is eminently desirable in the interests both of British Commerce and Imperial Unity, *it has not yet come within the sphere of practical politics*.[61]

Balfour had always sympathized in theory with Chamberlain's preferential policy, but had doubts about its practicality. His concise statement to the King that food duties were not yet practical politics represented a distillation of these doubts into concrete form, but did not constitute a change of policy.

At the cabinet of 14 September, the central point at issue remained not the specific uses of 'fiscal freedom', i.e. preference and food duties, but acceptance of the principle itself. Balfour insisted on this throughout the meeting and the free traders were aware of this. 'We were asked', Ritchie told Elliot, 'to swallow the principle and trust to Mr. Balfour and Mr. Chamberlain for details.'[62] Ritchie's comment reveals the fundamental misunderstanding of the free traders which Balfour deliberately fostered. They were not asked to trust both Balfour and Chamberlain for the details, but only Balfour. But because they did not know of Chamberlain's letter of 9 September they had no way of knowing this.

Nor could Balfour afford to tell them, for his acceptance of Chamberlain's resignation was conditional on resignations from the other side, and possibly even conditional on Devonshire agreeing to remain since there was little tactical purpose in losing both. Balfour could not separate from Chamberlain altogether. 'It must be borne in mind', he wrote to the King, 'that if Mr. Balfour made concessions in the direction of the Chancellor of the Exchequer's views, which, on its merits, he is not at all disposed to do, he would lose the services not only of Mr. Chamberlain and Mr. A. Chamberlain, the First Lord of the Admiralty [but also] others including the Lord Chancellor.'[63] His policy thus demanded a commitment for the future; the exclusion of preference for the time being, but a commitment to the policy of change irrespective of details, and a willingness to accept preference should it become 'practical politics'.

On these grounds Balfour distinguished between Devonshire and the other free trade ministers: 'I was convinced they were root and branch opponents of fiscal reform, and that they were resolved to leave the Government unless the fiscal reformers surrendered at discretion. I thought, on the other hand, that your attitude was one of not unfavourable suspense . . .'[64] It remains an open question whether Balfour would have taken the trouble to make this distinction, either in theory or practice, had he not considered Devonshire's support as vital. But Devonshire concentrated his attacks not upon the principle of fiscal reform but upon the proposed restraints to be placed upon Chamberlain, and had himself encouraged a distinction between his views and Ritchie's. Chamberlain's offer to resign thus removed Devonshire's objections, but did not affect Ritchie's. This assessment was not entirely incorrect. Ritchie had already determined his conditions for staying in office:

we must have some clear understanding that Balfour . . . *is not to commit the Cabinet as a whole to any portion of Chamberlain's policy*, and that Chamberlain is not to be at liberty to carry the fiery cross into all the constituencies during the autumn . . . An essential condition of this arrangement is, of course, that we are not to be asked at our next meeting to come to a definite decision on Balfour's paper . . . We cannot assent to the principles embodied in his paper until we have an opportunity of considering his plan in detail.[65]

Had Chamberlain resigned without corresponding resignations from the free trade side, Balfour would have been the prisoner of a free trade cabinet, with the progressive alienation of Chamberlain as he found it impossible to make concessions without destroying his government.

The free traders implied in their subsequent criticisms of Balfour's conduct that had they been informed of Chamberlain's resignation, which in fact had not taken place when the cabinet met, then they would have reconsidered their position. This attitude was inconsistent with their views at the time which were as hostile to retaliation as to preference, with their argument that the exchange of letters constituted Balfour's capitulation to Chamberlain, and with their continued pressure on Devonshire to resign from a protectionist government.[66] Knowledge of Chamberlain's resignation would not have induced the free traders to look more kindly upon the limited reform proposals which Balfour's policy embodied for the immediate future. Reconsideration of their position would have been based upon fear of resigning without Devonshire, and upon the calculation that the threat of resignation would give them effective control over Balfour's actions in the future when Chamberlain had gone. Under these circumstances the free traders had to go. Balfour's intrigues were designed solely to ensure that Devonshire did not go with them.

Apart from Chamberlain, Devonshire was the only individual whom Balfour made positive efforts to win over, partly because Devonshire indicated a desire to be reconciled, partly because of the influence he was reputed to have in the country. But Devonshire's decision to withdraw his resignation was not taken with conviction. 'I had, and still have', he told Chamberlain, 'difficulty in accepting the policy which Balfour will announce at Sheffield . . .'[67] Since this policy had been designed to retain Chamberlain's unofficial support, Devonshire's reluctance was not surprising. The Duke had allowed himself to drift into a false position, and by the end of the summer had contracted obligations both to the free traders and to Balfour. Both Balfour during the September crisis and the free traders after their resignations played upon the Duke's sense of honour. Under this pressure the Duke increasingly came to feel that his only course was to resign as quickly as possible. Balfour's speech at Sheffield, announcing the policy of 'fiscal freedom' for retaliation but excluding preference, gave him his opportunity.

Despite Balfour's protests that the speech contained no doctrine 'which was not equally contained in my "Notes on Insular Free Trade", and my published letter to Chamberlain',[68] the Duke remained unrepentant, and moved into the more comfortable position of ineffectual leader of the free trade faction. By resigning when he did Devonshire made matters worse than if he had resigned in September. It was to avoid such recurrent crises that Balfour attempted a clean sweep, and the Duke's resignation merely reopened old wounds and cast doubts upon the official government policy to which Balfour was now publicly committed. But in the short run, despite Devonshire's belated defection, Balfour's policy of postponing the imperial aspects of tariff reform indefinitely achieved his purpose. By blurring the edges of the ideological conflict between free trade and tariff reform, and turning the debate into one of details and timing, Balfour added considerably to the waverers in both extreme camps, prepared to await the outcome of postponement and in the meantime to support the government and its fiscal policy.

Chamberlain's Tariff Reform

With the break-up of the cabinet, Chamberlain began to 'carry the fiery cross into the constituencies'. He opened at Glasgow on 6 October, and for the next few months was the dominant political force in the country. His whirlwind campaign of speeches in major urban centres alarmed all his opponents, Unionist free trader and Liberal alike, who feared that he might carry the country by storm. The provisional programme of tariff reform which Chamberlain announced at Glasgow was simple—a duty of 2s. per quarter on imported foreign corn, excluding maize, and 'a corresponding duty on foreign flour', a 5 per cent duty on foreign meat and dairy produce, excluding bacon, 'a substantial preference to our colonies upon colonial wines and perhaps upon colonial fruit', and 'a moderate duty on all [foreign] manufactured goods, not exceeding 10%'. To make the new food duties acceptable to the electorate, Chamberlain proposed corresponding reductions in the existing duties on tea, sugar, cocoa, and coffee, making up the lost revenue from the duties on manufactured goods:

The principle . . . is that whereas your present taxation, whether it be on food or anything else, brings you revenue and nothing but revenue, the taxation which I propose, which will not increase your burdens, will gain for you in trade, in employment, in all that we most want to maintain, the prosperity of our industries. The one is profitless taxation, the other is scientific taxation.

Presented thus, the policy was no more than a readjustment of indirect taxation, 'a transfer from one item to another'. By this means, Chamberlain hoped to achieve the two objects of fiscal reform—retaliation or protection against foreign competition, and reciprocal preference with the colonies to further the unification of the Empire.[1]

The simplicity of the Glasgow programme was, however, deceptive. The arguments by which he supported his policy were distinctly protectionist and attacked free trade on broad ideological grounds as inconsistent with the new conditions of world trade, with the trend of British social legislation, and with the preservation of the Empire. Like the Fair Trade League and many of his contemporaries whose fears he reflected, Chamberlain took as his starting point the premiss that Britain's trade was declining, not yet in absolute terms, but in comparison with the rate of progress of her major commercial rivals. He explicitly rejected the explanation that the Liberal Imperialists gave for this domestic 'inefficiency', and their solution, improved technical education. The fault lay not within Britain herself, but in the unfair competition of her foreign competitors whose high tariffs were, he alleged, designed to exclude British goods. Under free trade, Britain was a 'defenceless village', her trade, her employment, her standard of living all at risk unless the existing system was changed.

Chamberlain directed his appeal in the first instance to the working classes on the basis of self-interest. If British workers wished to keep their employment and their living standards, standards protected locally against the rigours of an unfettered market economy by social and industrial legislation, they must accept protection against foreign competition as well. Social legislation

raised the cost of production; and what can be more illogical than to raise the cost of production in the country and then to allow the products of other countries which are not surrounded by any similar legislation, which are free from any similar cost and expenditure—freely to enter our country in competition with our own goods . . . If these foreign goods come in cheaper, one of two things must follow . . . either you will take lower wages or you will lose your work.

'You cannot', Chamberlain told the working classes, 'have free trade in goods, and at the same time have protection of labour.' In the last resort, they would be the losers. Capital was mobile, labour was not, and the capitalist could always invest abroad, whilst the workers had 'no recourse except, perhaps, to learn French or German'.

The choice of emphasis, to attack free trade as it applied to domestic social and economic conditions on ideological grounds, was primarily tactical, for it enabled Chamberlain to present free trade and extreme Cobdenite individualism as two sides of the same philosophy. Cobden, he reminded his working-class audiences, had been opposed to trade unions, and opposed to collectivist social reform. He reminded the working classes also that when free trade became the accepted fiscal policy they did not have the vote, and that 'the Radicals of those days', the Chartists, had opposed the repeal of the Corn Laws. Now, 'the matter is very much in your own hands. You are the judges. You are the Caesar to whom I appeal . . .' It was a direct attempt to win the working classes, and especially the trade unions, away from their attachment to the Liberal party and into the new radicalism of tariff reform.

The magnitude of the changes proposed made tariff reform in any case a radical policy. But Chamberlain deliberately emphasized its radicalism and the collectivist traditions of the Conservative and Unionist parties, drawing on the traditions of Tory Democracy, in contrast to the Liberals who, as free traders, were 'prevented from taking this course by the theories by which they have been governed'. In so doing, he sought to establish the same basis for Unionism as he had aimed at in the early 1890s, transcending class barriers to incorporate the working classes into the existing party system behind a radical Unionist party. To this end, the state regulation of tariffs and of social and industrial conditions was represented as the collectivist alternative to free trade and individualism.

Within this regulated society Chamberlain sought national unity, involving the unity of all productive classes, employers and employees, in contrast to class conflict. Conflict, including economic conflict, took place at the national level between competing states, not within nations between competing classes. 'There are some people', he declared:

who try to persuade the working men of this country that the whole thing is a struggle between themselves and the capitalists, and that if they can only squeeze the capitalist a little more, they will get more wages, and that it will only be the capitalist who will suffer. Now, everyone who has paid any attention to the condition of trade and industry knows this to be an absolute untruth. He knows that if you do not give the capitalist the reasonable profit that he has a right to anticipate, he will take his capital and go elsewhere, and in the long run, employment will go.

The interests of British workers and British employers were interdependent, whilst all British industry shared a common enemy, 'the foreigner', who robbed British workers of wages and work, and employers of their profit and capital. Chamberlain described himself in terms similar to those in which Asquith had described his idea of the Liberal party, as the representative of Labour, but Labour 'which

thinks not of itself as a class opposed to any other class in the community, but as responsible for the obligations of the country and the
Empire to which it belongs . . .'

On Chamberlain's arguments, the British working class had indeed
no choice but to recognize these obligations if it wished to maintain or
improve its living standards. For just as the interests of British producers were interdependent, combined in common competition with
the foreigner, so also they were dependent upon the maintenance of
the Empire. Throughout his career Chamberlain had maintained that
Britain's commercial supremacy, and with it her power and her
standard of living, were dependent upon the imperial connection.

> Is there any man in his senses [he asked in 1888] who believes that the
> crowded population of these islands could exist for a single day if we were
> to cut adrift from the great dependencies which now look to us for protection
> and assistance, and which are the natural markets for our trade? . . . If,
> tomorrow, it were possible, as some people apparently desire, to reduce by a
> stroke of the pen, the British Empire to the dimensions of the United King-
> dom, half at least of our population would be starved.[2]

This view he incorporated into tariff reform without change. Indeed,
it was central to the argument for tariff reform, for it was the only substantial link between the protectionist, or retaliationist, argument,
concerned solely with the defence of British trade and employment
against foreign competition, and the argument for imperial unity. As
Balfour had discovered, 'retaliation' and 'preference' could be separated from the purely domestic point of view, and retaliation would
secure most of the benefits Chamberlain promised from tariff reform,
including revenue, without the electoral disadvantage of food duties,
which were essential only for preference. The economic justification for
tariff reform as an imperial movement rested largely upon the acceptability of Chamberlain's contention that the future of British trade
depended upon the security of imperial markets. Because of this
contention, however, the imperialist and economic arguments by which
Chamberlain advocated tariff reform were mutually supporting. Britain,
and above all her workers, could not maintain their material standards
at home without an empire, and therefore had a vested interest in
taking advantage of any opportunity offered for furthering the movement towards imperial unity.

The moment for this was, according to Chamberlain, both propitious and critical—propitious because colonial participation in the South African war 'made possible an organised union of all the different parts of the Empire for common objects', critical because the colonies had already offered reciprocal preference at the Conference of 1902, and a rebuff would be worse than if the offer had never been made. Unless his programme was adopted Chamberlain prophesied the disintegration of the Empire and all that that involved. Trade was the key to the whole problem, for as trade depended upon the Empire, so the Empire depended upon trade. All sides of the tariff reform case were inter-related. Britain's trade, employment and living standards, her power, and imperial unity, stood or fell together. Chamberlain presented his listeners with a choice between going forward as a rich united Empire, or declining into a hungry little England, living on the sufferance of her more powerful neighbours: 'This is the parting of the ways . . . If you do not take this opportunity, it will not recur . . . We must either draw closer together, or we shall drift apart.'

But although Chamberlain based his propaganda in favour of tariff reform as an imperialist movement on the appeal to local material interests, and in particular the interests of the working class, the preservation of such interests was never the driving force behind Chamberlain's tariff reform movement. This line of argument was tactical, part of a general belief that with a mass electorate working-class support could not be obtained except by promising tangible benefits. But there was an idealistic side to the tariff reform movement, a particular vision of Britain and of the British race which, while not exclusive to tariff reform, was an essential part of its nature and motivated its most committed supporters. The economic debate which Chamberlain's tariff reform campaign stirred up was, for Chamberlain, a secondary issue, the questions raised secondary questions, about the means proposed not the ends sought. The choice he presented was not simply between prosperity and poverty, but between power and impotence, duty and irresponsibility. Tactics apart, Chamberlain was prepared to disregard the appeal to local vested interests as inessential:

I ask you to make this change for your own good, as well as the good of the empire, and . . . you will not be called upon for any sacrifice. I declare to you I wish I could say that you would be called upon for a sacrifice. I declare to you I would rather speak to you here and appeal to you as Englishmen, and ask whether you are not willing to do what your fathers would have done, and what in fact they did do; whether for some great good in which, indeed, you might have no immediate personal interest, you would not be willing to make a sacrifice for great imperial interests.

Sacrifice, not profit, was the essence of Chamberlain's 'true conception of Empire'. 'The British Empire', he declared, 'was acquired by sacrifice from first to last. It was won by sacrifice. It can only be maintained by sacrifice.' The government of the Empire was an imperial mission, a moral duty upon the race as a 'work of civilisation'. But, the 'faculties and qualities' which made the British 'a great governing race' were not innate. The Empire "has made us what we are—it has taught us the virtue of national sacrifice . . . It has ennobled our national life. It has discouraged that petty parochialism which is the defect of all small countries . . . all that is best in our present life, best in this Britain of ours . . . is due to the fact that we are not only sons of Britain, but we are sons of Empire."

Occasionally, in pursuit of this idealism, Chamberlain came close to contradicting those parts of his argument which emphasized the need for tariff reform for the protection of local interest:

I care very little whether the result will be to make this country, already rich, a little richer. The character of a nation is more important than its opulence. What I care for is that this people shall rise to the height of its great mission; that they who, in past generations have made a kingdom surpassed by none, should now, in altered circumstances and new conditions, show themselves worthy of the leadership of the British race and, in cooperation with our kinsmen across the seas, they should combine to make an Empire which may be, which ought to be, greater, more united, more fruitful for good than any Empire in human history.

But at other times both arguments reinforced each other, as Chamberlain argued that, if action was not taken along his lines:

we shall lose not only our commerce, but the whole character of the country will be changed; and, in the course of another generation, this will be much less an industrial country, inhabited by skilful artisans, than a distributive country with a smaller population consisting of rich consumers on the one hand, and people engaged in the work of distribution on the other . . . we may be richer, yet weaker.

Tariff reform offered a means to redress this economic imbalance, and restore the domestic foundations of power and idealism.

Chamberlain, and those imperial idealists who provided his movement with its activists, were primarily concerned with the Empire as a way of life and a governing tradition. Despite occasional references to other parts of the Empire, tariff reform was essentially a means to unite the mother country and the self-governing white Dominions as separate parts of a common race and civilization. Within this group, local British interests were absorbed into the general British imperial interest and Chamberlain, together with many other imperialists, could envisage a future in which the leadership of the Empire and its capital might move overseas. Already, in the tariff reform analysis, Britain could not cope with the task of governing the Empire alone, and the domestic changes to be wrought by tariff reform would not be sufficient in a hostile world of extensive empires with large populations to change this. In the self-governing colonies Britain could find partners to share the load, and at the same time a solution to her own defence problems. The same applied to food and to commercial warfare. Britain depended, according to Chamberlain, 'for four-fifths of our supplies [of wheat] upon foreign countries, any of which, by shutting their doors on us, might reduce us to a state of almost starvation . . .' But, 'we have an Empire which with decent organisation and consolidation might be absolutely self-sustaining . . .'

Immediate pressures and future prospects, material interest and moral duty, combined in tariff reform propaganda to demonstrate that Britain could only survive as a power by uniting with the Empire. Chamberlain presented the choice in apocalyptic terms:

The Colonies are no longer in their infancy . . . Now is the time—the last time—that you can bind them closer to you . . . We can, if we will, make the Empire mutually supporting. We can make it one for defence and for common aid and assistance. We are face to face at this time with complications in which we may find ourselves alone. We have to face the envy of other people who have noted our wonderful success . . . We shall be isolated . . . but our isolation will be a splendid one if we are fortified . . . by the affection and love of our kinsmen . . .

The character of the individual depends upon the greatness of the ideals upon which he rests, and the character of a nation is the same. The moral grandeur of a nation depends upon its being sometimes able to forget itself, sometimes able to think of the future of the race for which it stands. England without an Empire! . . . England in that case would not be the England we love. If the ties of sympathy which have been gradually woven between ourselves and our children across the seas . . . were weakened or destroyed . . . then this England of ours would sink from the comparative position which it has enjoyed throughout the centuries. It would no longer be a power, if not supreme, at all events of the greatest influence, generally well-exercised, on the civilisation and peace of the world. It would be a fifth-rate nation, existing on the sufferance of its more powerful neighbours.

Tariff reform, like Liberal Imperialism from which Chamberlain won a few recruits, reflected the anxieties of Chamberlain's class and generation about trade, food supplies, especially in wartime, defence, and to a much lesser extent about living standards and employment. But whereas the Liberal Imperialists proposed domestic remedies to problems which they saw almost entirely in domestic terms, Chamberlain sought help from outside, in the organization of the Empire, to make that, rather than Britain alone, 'efficient'. Even more than Liberal Imperialism, tariff reform was a competitive doctrine, believing in the inevitability of conflict between nations, and security and prosperity through strength. Its appeal, even in economic terms, was to national sentiment, albeit an extended nationalism which embraced loyalty to the Empire as a whole rather than to Britain alone. In the context of the recent past, of free trade and individualism, it was, with its collectivist stance, a radical doctrine. But it was a distinctly right-wing brand of radicalism, challenging not merely the 'old left' of Liberalism, but the 'new Liberalism' which was similarly collectivist, but which was anti-imperialist, anti-national in tariff reform terms, and had distinct overtones of class politics.

The opposition to tariff reform in 1903, however, came not from 'new Liberalism' which had barely begun to emerge from the books, journals, and debating societies of a new generation of Liberal intellectuals, but from traditional free traders on traditional free trade grounds, fighting, not a new economic or imperialist idea, but a revival of 'protection'. Their economic case, which Ritchie had already stated in his cabinet memorandums, rested on the necessity of low costs of production. Under Chamberlain's proposed system they predicted increased costs which would both hamper British penetration of overseas markets and reduce demand all round.[3] Under free trade Britain had progressed to become 'the richest nation in the world',[4] and the free traders saw no sign of impending collapse. 'Never', declared Churchill, 'was the wealth of the country greater, or the trade returns higher, or the loyalty of the Colonies more pronounced.'[5] Where there were special difficulties, the Unionist free traders fell back on the remedies already proposed by the Liberal Imperialists, 'scientific and technical education'.[6]

Nor did the free traders accept Chamberlain's contention that the unity of the Empire needed to be strengthened, or that it was possible to do so by means of preference. 'I fear', Churchill wrote, 'that a policy of Preferential tariffs will lead to much friction between the Colonies and the mother country, and if it is based upon the taxation of food, will estrange the masses of our countrymen from the Imperial idea.'[7] He stressed 'the almost insuperable difficulties of framing any scheme which will satisfy all the Colonies and the certainty of future bickerings and hagglings',[8] conflicts of interest which Lord Hugh Cecil believed would create discontent and disaffection in every colony. The result of Chamberlain's policies would thus, in the free trade view, be the very opposite of that which he intended, and precipitate the disruption he feared.[9] Only the revenue aspect of the question did not provoke total conflict. Chamberlain, after his promise to reduce existing food duties, shied away from the subject somewhat, whilst for the free traders it was not an ideological issue. 'The main propositions of Free Trade', wrote Churchill, 'do not touch methods of raising revenue. Money has to be found for carrying on the government of the country, and when revenue alone is the object of the tax no violation of Free Trade principles occurs.'[10]

In the summer and autumn of 1903, however, the free traders had some difficulty in making these principles widely known, a difficulty increased by Balfour's fiscal truce. 'While Mr. Balfour silences his followers in the House of Commons,' Churchill complained to *The Times*, 'Mr. Chamberlain is busy with their constituencies. Within the last few days, circulars have been sent to local Conservative agents inviting them, irrespective of the opinions of their members, to disseminate Protectionist propaganda.'[11] The tariff reformers also launched their attack on the national party organizations. Careful preparatory work on a tariff reform resolution and the whipping up of supporters ensured that the meeting of the National Union at Sheffield, where Balfour announced his official policy, was predominantly in favour of Chamberlain's views.[12] On 20 October the first step towards Chamberlain's eventual capture of the Liberal Unionist Association was taken, when the annual conference of the North Riding L.U.A. passed a resolution in favour of Chamberlain's policy in the face of a letter to the contrary from Devonshire, with the result that its free trade members resigned.[13] In the constituencies, by the end of December, Lord Hugh Cecil, Churchill, Lord George Hamilton, and Arthur Elliot had all been confronted with tariff reform resolutions passed by hostile constituency associations.[14]

Unable to make headway against Chamberlain in the constituencies in face of his swift capture of the organizations of their own party, the Unionist free traders looked to the Liberals, as they had done since the opening of the fiscal debate, for support in the defence of free trade, and even for the preservation of their own political existence. Even after the formation of the Unionist Free Food League, their organization was 'only a parliamentary committee with very meagre resources',[15] unable to provide on its own an effective counter to tariff reform propaganda. The Liberals in general shared their alarm at Chamberlain's activities and acknowledged the overwhelming importance of the issues he had raised. Chamberlain, according to Ripon, had already done

a degree of mischief to the political relations between the Mother Country and the Colonies which it will be almost impossible to remedy. If this country rejects these proposals now, the Colonies will be offended and alienated—if it accepts them and withdraws from them when their evil effects on the people of the United Kingdom and on our trade begin to be felt, the position will be still worse. If I were an Imperialist, I would denounce Chamberlain as the worst enemy of Imperial unity.

But that is not really the most important part of the matter. The abandonment of free trade, the taxation of food, if not of raw materials to which, whatever Chamberlain may say, his policy directly leads, the disorganisation of industry and the war of tariffs which are the inevitable features of this policy, render the present crisis by far the gravest in the last fifty years. It is the greatest political struggle even of my long political life . . .

Everything else sinks into insignificance. This battle must be fought to the end. We must be prepared to unite with anyone who will help and part company with anyone who will not.[16]

Ripon therefore advocated the establishment of a new non-party organization to combat Chamberlain's propaganda in the constituencies, a suggestion quickly taken up by Herbert Gladstone, which resulted in the formation of the Free Trade League.[17]

Co-operation in any other form, however, proved more difficult to achieve. The Unionist free traders were inevitably torn between their free trade principles and their party loyalty, a conflict which continually threatened to destroy their effectiveness as a group. Churchill, who favoured co-operation with the Liberals more than most, thus advised

Rosebery not to be 'drawn from your logical position to accommodate the programme of the Free Food League',[18] and added shortly afterwards that 'our difficulties in the Free Food League are immense. The pressure of local organisations upon the members is severe and there are 8 or 10 old women who . . . prate of loyalty, where it is not returned.'[19] The resolution of the cabinet crisis did little to ease this difficulty, even when Balfour's announcement of the official policy was followed by Devonshire's resignation, since it left the relationship between Balfour and Chamberlain imprecise. Balfour's success in clouding the issue by evolving his own 'half-way house' in fact made the dilemma, and hence the paralysis, of the Unionist free traders permanent: 'I am not at all clear as to the future of the Unionist Free Food League; and think it may not improbably dissolve,' Beach reported to Harcourt in September. 'As you know, it is a very weak organisation in point of numbers and means and many of its members are by no means prepared to oppose the principle . . . of . . . retaliation.'[20] Beach himself was of this last group. Liberal manœuvres throughout the year tended to revolve around the difficulties of co-operating with such irresolute allies. The Liberals, like the Unionist free traders, suffered from the uncertainty which tariff reform and Balfour's response brought into the political situation. Not until February 1904, when the failure of Chamberlain's autumn campaign became apparent and removed both the threat to free trade and the possibility of a snap general election, could the Liberal leaders review their position calmly and assess how much they really needed 'to unite with anyone who will help'. As long as it seemed as though Chamberlain might sweep the country, the Liberals were forced to take the Unionist free trade overtures seriously.

In seeking Liberal co-operation, however, the Unionist free traders were playing a complex double game, equalled in its duplicity only by that of the Liberals themselves. Whilst the defence of free trade was itself a non-party question, politicians were still organized into parties and the means by which free trade was defended could still be exploited for party advantage. Few of the Unionist free traders, even the most militant, had any serious intention of joining the Liberals, or even moving into open opposition to their own party. Their primary purpose was to defeat Chamberlain within the Unionist party and thus save the party from the disaster of protection for its own good. 'The new protection', wrote Strachey, editor of the *Spectator*, 'must be knocked

on the head within our own party and before it becomes an inter-
party fight.'[21] Initially Beach, whose support the free traders deemed
essential if their cause was to prosper, even opposed 'anything like the
start of a Free Trade organisation on our side; as if Joe is quiet, I don't
want to make any move to disturb him . . . My main object is to keep
the Government together and prevent Balfour from committing himself to Joe . . .'[22] Under pressure from his friends and from the increasing militancy of Chamberlain's supporters, Beach yielded and
agreed to participate in the formation of the Free Food League. But
his objective remained unchanged.

The tactics of the Unionist free traders were, therefore, of necessity
those of moderation, to avoid the sort of confrontation in which the
conflict between their principles and their loyalty would shatter their
unity. Lord Hugh Cecil thought:

at this moment nothing would be more calamitous than a division on a clear
issue. We might get thirty people on our side to vote with us. I want to get a
hundred or 150. Our game is at all hazards to avoid a division in which we
should vote with the Opposition. An immense section of the Party have not
yet anything like the courage, or 'disloyalty' to go into the lobby on a vote of
censure with the leaders of the Opposition. Yet they may be Free Traders at
heart. It is much better to begin an agitation on as large a scale as possible and
tempt trembling sheep on to our platforms . . . We must be most decorous
and respectable; and put Beach and Goschen (if he will come) in the forefront
of all we do . . . As much as possible we must throw the discredit for splitting
the party on Joe.[23]

Co-operation with the Liberals meant persuading them not to take
advantage of Unionist divisions for their own party benefit by raising
the subject in the Commons. To this end, Churchill wrote to ask
Campbell-Bannerman to withdraw an amendment he proposed to
move to Ritchie's budget: 'After all, we like the Finance Bill . . . the
position of those Conservatives who are unalterably opposed to the
impending fiscal change is one of great difficulty and danger . . .'[24]
Beach had already been to see Harcourt for the same purpose.[25] In the
first instance, the Unionist free traders' understanding of co-operation
was no more than an attempt to exploit the Liberal party to rescue the
Unionist party.

These were obviously not Liberal objectives and the Liberals were
aware of the difference. 'We do not leave out of consideration', wrote
Campbell-Bannerman to Harcourt, 'the fact that Beach and James and

hoc genus omne have objects in view which are not ours; in fact, as James avows, they want to prevent the Radicals from getting into office.'[26] But they were divided upon the response they should make. Their simplest course was to bring Chamberlain and Balfour out into the open, force the government to commit itself to protection, and thus make the issue a party question pure and simple, rallying all right-thinking free traders to the Liberal side. In view of the vacillation of the Unionist free traders, W. S. Robson concluded 'that the Free Trade Tories should be forced either to vote for Food Taxation or to attack the Ministry proposing it'.[27]

But there were dangers in such a hard-line course, the most obvious being that it risked staking all on one election which, if the Liberals lost, would be claimed by Chamberlain as a mandate for his policies. Additionally, whilst Balfour maintained a compromise position, such a move to press for clarification of the question, which would force the Unionist free traders to choose between free trade and their party, might, and probably would, reunite the majority of them to the main body of the party under the Balfourite umbrella. This, in turn, would make a Unionist electoral victory more likely. The alternative was to play the Unionist free trade game and avoid the issue, not for the sake of the Unionist free traders, but in order to prolong and deepen Unionist divisions, and make the final break, if it came, as disruptive as possible. This course, too, had its drawbacks. In particular, it involved holding back enthusiastic back-benchers for reasons which few of them could understand, with the risk of the loss of that morale which was only slowly returning to the party after its recent disasters.

Initially the Liberal leaders wavered inconsistently between these two policies. On 16 June, a statement was issued after a shadow cabinet meeting declaring that they did not intend 'to move a resolution in the House of Commons on the subject of the fiscal proposals of Mr. Chamberlain'.[28] But on 1 July Tweedmouth informed Churchill that the shadow cabinet had decided after all to raise the issue, and if the Unionist free traders pledged their support the terms of the resolution against preference would be for mutual arrangement. According to Tweedmouth, however, there was no hesitation in the shadow cabinet, which was determined to raise the matter even by vote of censure if Balfour would only permit a debate on those terms.[29]

But the dangers of forcing a division were too great for this tactic to be insisted upon in the face of Unionist free traders' reluctance to vote against their party. The effect, as Harcourt pointed out, would be to allow the government to rally its forces, 'thus halting the process of disintegration'.[30] Fully aware that 'we have nothing to expect from their cooperation in the House', Harcourt nevertheless advised acquiescence in the tactics of the Unionist free traders in order to avoid prematurely reuniting the Unionist party.[31] Harcourt's advice prevailed, and the Liberals, for tactical reasons, acquiesced in the truce of silence imposed by Balfour.

The effect of their actions on the Unionist party was only one of the factors which the official Liberal leaders had to take into account when devising their tactics in the summer of 1903. With the danger that Chamberlain might be successful in the constituencies, with Rosebery and the Liberal League on his flank, Campbell-Bannerman negotiated from a position that was neither strong nor secure. The Liberal League had lost considerable ground during 1902 as a result of the reunification of the party in opposition to the Education Act, and some initiative on its part was essential by the beginning of 1903 if it were to regain its influence. Herbert Gladstone thought the League was 'on the edge of a precipice. If Rosebery does not play an active game, he is likely to come a cropper. His own men are full of disaffection . . . [and] . . . their power for mischief is very small, for the real party organisation in the country . . . is about solid.'[32]

The League, however, had no intention of going down without a fight, whatever its parliamentary leadership might do, and friction between it and the Whips Office was frequent, particularly during 1903, demonstrating the difficulty of reuniting a party in which the differences of opinion had become institutionalized. This mutual distrust was well-illustrated by an abrasive exchange between Paulton and Gladstone early in 1903, after Paulton was reported as criticizing the inefficiency of the official Liberal organization. Jesse Herbert, one of the organizers thus condemned, demanded from Gladstone 'some defence against these party assailants who preach of unity and only mean "ascendency" '.[33] Gladstone's demand that Paulton justify or withdraw his remarks only provoked Paulton into a reaffirmation of his attacks and relations deteriorated further. 'The only evidence of falling to bits that I can see', wrote Gladstone, after Paulton had alleged that the national Liberal organization was 'falling to bits', 'is the formation of the Liberal League, which has abstracted men from the "official" organization, diverted funds, and in the supply of candidates, has certainly not yet justified its existence.'[34]

In the constituencies relations were worse. At Rye, Dr. Hutchinson created havoc by standing as a League candidate pledged to support Rosebery, even though the League did not want him. Hutchinson's action stirred up old bitterness between the rank and file of the two central organizations as to which, under these peculiar circumstances, should provide the agent for the constituency: 'it is not easy for us to act as subordinates of the League,' wrote Crook from the 'official' side. 'I rather fear the effect on the party of Bass as agent again, and Hutchinson a declared member of the League. It reopens old sores which were healing. That sort of thing is certain to produce reprisals sooner or later . . .' Bitterness was in fact so far aroused that Crook reported that H. S. Leon proposed a separate fund from opponents of the League for such emergencies to fight the League 'with its own weapon—cash':

The only card we have is their reluctance to offend Nash [the official agent] and all the agents who will resent a well-paid Liberal League agent always being stuffed into every vacancy. All prospects of 'plums' is thus denied them. They always have resented the same thing, even when done from Headquarters, and as rumour fixes the salaries at Victoria Street as still higher than at Headquarters, they resent it proportionately more.[35]

Freeman-Thomas nevertheless sent in Bass on behalf of the League, but pledged full co-operation with Gladstone, and agreed in regarding Hutchinson as a bad candidate: 'I fear his object [in joining the League] is to collect funds from all he can.'

Initially, however, Gladstone refused to back Hutchinson, not because he had joined the League but because Hutchinson refused to support Campbell-Bannerman. A formula was eventually agreed by which Gladstone found it possible to support Hutchinson's candidature, but the whole incident was indicative of the difficulties caused in the constituencies by the existence of two mutually suspicious Liberal organizations.[36] Crook still referred to 'considerable friction' in Rye as late as October 1903.[37] Hutchinson's disinclination to recognize Campbell-Bannerman as leader of the party, and his eventual agreement after being driven into a corner by Gladstone to recognize him as leader only 'as long as he was elected by the majority of the party', indicated also that Campbell-Bannerman was far from secure in his hold on the leadership, and that if Rosebery did choose to come forward he might still have the power to split the party.

Rye was no isolated incident, even if Hutchinson's antics made it worse than most. In March 1903 Jesse Herbert again howled with rage at League activities,[38] and later reported further problems with Bass and complaints about his activities in Leicester.[39] In November, Crook reported difficulties in Eastbourne where the local Liberals 'will not have Walker. They give no reason, but I feel it is because he is not a Leaguer.' He observed then that 'there is an admirable League candidate at their doors—F. W. Maude',[40] but Maude's membership of the League caused him difficulties later. In March 1904 Crook wrote again to recommend that Gladstone should back Maude ' "pontifically", as there is some opposition to him from the extreme Radical wing. He brought down Haldane to support him, and this caused the Radical leader in Eastbourne to make a violent speech against "wolves in sheep's clothing" '.[41]

Further problems broke out in Hallamshire in October, where the League was opposed to Compton Rickett,[42] and in January 1905 difficulties again erupted at Rye over the obliging, but nevertheless unpopular, Dr. Hutchinson and his election expenses.[43] By 1905, however, progress towards unity within the Liberal party had gone far enough to make agreement between the two organizations possible. The League, Freeman-Thomas told Gladstone, had 'no intention of making any appeal for funds for the General Election, which would interfere with the Central Fund', and he promised full co-operation in allocating money.[44] Both were symptomatic of the decline of the League as an independent organization by that time. But as long as the League continued, and the possibility existed that Rosebery might pick up the old threads and 'play an active game', the Liberal Imperialists could not be written off.

The split in the Unionist party offered such an opportunity to transform their situation. The Unionist free traders were as frightened of the radicalism of the Liberal left with which they associated Campbell-Bannerman, as they were of the protectionist views of Chamberlain and the tariff reformers within their own party. Several of the leading spirits among the free traders were Conservative, even within the ranks of the Unionist party, in particular the Cecils. Their Conservatism as much as their comprehension of economics led them to take refuge in a doctrinaire adherence to free trade, and to identify the 'interventionist' economic and social policies of tariff reform with socialism. The possibility of fusion, or co-operation at least, with the Liberal Imperialists, appealed to a broad spectrum of Unionist free trade opinion. It was for these Unionists the natural second line of defence.[45]

The overtures which the Unionist free traders made to the Liberal party were thus as great a threat to Campbell-Bannerman's position as they were to Balfour's: 'we ought not to act with C.B. at all', Lord Hugh Cecil wrote to Churchill. 'Rosebery and Grey are our friends. We must try and split their party as well as our own.'[46] 'A large number of Unionist free traders could not in honesty and patriotism permanently co-operate with the Liberal party as now constituted,' he wrote later to Devonshire:

If . . . the dominant force in that party were Lord Rosebery and the Liberal Imperialists, the case might be different. But . . . the mainstream of Liberalism . . . is Gladstonian in foreign, colonial and Irish questions, it is Nonconformist in ecclesiastical and educational questions, it is Radical in questions affecting property, it is Trade Unionist in questions affecting labour and capital. For those of the Free Food League who are Imperialists and Unionists and Churchmen and Conservatives, a permanent cooperation with such a party could not be otherwise than immoral . . . [47]

Campbell-Bannerman, who tended to share the views of his radical supporters on this subject, in turn condemned the Unionist free traders as 'a feeble lot . . . time servers almost to a man'. Even Churchill, who in 1904 defected to the Liberal party, he regarded as 'hardly worth any increase of complications'.[48] But in 1903 Churchill was thinking in terms of a 'reconstituted Liberal party' under Rosebery's leadership, or a Rosebery–Devonshire coalition, either of which would have destroyed Campbell-Bannerman's position.[49]

The doubts which Campbell-Bannerman voiced about the usefulness of such allies were confirmed by Beach in November. In pursuit of his policy of supporting Balfour against Chamberlain from within the Unionist party, Beach had secured Balfour's personal assurance that he had no intention of going beyond the policy announced at Sheffield. With that Beach was, or professed to be, content, and he publicly declared his satisfaction with the official party policy.[50] His desertion was a vivid reminder of the tenuous position adopted by the Unionist free traders whilst Balfour maintained his central position. In any outspoken protest they would lose the majority of their nominal supporters. Conversely, to keep up the appearance of a following they were forced into inactivity. Either way they were doomed to be ineffective as long as politics remained confined in the existing party system.

The loss of Beach in November was apparently more than compensated by the gradual emergence of Devonshire as a militant free trader. Initially the Duke had counselled caution,[51] but under pressure from more extreme free traders and from Chamberlain's apparent success in the country at the end of the year, Devonshire came out more strongly in opposition both to Chamberlain and to Balfour. In the autumn of 1903, the Unionist free traders attempted various demonstrations of their strength. On 23 October, the Unionist Free Food League issued its manifesto; on 11 November, Lord Hugh Cecil and Churchill spoke in Birmingham, the very centre of Chamberlain's power. But the hopes of the Unionist free traders were really pinned on the appearance of Devonshire as their leader in their efforts to withstand Chamberlain.[52]

These hopes were fulfilled when Devonshire addressed a major rally at the Queen's Hall with a platform which contained nine former cabinet ministers. Even Campbell-Bannerman was moved to admit that 'the Duke of D.'s speech is a huge help'.[53] On 12 December, with the full support of the Free Food organization, Devonshire went further and published a letter to the electors of Lewisham advising them not to vote for a candidate who supported Chamberlain's policies.[54] The results were disastrous, both for Unionist free trade hopes and Devonshire's reputation. Contrary to the expectations, not only of the Liberals and Unionist free traders but of the tariff reformers themselves, the by-elections at Dulwich and at Lewisham were won by Unionists who supported the full Chamberlainite programme. A Chamberlainite also held Ludlow on 23 December.[55] These by-elections were the first practical test of the success of Chamberlain's autumn campaign, and nothing demonstrated more clearly the ineffectiveness of the Unionist free traders or the dangers of Chamberlain to the free trade cause. Churchill had summed up their problem earlier, when appealing to Rosebery to come forward against Chamberlain: 'Beach and Goschen are old and husky. We are children. Joe's electric strength carries all before it.'[56] At that time Churchill still had hopes of Devonshire. After the Lewisham by-election Devonshire seemed equally ineffectual.

Chamberlain's apparent success forced both the Unionist free traders and the Liberals, despite their mutual distrust, to renew the search for a compromise which would permit more effective joint action. The Executive Committee of the Unionist Free Food League on 10 December agreed not only to issue the Lewisham letter but to reopen negotiations with the Liberals regarding the seats of Unionist free trade M.P.s.[57] Typically, however, it was to Rosebery rather than to Spencer, the official Liberal leader in the Lords, that Devonshire wrote to establish contact, even if his letter eventually arrived in the unwelcoming hands of Campbell-Bannerman.[58] For Campbell-Bannerman it was a particularly trying time. Although in November, Herbert Gladstone was inclined to dismiss the Liberal League,[59] Rosebery, speaking at Leicester on the seventh of that month, urged the Liberal party to unite against Chamberlain in terms which, to Campbell-Bannerman at least, seemed like a renewed bid for the party leadership.[60]

Under these circumstances Campbell-Bannerman could not but be suspicious of any overtures from the Unionist free traders in view of their open bias towards the League, and their desire to split the Liberal party. By the end of the year the air was again thick with rumours of an impending coalition between the Unionist free traders and the Liberal Imperialists. A speech by Rosebery on 25 November, the day after Devonshire's Queen's Hall rally, was interpreted as paving the way for a Devonshire–Rosebery ministry of the centre.[61] Gerald Balfour interpreted the Duke's Lewisham letter in this light,[62] and Balfour himself exploited these rumours to resist pressure from Austen Chamberlain to advance beyond the Sheffield policy. Campbell-Bannerman's position was the more difficult since his view of Rosebery's actions was not universally shared within the official wing of the Liberal party. Herbert Gladstone urged him to take advantage of the Leicester speech to heal the breach as the party desired 'to wipe out the past altogether, and to drop everything which may tend to keep up friction. I am quite certain that our people look upon the Leicester utterance as Rosebery's share of a concordat.'[63]

Gladstone's concern, as it was the concern of many Liberal leaders, was to secure the widest possible coalition against Balfour and Chamberlain in case Balfour decided upon a snap general election in January or February,[64] and this involved conciliating both the Liberal Imperialists, who had taken a leading part in the free trade campaign against Chamberlain, and the Unionist free traders. Yet during the autumn the official Liberals had made little effort to investigate how far the difficulties facing co-operation with the Unionist free traders could be overcome, nor even to define their own attitude. Desultory conversations had taken place between individuals on both sides, but these had been almost exclusively concerned with the future of those Unionist free trade M.P.s who appeared most likely to come over to the Liberal party. Gladstone thus reported that Churchill, Guest, and Seely were thinking of resigning their seats and seeking re-election as free traders pure and simple,[65] and Tweedmouth returned to this possibility at the end of November, expressing the hope that 'a helping hand will be extended to the free fooders, or to such of them as are willing to grasp it'.[66] But Campbell-Bannerman was, as usual, sceptical both of the public impact of such a 'melodramatic coup', and the utility of 'half a dozen doubtful or difficult recruits'.[67] Spencer shared these doubts.[68]

By December, however, after the recent election results, Gladstone was becoming anxious and demanding instructions: 'Time is slipping away, and excepting certain actions which I can take here and there, nothing is being done for the serious and practical consideration of our relations with the Conservative free traders . . . the Party leaders should meet at the first opportunity to determine whether any definite step can be taken to find some modus vivendi.'[69] Under this pressure Campbell-Bannerman relented slightly, and admitted that private conversations between Spencer and Devonshire might be useful. But he remained cautious and opposed the suggestion that the Liberal leaders might appear publicly with the Unionist free traders, which might 'deter the timid Conservatives and alarm some of our people also; we must be careful to shed none of our Nonconformists'.[70] Spencer agreed, but he was willing to open discussions to see what might be achieved.[71]

By the time Spencer wrote, however, the Unionist free traders had taken the initiative, again directing their approach to the Liberal Imperialist wing, rather than the official leadership. In addition to Devonshire's letter to Rosebery, James saw Asquith on 21 December and subsequently drew up a memorandum to clarify the Unionist free trade attitude. He rejected fusion of the two parties as a practical impossibility, but stressed the need for co-operation in the constituencies.[72] But as he subsequently conceded, in return for help to keep their seats few Unionist free traders would be prepared to support the Liberal party in the House of Commons, even if this was recommended by Devonshire, and he reiterated Unionist free trade objections to Campbell-Bannerman's leadership.[73] It was an impractical attitude. Yet James, who held it, was among the more 'Liberal' of the Unionist free traders. Lord George Hamilton speaking as a Conservative, declined to take any part in the negotiations at all.[74]

The Liberal leaders did take the Unionist free traders seriously enough to make inquiries of their Nonconformist supporters whether any arrangements could be arrived at on education.[75] Campbell-Bannerman asked Bryce to write to Clifford,[76] and Asquith consulted Perks, but both were discouraging. As Perks reported, his conversations with 'prominent free Churchmen' revealed that 'they all without exception refuse to have anything to do with any Education concordat . . . It is clear therefore that an attempt to reach union along these lines is hopeless.'[77] The only practical result[78] of the talks was a plan devised by Devonshire and Spencer whereby the Unionist free traders would be urged to support an amendment to the Address on the fiscal question, and the Liberals would consider constituency arrangements in the light of their votes.[79]

Campbell-Bannerman's attitude during these negotiations showed that after his brief lapse in November, when he over-reacted to Rosebery, he retained his usually sharp grasp of political realities:

James does not seem to recognise that they are in a cleft stick, and that the time comes with the opening of Parliament which will show how many of the fifty-three are really in earnest and have the courage of their opinions . . .

In short we are under no necessity to go to them, and indeed cannot go to them: it is they who must come to us. This need not be proclaimed, but it is the essence of the situation and cannot be ignored.[80]

His hand was strengthened by the radical wing of the party which reacted to the rumours of a coalition by renewing its protest of the previous May against any compromise with the socially conservative Unionist free traders. Lloyd George declared that he could not co-operate with a reactionary like Devonshire, and Campbell-Bannerman, to reassure them, emphasized that the Liberals would make no compromises in a speech at Maidstone on 13 January.[81] In the light of James's memorandum and the unacceptability of Campbell-Bannerman's leadership to the Unionist free traders, this was to consign the negotiations to the fire. Campbell-Bannerman was the only acceptable leader to the radical Liberals and he, in turn, identified himself with them.

Throughout the crisis provoked by Chamberlain's apparent success Campbell-Bannerman was fortified not merely by the need to retain the confidence of his radical supporters, but by his belief that Chamberlain's triumphs had no real foundation. Much of the urgency for negotiations with the Unionist free traders came from Herbert Gladstone because of rumours of an imminent general election, and in resisting concessions Campbell-Bannerman was justified by subsequent events. Chamberlain's campaign collapsed after the victory at the Ludlow by-election. The Mid-Devon by-election was an easy Liberal victory and thenceforth 'tariff reform was routed in a series of by-elections between 15 January and 13 February' at Norwich, Gateshead, Ayr Burghs, and Mid-Herts.[82] With the removal of this pressure from Chamberlain, the last lever which the Unionist free traders could use against the Liberal party disappeared. The by-elections in 1904 sustained Campbell-Bannerman's contention that free trade was in no real danger, and with this the opinion that no concessions to the Unionist free traders were necessary.

The occupation of the middle ground, which the Liberal Imperialists and the Unionist free traders both allegedly sought, depended upon the break-up of the Liberal as well as of the Unionist party. Implicitly, Unionist free trade overtures were based upon this assumption, even when the outlook for free trade was at its bleakest in November and December 1903. In the unstable political situation of 1903 such an outcome was not impossible. Rosebery's speeches in defence of free trade attacted large and enthusiastic audiences and placed him again in the front line of Liberal leaders, yet he consistently refused to co-operate with Campbell-Bannerman, Haldane remained outspokenly hostile, and Grey still refused to consider taking office whilst Campbell-Bannerman remained leader. The League was active and frequently in conflict with the official organization and Home Rule still divided the Leaguers *en masse*, including Asquith, from the Bannerman wing of the party. But the negotiations failed, and Rosebery did not come forward as the leader of conservative free traders, Liberal or Unionist. In December he declined Spencer's invitation to give the traditional dinner to the Liberal peers,[83] and thus made it clear that his speeches in November were no more than another of those isolated forays into politics with which his career had been studded since 1896. In the spring of 1904 both Unionist free traders and Roseberyite Liberals began to drift away from their central position, and to take sides on party lines. Unionist free trade waverers followed Beach back into the Balfourite fold whilst militants like Churchill crossed the floor to the official Liberals. Rosebery's followers similarly began to realize that the lead for which they hoped would never come and melted away. The League itself, still occasionally troublesome in the constituencies, began to collapse at the top.

Chamberlain, too, was in trouble. By the spring, it was clear that his campaign to win the working classes over to tariff reform and preference had fallen on deaf ears. The imperial and 'cultural' aspects of his programme appear to have been more successful, but to have appealed largely to established Unionists. In February 1904 Balfour thought the leaders of the local associations of the party were 'in the main "whole-hoggers" ',[84] an opinion confirmed by Beach.[85] Certainly Chamberlain had secured enough support within local organizations to put pressure on the leading Unionist free traders by the end of the year. But these were not the classes which Chamberlain had primarily set out to win by a campaign of radical Unionism, nor was it to the advantage of the Unionist party if he made existing Conservatives more conservative. Chamberlain left the cabinet in the autumn to demonstrate that the hostility of the working classes to food duties had been overestimated and that the full programme of tariff reform, including preference, was really 'practical politics'. Whatever else he may have done in laying the foundations of the tariff reform movement, in this he had clearly failed.

4

Factions at Play

The test of almost a year of intrigue within both major parties and their dissident groups came with the opening of Parliament and the debate on Morley's amendment to the Address on 8 February 1904, a debate conducted in Balfour's absence. For the Unionist free traders their votes would determine the extent of Liberal co-operation, if any, in the constituencies. For the Balfourites the test was more subtle and turned on the effectiveness of Balfour's devious policy when advocated by less subtle minds. In general terms, both groups failed to rise to the standards required, and the debate exposed the divisions within both. Furthermore, the difficulties of each group reacted upon and aggravated the difficulties of the other. The government was well aware of its own problem—its dependence upon the votes of at least some of the free traders to stay in office, yet the need at the same time not to alienate the tariff reformers and provoke them to revolt. In the absence of Balfour no solution was found to this dilemma, and individual government speakers varied their emphasis to the point of contradicting their colleagues in their efforts not to alienate either wing. Similar disunity befell the free traders. Caught between the pressures of party, of free trade principles, and fears for their seats if they did not come up to scratch in the eyes of the Liberals, 'their views oscillated with each Government speaker'.[1] In the end, twenty-six voted with the Liberals, fourteen with the government, and twelve abstained. Sandars thought this result good: 'The fiscal malcontents were hopelessly split on the question . . . the moral of which is that the cave does not afford a permanent habitation . . .'[2]

The eventual free trade revolt was, however, of sufficient size to cause the government concern. Sandars pointed the moral here also: 'If we avoid either frightening or irritating these twenty-five Unionists, we shall carry on—if, on the other hand, we alarm or annoy them on the fiscal question, they can turn us out at a moment's notice . . .' This, above all, would prevent Balfour moving towards Chamberlain. The Chamberlain bubble had burst. Sandars informed Balfour that:

it has been necessary to disclaim any idea of protection, any idea of the taxation of food or raw material, and any idea of diminishing the control of the H. of C. over our fiscal arrangements . . .

The majority of our men can hardly hear a sympathetic toleration to be expressed for the aspirations of the Birmingham school; and we have certainly not, *in your absence*, a speaker who can hold our men on the Sheffield lines, and yet avow a modicum of sympathy with Colonial preference and food taxation. The moment a man says that he is for the Government policy, but that with public opinion in its present state, the taxation of foodstuffs is not within the range of practical politics, then he is dubbed a Protectionist in disguise . . .

Consequently, any avowal by their leaders that the idea of Fiscal Union with the Colonies has an Imperial value, and that, if and when the country is ready to make the necessary sacrifice of its existing prejudice about food taxation, the proposal might be entertained, frightens them out of their wits . . .[3]

It was an assessment which Balfour, with his constant insistence on the impracticality of food duties, had no difficulty in accepting.[4] This view, and the instability of his parliamentary position caused by the doubtful loyalty of the Unionist free traders, dominated Balfour's actions until 1906. Should he ever have been inclined to forget, successive Liberal resolutions on the fiscal question during 1904 and 1905 acted as constant reminders of his insecurity.

Yet Balfour's dependence was not on one side only. He had opted in 1903 for a middle course between free trade and tariff reform, and if the first Liberal challenge brought out the difficulties of such a course in relation to the Unionist free traders, the second, in March, revealed similar problems with the tariff reformers. On Morley's amendment, Sandars commented, 'Joe's men are behaving very well. They see it is no use to force the pace and they trust that time will help on their policy . . .'[5] But good behaviour from the tariff reformers could also only be had at a price. On 9 March a resolution condemning 'agitation in favour of preferential and protective tariffs', moved by the Liberal back-bencher, Pirie, was met by a government amendment, in the name of Wharton, dissociating it from 'a general system of Protection or Preference based on the taxation of food'. The Wharton amendment was a direct rebuff to Chamberlain, and hardly in accordance with

Balfour's expressed sympathy with imperial preference, but it illustrated the government's alarm at the revolt of the Unionist free
traders the previous month. On this occasion, however, appeasement
was taken too far. A meeting of 112 tariff reform M.P.s, chaired by Sir
Herbert Maxwell, informed the whips that in the light of the Wharton
amendment they might have to reconsider their support of the government. This was enough to force the withdrawal of the amendment. On
a vote on Pirie's unamended resolution 24 Unionist free traders voted
with the opposition, but the government survived.[6] The divisions
within the Unionist free traders and the continued loyalty of the tariff
reformers, indicated that if Balfour pursued a careful policy of balance
he could carry on. The Unionist free traders would not vote against
him *en masse* as long as he showed real independence of Chamberlain,
and Chamberlain's weakness after December 1903 ensured that he would
not prove irresistible, as had originally been feared.

Chamberlain himself was not put out by the reversal of his fortunes.
'I do not expect, and indeed never have expected to carry the country
with a sweep at the next election,' he wrote to Northcote in April.
'*All my efforts and hopes are directed to the election after next* . . . My object
is, first, to unite the Unionist Party on the policy of fiscal reform and
Colonial Preference. *This will, I believe, be accomplished at the next general
election where the so-called free-fooders will go to the wall* . . .'[7] Chamberlain,
like Sandars, had read the moral of the fiscal debates of February and
March. He could do nothing to remove Balfour's dependence on the
Unionist free traders in the existing parliamentary situation. A further
reminder of this had been given in May, when the Liberal, Black,
introduced another resolution condemning food duties which Balfour
converted into a vote of confidence. Even so, 22 free traders again
voted with the opposition.[8] From the middle of 1904, an early general
election and the undermining of the Unionist free traders in their
constituencies became a central feature of Chamberlain's tactics.

Chamberlain's difficulty in hoping to put any pressure at all on
Balfour was that he had so little to bargain with. His strength, whatever it was, lay in the country, and was hardly in evidence. Apart from
the capture of the Liberal Unionist Association,[9] the foundations for
which had been laid the previous winter, he achieved virtually nothing
of value. Three publicly impressive demonstrations—a banquet to
celebrate his sixty-eighth birthday attended by 177 M.P.s who expressed their support for preference;[10] a mass meeting at the Albert

Hall to inaugurate the new Liberal Unionist Council with the cabinet ministers Lansdowne and Selborne in attendance as vice-presidents, and the first annual meeting of the Tariff Reform League on 21 July[11]—did something to keep up appearances, but were meaningless as levers against Balfour. More significant were the by-elections. After the disasters of February, none of the 9 Unionist candidates in the by-elections which followed had dared to adopt Chamberlain's full programme, and took refuge instead in Balfour's obscurities. In July and August, when two whole-hoggers contested by-elections in Oswestry and NE Lanark where the initial auguries were thought to be good, both were defeated.[12]

Nevertheless, passive acceptance of his position was neither in Chamberlain's nature nor in the nature of the situation. It was implicit in the policy of postponement that Balfour adopted that Chamberlain should attempt to force the pace. At the end of June 1904 Chamberlain began to evolve a policy which he thought might make it possible for him and Balfour to work together again. Balfour had always based his objections to food taxes on their impracticality. Chamberlain, speaking on 1 August, proposed that this practicality should be tested by calling a colonial conference to ask 'what it is that the Colonies really wish, and what it is that they are prepared to do . . .'[13] Austen Chamberlain elaborated upon this theme, and took over the task of applying pressure to persuade Balfour to announce that, if he won the next election, he would summon a colonial conference to discuss imperial preference, and that, if he was satisfied with the result, he would propose the necessary legislation. In return, Austen offered the solution of Balfour's problems by promising that if the result was unsatisfactory, the tariff reformers would give no further trouble. Moreover, Balfour was offered a virtually free hand with the details, provided he committed the government officially to preference.

Balfour responded with a scheme of his own which he had apparently discussed with Austen before the exchange of letters. Whilst he agreed on 'the extreme desirability of having a full and free discussion with our Colonies on the present position and future organisation of the Empire', he laid the greatest stress on such a conference being 'full and free', which he felt would be impossible if its members were pledged to carry out its recommendations immediately, without any further reference to the electorate. He, therefore, proposed a 'double election' scheme, whereby he would pledge the party to call a conference after the next election, and to enact the resolutions of the conference if they were confirmed by a second election. Austen Chamberlain thought this disastrous, but the purely tactical nature of his objections betrayed that the tariff reformers had really raised the colonial question not to consider the details of policy but as an expedient to push Balfour further along the road to tariff reform and enable the tariff reformers to present their policy as the official policy at the next election. Chamberlain's letters were almost solely concerned with tactics, and if Balfour on this occasion concerned himself more with abstract policy than with tactics, it was only because a discussion of policy was likely to prove less divisive.

The most significant aspect of Austen Chamberlain's letters of 24 August and 12 September was not the new policy put forward, but the arguments used in support of that policy. Chamberlain and Balfour disagreed fundamentally about the political situation. The difference began as a disagreement about facts—why the Unionist party was losing by-elections, and the mood of the electorate which these defeats reflected. According to Austen Chamberlain, the party's record had been no worse after his father's Birmingham speech than it had been before, and 'we have fared no better where our candidate has been a "half-hogger" than where he has been a "whole-hogger" . . . both Bridgeman at Oswestry, and Touche at Lanark, think they would have done worse with the more restricted policy.' From the Balfourite camp, Sandars dissented completely from this view. Chamberlain, he thought, 'is wrong in his estimate of the forces at work in elections now-a-days. Oswestry would have been won but for the "dear loaf". We beat them on Chinese Labour, we were worsted in the villages on the cry of dear food . . . Lanark was clearly against us on fiscal policy.'

Behind these disagreements lay differing conceptions of the nature of democratic politics, the role of political leadership, and the function of policy. Austen Chamberlain urged constantly the need for a 'constructive policy', a 'positive policy', to awaken the enthusiasm of the party. From his point of view, elections were won by the 'party which can raise a great ideal, and touch the spirit of the nation . . . acting on the offensive and substituting an active policy of the future for a mere passive defence of the past'. Colonial preference fulfilled this function, and was 'the greatest object to which we in our time can devote ourselves, not only for itself but for all to which it may lead, and which we cannot realise without it . . . worth great and immediate sacrifice, if such were called for, both from the party and the nation'. Alfred Lyttelton saw matters in the same light: 'After all, what does it matter if there are some obstacles—the spirit of greatness is in that ideal, and to fail in it is worth most successes.' Lyttleton, like Chamberlain, believed that 'the real heart of the nation is as ready now as it ever was to make sacrifices for great causes . . .' This idealism, and a consequent tendency to see politics in black and white terms, was perhaps the most salient characteristic of the imperialist mentality, which gave the tariff reform movement its most dedicated adherents.

But none of this had any appeal for Balfour. He admitted that the official policy did not inspire; he was not convinced that this was necessarily a fault. Beyond noting that Austen Chamberlain wanted 'a policy which, when agreed to, will tap deeper springs of enthusiasm than can ever be reached by the Sheffield programme taken *simpliciter*', and that this could only be found in the direction of colonial unity, Balfour was more concerned with the fears of the timid than the enthusiasm of the converted. His crucial objection to Austen Chamberlain's policy was that it would 'frighten the Colonies; and it would certainly frighten an important section of opinion in this country'.[14]

When Balfour looked to the country, he sought to appeal to its reason, not to its heart, to 'sober' public opinion, not to enthusiasm. His ideological relativism permitted no great beliefs and few permanent features in politics—the Church, the Conservative party, and conservatism in an ever-changing, ever-adapting form, and possibly the Union, institutions but not policies. The effect was to deny charisma, to play down the role of the leader except as manipulator, and to reduce policy to a thing of the moment against an eternity of institutional tradition. In 1904, this distinction between the Chamberlainite and the Balfourite approach to democratic politics was barely visible. But in the future, especially once the party was in opposition and Balfour's negative approach to policy became more evident, the demands for positive leadership and a constructive policy from the followers of Chamberlain's brand of radical Unionism began to undermine Balfour's position.

In 1904, however, Chamberlain had little or no support. As Sandars wrote to Balfour:

Austen now calls upon you to make a bridge. For whom? Not for the great mass of our party. They do not want to walk, as I believe, on any bridge which brings them any nearer to taxation of food, and to the policy of Joe and Protection. Personally, I think . . . that it is all the other way. Our people want a way out, not a way in . . . [15]

More significantly, Selborne, who technically ranked amongst Chamberlain's followers by virtue of his appearance as a vice-president of the Liberal Unionist Council, shared Sandars's views on this occasion.[16]

Both Selborne and Wyndham, whom Balfour consulted during this dialogue with Austen Chamberlain, made a further point, that since both Chamberlain and Balfour agreed that the Unionists would lose the next election, the controversy over one election or two was academic. The policy which Balfour would announce would be binding for the forthcoming election only, and afterwards future policy could be decided in the light of new circumstances.[17] Balfour agreed with this also, and felt that the Chamberlains were exaggerating the difference of opinion to pressurize him.[18] Reinforced by Selborne, Wyndham, and Sandars, who discounted 'the risk of an open breach with Joe',[19] he ignored the threatening murmurs of independent action at the next election from the Chamberlain camp,[20] and went his way undeterred. 'At Edinburgh,' he told Selborne, 'I propose, as at present advised, to make a short but quite explicit speech upon the lines of my letter to Austen.'[21] Preferentialists, if not protectionists, were satisfied that Balfour had at least found some place for their policy in the Unionist programme. 'Arthur's Edinburgh speech perfect,' Wyndham wrote to his sister. 'It has rallied all "bien pensants" Free Fooders and yet enabled Imperialists like your little brother to pursue their mission which has nothing in common with protection, and very little with Retaliation.'[22] Chamberlain initially had high hopes of the conference proposal and of the National Union Conference at Southampton where he thought it might be announced, hopes which he retained until the end of September.[23] But in reality the emphasis which both Austen and Joseph Chamberlain put on this proposed compromise, and Joseph Chamberlain's insistence on a vote of support from the annual party conference, revealed the sense of failure and frustration which was, as Sandars noticed, creeping into the tariff reform movement. After the failures of the year in general, Chamberlain needed some demonstration of influence within the party to maintain the momentum of his campaign, and he went so far as to threaten withdrawal from its leadership if the vote of support was not forthcoming.

His hopes were shattered by Balfour's announcement at Edinburgh on 3 October of the 'double election' policy. It was a statement which

Chamberlain could not accept, and in his speech at Luton on 5 October he dissociated himself from it.[24] 'I most deeply regret it,' he wrote to Lyttelton, 'but I will make the best of it . . . the time has gone by for argument and I can only attempt to minimise the difference'.[25] To 'minimise the difference', the tariff reformers put their own gloss on the Edinburgh policy, as they did with all Balfour's statements. Sandars found that:

Henry Chaplin and Henry Granby . . . claim that their case has made substantial progress with you, and they suit their argument thus. The Colonies want Preference. *You* would not have supported the proposal of a Colonial Conference unless you were prepared to meet the desire of the Colonies for Preference. Preference involves the taxation of foodstuffs, ergo *you* may be said to be in favour of food taxes . . .[26]

Lyttelton had hinted at this approach during the discussions on the compromise, and argued that to get Balfour 'as far as advocacy of a Conference' was the essential thing: 'if we fight on that issue . . . we commit ourselves impliedly, but inevitably, to readjusting our food taxes if the Colonies make a reasonable offer'.[27] It was by reasoning along these lines that Chamberlain was able to say to Leverton Harris: 'The recent speech by Balfour leaves the way open for a unanimous meeting at Southampton.'[28]

Nevertheless, under these circumstances Chamberlain's victory at the Southampton Conference was a hollow one, made even more so by the chance attack by the Russian fleet on British trawlers fishing off the Dogger Bank. At Southampton the Chamberlainite resolution gained an overwhelming majority, and as a consequence of a free trade amendment in favour of the Edinburgh policy, the tariff reform success was even 'better than anyone could have expected for . . . what the idiots have succeeded in doing is to get the Conference to negative a resolution approving of the policy laid down at Edinburgh, with this result, that the only part of that policy which they approve is what is embodied in our resolution and the rest is condemned'.[29] But despite their tactical error, the free traders had no reason to feel displeased with the situation at the end of 1904. Balfour, in his speech to the Southampton Conference, took advantage of the diversion provided by the antics of the Russian fleet to ignore the tariff question altogether, and the Edinburgh speech was widely greeted with approval on the free trade side,[30] even though Devonshire's 'mood was one of profound suspicion'.[31] The Edinburgh policy held the Balfourite position together during the autumn and winter of 1904–5. Both the Unionist free traders, only three of whom supported Asquith's fiscal amendment early in 1905, and the tariff reformers could, by putting their own interpretation upon the speech, find comfort in the policy. As a compromise, however, it would not guarantee Balfour peace from Chamberlain's pressure for long.

In February 1905 Chamberlain asked Balfour for a meeting, pointing out the danger that they might 'insensibly drift apart', and made a further effort to persuade Balfour to drop the 'double election' pledge.[32] As in 1904, the attempt produced more friction than harmony. Chamberlain could still produce no acceptable answer to Balfour's fundamental objection:

The prejudice against a small tax on food is not the fad of a few imperfectly informed theorists: it is a deep-rooted prejudice affecting the large mass of voters, especially the poorest class . . . the obstacle with which the Candidate is confronted is not the opinion of the local leaders, but the absolute impossibility of inducing the mass of the voters to do anything which they can be made to believe would increase the price of bread.[33]

It was a perceptive comment on both the failures and successes of Chamberlain's campaign so far. But Chamberlain thought he had done more, and that 'the prejudice . . . has already largely disappeared among the artisan population, and even in agricultural districts I am sure that where a proper house to house education has been undertaken the labourers are open to conversion'. It was the same dispute about facts as had divided Chamberlain and Middleton in 1902, and Austen Chamberlain and Sandars in 1904, and the difference produced the same disagreement about tactics. The whole question still revolved around making tariff reform 'practical politics', the task Balfour had set Chamberlain on his resignation. Tactically, Chamberlain had a reasonable case in arguing that candidates who took Balfour's line deprived themselves of the enthusiasm which the imperial side of tariff reform evoked and the arguments in favour of reciprocal preference and imperial unity, as well as putting themselves wrong with the farmers 'who will otherwise be inevitably estranged by a policy which threatens them with increased prices for all that they buy, and gives them no corresponding advantage in what they have to sell . . .'[34] It was his weakness that the final decision lay with Balfour.

By the beginning of 1905, relations between Chamberlain and Balfour were breaking down, and the tensions between principle and party becoming increasingly apparent. 'My information', Sandars told Balfour in January, 'points to an early, rather than a late, disruption of our forces.'[35] Even Balfour's decision to meet Parliament again was an affront to Chamberlain's desperate desire for an election, reiterated again in the debate on the Address in February. Chamberlain was restrained from precipitating the downfall of the government by the party loyalty of his followers. But the 'cordial support' which he had promised Balfour when he resigned had now evaporated completely.[36]

The weakness of the government was cruelly revealed by successive Liberal resolutions on the fiscal question. On 8 March, Churchill introduced a motion condemning preference, and the government was able neither to devise an amendment to unite its nominal supporters, nor feel confident that it could hold the Unionist free traders on a straight vote. The disaster was only evaded by moving the previous question. At the end of March, the collapse moved one stage further when the Liberals gave notice of four more resolutions. Two in particular, Ainsworth's resolution of 22 March condemning a 10 per cent general tariff, and Osmond Williams's of 29 March condemning Chamberlain's policy by name but not Balfour's, were aimed at splitting Chamberlain and Balfour. The whips felt unable to hold the party together by moving the previous question on Chamberlain's policy alone, and advocated a free vote. Chamberlain responded by threatening a tariff reform revolt on those resolutions which also condemned Balfour's policy. Thus trapped between the two wings of his party, Balfour recommended abstention on all four resolutions unless they were made into votes of censure. In effect, the precarious unity of the party on the fiscal question had been destroyed. When the resolutions were moved the party, led by Balfour, walked out of the House. Even so, 35 Unionist free traders voted with the Liberals on Ainsworth's resolution against the general tariff.[37]

Balfour's humiliating tactics brought the tariff reform extremists almost to the point of revolt. 'The state of affairs here', wrote Griffiths Boscawen, 'is very unsatisfactory. We decided, after consultation with Austen, to fall in with the Government's plan of abstaining . . . but I am convinced that it has done a lot of harm . . . there is a very general feeling of discontent and dissatisfaction—failure almost'.[38] Chamberlain's public acquiescence in Balfour's tactics, whatever his protests in private, produced sentiments of rebellion not only against Balfour, but against Chamberlain himself. J. L. Garvin, wrote to Maxse:

As for the political situation, believe me, if Joe doesn't force a General Election by July, at any cost, *he* personally is done. And we others who have more life to spare must lay ourselves out to work a decade longer. Yet what is the good of starting a General Election campaign before we are sure he will not stultify [?] us, by allowing Balfour to go on?[39]

To rally his forces, Chamberlain held a meeting of tariff reform M.P.s on 13 April, and led a deputation to present a memorandum to Balfour requesting a clarification of Balfour's policies. Although it had been implicit in the two previous attempts to induce Balfour to accept Chamberlain's programme, the open accusation that Balfour's policy was unclear and made for confusion was a new weapon in the Chamberlainite armoury, one which would in future be increasingly used to attack Balfour's leadership. The fact that Chamberlain spoke so openly indicated the degree to which he and Balfour had in fact drifted apart, and Chamberlain's dissatisfaction not simply with Balfour's policy but with his leadership as a whole. The memorandum itself made evident this separation by spelling out the specific points of difference between the two policies. Defining Balfour's policy as a repudiation of protection, freedom of fiscal negotiation, and closer commercial union with the colonies after a free conference, the tariff reformers declared their support in principle but demanded the details. This, however, was precisely what Balfour wished to avoid, since it was upon the details that division arose. On retaliation, the tariff reform memorandum maintained that 'no such policy can be successful, unless it embraces the system of a *general tariff* . . . such a tariff would be a revenue tariff, moderate in amount . . .' and varied to prevent dumping and negotiate reciprocity treaties. This, and the demand that Balfour drop the 'double election' pledge, were the two essential points upon which the tariff reformers wanted change in the official policy.[40]

As a result of this memorandum, further discussions were held between Balfour and Chamberlain during May. Balfour, perhaps influenced by the degree of tariff reform discontent, was initially conciliatory and accepted both that tariff reform, including colonial preference, should be the foremost article in the programme submitted by the Unionists at the approaching general election and the principle of an all-round tariff. A new device to get around the Edinburgh policy was also apparently agreed—that if the government survived in office until after the next Colonial Conference scheduled for 1906, the 'double election' pledge would no longer apply. Free trade and Balfourite pressure ensured that Balfour's advance was not long maintained. Balfour informed a free trade deputation on 16 May that he had given Chamberlain no promises, and despite a statement in the Commons that there was nothing in his 'double election' pledge which excluded the discussion of preference with the colonies at the 1906 Conference if the government was still in office, Balfour informed Chamberlain when their talks resumed on 26 May that 'owing to the construction put upon his Edinburgh speech by some of our party, he felt debarred from allowing the Conference to assemble before the General Election'. The reversal in Balfour's attitude had been produced by a censure motion which the Unionist free traders threatened to support.[41]

There still remained, however, the apparent gain of Balfour's agreement that tariff reform must be the first plank in the Unionist election platform, and his acceptance of the principle of a general tariff. Chamberlain agreed to support the government if Balfour announced during the censure debate that 'Tariff Reform, including Colonial Preference, will be the foremost article in the programme submitted at the next general election', and that if the Unionists lost the election, the 'double election' pledge would lapse. Chamberlain apparently accepted that in the censure debate Balfour would have no opportunity to raise the subject of the general tariff. Balfour's reaction indicated that his mind was working along different lines, and that he still evaded the issue:

if by 'Colonial Preference' is meant (as I suppose it is) closer commercial union with the Colonies (as per half sheet of notepaper) and if by 'first item in my programme', is meant (as I suppose it is) that I regard it as the most important part (though the most difficult) of fiscal reform, and fiscal reform itself as the most important part of the Unionist policy, why should I not give the assurance asked for?[42]

In the event, the censure debate was postponed, and Balfour made his announcement at the Albert Hall on 2 June. The speech did not mark a major advance on Balfour's part. Balfour stated publicly, as he had admitted privately in 1903, that preference was the most important but the most difficult part of fiscal reform, and was 'the greatest, the most important . . . the most urgent of all the great constructive problems with which we have to deal'. He also declared that the Edinburgh policy only applied to the next election, but he did not mention the

general tariff.[43] Wyndham, who wholeheartedly supported the speech
as the best practical position for fiscal reformers, whether protectionist
or Balfourite, felt that 'all is as well as it can be' after having 'discreetly
collected opinions', and suggested that Balfour had again successfully
ridden both the free trade and tariff reform horses. But he also learned
from Amery that the 'Tariff Reformers were disappointed because—as
he put it—they expected a more definite lead in respect of the Future'.[44]
This lead Chamberlain provided the next day. His interpretation of
Balfour's speech made definite that which Balfour had, as usual, left
vague. In so doing, as in May 1903, he completely altered Balfour's
meaning: 'What did Mr. Balfour say? He said last night, tariff reform
will be the most important part of Unionist policy. He said Colonial
Preference is the most important part of tariff reform. He said Colonial
Preference will therefore be the first item in the future Unionist programme.'[45]

Unlike the Commons debate, there was nothing to prevent Balfour
from referring to the general tariff at the Albert Hall meeting, and the
omission was perhaps deliberate for Chamberlain had specifically
mentioned it as one of the conditions Balfour must meet in his speech.
Despite Balfour's own acceptance of the principle, however, free trade
opinion against it was strong, and there was the danger that it might
prove to be the final straw in alienating the Unionist free traders.[46]

Balfour's refusal to call a colonial conference before the next
election, and the absence of any reference to the general tariff in his
Albert Hall speech, were both indications of the continued strength of
the Unionist free traders. Such strength, however, depended entirely
on the Unionist free traders' ability to hold the parliamentary balance
and would, as Chamberlain saw, disappear overnight when Balfour left
office. But after the failure of their negotiations with the Liberals in
1903–4, the Unionist free traders had made no further progress
towards strengthening their position in the country. Chamberlain
on the other hand had increased the pressure upon them in their
constituencies as the logical extension of his desire for an early
election.

In February 1905, Lord Robert Cecil compiled, for Balfour's
information, a memorandum on 'The Attack on Unionist Free Trade
Seats', in which he quoted a letter by the Tariff Reform League
secretary, Ratcliffe Cousins, to *The Times* of 13 January 1904 stating
that 'The League . . . is . . . determined to oppose the return of all

Free-fooders, whether Unionist or Radical, and we shall use the whole of our organisation for that object.' Lord Robert listed 25 seats in which such attacks had taken place, and thought there were 'probably others'. To this list he added a further four seats in which the sitting Unionist free trader had escaped attack only by promising to withdraw from Parliament at the general election. 'The attacks have been commonly initiated or supported by the Tariff Reform League, or persons connected therewith', and, according to Lord Robert, had the personal support of Chamberlain.[47] 'Nothing', wrote Lord Hugh to Balfour in December 1904, 'has done so much to embitter the feelings of Free Traders as the attacks and threats in respect to their seats.'[48]

> The truth is that all along, Joe has been the aggressor, and has striven to drive us out of the Party. He began the Tariff Reform League, and we replied with the Free Food League. He started his 'raging tearing propaganda' and we had, with great difficulty, to try to hold meetings on the other side. From a very early period down to the present time trouble has been made— or has arisen— in our constituencies . . . in view of this unrelenting attack, it is surely unreasonable to ask us not to retaliate when we have the chance . . . If you want peace within the party, you must persuade Joe to change his whole tactics. At present he is making war and we must do so too.[49]

The free traders, however, could reach no agreement amongst themselves on the best means to prosecute their 'war'. Cecil and his wing of the Unionist free trade group still believed that Balfour remained sympathetic to free trade and that he should be supported against Chamberlain from within the party. Their desire in the first instance was not an agreement with the Liberals for joint work in the constituencies, which might brand them as rebels, but a denunciation of tariff reform and its methods by Balfour, which would secure for them the support of the Unionist moderates. From free traders as from tariff reformers, Balfour was constantly harried for a statement in their favour.[50] In return, the Unionist free traders were prepared to make what were, in their view, considerable concessions. Informing Balfour in March 1905 'of the grave danger that the free traders will break loose altogether', Lord Hugh expressed the wish 'to establish more conciliatory relations between Unionist free traders and yourself, and [I] am prepared to stretch my economic conscience to cover some sort of retaliation—as far as it will go . . . But I am not prepared to desert my friends . . .'[51]

Balfour was no more inclined to be driven from his central position

by free trade pressure than he was by Chamberlain, and he counter-
attacked rather than apologized for his unco-operative behaviour,
accusing the free traders of doing

great injury to free trade by their appeals to ignorance and prejudice and by
the exaggerated importance they have given to any objections that may be
made to a rearrangement of our duties on food. They have defended free
trade . . . with zeal, with earnestness, but with . . . little comprehension
apparently that there was any standing ground between the free trade of Mr.
Cobden and the Protection of Lord George Bentinck . . . They have certainly
not always smoothed the course of those who, as I think, took a more
rational view of the subject: and, by the narrowness of their outlook, they
have greatly aided the opposition . . . [52]

Balfour would, therefore, not intervene, partly out of principle, and
partly out of disapproval of the Unionist free traders and their actions:
'You must always remember that some of the members who have
taken a prominent part in the so-called Free-Food business are persons
who have *always* taken every opportunity of attacking the Government:
are indeed no more than professional critics of their own side.'[53]

Positive action in their own defence was for the Unionist free traders
essentially intertwined with the problem of defining their attitude to
the Unionist party, its leader, and its official policy. In fact their disagreement on these subjects was so great that no collective policy was
ever achieved. Rather, the question threatened to destroy the group
entirely every time it was raised. By the spring of 1905, Balfour's
consistent refusal to back up the free traders who had been anxious
to keep the peace provoked a revolt from those Unionist free traders
who suspected him of tariff reform inclinations. As Lord Robert Cecil
warned Sandars:

Unless something can be said in public to remove the impression, i.e. a
definite public reprobation of the attempt by the Tariff Reform League to
proscribe Unionist free traders, we shall not only have reprisals against the
extreme Tariff Reformers—which I should not regret—but there will be
a danger of repudiation of all connection with official Unionism which would
be deplorable.[54]

Repudiation took the form of a proposal of the Executive Committee
of the recently formed Unionist Free Trade Club that a letter be sent to
candidates urging them to disavow all taxation not imposed for revenue
purposes. In addition, the U.F.T.C. also considered the question of

reprisals against tariff reformers in their own constituencies. Two memorandums from Manners Sutton were sent out as preliminary inquiries, although with the emphasis that nothing was as yet decided. The reprisals on seats named in memorandums were to be proportionate to tariff reform attacks on free trade seats, with the idea that 'if later on, the tariff reformers should make an onslaught on all the Unionist Free Traders—no unlikely event—we ought to be prepared to make a corresponding movement, and plans should be laid accordingly'.[55] This, at least, obtained united support. Lord Robert Cecil co-operated with Elliot in attempting to organize reprisals, and approved of his negotiations with Herbert Gladstone for an arrangement on seats. But he drew the line at the letter to candidates which condemned Balfour and Chamberlain alike:

I certainly would not pledge myself not to support under any circumstances taxes for other than revenue purposes . . . but . . . it is very much more important that such a test would exclude almost all the Unionist Free Traders in Parliament. It would also mean a definite and open breach with all Ministerialists, and it would create the impression that we were extremists and fanatics—a character which means the loss of all influence with our countrymen.[56]

The question of Balfour's intentions was the real cause of division within the Unionist free trade group, as Balfour intended it should be. But even if Balfour was regarded, as many Unionist free traders regarded him, as a secret tariff reformer, the Cecil faction within the Unionist Free Trade Club still saw advantages in maintaining contact with the Balfourites 'by saying smooth things, or at any rate abstaining from saying sharp things, about the Government'. By so doing, the Unionist free traders, Lord Hugh Cecil thought, retained 'their place in the party, and their influence with its moderate members . . . The half-hearted Free-Traders are very numerous and important, and . . . I am anxious not to quarrel with them.'[57] Moreover, far from weakening their position, Lord Hugh regarded such co-operation as giving them a hold over the government without being forced into any compromises on principles, since by remaining within the party they kept 'the power to break it up whenever we may think necessary'. In mid-1905, Cecil 'never felt more confident of the success of my tactical system than I do at this moment'.[58]

But the private line which their family connection with Balfour gave to the Cecils was a two-way affair which aided in spreading disunity in

Unionist free trade ranks. Balfour's ability to argue his case with the Cecils enabled him to do with the Unionist free traders what he could not do with the tariff reformers under their firmer leadership, to interpret his own speeches in a light favourable to himself, and to do so privately so that he was never forced to contradict Chamberlain's 'interpretations' in public and provoke an open breach.

Strachey, at least, realized the dangers, and preferred to 'remain in active revolt . . . boldness will pay us much better than timidity'. In his view, 'The prospect of reuniting the party on a Free Trade basis will become brighter the more complete is the ruin of Chamberlainism . . . When the bulk of the Unionists realise fully that nothing will restore the party but the abandonment of Protection, I believe they will abandon it,'[59] and he thus repudiated Cecil's 'tactical system' completely. But his tactics were no more sound than Cecil's under the circumstances, since so few Unionist free traders adopted Strachey's analysis of either Balfour's position or their own, that the defection would go almost unnoticed. Activity by the Unionist free traders in the country was rendered almost completely ineffective by these divisions. They were discredited in the eyes of the Liberals by their apparent loyalty to Balfour, which the Cecils insisted upon, and in the eyes of the Bal-fourites by their association with the Liberals.

Co-operation with the Liberals, in so far as it could be organized by Elliot and Gladstone, almost certainly benefited the Liberals more than the Unionist free traders in the election of 1906, since both Devonshire and Strachey in the *Spectator* advised voters to support Liberal candidates whilst the Liberals, in return, made few concessions in regard to seats. In the election only seven Unionist free traders stood without Liberal opponents, and three of these were for University seats.[60] To Chamberlain's attacks the Unionist free traders found no answer, either from Balfour or from the Liberals, whilst Chamberlain, despairing of concessions from Balfour as long as he remained in office, came increasingly to rely on an election to purge the Unionist free trade block to the progress of tariff reform.

The discussions of May 1905 were Chamberlain's last attempt to convert Balfour before the general election. From then on his critical, if not hostile, attitude already apparent in the May memorandum became more and more openly expressed. Although he affected to believe that there was no real distinction between his position and Balfour's, except 'a difference of expression which results from different temperaments', Chamberlain had, by mid-1905, lost patience with Balfour's leadership. What had begun in October 1904 as criticism of a timid policy became criticism of timid leadership which sought refuge in obscurity.[61] Chamberlain's attacks henceforth concentrated on this official 'ambiguity' as much as on the differences of policy. On 7 June, at the annual meeting of the Tariff Reform League, he thus contrasted the clarity of his own position with discreet obscurity.[62] As Lord Hugh Cecil commented to Balfour, 'he not only excommunicates us . . . but . . . under a very transparent veil, he denounces you'.[63] The speech, as Wyndham saw it, 'will revive discussion and precipitate conflict'.[64] Possibly this was Chamberlain's intention. He hoped for a dissolution in the autumn and it was in his interest to weaken Balfour to the point where he could not carry on.

Consequently he intensified his attack on 'the path which has been born of timorous counsels and of half-hearted convictions'. Londonderry, who had urged caution on the fiscal question, came under a scathing personal attack.[65] Hood, as chief whip, saw 'grave troubles ahead' in the face of this Chamberlainite onslaught,[66] and Wyndham found 'much . . . that exercises my mind, and for *the first time* since Chamberlain's speech on the Whitsun adjournment of 1903, makes me uncertain whether the Party can be saved'.[67] At the National Union Conference at Newcastle Chamberlain's policy was again adopted by an overwhelming majority, and Balfour's policy rejected.[68] At Bristol on 21 November, despite Balfour's pleas for unity at Newcastle, Chamberlain directly attacked both Balfour's leadership and his policy: 'No army was ever led successfully to battle on the principle that the lamest man should govern the march of the army.'[69]

Against these Chamberlainite attacks, Balfourite hostility to Chamberlain himself increased considerably. By then, the steady succession of by-election losses had lent substance to Balfour's argument that food duties were unpopular, and his personal advisers continually reiterated both the disastrous effects of Chamberlain's policies and the need to maintain a distinctive Balfourite position.[70] 'I feel sure', Sandars told Balfour, 'that we could strengthen the *Conservative* position by reiterating the fact that under the Sheffield policy neither raw material nor "Food" would be taxed . . . The most pressing thing . . . is to develop the Sheffield policy as an independent platform . . .'[71] He therefore advised Balfour to make 'a declamatory statement of your own policy . . . [which] . . . should exhibit the particular points in which your speeches as to immediate policies differ from Joe's . . . The two policies are known to exist, and you have to consider the case of the large majority of the Party . . . who are really asking for a distinction to be drawn.'[72]

What all this amounted to was a conviction in the Balfourite camp that Chamberlain's tariff reform campaign had failed. They did not deny Chamberlain his successes, but he had failed in the wrong places and, in his own terms, with the wrong people. 'The portion of the Birmingham policy which offers the greatest attraction to average Conservatives', thought Sandars, 'is that which appeals to their Imperial sentiments, and it, therefore, seems the greater pity that the idea should be based upon the unpopular proposal to tax food.'[73] But so it was, and as such it was still not, the Balfourites thought, 'practical politics'. But Balfour himself was 'determined that under no circumstances would [he] be provoked into an open quarrel with Joe . . .'[74] and Chamberlain acted under a similar sentiment, although he felt that Balfour 'does not play the game and makes a real sympathy very difficult'.[75] The agreement of the leaders, on this point at least, was sufficient to hold the party together, but it precluded that emphasis on their differences which the Balfourites sought. Below the level of the leadership the party was in a state of total disintegration, with Unionists opposing Unionists, members leaving the party, candidates hard to find, and subscriptions low.[76] It was a gloomy picture, but one which Herbert Gladstone would have had no difficulty in recognizing from his experiences in 1900—it was the condition of a divided party entering an election it could not hope to win.

By the end of the year Balfour himself had had enough of the humiliations of the previous session.[77] For Balfour the question was simply one of timing. His opinion that it would be better to hold out to February was based largely on the general desire of the party to postpone for as long as possible an election from which many of them would not return, supplemented by special pleas from Long in Ireland and Selborne in South Africa that their work needed more time. All along, Balfour had been in favour of resignation rather than dissolution in the belief that even a brief period in office before the election would reveal the divisions of the Liberal party, and assist the Unionists. At the end of 1905, he thought those divisions had broken out once again. Campbell-Bannerman, speaking at Stirling, announced his acceptance of the 'step-by-step' policy of Home Rule, a policy which Rosebery swiftly condemned at Bodmin on 25 November. On 4 December Balfour resigned hoping that the Liberals would find the formation of a strong government impossible in the light of these differences on Ireland.

Ireland was the one remaining subject of importance which still divided the Liberal Imperialists from the official party. The dispute which led to Campbell-Bannerman's speech at Stirling had been reopened by Morley at Forfar on 20 October. Asquith wrote of this:

I am afraid that J. M.'s speech on Home Rule will be taken seriously, and not (as in all probability it really was) as a mere splenetic outburst directed at me.

If it secures any countenance, open or ambiguous, from C. B. . . . it will do incalculable and perhaps fatal mischief.

If we are to get a real majority in the next House of Commons, it can only be by making it perfectly clear to the electors that—as I said the other day—it will be no part of the policy of the new Liberal Government to introduce a Home Rule Bill in the new Parliament.[78]

Campbell-Bannerman, who intended to lead the party '*on the old lines*', thought both Asquith and Morley 'a little too emphatic and peremptory', but whilst his sympathies were with Morley, he viewed the future in the same way as Asquith. From Campbell-Bannerman's point of view, however, the essential point was to ensure that Ireland did not again divide the party: 'It would not be very difficult to frame a "formula" (Spencer has always said we must do this) before the election, expressive of our attitude.'[79] In this he had the full support of the party, even the League section, who had no wish to see old wounds reopened.[80]

The re-emergence of the controversy in the autumn of 1905, a controversy in which Rosebery joined when speaking at Stourbridge on 25 October, embarrassed everyone and stimulated Campbell-Bannerman to find the formula which he announced at Stirling. Unknown to either Rosebery or Balfour, however, he had agreed this policy beforehand with Redmond and with the Liberal Imperialist leaders in the Commons. The failure of the Liberal League to work out its policies in detail, one result of which was that Rosebery and his vice-presidents could, for almost four years, advocate different policies on Ireland while believing themselves to be in agreement, took its toll when the differences became obvious.

Rosebery's Bodmin speech, far from dividing the Liberal party again as Balfour expected, merely completed Rosebery's isolation.

'Rosebery is deplorable', wrote Lawson Walton: '. . . The Liberal
League has stood for many unpleasant opinions, it shall not stand for
anti-Home Rule. I fancy Lord Rosebery meant to commit "hara-kiri",
I think this is the word—in some dramatic way.'[81] Hudson, secretary
of the N.L.F., found 'the indignation against Rosebery is extreme.
I had two members of the League in here yesterday cursing his speech
up hill and down dale',[82] and even Herbert Gladstone, so long a
softening influence on Campbell-Bannerman's distrust of Rosebery,
thought the speech 'the speech of an enemy, not of a friend'.[83] But
Rosebery would not back down unless given the opportunity by
Campbell-Bannerman.[84] 'Rosebery', Herbert Gladstone informed
Campbell-Bannerman, 'is in a savage and despairing mood. He
denounced Asquith and Grey in unmeasured terms, accusing them of
having abandoned him, saying he had done with public life, having no
party and no friends.'[85] After the Bodmin speech his future as a Liberal
leader lay in Campbell-Bannerman's hands and Campbell-Bannerman,
who had been insecure for so long, made no effort to rescue his rival.

In the light of the negotiations of 1903–4, when the Unionist free
traders had attempted to prise Rosebery and the Liberal Imperialists
away from the Liberal party, the situation was ironic. Gladstone's
willingness to sacrifice Rosebery in 1905 stemmed directly from his
concern for Unionist free trade votes and for the votes of the weak
Liberals whom Rosebery represented:

The advanced Home-Rulers and Radicals are of course all right and entirely
with you whatever turn you give to Home Rule utterances . . . But the vote
which will make or mar our majority is composed of Un. F.T.s. and Edu-
cationalists and Anti- or weak Home Rule Liberals.

Your Stirling speech was accepted by all 'til Rosebery's monstrous
outburst. Since then letters have been coming in to me from quite good men
in different parts of the country reporting disturbed minds.[86]

Rosebery was thus left in the void as he himself finally recognized in
December. 'The difficulty', he informed Spender, 'is that C. B. cannot
make his statement in time. He has lost two opportunities and there is
no third. For I speak before he does and must explain my interpretation.'[87] Balfour still attempted to raise the 'Home Rule bogey',
but the Liberals, by ignoring Rosebery completely, prevented the
issue from achieving any prominence.

But Campbell-Bannerman's path was not quite clear, and Herbert
Gladstone was premature in believing that 'Grey and Asquith are now

both on the right side'.[88] Grey was far from happy with the situation, even though he adopted the official interpretation of the Stirling speech,[89] and the Liberal Imperialists were still not fully reconciled to Campbell-Bannerman's leadership. In 1903, Asquith, Grey, and Haldane had met to discuss their position in relation to the formation of a future Liberal government, and had agreed, in what became known as the 'Relugas Compact', that none of them would accept office unless Campbell-Bannerman agreed to go to the Lords and Asquith led the Commons. The compact itself broke down rapidly when Campbell-Bannerman stood firm. Asquith gave way, justifying himself on the grounds that Balfour's decision to resign rather than dissolve made it necessary to go into the election with a united front for the sake of free trade. Haldane, too, quickly lost his objections once Asquith had accepted, but Grey proved difficult to convince, and only the intervention of Acland finally secured his participation in the new cabinet. Some days of intrigue, rumour, and counter-rumour preceded the formation of the first Liberal government for a decade.[90]

The inclusion in that government of the four Liberal League vice-presidents confirmed Campbell-Bannerman as the real victor of the intrigues between 1903 and 1905. For Chamberlain these had been wasted years. If anything, his apparent acquiescence in Balfour's policies had damaged his movement by creating a distrust even of Highbury amongst his most committed supporters which Austen Chamberlain, when he succeeded to the leadership of tariff reform in 1906, was never fully able to overcome. Balfour, too, was damaged by the years spent clinging to office. His achievements in other fields did not compensate for the decline in his reputation that occurred as a result of his handling of the fiscal question. From these years stemmed the damaging charges of vacillation and obscurity which were eventually to undermine his position and bring about his resignation. For the Unionist free trade group and the Liberal League, these years were disastrous: the coalition of the centre never materialized, and neither succeeded in coming to terms with its own official party; both were to be shattered in the forthcoming election.

Valentine

The Liberals won a landslide victory in the general election of 1906. With 377 seats, they had an independent majority of 84, and with the addition of their allies, the Irish (83) and Labour (53), the government could call on a total of 513 votes in most divisions. In contrast, only 157 Unionists struggled back to the new House of Commons. But if the election as a whole confirmed and even exceeded Liberal expectations, within the limited arena of the Unionist party victory undoubtedly lay with Chamberlain. It was not simply a numerical victory, and future events were to show that he did not control the majority with which he was initially credited. Contemporaries divided the party into 109 tariff reformers, 32 Balfourites, and 11 or 16 Unionist free traders, depending on the members 'not classified'.[1] Recent historians have to some extent questioned these figures. R. A. Rempel lists 27 Unionist free traders in the House of Commons of 1906–10,[2] Neal Blewett lists 31,[3] and if the two M.P.s included in Rempel's list, but not in Blewett's, were added,[4] a gross figure of 33 could be given. Blewett gives the Unionist party a further free trade inclination by reducing the whole-hoggers to 79 and enlarging the Balfourite contingent to 49, and even this may be an overestimate of Chamberlainite strength.

But the three-faction analysis, while facilitating an apparent numerical precision, only obscures the real situation. Even on the criterion of policy alone, the impossibility of defining the Balfourite or the Unionist free trade position precisely makes such calculation of doubtful value, irrespective of the conflict of priorities between the fiscal question and other issues, and between loyalty to principle and loyalty to party, which inevitably influenced the attitudes and actions of individual Unionists. After 1906, as before, the Unionists were strung out, individually or in small groups, all the way between the extremes, with the majority seeking to be as Balfourite as they could. Thus of the 56 so-called Unionist free traders who stood in the 1906 election, 48 former M.P.s and 8 new candidates, some 35 were prepared to accept the essentials of Balfour's policy, 'retaliation against hostile tariffs and . . . a "free and unfettered" colonial conference . . .'[5] All that can be said is that the Unionist factions were very divided within themselves, and that the greater the numbers attributed to them, the wider these divisions become.

Although they were not irrelevant, the Balfourite free traders caused Chamberlain less concern than the hard-core activists, that fluctuating 20–40 who, by voting against the government on Liberal fiscal resolutions, had jeopardized Balfour's government and thus, in Chamberlain's eyes, held him back from preference. It was on the reduction of this group to 'nine or ten' activists that Chamberlain could congratulate himself after the election. Several factors combined to produce this result: 12 Unionist free traders, including some of the most aggressive younger men such as Churchill, had crossed the floor to the Liberals before the 1906 election;[6] 23 more, including Beach, Lord George Hamilton, and Ritchie, had either retired from the House of Commons or died before 1906;[7] and of those who remained, the most active were opposed by tariff reformers in the constituencies.

By 1906 Chamberlain felt as Campbell-Bannerman had felt in 1903, that the Unionist free traders should be the ones 'to make advances. They are the people who, being in a very small minority, have set themselves against the wishes of the majority of their party . . . and if they want to save themselves, they should bring forth fruits meet for repentance.'[8] One further factor contributed to Chamberlain's apparent dominance of the party in the immediate aftermath of the election, the defeat and consequent absence from the House of Commons of Balfour himself. Chamberlain was the natural candidate for the temporary leadership whilst Balfour sought a new seat, much as the Unionist free traders and the traditionalists within the party might dislike the idea.[9] On 23 January, against a background of demands from his own supporters that he should replace Balfour permanently, he opened negotiations for the reunification of the party.

Chamberlain was determined to use his position 'to secure agreement . . . on a programme of more definiteness',[10] which he intended to achieve by having the party policy determined at a party meeting where he could exploit his numerical majority. If Balfour would not accept this then he would not lead but would retire from the front

bench and act 'as an independent though friendly member'.[11] The
threat to refuse the leadership was one which Balfour could not ignore.
Even Sandars, before he had seen Chamberlain's letters, thought
Chamberlain the only possible leader, and that none could lead over his
head in Balfour's absence.[12] Moreover, Chamberlain's absence from the
already depleted Unionist front bench would advertise the divisions
within the party, and be an open admission that Balfour's policy of
unity had failed. Chamberlain's letters of 23 and 26 January in which
he made his demands changed opinion within the Balfourite camp.
'Be it so', was Sandars's reaction on 27 January to Chamberlain's threat
to withdraw to the back-benches:

The attitude taken by Joe—if he maintains it—involves . . . a breach in the
party . . . you have your followers, Joe has his. Joe recommends that there
should be a trial of strength before parliament meets. This I don't believe the
party desires for one moment, whatever their opinions may be. They want
both you and Joe to help them in the fighting line.

Sandars, therefore, assumed that Balfour would make no concessions
to Chamberlain on either policy or tactical grounds, since Balfour
could accept neither the scientific tariff, nor anticipate a colonial conference, whilst it was madness to call a party meeting to settle 'such a
quasi-academic question as its own particular policy (a policy just
rejected by the country) which won't be before Parliament for years,
before it knows what revolutionary legislation may engage all its
efforts in the House of Commons and the country . . .'[13]

When the two leaders met on 2 February, Chamberlain was left
completely dissatisfied with Balfour's attitude.[14] Like Sandars, Balfour
regarded the result of the election as a shattering defeat for Unionist
policy as a whole, including tariff reform, rather than a victory for
tariff reform within the party. Chamberlain found him unimpressed
by the numbers which the press attributed to the tariff reform section
of the party in the new House of Commons and 'more definitely against
a General Tariff than he ever was before . . . What he evidently desires
is that Tariff Reform should be put entirely on the shelf during this
Parliament when, he says, it cannot be practical politics . . .'[15] The
interview, at which Chamberlain 'saw no signs of advance or of
concession on any single point', thus produced not the intended
rapprochement but even greater separation.

On 6 February Chamberlain wrote a letter to Ridley for publication
to clear up any 'misapprehension of our position as Tariff Reformers',

in which he restated his intention not to challenge Balfour for the leadership but only to seek clarification of future policy. Chamberlain identified the crucial areas of difference as food duties, where the advanced tariff reformers 'think that the probability of our having to place a moderate duty on corn from foreign countries in return for a substantial preference to be given by the Colonies to our manufactures should be frankly admitted and defended . . .', and the general tariff, where 'in our opinion, it is impossible without it to have any practical or effective scheme of Retaliation . . .' He thought the party 'would welcome a declaration by Mr. Balfour which would show clearly that Tariff Reform was not to be dropped', but if it did not, then tariff reformers, whilst not formally leaving the party, 'may very properly constitute themselves into a parliamentary group or Committee'. There may have been 'no question of repudiating the leadership of Mr. Balfour', but as a published letter the statement was not without menace.[16]

On the same day Balfour himself wrote to Chamberlain, feeling his way towards a compromise. After reflection, Balfour was prepared to make one concession: 'I have come round to your view that, *if you desire it*, a Party meeting must be held.' Typically, however, most of the rest of the letter was devoted to 'several minor questions of considerable difficulty', the sum effect of which was to demonstrate the impracticality of such a meeting. In particular the question of procedure, which Balfour called 'the most difficult', was one which Balfour could turn to his advantage. 'Are you and I to agree upon some question on which the meeting can vote "aye" or "no" . . .?',[17] an apparently innocent question which concealed a trap which Chamberlain failed to notice in his reply: 'of course there will be no question whatever as to Leadership,' he wrote, 'but as I have already explained, I think the party as a whole should be asked to express freely their opinion as to the best policy for the future, and to vote as between the alternatives suggested'.[18] Balfour's reply of 8 February sprang the trap: 'if . . . we take the course you propose, it seems to me that, should the vote go against *you*, your position will not be made easier; should it go against *me*, *mine* will become impossible, and you will have to reconsider your decision to "refuse the leadership under all circumstances". '[19]

Balfour refused to separate policy and personality, as Chamberlain wished. He was well aware of the distrust in which Chamberlain was held by large sections of the Conservative party, and had commented

to Lord Hugh Cecil that Chamberlain would never be elected leader:
'If he was, the party would no doubt for a time be broken up.'[20] On
the same day that Balfour threw his leadership into the scales, and tilted
them firmly in his direction, Chamberlain had written to Ridley: 'with
such a Party as ours, my leadership would not have been possible for
twenty-four hours'.[21]

Chamberlain's refusal to contest the leadership was, as Ridley saw,
a critical weakness,[22] and he even attempted a little discreet pressure,
informing Chamberlain on 12 February that 'some of our friends, both
in conversation and writing, feel very strongly that the weak point in
your position is your refusal in any event, to lead'.[23] But Chamberlain
would not be moved.[24] The more realistic of the tariff reformers,
despite their dislike of Balfour's policy, agreed with Chamberlain's
analysis of the position. 'As to Balfour,' Garvin wrote to Maxse, 'we
differ only as to tactics . . . A united party will not follow Joe, and he
never was wiser than in refusing to lead. I am perfectly certain that at
least a score of nominal tariff reformers (according to the present lists)
will rat to Balfour if there is a split.'[25] The situation pointed to an
insecure future for Balfour as leader, accepted as he was by the whole-
hoggers, or the more realistic of them, because they could not see a way
of getting rid of him. Nevertheless, such was the situation as long as
Chamberlain wished to use the Unionist party, with its predominantly
Conservative composition, as the vehicle of his policy.

Conservative distrust of Chamberlain was strong and many-sided.
Even on the straightforward question of policy on which Chamberlain
wished to fight, Balfour had his supporters. Lansdowne, despite being
a vice-president of Chamberlain's Liberal Unionist Council, urged
Balfour to reject any compromise:

If Joe insists on pushing his views, the schism will become deeper, and the
Unionist party will degenerate into two feeble and mutually suspicious
groups. Surely we may, so far as the near future—certainly so far as this
Session—is concerned, relegate the fiscal question to the background of our
political life, and devote our attention to the many grave questions which
members of H.M. Government have told us will be taken up . . .

It is not necessary that we should recant our opinions as to retaliation or
Colonial Preference, but the country has pronounced decisively against them,
and we must accept the verdict . . . With a majority of over 200 against us, we
are—for the moment at all events—relieved of the necessity of bringing
forward a constructive policy of our own.[26]

Sandars thought Lansdowne 'is very frightened about Joe and protection',[27] but noted also that Lansdowne was not alone in the Lords as
Salisbury, Cawdor, and Londonderry were all against Chamberlain.[28]

Lansdowne, as a Liberal Unionist, was perhaps not in the best
position to judge, but on this occasion his view was confirmed by both
Douglas and Sandars, Balfour's eyes and ears in the clubs and amongst
the rank and file of the party. According to Douglas, 'There is a strong
anti-Joe feeling in the party Club—thinking he is the author of our
ills',[29] whilst Sandars thought that

Joe would be worsted in this encounter at a party meeting. More men than
he knows of are very sore with him, men who with safe seats have had to
fight for their lives, men who have seen their friends and neighbours in
other constituencies fall before the 'big and little loaf' cry which they owe to
Joe, or have lost their seats because of the intrusion of a Tariff Reform
candidate.[30]

But the distrust of Chamberlain was far deeper than resentment
engendered by recent defeats, and the Balfourite position always rested
on stronger foundations than that of confused party loyalists seeking
shelter from the fiscal storm. The basis of Balfourite strength was the
traditional Conservative party, the landed gentry, whose conservatism
outweighed the appeal of Chamberlain's hints of protection for agriculture. In the first instance, this conservatism expressed itself as a
concern for the greater priority, now that the party was in opposition,
of the other causes for which conservatism stood, and which Chamberlain's obsession with tariff reform appeared to neglect or even endanger.
Balfour explained to Cawdor:

The difficulty arises not from a certain ambition on the part of Joe, but from
his absolute concentration upon one idea. He desires that the party at the
end of this Parliament should find itself absolutely united not merely on the
broad question of Fiscal Reform, but on Fiscal Reform as he individually
conceives it, and he desires nothing else. For this he would sacrifice all other
interests which he regards as mere dust in the balance . . .[31]

'It is quite clear', came the answering echo from Cawdor,

that Joe considers things as 'dust in the balance' which we consider to be of
much importance—e.g. Education and Church—possibly he would put Home
Rule in his dustheap too . . . We may have to face throwing out some Government Bill in the Lords, thereby forcing an election on a definite issue, and we
ought not to be hampered if such an occasion arises, by Tariff Reform.[32]

Lansdowne, too, particularly disliked 'tarring the House of Lords with the brush of Protection'.[33]

It was this concern for traditional institutions which he shared with the majority of the Conservative party that made Balfour the only possible party leader in Conservative eyes. Chamberlain in contrast was not safe, partly because of what he might sacrifice in his 'absolute concentration on one idea', partly because he was, personally, a radical. It was, perhaps, in origin no more than a difference of temperament, but it led Conservatives to regard the tariff reform movement throughout its existence with great suspicion. 'The more I think of the matter,' Salisbury wrote to Selborne:

the more impressed I am with apprehension at the violent nature of the changes proposed. The whole of my Conservative training revolts against the catastrophical theory of politics. Chamberlain and Milner and Ashley all in their several ways, adhere to that theory . . . My conception of Tariff Reform is to go a step—and that only a short step—at a time . . . only a policy of this kind . . . has the least chance of real approval by the mass of the Conservative party.[34]

Seen in this light tariff reform was a disaster for the Conservative party, not just because its proposals to tax food were unpopular but because it diverted the party from its real purpose and distorted its nature. The débâcle of 1906 was 'not all because of tariff reform', Salisbury thought:

perhaps not mainly because of tariff reform. But tariff reform is the most fatal of the poisons that are at work. Education has done much harm, but it split politics on normal lines, the wounds it deals are healthy. Labour is most formidable, but it is essentially a force which leads to a reaction. Chinese Labour will not be of permanent interest here—it has done all the harm it can. But tariff reform is an effort to drive the Conservative elements of our society into a policy of far-reaching change. It is not put forward as a moderate but as a revolutionary new departure. It *might* have been moderate, but it is not in the hands of moderate men.

As such, Salisbury thought, 'it will remain a fatal handicap for years'.[35]

From the Conservative point of view this was fair comment. Chamberlain had never joined the Conservative party, aimed many of his speeches at the trade unions, and stressed the social reforms which would result from his proposals in a way which could have little appeal to Conservatives of Salisbury's outlook. Moreover, the 1906 election, and the impact made by the appearance of a distinctive Labour vote on minds unprepared for such an outcome, opened the possibility that Chamberlain might extend the radical or 'socialist' implications of his policies to regain this vote. Chamberlain certainly saw 'no reason why the Labour party should be more hostile to us than to the Radicals'.[36] It was just such a vision—or lack of it—that concerned the Conservatives.

Many of Chamberlain's whole-hogger following, however, welcomed the new development. W. J. Ashley, for example, admired Chamberlain's way of making tariffs his one cry:

But I do hope that, while keeping this very much in the front, we shall not be silent or merely negative on social reforms. I think they are both necessary in themselves and expedient in a party sense. I know Jesse Collings has long felt that Chamberlain will be compelled to take an interest in proposals for the benefit of the agricultural labourer, and I am anxious also that our party should not fall foul of Trades Unionism. My own earlier enthusiasm led me to look at Trades Unionism in a very favourable light . . . I do hope that the naturally important place of some of the big manufacturers in the Tariff Reform movement, regarded as a Protectionist movement, will not tempt our people to identify themselves *too much* with the ordinary manufacturers' attitude towards Trades Unionism.[37]

One reason why Salisbury and the Conservatives regarded tariff reform as such an electoral handicap was because they rejected, as Conservatives, the 'constructive' social programme which Ashley's attitude implied, and which Chamberlain attempted to associate with his fiscal proposals. They thus feared Chamberlain both for what he had already done, propose food duties which made their negative position more difficult, if not impossible, to maintain, and for what he might do.

The Labour party [wrote Salisbury] have come forward in the consciousness of strength, and have formulated enormous demands. The Radicals will attempt to meet them—so will Joe, I suppose. But we wretched Conservatives, if we are honest, can offer them very little. Into this is mixed tariff reform, and our position as a party and in the Lords' trying to stem the current is to be this—we cannot give you old age pensions, land nationalisation, compulsory minimum wages, etc., but this is what we will do, we will give you a tax on your bread. It is an impossible situation. The food tax was always a very heavy weight to carry but with a suspicious and importunate proletariate, it is a prohibitive handicap—for Conservatives.[38]

As long as it remained in the Unionist alliance but failed to dominate it completely the Conservative party proper, Salisbury's Conservative party, was caught between two alternative concepts of Unionism and of mass politics, and suffered the worst of both worlds.

But by Salisbury's standards Chamberlain could not be classed as a Conservative, honest or otherwise, and as such he could not lead the Conservative party. 'The Unionist M.P.s may want Joe,' wrote Pembroke:

but the mass of the Conservative party in the country do not quite look upon him as a safe man to whom they can entrust the future of the Party . . . I am afraid that Joe Chamberlain will bid for the Trade Union vote, by giving up principles which are the mainstay of our party. Arthur Balfour is absolutely to be trusted. The best leader of the House of Commons, whether in or out of office that we have ever had . . .[39]

The trial of strength, as Sandars termed it, which arose after the 1906 general election was, because of the policy issues involved, as much a conflict between two concepts of Unionism, Radical and Conservative, as a dispute over the details of one particular policy.

After the election the resentment of the tariff reform rank and file was as great against Balfour, whose negative leadership they blamed for the magnitude of the defeat, as Conservative feeling against Chamberlain. Ridley was 'deeply convinced that it is quite impossible for Balfour to continue as leader. The present elections have in the main been a revolt against him and all that he stands for.'[40] Maxse echoed this:

One obvious inference from the voting is that we have lost the Tory Democracy, thereby fulfilling the remarkable prophecy of Randolph Churchill when he heard that Balfour had become leader of the Party in the House of Commons. 'So Arthur Balfour is really leader—and Tory Democracy, the genuine article, at an end . . .' unless the Party is prepared to fearlessly face the situation as it is, and to realise the impossibility of recovering the confidence of the country under the present regime, we may remain in opposition for half a generation.[41]

Between the rank and file of the respective factions, Chamberlainite and Balfourite, the conflict was indeed more open and more bitter than within the leadership where personal contact and a greater awareness of political practicalities blunted the edge of confrontation. As Chamberlain remarked, some of his friends were not always discreet,[42] and their indiscretions provoked retaliation. Iwan-Muller, of the Balfourite *Daily Telegraph*, was infuriated by Maxse's attacks on the 'Balfour clique' in the *National Review*, and sent Maxse a declaration of war:

you in the N.R. *would* have nothing but absolute submission on the part of the Tory wing of the Unionist party . . . Of course I am a Tory, and sincere as is my admiration for Mr. Chamberlain, I have never pretended a desire to hand over the control of the Tory party to Liberal Unionists. We are allies on honourable terms and our Tory share is four-fifths of the alliance . . . I am willing to stretch compromise to its most elastic limits but I am not going to sacrifice Toryism to an unknown Liberalism temporarily in alliance with my party . . .[43]

'What it seems to me you ignore,' he wrote in a cooler moment three days later, 'is that the Tory party is not a Liberal–Radical–Unionist party. Sometimes I doubt if you believe in the existence of a Tory party at all.'[44]

But although the extemists of either camp were the most vocal, they were far from the most numerous. The tariff reformers were split on their attitude to Balfour, with even strong tariff reformers in principle being reluctant to press the issue to a clear separation. Gilbert Parker found 'a willingness to fight for Tariff Reform *within* the party . . . but no one will go into a separate Camp and form, as it were, a new party. It is perfectly hopeless to canvass men on that basis.'[45] Chamberlain and Balfour were tied together as before. Both had the power to destroy the effectiveness of the party; only together could they successfully preserve it. However unlikely a compromise seemed during late January and early February, all the pressures were in that direction.

The conflict between the two leaders produced confusion rather than strong feelings one way or the other amongst the bulk of the party, which desired unity above all, but desired it with Chamberlain's policy and Balfour's leadership. If this was, at this stage, to want the impossible—Balfour as tariff reform leader—then the party wanted the only practical alternative, the continuation of the duumvirate of Chamberlain and Balfour working together. In the whole controversy this was the critical influence. The centre of the party had sufficient strength to bring about its wishes and force Chamberlain into compromise with Balfour, and to force Balfour to make compromise possible by meeting Chamberlain more than half-way on the question of policy.

Nevertheless, by introducing the leadership issue at the personal as well as at the policy level, Balfour had regained the initiative in the negotiation of such a compromise. Chamberlain had no ready answer to Balfour's letter and was forced to temporize, promising 'some

suggestions' after he had had time to think.[46] The line along which his
thoughts ran, he indicated to Ridley: 'I am inclined to try my hand at
a Resolution which would reaffirm the importance of fiscal reform as
the first constructive item of the Party policy and claiming that the
idea of a general tariff and 2/- on Corn, should be left to the future
without any premature committal.' This was an attempt to get round
Balfour's proposal of a party meeting and a general discussion, but no
vote, which Chamberlain considered 'would not be satisfactory'.[47] At
the same time, such a resolution was a long way from insistence on
the Glasgow programme.

On 10 February Chamberlain sent his reply, pleading that 'the suspicion of dual aims' should be removed 'to give the Party a lead which
will certainly be accepted by the great majority as an official policy . . .
Cannot you and I devise some compromise?' It was, as Chamberlain
said, 'a really persuasive letter',[48] and the compromise suggested
'although it is not nearly as definite and does not go nearly as far as the
Glasgow programme . . . *does* officially deprecate any premature
decision against either a general tariff or a small duty on foreign
corn'.[49] Chamberlain was clearly on the defensive. Balfour's control of
the situation was revealed by his reply, postponing any decision until
after his speech in the City on 12 February. Balfour agreed to meet
Chamberlain on 13 February,[50] but no compromise was found then,
and a further meeting was arranged for 14 February. From this emerged
the 'Valentine letters', which finally settled the post-electoral disagreement on the basis of compromise, avoiding, by the exchange of
letters, both the resolution at a party meeting to which Balfour objected,
and a policy speech by Balfour which Chamberlain, warned by previous
experience, could not accept. Balfour agreed that

Fiscal Reform is, and must remain, the first constructive work of the Unionist
Party:
   that the objects of such reform are to secure more equal terms of competition for British trade and closer commercial union with the Colonies:
   that while it is at present unnecessary to prescribe the exact methods by
which these objects are to be attained, and inexpedient to permit differences
of opinion as to these methods to divide the Party, I hold that, though other
means may be possible, the establishment of a moderate general tariff on
manufactured goods, not imposed for the purpose of raising prices or giving
artificial protection against legitimate competition, and the imposition of a
small duty on foreign corn, are not in principle objectionable, and should be

adopted if shewn to be necessary for the attainment of the ends in view or for purposes of revenue.

With the addition of the qualifications that it was inexpedient to allow differences of opinion about methods to divide the party, and that the general tariff should not be imposed for protection, this undertaking embodied, almost word for word, Chamberlain's compromise resolution which he had sent to Balfour on 10 February, and he was able to accept the policy gladly.[51]

Superficially, the Valentine letters appeared as a Chamberlainite victory. Unionist free traders certainly saw them as such. Lord Hugh Cecil complained of Balfour's sudden identification with Chamberlain, 'even to the point of treating opposition to the taxation of corn as grounds for exclusion from Parliament',[52] and on their militant wing, Strachey, who had always suspected Balfour of being a secret protectionist, congratulated his opposite number and former fellow Liberal Unionist, Leo Maxse, on the 'Balfour climb-down', as a 'great triumph for the *National* . . .'[53] The Conservative Balfourites, Balfour himself excepted, also gave the letters this interpretation. On 25 February Salisbury wrote to Selborne:

The world—at least the world with which I am in contact—thinks these letters are a surrender by Arthur. Arthur thinks it is a surrender by Joe. The free-fooders are in despair. I am sick of politics . . . Linky [Lord Hugh Cecil] may go over to the other side if the education question is out of the way. For the present, we are shattered.[54]

Such appearances were deceptive. Balfour, in agreeing to the Valentine letters, did not consider that he had advanced doctrinally, and continued, as before, to interpret his public statements literally. Within a week of the publication of the letters he wrote to an inquisitive correspondent: 'The party is not committed, so far as I am concerned, to a general tariff. What it is committed to, is the proposition that a moderate general tariff not framed on protectionist lines is "not in principle objectionable", etc.'[55] Tariff reformers, if ever they shared the illusions of the Unionist free traders, quickly lost them. From their point of view, W. Howard Gretton commented in February 1907: 'In the history of party politics, there are happily few examples of a more specious manifesto. Vague, indeterminate, elaborately guarded, it is susceptible of fully a dozen different meanings . . .'[56]

But as a compromise to which Chamberlain had agreed the Valentine letters temporarily took the steam out of direct attacks on Balfour's leadership. They did not, however, remove the sources of discontent, and during the early part of 1906 alienated whole-hoggers turned their attention to the inadequacies, as they saw them, of the party organization. A resolution by Leverton Harris, passed by an overwhelming majority at the National Union Conference at Newcastle in 1905, calling for the democratization of the party machine, served as a lever against those whom the *National Review* called 'The Organisers of Disaster'.[57] Here too, however, the Young Turks of the Tariff Reform League, even with the backing of Chamberlain,[58] were no match for the experience and power of the Central Office, which kept a careful control of the various committees set up to implement the 1905 resolution.[59] In June Maxse voiced the tariff reformers' concern that there was 'little or no prospect of a serious reorganisation of the Unionist party . . . Reorganisation committees have been set up, but power will be in the hands of the irresponsible and incompetent Junta which organised the recent debacle.'[60] It was tantamount to a confession of defeat.

In outmanœuvring the whole-hoggers Hood, as chief whip, had been careful to keep the management of the Central Office out of the discussions, and had interpreted the conference resolution as a demand for the reform of the National Union alone, with propaganda work removed to the National Union, and with closer liaison between the National Union, the Central Office, and the leadership. On these lines he made concessions, in particular the establishment of an advisory committee to provide the necessary liaison. It was not, however, what the tariff reformers had intended. They had controlled the National Union conference since 1903 and had, in every year since then, passed resolutions in favour of Chamberlain's programme. Their difficulty was that such resolutions, apart from their moral force as expressions of rank-and-file opinion, were in no way binding on Balfour with whom final decisions of policy rested. What they now sought was a share in formulating policy and control of the Central Office, especially in regard to funds and the selection of candidates. They gained none of this. The Committee eventually set up was purely advisory, and its composition ensured that it remained firmly under the control of the chief whip.[61]

Tariff reform frustration boiled over at the special conference of the National Union which met on 27 July to approve the scheme of reorganization. Leo Maxse, a Liberal Unionist who qualified for membership of this Conservative body at 10.30 on the morning of the Conference itself,[62] put down a resolution that 'no reorganisation of the National Union meets the unanimous demand of the Newcastle Conference for the reform of the Central Management of the Conservative Party, which can only be satisfied by bringing the Central Office under more effective popular control'. This was neither an isolated nor a spontaneous outburst on his part, and some attempt had been made to pack the meeting beforehand.[63] The plan misfired badly. Hood, confronted with a direct challenge, replied by stressing the concessions made and the dangers of management by committee. It was a masterly defence, and combined with the thinly veiled threat that both he and Balfour might resign if the tariff reformers went ahead, it proved irresistible. Chaplin, who had been predisposed to favour Maxse's resolution, now commented that the entire scheme of reform would collapse if the resolution was carried, and after Chaplin's speech Maxse was forced to withdraw.[64]

The tariff reformers had committed a cardinal error in publicizing their hostility to the leadership so soon after the Valentine letters had brought relief to an anxious party. In this Maxse's outspoken attacks in the *National Review* upon Hood personally,[65] and upon the 'Balfour clique' in general, played a crucial part. After the débâcle of the general election, preceded as it had been a few weeks before by the resignation of a chief agent admitted on all sides to be incompetent, the Central Office and the party officials were vulnerable. But to attempt to transform dissatisfaction with the organization into an all-embracing attack on the leadership, including Balfour himself, was to ignore all those factors which had defeated such a move in January and forced Chamberlain to agree to the Valentine compromise.

After the conference, Lawrence complained to Chamberlain of the poor tactics of the tariff reformers. He pointed out that, even though they knew beforehand that Chaplin, Vincent, and other stalwarts were not prepared to support Maxse's resolution, no one had done anything about it. He also noted, as was obvious, that after his 'bitter article' Maxse was the wrong person to lead the attack, and that he had merely played into Hood's hands.[66] Lawrence himself felt that it was his duty, after the *National Review* article, to make his own peace with Hood[67] and even W. C. Bridgeman, who had seconded Maxse's resolution, felt it desirable to excuse his conduct to Balfour, although his excuses fell on deaf ears.[68] Sandars, who drafted several replies to Bridgeman, felt certain that he 'hatched the plot in concert with Maxse . . .', and rejected his professions of loyalty. In common with the bulk of the party he also concluded, as was in fact obvious from Maxse's role in the affair, that the tariff reformers were less concerned with reorganization for its own sake than to capture the Central Office and change its personnel.[69]

Circumstances were against such an attempt in the summer of 1906, not only because the Valentine compact was still fresh and an apparent concession by Balfour to the tariff reformers, but because tariff reform itself was not the primary issue of politics. Early in the new session the new Liberal government had introduced a resolution in the name of Sir James Kitson declaring that the recent election had demonstrated the decisive rejection of tariff reform by the electorate, and the resolution had inevitably been carried by a large majority. With this vote went any claim tariff reform had to immediate political relevance.

The Liberal legislative programme, particularly its Education Bill, turned politics back into well-trodden, and for the Unionists less divisive, paths. As the prime mover of the Unionist Education Act of 1902, Balfour was exceptionally well qualified to lead the opposition to its modification and the vigour with which he did so led the ever-suspicious tariff reformers to see in his performance another attempt to side-track tariff reform. To the majority of the party, however, his distinction on this question confirmed their belief that he was the only possible leader for a Conservative party. Nor did the condition of the economy intrude upon the political situation in 1906, as it had done in previous years. On the contrary, as Chamberlain remarked, the trade returns showed unprecedented prosperity, and consequently this was not the time to look forward to a sensational agitation in favour of a change in the fiscal system.[70] Moreover, in July the tariff reform movement suffered its greatest set-back of all when Chamberlain suffered a stroke which, as it turned out, removed him from the centre of politics forever. The most serious rival, perhaps the only serious rival, to Balfour's position had gone. The extent of Chamberlain's illness was not revealed for some time, and his followers continued to hope for his return. In the interim, leaderless and defeated, the tariff reform movement drifted into the autumn of 1906 without force or direction.

6

Socialism

The radical imperialists who attacked Balfour's leadership in the first half of 1906 did so, not because of his attitude towards tariff reform alone, but because a policy of criticism such as he desired whilst in opposition seemed to offer the party no prospect of recovery in the future. The difficulty was the emergence of the Labour party. In a two-party system, they argued, the opposition could rely on the swing of the pendulum and the accumulation of dissatisfaction which attached to any party in office. But with Labour offering a third alternative these conditions on which Balfourite tactics were based no longer applied. 'Our leaders who live in a world of their own, do not realise that we have to beat Labour as well as Liberalism before we can hope to regain power,' Maxse wrote in the *National Review* in September 1906, adding a month later in the same review:

though the growth of the Labour party may portend the disappearance of the Liberal party, it will effectively prevent the reappearance of the Unionist party. Outside Birmingham, the Labour party is robbing us of the Tory democracy which has been the mainstay of the Unionist cause for the past twenty years.[1]

In the aftermath of defeat it was this sudden appearance of Labour rather than the size of the Liberal majority that the Unionists found most noticeable: 'what is going on here,' wrote Balfour, 'is a faint echo of the same movement which has produced massacres in St. Petersburg, riots in Vienna, and Socialist processions in Berlin'.[2] The reaction which many of Balfour's leading colleagues shared in various ways, was in part one of surprise. Despite Chamberlain's concentration on the working-class vote in his tariff reform campaign, the Unionists, tariff reformers and Balfourites alike, had taken very little notice of trade union discontent after the Taff Vale decision or of trade union willingness to participate in an independent political movement, and had lost touch with the real feelings of Labour. Rudely awakened in 1906, even those who did not fully accept Balfour's global view saw local issues in this context. Salisbury thought that

the Labour Movement and Organisation (of the magnitude of which our clever wirepullers never seem to have had a glimmering, though it must have been going on under their very noses for months or even years) has been of incomparably greater importance than anything else. [Thus, Chinese labour] fitted in with the labour fever here. Men who were rising against what they consider the tyranny of capital have had no difficulty in believing that capital was guilty of every atrocity in South Africa. So this issue was merely an expression of the labour movement, and so I say that the labour movement has left the fiscal question a long way behind in importance . . . To these working men, a food tax is probably another example of the indifference of capital to the struggles of the poor . . .[3]

Salisbury was, as always, perceptive, pragmatic, and moderate. Even though he was still a Balfourite at this stage of his career, George Wyndham's way of making virtually the same points as Salisbury illustrates, as nothing else could, the essential difference between the attitudes of the Balfourite and the tariff reform Unionists. Wyndham wrote to his father:

Now, today in England, we are fighting to a finish—'damned badly', I admit.

But in the course of the fight, the Education Act, and Home Rule, and Chinese Slavery and 'Dear Food' are so much ammunition which has thinned our ranks, but is *now* expended.

Two ideals, and only two, emerge from the vortex:—

1. Imperialism which demands Unity at Home between classes, and Unity throughout the Empire; and which *prescribes* Fiscal Reform to secure both.

2. Insular Socialism, and Class Antagonism . . .

Between these two ideals a great battle will be fought. I do not know which will win. If Imperialism wins, we shall go on and be a great Empire. If Socialism wins we shall cease to be. The rich will be plundered. The poor will suffer. We shall perish with Babylon, Rome and Constantinople.[4]

Both Salisbury and Wyndham reflected the wide consensus that particular policies had made little difference to the eventual outcome of the election, which was determined by forces beyond the control of individual politicians, factions, or parties. The election, for the Unionists at large, demonstrated not the victory of free trade as represented by the huge Liberal contingent in the House of Commons, but 'the solidarity of labour . . . the conviction for the first time born in the working classes, that their social salvation is in their own hands . . .'[5]

Convinced as they were that the Unionist party was the democratic party which rested on working-class votes in opposition to the 'blatant, lower middle-class fraud, called Liberalism',[6] the radical imperialists saw the Labour party as the real enemy to be confronted, not the Liberals. In practical terms it was the Labour party which had taken votes from the Unionists, and thus destroyed Toryism in such old strongholds as Lancashire. In theoretical terms both Labour and Unionism appealed to the voters for the same reasons. Both were ideologies based upon the necessity of state intervention in the workings of society and upon the inevitability of conflict. Where they differed was in the nature of that fundamental conflict—whether it was between races organized as nation states and empires, or between classes organized internationally. For both, Liberalism, defined as a belief in the possibilities of national and/or international harmony achieved through rational discussion, arbitration, and disarmament, was irrelevant, condemned by a denial of conflict which seemed unrealistic, and a *laissez-faire* individualism which appeared both cruel and inefficient. Unionists themselves were struck by the similarities between their objectives and those of the Labour party. 'Labour and Imperialism', Wyndham commented, 'aim at the same goal: a better life for more of us. I believe in my method, they believe in their method. We shall see. But whether we are socialists or Imperialists, we are living men. The others are old women and senile professors. They have got to clear out of the ring . . .'[7]

Awareness of Labour was strong enough, even amongst the Balfourite leadership, to exercise a decisive influence on parliamentary tactics. With their control of the House of Lords the Unionists could reject any measure they chose. Yet, believing that it was the defection of their working-class supporters which had brought about the defeat of 1906, they felt they could not, without condemning themselves to permanent opposition, oppose Labour-sponsored reforms, however great their distaste for them. As Garvin explained the difficulty to an unwilling Maxse:

this is *the* crucial issue of Unionist policy . . . the Unionist party has suffered extremely in the last twenty years by absorbing the middle classes, and . . . is much less vital and daring in the sphere of social reform than it was when it passed the Factory Acts, when Randolph Churchill's Tory Democratic campaign was at its height and when Mr. Chamberlain's Unionist radicalism was fresh . . . if the party of fiscal reform is to echo Mr. Cobden's own original sentiments about Trades Unionists and Trade Unionism we shall be dubbed and dumped as an Employers party . . .

The alternative before us is plain. If we adopt an attitude which the House of Lords does not follow up, the party practically stultifies itself by drawing back from its brave words at the last moment in the place where it has power. But if the House of Lords does follow it up, then you have a conflict between the House of Lords and industrial democracy upon a direct Labour issue. I am absolutely convinced that that will imperil, as nothing else in the world can do, the existence of the House of Lords itself, and will make that Chamber useless on other questions where its opposition would be justified, wise and successful . . . Because there is a lot of froth upon the top of the Labour movement, do not let us forget the bed-rock which is under that movement. We shall never come back to power by the support of the middle classes.

The House of Lords will have plenty of big business to take on, and it must not take on too much . . . If it opposes Labour to begin with, Labour being compelled at the outset to oppose it upon the Trade Union issue, will oppose it on everything . . . which would result in making some of the adverse conditions of the last General Election permanent and would threaten the loss of all our causes as nothing else could . . .[8]

Balfour had arrived independently at similar conclusions regarding the tactics to be pursued by the Lords on both the Trades Disputes Bill and the Education Bill, and for the same reasons.[9] The Education Bill was amended beyond recognition by the Lords and dropped by the government in consequence. The Trades Disputes Bill passed unscathed to become the major legislative product of the session.

In January 1907 Sandars reported the defection of 'some Radical manufacturers' who had subscribed to the Tariff Reform League, 'being afraid of predatory socialism, and being aware of the possible advantages of a tariff'.[10] The problem of finding the revenue to pay for social reforms admitted on all sides to be necessary, combined with the fear that the Labour party might drive the government into confiscatory taxation, gave new weight to tariff reform arguments and dragged the party, including Balfour, in their direction. Apart from a small minority of free traders, the universal view that Labour had stolen the Tory Democracy in 1906, that if the Unionist party was ever to regain power this vote had to be won back, and that it could only be won back by a policy which promised social reform, put the party well on the way to accepting tariff reform as the constructive policy it needed. This was the essence of Parker Smith's message when he lamented the loss of the lower-class voters to Labour in Scotland. Tariff reform, in his view, was vital not for imperialist reasons, but as the 'only effective argument against the spoliatory schemes of taxation which will be put forward. Fresh sources of revenue are required by men of all parties for social schemes . . . In opposing confiscatory proposals, we must have an alternative policy of taxation.'[11] The alternative he proposed was an all-round moderate tariff.

Before 1906 the question of revenue had remained in the background. George Wyndham, after his resignation from the Irish Office in 1905 when he had 'at last begun to study "fiscals" seriously', rejected out of hand Chamberlain's programme of 'an all-round tariff for the double object of (1) giving employment, (2) raising surplus millions to relieve rates and promote social legislation'. But he nevertheless concluded: 'My difficulty begins with "broadening the basis of taxation" . . . I preach economy, honestly. But in my heart of hearts, I *know* that Imperial Defence—developing the Unity of the Empire—bettering the conditions of life at home, *must* mean greater expenditure . . .' His solution was a purely revenue tariff.[12] But in the circumstances of late 1905, with Chamberlain and Balfour quarrelling bitterly over tariff reform, such a policy was politically impossible. As Wyndham himself had noted in a letter to Sandars two days earlier, his proposal was so close to tariff reform that it was unsafe to announce it.[13]

After 1906, when Socialism, both as an ideological challenge and as a threat to property by its confiscatory proposals, became for many Unionists an immediate political threat, the dangers of the similarities between tariffs for revenue alone and tariffs for the general purposes of the tariff reformers became less serious. By January 1907 Wyndham, while still dealing with the revenue problem, saw the question in a different light:

I maintain that no probable increase in taxable income will meet the probable demand for increased revenue.

The Government will try to cut down Army and Navy. But they cannot go far enough to make any material difference . . .

On the other hand the Government must find money to meet the growing and excessive demands of their supporters. Some day Old Age Pensions will be voted . . . If the population increases—as it does—and at the same time insists on state aid, as it does, by way of costly education, costly Poor Law; perhaps direct pensions; and by way of Housing schemes, and Small-Holding schemes, guaranteed by the State at low interest and long periods of repayment, there is no possible ultimate solution except that the people should pay for all this. And there is no way in which they pay except by broadening the basis of taxation . . .

That is the way in which Fiscal Reform will come.[14]

Even Acland-Hood, speaking on 29 October, urged redistribution of taxation as the great subject for the Unionist party to take up, a statement which the official Tariff Reform League magazine, *Monthly Notes on Tariff Reform,* called an 'unequivocal demand by the chief Unionist Whip for the full policy of Tariff Reform plus Imperial Preference'.[15] This was wishful thinking, but the basic point was sound enough.

Yet Balfour appeared during 1906 to be taking too long to reach this generally accepted conclusion. Although aware of the dangers of alienating the working-class vote, he showed no inclination during 1906 to formulate a policy to win this vote back. In opposition, however, Balfour no longer had the power to control events to the degree that was possible whilst he was Prime Minister. Nor was Chamberlain's presence indispensable to tariff reform activity in the long run. Indeed, many of the more extreme whole-hoggers suspected that Chamberlain's loyalty to Balfour jeopardized their chances of ultimate success, and were alarmed at his apparent inability to pierce Balfour's smoke-screen or control Central Office malevolence.[16]

Tariff reform discontent began to boil over again in the autumn as Balfour's silence on the fiscal question became increasingly noticeable. The Tariff Reform League's autumn campaign was largely in the hands of the extremists who had led the attack on the Central Office, and who were now losing faith not only in Balfour, but in the hierarchy of the Tariff Reform League as well.[17] As a result, the malcontents began to organize themselves into the 'Confederacy'.[18] Bernard Wise sent out a circular invitation on 12 December in the name of Henry Page Croft to a meeting at the Isthmian Club, Piccadilly:

to consider what steps should be taken to compel the selection of Tariff Reform candidates by the Central Office.

It is proposed to form a small association of Unionist members and candidates pledged to organise Tariff Reform meetings in the constituencies for which Free Trade Unionists have been selected with a view to creating a sufficiently strong public opinion to compel the acceptance of Tariff Reform views.[19]

With this the extremists were prepared to go it alone, 'in independence even of Highbury . . . Otherwise, we shall be more effectively killed by the policy of silence than we could have been by a policy of repudiation.'[20]

In fact independent action proved unnecessary. For the first time since the election, conditions in the autumn and winter of 1906 moved in favour of tariff reform. The Labour difficulty had not disappeared with the Trades Disputes Act. On the contrary, the Labour party continued to reaffirm its independent existence as an alternative to both Unionism and Liberalism. The candidature of Robert Smillie in the Cockermouth by-election in August, even though he came a poor third, alarmed both Unionists and Liberals alike. In the same month the Master of Elibank called for a Liberal 'crusade' against Socialism, and Maxse used the Cockermouth by-election as the basis for a reassertion of the Labour threat to Tory Democracy.[21]

Moreover, in December Milner appeared as a possible alternative leader of tariff reform to replace the ailing Chamberlain. Hitherto Milner had played little part in domestic politics, concentrating on the defence of his South African settlement against Liberal proposals for self-government. In December, however, he addressed major public meetings at Manchester and Wolverhampton, and the simple fact of his speaking was sufficient to inject new life into the tariff reformers, and to spread alarm amongst the Balfourite hierarchy. Sandars hurried off to find out what Milner was up to, and reported to Balfour on 13 January that there was no immediate danger to Balfour's leadership from that quarter.[22]

Sandars, with his fixation on the personal threat to Balfour, underestimated the damage that Milner's speeches might do to Balfour's position, particularly in the context of the changing mood of the party in relation to socialism. Tariff reform had always pressurized Balfour and the recalcitrants in the parliamentary party through its strength in the country, and although Milner himself was no danger, the content of his speeches made a great impression. Partly as a result of Balfour's own treatment of the subject, the difficulties of making tariff reform acceptable to the electorate had come to overshadow all other aspects of the policy. Milner restated again the basic connection which imperialists made between imperialism and collectivist social reform. For Milner these were 'inseparable ideals, absolutely interdependent and complementary to one another'. They were so for the old Chamberlainite reasons, the need of a prosperous people to 'sustain this vast fabric of the Empire' and the dependence of a small state like Britain upon the Empire for the maintenance of the power upon which her prosperity depended.[23]

This was the core of radical imperialism upon which the support for tariff reform was based, and it had not been put with such conviction since Chamberlain's first campaign of 1903. Milner indeed had no objection to the label 'socialist' for his advocacy of state intervention, provided the distinction between 'odious' and 'noble' socialism was maintained, and refused to join

in the hue and cry against socialism . . . there is an odious form of Socialism . . . which attacks wealth simply because it is wealth, and lives on the cultivation of class hatred. But . . . there is a nobler Socialism which . . . is born of a genuine sympathy and a lofty and wise conception of what is meant by national life. It realises the fact that we are not merely so many millions of individuals, each struggling for himself, with the State to act as policeman, but literally one body-politic; that the different classes and sections of the community are members of that body, and that when one member suffers all the members suffer. From this point of view the attempt to raise the well-being and efficiency of the more backward of our people—for this is what it all comes to—is not philanthropy: it is business.[24]

The speeches were a much needed statement by an authoritative Imperialist and tariff reformer of the ideals of tariff reform and their relationship to other policies of the day. In the absence of a lead from Balfour on the fiscal question, Milner's approach, despite his denial of claims to the leadership, would commit the party by default. 'It struck me', wrote Robert Filmer to Balfour after the Manchester speech, 'as a very fine declaration of the Imperial ideal, imbued with the very natural more local ideal of Social Reform, and I feel sure no Unionist who has at heart the good of this country and the Empire could refuse to follow the essence of such a policy . . .'[25] Such sentiments amongst the party faithful made a response by Balfour essential to maintain his authority.

By December Balfour was also losing touch with the tariff reform leadership proper, and Austen Chamberlain was well on the way to join the rebels in protest against 'the persistent silence of most of our leaders, and of Mr. Balfour in particular',[26] on tariff reform. Consequently he accepted an invitation from the new proprietors of the *Outlook* to write a 'New Year's Message' on the position of tariff

reform in the Unionist programme.[27] The message was widely interpreted as a condemnation of the policy Balfour had pursued while in
office, and a call for a forward move. The activists who met at the
Isthmian Club to organize themselves for independent action were not
far ahead of the main body of tariff reformers. Disloyalty to Balfour
had become the order of the day. Hood, describing Austen Chamberlain's article as 'a dangerous one', predicted that the party would have
'a very difficult task this year, and unless the chief can show that he is
in favour of a cautious and moderate policy of Fiscal Reform in
accordance with the "Valentine" letters, I very much fear a serious
revolt . . .'[28]

During January, tariff reform pressure continued to build up as
discontent became more vocal. 'I continue to hear reports', Sandars
told Short, who had gone to Whittinghame with Balfour, 'of the
increased activity and financial strength of the Tariff Reform movement',[29] and there was

a widespread belief that in the course of the next month we shall see a forward
move taken by the Tariff Reform party. Something has happened to give
them a new lease of life. They recently held a dinner at Stafford House,
where £10,000 a year was guaranteed for five years and they expect to get
more . . .

Now it is obvious that this development is much to the detriment of the
party proper (1) It raises a party very hostile to the recognised leader of the
party, (2) It drains our coffers, or rather it interferes with their supply,
because this money *ought* to come to the Whips, and (3) It is having the
effect of inducing many of our best local committee men to leave our local
associations and to join and work for the T.R.L. branches.

According to Sandars, the tariff reformers had also virtually captured
the Council of the remodelled National Union, and at the county meetings held as a result of that reorganization they had exploited the opportunity to denounce Balfour's silence on their policy. Their criticisms
found a sympathetic audience in the rank and file of the party who
were no longer satisfied with a negative policy but demanded 'some
broad line of policy . . . above and beyond the policy of resisting and
denouncing a Government, no matter how pernicious it may be'. Both
Sandars and Hood agreed that in this situation even the moderates in
the party were likely to 'drift away from us, and become members of
the Tariff Reform League branches' if Balfour did not take immediate
action. They recommended

a speech ... at the National Union meeting on February 15th ... the fortunes of the party ... depend upon this speech. If you do not speak on the Fiscal Question at this meeting, then the malcontents will declare that their contention is well founded and that you are indifferent to the Tariff issue ... The bulk of the Party do not for a moment desire that you should commit yourself to details ... But they do want a statement on broad lines touching Fiscal Reform in its relation to finance both Imperial and local; they would like a sympathetic reference to closer commercial union with the Colonies; they would like a point made of the fact that schemes of social reform depending upon public money cannot be accomplished without the elasticity of revenue which alone can be obtained from a wider basis of taxation, and that, finally, until the fiscal question is tackled the British manufacturer will never get better treatment for his wares abroad.

A speech on these lines, without the refinement of argument, but delineatory of your own personal belief would, in Hood's opinion, pull the party together—

The point is—are you disposed to make it? It may, in your judgement, be unwise . . . but then says Hood, we shall practically lose our army—very likely not all at once, but by degrees until anarchy is succeeded by a new authority.[30]

Balfour was well aware of events within the party. But in November he was inclined to dismiss the conspiracy as 'largely a press conspiracy', and watched 'the matter . . . with a philosophical calm'.[31] Of all the news in Sandars's long report of 22 January, only the fund-raising meeting of the Tariff Reform League at Stafford House was new to him.[32] 'The party,' he commented to his cousin, Lord Hugh Cecil, 'so far as I can see, is determined to go to the devil.'[53] But the 'philosophical calm' which Balfour affected was a public posture which bore little relation to his qualities as a political manipulator. Nor, in 1907, was he prepared to yield to a successor who would be more aggressive on tariff reform, not because he clung to the leadership for its own sake, but because he considered his leadership, and moderation on the fiscal question, as indispensable to the revival of the party and the achievement of unity. Least of all was he prepared to make concessions to his critics. Rather he proposed

telling the party the 'truth in love' at Hull, and not waiting for the 15th when, however, I could repeat the lesson if it were necessary. I shall, of course, have to touch on Tariff Reform, and say what I have so often said before, but what apparently our Tariff Reform friends are never tired of hearing. I am by no means sure that we shall not have to carry the war into the enemy's camp and make it quite clear that if the Party is to be destroyed—which can easily be done by either wing—the disloyal Tariff Reformers have at least as much to lose as anybody else.[34]

At Hull Balfour did precisely this. Whilst reaffirming his commitment to the policy of the Valentine letters in order to satisfy the moderates, he reiterated his own objections to the formulation of programmes whilst in opposition, and warned the whole-hoggers of the dire consequences to tariff reform, as well as to other Unionist causes, which would result from their pushing their views so hard as to split the party. The speech was a test of the prevailing mood of the party. Balfour had no wish to advance his policy on tariff reform nor to emphasize its place in the party programme, if he could satisfy the moderates and isolate the whole-hoggers, as Hood had suggested, without doing so. If he had to say more it could be said to the National Union a fortnight later. The whole-hoggers were naturally frustrated. 'Nothing', thought Garvin, 'could be cleverer than the Hull speech for Balfour's purposes, nor emptier for our purposes.'[35]

Nevertheless, the tariff reformers kept up the pressure. Austen Chamberlain accordingly interpreted the Hull speech as the preface to a fiscal amendment to the Address, and expected that in the light of the coming colonial conference, the amendment would raise the question of preference. He also insisted that the amendment be moved from the front bench, although he was prepared to accept a formula which would make party unity on it as easy as possible, provided it satisfied 'honest tariff reformers'. The threat was thinly veiled: 'I am sure that if we do not move some of our men will, and of course in that case I should be bound to both speak and vote with them.'[36]

The inclusion of some front-bench statement on preference with the commitment to food taxes that it involved was an essential part of Austen Chamberlain's strategy to induce Balfour to advance in a tariff reform direction. Balfour had intended no such thing by the Hull speech. The speech was designed to close the discussion of the fiscal question not to extend it. But Chamberlain was only reflecting back-bench feeling. Ridley, as president of the Tariff Reform League, had informed Chamberlain in the middle of January that 'the feeling (of want of leadership) in the party is growing very fast indeed' and had 'now spread far beyond the Maxses and the Wares'. The Tariff Reform League had therefore set up a committee to confer with Chamberlain and Law on the possibility of raising the fiscal question 'constantly' in the House and of sending a deputation to Balfour to press for greater activity.[37]

Chamberlain's initial response to this move was almost as negative as Balfour's might have been. He emphasized the difficulties of parliamentary action because of the weakness of tariff reformers amongst the party leadership, and offered little hope of a front-bench amendment. He himself, however, suggested the possibility of independent action by the whole-hoggers on the back-benches as a means of putting pressure on Balfour, and instructed Ridley to take soundings on whether there would be sufficient support to make such a move possible.[38] Apparently there was. Ridley replied on 19 January that there were grounds for hoping that they could 'give Balfour another push'. He reported a letter from Imbert-Terry, a Balfourite believed to be in close contact with Hood, seeking some compromise on tariff reform on the basis of excluding food duties. Ridley opposed any compromise (and was backed up by Chamberlain), at least in part because Terry's letter itself gave him the scent of victory.[39]

Thus assured of support, Chamberlain himself took up the task of forcing a front-bench tariff reform amendment on the unwilling Balfour. As a result, the split in the party opened up again within the shadow cabinet itself. Balfour's first reply to Chamberlain was non-committal, requiring only a meeting of the shadow cabinet before any decision was taken, and reiterating his Hull text.[40] Chamberlain in turn urged speed, since 'the sooner we can indicate to our friends that we intend to move, the better, as it prevents them taking separate and possibly inconsistent action', and gave Balfour notice of a tariff reform meeting on the subject on the Monday.[41] Since Chamberlain was encouraging, if not leading, the tariff reform movement for independent action, his letter was less than open. On 9 February Balfour wrote again to say that he had only been able to consult Long, who was opposed to a front-bench amendment, and to put an argument 'which I think you will agree is almost conclusive against any Amendment in the form you suggest'—that whilst an amendment could be found which would unite the party, it would not be possible to prevent a further amendment being moved by the government 'to divide us hopelessly'. Since Chamberlain still did not seem to have grasped the point of either his speech or his letter, Balfour also repeated the lesson at greater length:

my whole object is to restore the Party to the position of an effective fighting machine, which is the necessary preliminary to our being able either to arrest the disintegrating forces of modern Radicalism or to carry out a constructive policy of our own. I am confident this cannot be done by a policy of ostracism. If such a policy succeeded in making the party unanimous, it would be at the price of keeping it small. The wise course for us to adopt is, on the one hand, to make it quite clear what are the ideals at which we aim, and then to make it as easy as possible for the varying elements of the Party to fall into line . . . everything which induces people overtly to proclaim themselves in different camps, everything which drives them into different lobbies, everything which tends to the formation of sharply defined and antagonistic sub-organisms within the great organism of the party must, in my opinion, militate against the ultimate triumph of Fiscal Reform, as well as every other policy to which we wish to give effect . . .[42]

No clearer statement could be found either of Balfour's priorities, or of his policy of blurring the edges of ideologically opposed factions for the sake of preserving unity. Not surprisingly, Austen Chamberlain found this letter 'unsatisfactory'.[43]

Balfour, however, was less against an amendment as such than against specific references to the divisive question of preference and food duties, and he suggested a compromise. The idea itself came from Hewins who had been active in communicating both with Balfour and Chamberlain in an attempt to keep the party together, whilst at the same time persuading Balfour to advance on tariff reform. Hewins met Balfour and Alfred Lyttelton on 8 February and devised a new amendment altogether. 'The essence of the plan', as Balfour summarized Hewins's proposals to Austen Chamberlain, 'is so to draw the amendment as to concentrate attention upon the critical position which this country stands in towards the Colonies, and especially Canada, in view of the Tariff changes which Canada is proposing, and the subsequent change in her fiscal relations with Germany, with the United States and with the Mother Country . . .'[44] Hewins wrote in the same sense to Chamberlain and was fairly optimistic as to the outcome. In his belief, 'there is no substantial difference between what we desire and what Mr. Balfour desires. It is really very much a matter of expression . . .'[45]

Progress came to an abrupt halt at the meeting of the ex-cabinet at which the chief whip (Hood) was present: 'It was the emphatic opinion of those present, with the exception of Mr. Austen Chamberlain, that no amendment raising the Fiscal Question should be moved to the Address.'[46] Chamberlain, however, had made sure before he began his campaign for an amendment that he had support enough to carry him through, and the tariff reformers were ready for such an eventuality. They met the following day with nothing left to chance, and despite a weak denial by Austen Chamberlain, all the evidence suggests that the meeting was packed. Leading men such as Long, normally regarded as tariff reformers but known to be hostile to the amendment, were ignored for reasons which were patently spurious.[47] Shortly before the meeting Chamberlain attempted to see Balfour to get some message to take in, but Balfour was not in his room. According to the memorandum on 'the Fiscal Question in February, 1907', Balfour arrived after Chamberlain had left for the meeting, and sent in a message which, while sympathetic to the 'natural and legitimate' wish of the tariff reformers for a purely fiscal amendment, reaffirmed his reservations in practice, and deprecated a premature decision.[48]

Exactly what happened at the tariff reform meeting is far from clear. According to the 'Fiscal Question' memorandum, Austen Chamberlain was playing a double game, appearing to be in pursuit of compromise, but in reality egging on the extremists so that he would not have to make concessions. Thus, although he received Balfour's note during the course of the meeting, he did not read it out. Hood heard subsequently that had Balfour's strong feelings against the amendment been made known to the meeting, the result might have been different. As it was, the 43 members present agreed to insist upon a fiscal amendment with Mason and Lawrence Hardy dissenting.[49] A report in *The Times* of 15 February confirmed much of this. According to *The Times*, Chamberlain informed the meeting that Balfour would not accept a tariff reform amendment, and Law made a strong plea for independent action. When Mason replied that this would be a tactical blunder, there was a row, but eventually resolutions were carried to the effect that a front-bench amendment would be demanded of the leaders, and if they refused the amendment would be moved independently.[50]

The Times's report was strongly denied by several tariff reformers who had been present at the meeting,[51] but the incident left feelings of bitterness[52] and the ex-cabinet meeting that evening was a tense affair. Balfour then restated the strong objections which he and his colleagues felt to the proposed amendment, but after Austen Chamberlain had reported that the tariff reformers had decided upon independent action, Balfour was left with no alternative but to give way and give the amendment his official blessing. The amendment was placed upon the order paper that evening.[53]

The fiscal amendment demonstrated the failure of Balfour's tactics at Hull. He had tested the mood of the party to see if he could get away with a simple reassertion of the *status quo*, and discovered on 13 February that he could not. But it was a basic presupposition of such tactics that if pressed he would say more, and it was those tactics and that presupposition which made Austen Chamberlain's dubious intrigues justifiable. Balfour's commitment to the maintenance of party unity as the highest priority made the party the ultimate arbiter in disputes on fiscal policy, and the conversion of the party entailed the conversion of Balfour. Both Chamberlain and Balfour knew this, just as they knew what the other was attempting to do. The split in the leadership, real though it was on policy and tactics, was none the less artificial to the extent that both men were prepared to give way once it became clear to which side the party inclined. After the trial of strength even Balfour was convinced that a change of approach to tariff reform and to the tariff reformers was necessary.

In reaching such a conclusion from the pattern of recent events, Balfour was not forced into a sudden reconsideration of his policy or position. He had been thinking hard about fiscal reform throughout the winter, and had reached similar conclusions to the bulk of his party. He was guided along this wide road to tariff reform by Professor Hewins who, as Secretary of Chamberlain's Tariff Commission, was the economic expert of the tariff reform movement, responsible for working out the details of tariff reform policy. In December 1906 Balfour discussed fiscal reform at a small dinner given for the purpose by Austen Chamberlain,[54] probably with the deliberate intention of bringing Hewins and Balfour together. If so it was an intelligent move. Hewins's intellectual approach and his clear appreciation of the intricacies of the subject made an immediate impression on Balfour.[55]

The mutual regard of Hewins and Balfour made Chamberlain's dinner a great success.[56] A further meeting to continue the discussion was cancelled when Balfour became ill with influenza. In the middle of January, however, Balfour invited Hewins to come to Whittinghame to continue the interrupted talks, which Hewins accepted with the full approval of Austen Chamberlain.[57] With these discussions began a long association between Balfour and Hewins which lasted until the general election of December 1910, as long that is as tariff reform remained the central issue of Unionist politics. During this period, Hewins became Balfour's *de facto* adviser on economic affairs, summarizing and commenting on changes in the tariff policies of foreign and colonial states, providing statements of the theoretical basis for tariff reform, and criticism of Liberal policies. The precise degree of influence which these countless memorandums, notes, and conversations had on Balfour is impossible to determine. As party leader, the final decision on policy was Balfour's, and he retained mastery of the situation. But Balfour was accustomed to seek expert advice, particularly on economic affairs, and had indeed done so in 1903 when the tariff controversy first broke out in order to draw up his 'Economic Notes on Insular Free Trade', and there is no doubt that he found Hewins particularly useful both in providing material for attacks on the government, and in drafting statements of his own policy. During 1907, when the major redefinition of Balfour's attitudes towards tariff reform was taking place, it was in the latter role that Hewins's influence was most marked.

At Whittinghame in January 1907 Hewins discussed the whole range of tariff reform topics with Balfour. The argument Hewins presented to Balfour started from the fact of colonial development and the immense potential of the colonial market if the growth of foreign trade with the colonies was checked by preference, considered the revenue needs of Britain herself and the inadequacy of the present fiscal system, and returned from the need to broaden the basis of taxation to the effect of revenue duties upon imperial relations. Against this, the development of Germany, the relative decline of the United Kingdom as reflected in her naval position, dumping and employment, all of them basic tariff reform arguments were, to Hewins, 'other lines of approach', but of clearly secondary importance. His real case, as it was to become Balfour's, was the necessity of more revenue, and the use of indirect revenue taxes imposed for that purpose to serve as a basis for preference and thus secure to the mother country the colonial market.[58]

A memorandum on food taxes sent to Balfour on 11 February followed up these propositions, and justified food duties, not because they were essential for preference and imperial commercial unity, but from 'the Revenue standpoint'. Britain, Hewins argued on traditional tariff reform lines, already had food duties. All the tariff reformers proposed was a scientific readjustment to 'substitute revenue duties on imported agricultural produce, some portion of which would almost certainly be paid by the foreigner', for the existing duties on tea, sugar, tobacco, etc., all of which were paid by the consumer. Increasing expenditure made the broadening of the basis of taxation inevitable, and this could 'only be done by enlarging the area of indirect taxation'. Nor could this development be prevented by abandoning social reform. 'A state of war, or even serious complications would at once smash the present fiscal system.' The problem of revenue would of itself force on the question of food duties, and thus of preference, independent of imperial considerations in favour of their re-imposition.[59]

The result of these two influences, pressure from the party and argument from Hewins, acting on Balfour's own concern for party unity, was his speech to the National Union on 15 February at the Savoy Hotel. Originally intended as an occasion for the repetition, if necessary, of the lessons of the Hull speech, Balfour instead outlined a new 'safe, sound, sober policy of fiscal reform'. This consisted essentially of four basic points—arguments for, or approaches to, the fiscal question—the broadening of the basis of taxation; the safeguarding of the 'great productive industries' from unfair foreign competition; the recapture of foreign markets; and the maintenance of British colonial markets. The approaches were, as Balfour argued, logically distinct but practically connected, since the party could not carry out its domestic programme without broadening the basis of taxation, and in that lay the solution to the other three problems. The order of priority was, however, clearly set out, and the first point, revenue, was to Balfour both the most important and the most practicable: 'I am sure that some revision of our fiscal system—some broadening of our basis of taxation—would be absolutely necessary if we were the only commercial nation in the world, and did not have a single colony.' Balfour was loudly cheered by the delegates for the speech. 'He was', commented the *Standard*, 'somewhat brief in his treatment', but there were 'no grounds for suspicion as to the sincerity of his convictions or as to his determination to press forward in what he has defined as the first constructive work of the Unionist party'.[60] Sandars thought the speech 'a very good one and highly agreeable to the Tariff Reformers. I sat next to Lawrence who was delighted with it.'[61] Further satisfaction came in the following week with Balfour's speech in the debate on Hills's fiscal amendment, to which he had so grudgingly consented.[62] Some of the more hostile, like Maxse, remained unconvinced,[63] but in general these two speeches achieved what the Hull speech had failed to do—restore the confidence of the moderates in Balfour's leadership.

The Savoy Hotel speech marked a crucial stage both in the development of Balfour's relationship with tariff reform, and in the development of tariff reform itself as a policy. The most striking feature of
a speech which dealt with imperial commercial relations was its
emphasis on purely domestic problems. In many respects, Balfour's
policy was a reversion to Chamberlain's original scheme, proposed at
the time when Beach's registration duty was still operative, of making
remissions of revenue taxes for imperial purposes. But in general
Balfour completely overthrew Chamberlain's priorities. Chamberlain
had come to tariff reform as a means of achieving imperial unity when
all other avenues had failed. Protection, retaliation, and revenue were
all by-products of the original imperial design. In the Savoy Hotel
speech Balfour made preference and imperial unity the by-products.
Preference became, despite Balfour's denials, both last and least in his
four-point programme of fiscal reform. During 1907 it was on domestic
and revenue, not imperial, grounds that he defended his attitude to
food duties against free trade criticism.[64]

Contemporaries largely missed the significance of the Savoy Hotel
speech. In the debate on Hills's fiscal amendment the following week
Rowland Hunt openly attacked Balfour's leadership on the fiscal
question, and the Unionist whip was withdrawn from him as a result.
Maxse, in the *National Review*, supported Hunt, condemned the withdrawal of the official whip, and made no reference to the advance in
Balfour's position.[65] Even in the Balfourite camp, the speech was not
noted at the time as marking a new departure, and at the end of the
year Sandars felt it necessary to remind Balfour that he had made it,
and that it was so well received that he should look it up.[66] The reason
for this is not hard to find. The speech marked the beginning of a
process which tariff reformers, especially Balfour's most hostile critics,
found incredible, the emergence of Balfour as a tariff reform leader.
But it was only the beginning, and the development continued throughout the whole of 1907. It was not until the end of the year, in Balfour's
speech to the National Union Conference at Birmingham, that this
transition became apparent and Balfour's 'conversion' to tariff reform
conclusive. As a result it was the Birmingham speech which attracted
the recognition and finally reconciled the extreme whole-hoggers to
support of Balfour's leadership, and the Birmingham programme
which became the official party policy.

In the early stages, this development of Balfour's attitude was sufficiently hesitant and uncertain to lend substance to extremist suspicions. In April Balfour made a speech of welcome to the colonial delegates to the Colonial Conference at the Albert Hall which left Amery fuming with rage[67] and in May Collings likened the party to 'sheep without a shepherd'.[68] In general, however, the tariff reformers were satisfied, and with good reason. In the same month as Collings's complaint, Joseph Chamberlain wrote to Halsbury to say how much he had been struck by the progress made in the last six months,[69] and Milner too thought that 'Tariff reform seems to be making great progress in this country.'[70]

May marked the realization that the turning point had been reached as far as Balfour was concerned. Austen Chamberlain had been inclined to agree with Amery about Balfour's speech in April to the colonial delegates,[71] but the setback was temporary. A fortnight later, on 3 May, in the same hall, Balfour addressed the Primrose League. The subject was tariff reform and preference, and was chosen voluntarily by Balfour. 'He is', Austen Chamberlain reported to his father, 'impressed by the [Colonial] Premiers' attitude and speeches, and is going strong on broadening the basis of taxation, but I do not myself anticipate that he will materially advance his position.'[72] After the speech, he had changed his mind and was 'pleased with Balfour's speech . . . even though he still leaves his 'i's undotted and his 't's uncrossed'.[73] By 6 May events had convinced him that with this speech the corner had been turned.[74] Chamberlain also informed Highbury that Balfour had taken the initiative in suggesting to him that there should be a censure debate on the handling of colonial preference by the government at the recent Colonial Conference, in addition to an amendment to the budget stressing the need to broaden the basis of taxation. The tide, as Chamberlain commented at the end of the month, 'is turning . . . Our danger now is not Liberalism, but "Labour" working with and through Liberalism. But if we could hold our own and even gain ground before the Conference, everything is possible to us now after the Conference.'[75]

The Colonial Conference indeed made a great impression upon Balfour and made him more sympathetic to the preferential aspect of the tariff reform programme as he became aware for the first time of the real extent of colonial enthusiasm. Joseph Chamberlain, watching events from his sickbed, felt that the Conference 'has been of great importance in the effect it has had upon English public opinion',[76] whilst Hewins, closely involved as he was with Balfour, remarked that

'Balfour is getting very keen and interested'.[77] In other respects, however, the Colonial Conference was only of temporary importance, an imperial interlude which brought preference briefly to the fore in tariff reform thought, but which was quickly superseded after the departure of the colonial leaders by pressing domestic issues. The political initiative in determining the vital issues of the day still lay with the government and its heterodox majority, and both policy and interest dictated that it would keep domestic issues prominent and divisive imperial problems in the background. This in turn meant social reform, and for the opposition the problem of 'Labour working with and through Liberalism', the revival of the revenue question, and 'predatory' socialism.

It was this aspect of tariff reform, not preference and imperial unity, which returned to dominance in the autumn. There were various reasons why this should have been so. In February Barnes had put down an amendment on old age pensions on behalf of the Labour party, and in his budget in May Asquith reacted to this left-wing pressure with a promise that the government would enact a scheme. This inevitably and immediately brought up the question of revenue. Hewins, commenting on the budget in a series of letters to Balfour, made the argument that 'the existing fiscal system is inadequate to the needs of the United Kingdom and the basis of taxation should be enlarged', the focal point of his many criticisms.[78] To Balfour and to many of the moderate Unionists like Wyndham, for whom the question of revenue was intimately bound up with the question of the navy and national defence, Hewins's arguments carried considerable weight.

Outside Parliament, socialism also made a deep impression in 1907 both in by-elections and in industry. Cockermouth had been only a prelude. In July, Pete Curran won at Jarrow for the official Labour party in a four-cornered contest, whilst in the Colne Valley Victor Grayson also triumphed over both Unionist and Liberal rivals. The gloomiest predictions of 1906 appeared about to be confirmed in the demise of both the Liberal party and the Tory Democracy. These socialist successes coincided with a marked change in the prevailing economic climate. The boom of 1906 collapsed, and a brief depression set in in 1907. Perhaps because tariff reformers had for so long been predicting a depression, that of 1907 excited far more political comment than its economic significance justified. It made no appreciable difference to the general pattern of the Edwardian era of prices rising more rapidly than wages which did much to account for the increase of labour militancy. Hewins, who put the rise in prices between 1903 and 1907 at 17 per cent and thought the process was still continuing, pointed out the connection to Balfour. 'It appears to me', he wrote, 'that this alone is sufficient to account for the very general demand for an increase in wages in the country, to which employers are bound to give way unless they are willing to sacrifice their trade.'[79] Both the depression of 1907 and the long-term pattern were, however, further factors in favour of tariff reform, one of the standard arguments of which was that high wages depended upon the protection of trade and employment.

It was inevitable under these circumstances that socialism should figure prominently in the Unionists' autumn campaign, with Balfour being personally consulted for suggestions on the line party speakers should take on the critical question of social reform.[80] The Central Office planned 'a general campaign throughout the country and some 20 or 30 vans with speakers will shortly leave London . . . they are determined to counter the Socialists in their street corner meetings'.[81] Balfour himself was subjected to a barrage of letters on the need to counter socialism from all sections of the party during the run in to the annual conference of the National Union to be held at Birmingham in November. 'As far as I can judge,' wrote Rutland, the Chairman:

there will be—as must obviously be the case—resolutions on the Socialist danger and the means to fight it. These will be coupled with fiscal reform resolutions based chiefly on your Albert Hall and National Union dinner speeches.

What I find universally hoped is that you will go tooth and toenail for the Socialist party, tacking the Radical party on to them; and stick firmly to your utterances to which I have just referred . . . the whole party is waiting for a definite and clear utterance on your part . . . and encouragement given to our workers and the *middle classes* or we shall lose the latter . . .[82]

The details of the line the party should take in its reaction to, and exploitation of, the socialist danger were, however, more divisive. Ailwyn Fellowes, stressing that even the countryside was threatened by 'the Black Flag of Socialism', urged Balfour to rebuild party unity by making concession to free trade opinion. But even within the countryside, divided opinions made the unity that Fellowes wanted almost impossible since the farmers were usually 'out and out Protectionists', whilst the labourers '*will not have their bread taxed*'. All that

Fellowes could propose in such circumstances was that the Unionists should abandon food duties so called, and replace them by the imposition of the old 1s. registration duty on corn. On this policy he optimistically expected that 'many Liberals and thousands of the working classes who see the danger ahead would join you to fight against the Socialist programme'.[83] Sandars found the proposal feeble, and pointed out that changing the name of the tax meant nothing to the labourers whose only concern was 'whether the duty is a small one or a big one'.[84]

The suggestion was a non-starter in other respects. Whilst both free traders and tariff reformers were concerned about Socialism, their very different views of the nature of the enemy in fact drove them further apart. Moreover, neither at this stage was any more willing to compromise than they had been in the past. The Unionist free traders were seeking new allies amongst the Liberal League, and the Cecils at least had still not lost hope of Balfour. The tariff reformers, buoyed up by the triumphs of the preceding months were waiting for the bulk of the party to come over to them in the natural course of events, as the reaction against socialism gathered momentum.

The tariff reform concept of an anti-socialist platform differed considerably from that of moderates such as Rutland and Fellowes. Rutland was concerned to reassure the middle classes of Unionist firmness whilst at the same time frightening them towards the Unionist party by associating the Liberal government with socialism. Fellowes, still concerned with the somewhat archaic question of food duties, was prepared to sacrifice revenue to placate free trade opinion. Both policies severely restricted the nature of the 'constructive alternative' to socialism that the Unionist party could put forward, the former because of the susceptibilities of the audience of rate payers and taxpayers to whom it was directed, the latter by lack of revenue. Tariff reformers, on the other hand, still sought the solution to the party's problems in the recovery of the Tory Democracy. Both sustained and alarmed by reports upon working-class opinion that socialism was 'the only thing which is making strides among that class . . . the Liberals are practically wiped out and they [the working classes] are now divided into Socialists and Conservatives',[85] tariff reformers sought to develop further their positive policy. Austen Chamberlain gave Balfour an idea of the direction in which tariff reform thinking was tending in a long letter on 24 October in which he requested a lead on fiscal reform, including tariffs on both imported foreign manufactured goods 'for the purpose of revenue and retaliation', and on foreign imports of corn and meat to establish imperial preference; a contributory old-age pensions scheme 'somewhat on the German model—one-third from the workmen, one-third from the employer, one-third from the state', as an alternative to the government's universal non-contributory scheme which he considered 'vicious in principle and impossible in practice on account of the cost'; a policy of land purchase and land ownership as 'the true Conservative policy . . . in opposition to hiring and tenancy as adopted by the Government and the Socialists'; and on Housing and Sweated Industries. 'Surely,' he pleaded, 'we have here the elements of a fine programme, conservative in the best sense of the word, yet popular and capable of arousing great enthusiasm . . .'

This was not a clear-cut tariff reform programme which Chamberlain sought to impose on Balfour or make the test of party orthodoxy as his father's Glasgow programme had become. The tone of Chamberlain's letter was more a plea for 'sympathetic consideration' for what he called 'his thoughts'.[86] Nor, however, were the contents of this letter the product of Austen Chamberlain's solitary reflections. The section on the Land Question shows clear signs of Jesse Collings's influence, and that on sweated industries bears Milner's trade mark. Chamberlain had indeed been discussing the question of an alternative policy with Milner,[87] and the entire letter is Milnerite in conception, as was the whole idea of extending the advanced programme from tariff reform alone to that of tariff reform in 'a sound national policy'.[88] Milner had never considered tariff reform as a purely fiscal policy but regarded fiscal reform 'as an element . . . of a larger policy'.[89] He wanted a wider programme of domestic and imperial reorganization, 'a policy of constructive Imperialism, and of steady, consistent, unhasting and unresting Social Reform', and stressed more than anyone, including even Joseph Chamberlain in his first tariff reform campaign of 1903, the connection between the Empire and social reform in the interests of efficiency. The prosperity of Britain depended upon 'the Empire and all that it provides'; the Empire, upon 'a healthy, thriving manly people at the centre. Stunted, overcrowded town populations, irregular employment, sweated industries, these things are as detestable to true Imperialism as they are to philanthropy.'[90] Tariff reform was the essential base of Unionist policy, the means by which industries were protected against illegitimate foreign competition, reciprocal preference was established with the colonies, and revenue obtained 'for a policy of progressive Social Reform'. But it was not the end of that policy.[91]

It was the radicalism that underlay many of the attitudes of the more fervent tariff reformers, and of which Milner himself was an extreme example, which set their concept of an anti-socialist policy apart from the conservatism of moderates like Fellowes and Rutland. This radicalism, which found expression in Milner's speeches in the autumn of 1907, was conscious and deliberate, and Milner conceived of his speeches as a whole, forming a statement of radical imperialist doctrine in opposition to the negative, anti-socialist policy which he feared the party would adopt.[92] Nor was Milner speaking only for himself. 'Anything he says about old age pensions', Ware wrote, 'will be after consultation with Austen Chamberlain, and will represent the policy of the tariff reform wing.'[93] Milner's Guildford speech particularly made tariff reform thinking clear on socialism and the Unionist alternative:

My objection to anti-Socialism as a platform is that Socialism means so many different things . . . Correctly used, the word only signifies a particular view of the proper relation of the State to its citizens—a tendency to substitute public for private ownership, or to restrict the freedom of individual enterprise in the interests of the public. But there are some forms of property which we all admit should be public and not private, and the freedom of individual enterprise is already limited by a hundred laws. Socialism and Individualism are opposing principles, which enter in various proportions into the constitution of every civilised society; it is merely a question of degree . . . The danger, as it seems to me, of the Unionist party going off on a crusade against Socialism is that in the heat of that crusade it may neglect, or appear to neglect, those social evils of which honest Socialism is striving, often no doubt by unwise means, to effect a cure . . .

The true antidote to revolutionary Socialism is practical social reform . . . the revolutionary socialist . . . would like to get rid of all private property . . . He is going absurdly too far; but what gave birth to his doctrine? The abuse of the rights of private property, the cruelty and the failure of the scramble for gain, which mark the reign of a one-sided Individualism. If we had not gone much too far in one direction, we should not now have had this extravagant reaction in the other . . . While resisting the revolutionary propaganda, let us be more, and not less, strenuous in removing the causes of it . . . it is not to the objects which many Radicals have at heart that we, as Unionists, need take exception . . . the multiplication of small landholders and . . . landowners, the resuscitation of agriculture; and . . . better housing in our crowded centres; town planning; sanitary conditions of labour; the extinction of sweating; the physical training of the people; continuation schools—these and all other measures necessary to preserve the stamina of the race and develop its productive power—have we not as good a right to regard these as our objects . . . It is not these objects which we deprecate . . . What we deprecate is the spirit in which they are so often preached and pursued.[94]

The practical result of these views was further tariff reform pressure upon Balfour, not so much to say more about tariff reform policy itself, but to commit the party to a constructive policy built upon tariff reform in order to retain the support of the working classes. Ridley echoed Milner's conviction that socialism progressed only because it was the only programme proposing concrete collectivist reforms, and in objecting to a negative campaign of opposition. He wanted, as the Chamberlains and Milner wanted, a policy of 'social reforms as well as what you have said about reform of the tariff', in order to retain 'the moderate working men who will then be ready to fight with us against Socialism'.[95] In Milner's hands, the imperial aspect of tariff reform was always kept prominent. But the emphasis on the need for revenue and the elaboration of a programme of purely domestic reforms upon the basis of indirect taxation, not only provided a common ground with Balfour's own fiscal policy as it was emerging during 1907, but pointed similarly in the direction of relegating the imperial aspect of tariff reform into the indefinite future.

As Balfour thus moved closer to the tariff reformers in terms of action, the tariff reformers in some respects moved closer to Balfour. In this process it was again the Savoy Hotel speech which proved vital. The Introduction to the 1907 edition of the tariff reform *Speakers' Handbook* founded its treatment of tariff reform squarely on the four points which Balfour had elaborated, and the speech itself was quoted at length in Chapter 6. The contrast with the handbook of 1905 was striking, and demonstrated the impact of the revenue argument. In 1905 the arguments for tariff reform were based largely on comparative statistics demonstrating Britain's relative decline and her dependence upon colonial trade. Food duties were justified as essential to preference, and the Handbook attempted to show that they would not raise the cost of living. Nowhere was the need for revenue used as a reason for tariff reform, nor were food duties defended as part of the general redistribution of revenue taxation, and social reform was only included on the old lines of employment and higher wages. The 1907 edition was not only a more sophisticated production, making use of the argument of the economy of scale, and the consequent need for larger and more secure markets to induce colonial corn producers to extend the area under cultivation, but presented food duties within the context of indirect taxation in general, and related them to the purely domestic need for increased revenue.[96]

Nevertheless, Balfour remained cautious about committing himself too far. Convinced he may have been by October 1907 that fiscal reform was inevitable, and the party 'definitely committed',[97] but his policy statements remained unchanged. He thus wrote to Ailwyn Fellowes that he had 'never committed myself or the Party to the necessity of a tax on corn', although he added that the needs of social reform, the relief of local taxation, and imperial preference all depended on 'widening the basis of taxation, and I doubt whether this is practicable unless a small duty is placed upon corn—not for Protection but for revenue and Imperial purposes'.[98] There was a considerable amount of support for this cautious approach. The party was moving towards unity, but tariff reform remained a divisive issue, and the elaboration of a collectivist programme of social reforms based upon the revenue from import duties only made it more so, given the antipathy of the free traders and some of the old-style Conservatives to state interference in any form.

Balfour and the Balfourites sought unity above all from the Birmingham conference. But to them this meant reconciling the moderate free traders rather than adopting an even more explicitly radical version of tariff reform. There was a general consensus amongst the Balfourite leadership as to the line Balfour should take at Birmingham to achieve this unity. The recipe should be the same as before, but served with more spice. Long dwelt on the 'general desire among all loyal men' that at Birmingham Balfour should follow the lines of his Albert Hall speech,[99] 'going for Tariff Reform, but not in such a way as to enable the extremists to say that they have "got you", and for social reform . . .'[100] Long was particularly concerned lest Balfour should go too far in the direction of the extreme tariff reformers.[101] He was, at this time, involved in negotiations with Lord Robert Cecil with a view to reconciling the Conservative wing of the Unionist free traders to the party, and thus had special reasons to emphasize this point, but his fears were not entirely unshared. Sandars wrote to Douglas to enlist his aid in keeping Balfour on the path of virtue (as did Long), and to concentrate on attacking the government by identifying them with socialism rather than by manufacturing programmes, even at the risk of alienating those who clamoured for an alternative policy.[102] Douglas needed no convincing,[103] and the Balfourites were indeed unanimous. Rutland made the same point as Long, that the programme required was that of the Savoy Hotel and Albert Hall speeches, as did Wyndham,[104] and Sandars and Hood agreed.[105]

The preconditions for the reunification of the large body of the party on some moderate programme of fiscal reform were thus in existence before the Birmingham conference itself. By the end of October Sandars was already looking out previous speeches by Balfour on socialism,[106] and Balfour himself had replied to Ridley that he agreed with his views on the need for some policy of social reform.[107] He had also consulted the inevitable Hewins on 'Socialism', 'Productivity', and 'The Tariff Reform Alternative' in preparation for his speech.[108] The resolutions at the Birmingham conference in Chaplin's name followed Rutland's expectations. The party was asked to commit itself to fiscal reform as its first constructive policy in order to broaden the basis of taxation, safeguard home industries against unfair foreign competition, strengthen the government's hand in commercial negotiations, and to establish a system of imperial preference—in that order.[109] Balfour had no difficulty in strongly supporting these resolutions which were, as he recognized, lifted bodily from his Savoy Hotel speech.

Balfour's Birmingham speech was therefore more significant for its political impact than for any new policy which it put forward. Balfour appealed for unity, and against the 'courts martial' of 'those who had difficulties with items in the party programme', to a party which was already largely united on the policy of his speeches earlier in the year, and particularly that at the Savoy Hotel. Most of the speech was devoted to fiscal reform, socialism, and social reform, as the audience desired, but still did no more than lay down the general principles upon which these questions should be approached, principles which had already been set out in his Savoy Hotel speech. The new feature was the emphasis which Balfour placed on tariff reform, which effectively committed him to imposing revenue duties when he returned to office, and to summoning a colonial conference to discuss the question of preference on the basis of these duties. What these duties were to be was defined only by the negative qualifications to which Balfour had adhered ever since 1903—they should be small, widespread, should not fall on raw materials, and should not increase the cost of living of the working classes. But this, in view of the reaction of the whole-hoggers to socialism during 1907, was enough, for they, like Balfour, had come to see revenue as the first, and most important, purpose of tariff reform.

On socialism and social reform also, Balfour struck the right tone for the moderates, without going beyond generalizations. He admitted none of the ambiguity which had characterized Milner's treatment of these subjects. Socialism had 'one meaning only', that the state should take over all the means of production, and all private property. Social reform 'is when the state based upon private enterprise, based upon private property, recognising that the best productive results can only be obtained by respecting private property, and encouraging private enterprise, asks them to contribute towards great national, social and public objects'. Social reform for Balfour was not a half-way house to socialism, but a completely distinct concept. 'What matters', he said the following day to a working-class audience, 'is that the mutual well-being of the community . . . is fundamentally and essentially built upon the productive energy and efficiency of the people. Production, not distribution is the fundamental fact . . .'[110]

With this dependence upon private enterprise in mind, Balfour laid down the essential limits beyond which Conservative social reform could not go: 'if you ask from the community at large too great a contribution even for the best of objects you defeat your own end by destroying the productive efficiency of the community upon which all your philanthropic efforts must ultimately be based'. The 'happiness of the crowded centres of our great towns', working-class housing, the extension of small landownership, reform of the poor law and old-age pensions were all mentioned as subjects for the party to take up, but with none of the definiteness which had characterized tariff reform planning in this direction. The basic assumptions of Balfour's social reform policy were a long way from the radical imperialism of Milner and his sympathizers for whom social reform was not philanthropy but business, because productive efficiency and social conditions were interrelated. Balfour saw social reform in simple terms as a levy by the public upon the private sector of the economy, another burden which private enterprise and private property had to bear for humanitarian reasons, but which was, in economic terms, all loss. However convincing and sincere his new enthusiasm for fiscal reform, Balfour was not, and was never likely to be, at one with the committed radicals of the imperialist movement.

Nevertheless, the speech went a long way to satisfying the demands of even the most extreme whole-hoggers. In the debate on Chaplin's resolutions, Maxse had openly declared that there was no point in passing further fiscal resolutions, since all previous efforts had ended up in the whip's wastepaper basket, and had called upon 'the oracle' to declare 'in language understanded of the people' that the party was committed to preference and a general tariff, and that all members of the party were expected to subscribe to this programme. But Maxse, as *The Times* commented, 'struck a jarring note' at the conference, and in the December issue of the *National Review*, Maxse came into line, claiming that Balfour's speech, 'singularly free from ambiguity, qualifications or refinements . . . should become a landmark in British policy . . . acceptable to all reasonable tariff reformers'.[111]

The change was as much one of tactics as of feeling about Balfour himself. The Birmingham speech would suffice, and the line, even of men like Maxse, was now to support Balfour as the leader of a tariff reform party, and to interpret the Birmingham speech as a declaration to that effect, to which all members must subscribe. Joseph Chamberlain himself took this line, and exerted himself to ensure that his opinion was known to possible dissenters like Maxse.[112] But Maxse had reached similar conclusions before Chamberlain's warning, and his doubts were no longer for public consumption.[113] At the conference itself, Chaplin hailed Balfour as the successor of, and rival to, Disraeli,[114] and publicly at least radical Unionists rallied to Balfour as the new leader of Tory Democracy. The fears which had led Ridley in 1906 to denounce Balfour for having 'undone all the good that R. Churchill began, and given Socialism a new impetus',[115] and which had been the basis of tariff reform criticism of Balfour since the beginning of the controversy, were swept away in the enthusiasm of the party's newly discovered unity and purpose. Outwardly this unity was the result of a signal tariff reform triumph during the course of 1907. Balfour had finally been captured.

The 'capture' of Balfour for tariff reform was, however, a double-edged success, and his apparent espousal of tariff reform far more complex than a simple conversion to whole-hogger policies. His speech to the National Union Conference at the Savoy Hotel in February 1907 in fact marked the beginning of a Balfourite capture of tariff reform as much as a tariff reform capture of Balfour. During the course of 1907, culminating with the Birmingham speech, Balfour had converted what had been a radical approach to the problems of imperial unity into a conservative policy related primarily to domestic affairs, and even more to the domestic preoccupations of the propertied classes.

Such a take-over had always been possible in view of Balfour's position as party leader, as long as the tariff reformers determined to make the Unionist party the political vehicle of their programme. But until his stroke in 1906, Joseph Chamberlain had acted as a counter-weight to Balfour, with the result that tariff reform and the Unionist party existed as separate, independent, and often antagonistic movements, and the leadership operated as something of a duumvirate. But after Chamberlain's removal from active politics no other tariff reformer came forward to fulfil his role. Austen Chamberlain lacked both the authority and the personality to challenge Balfour, and Milner, although possessing the charisma and independence, was too remote from the day-to-day politics which he despised. That tariff reform had become so closely identified with one party was the direct result of Joseph Chamberlain's tactics based upon the assumption that the only practical avenue to success was through the medium of an existing political party. But once this choice had been made it was impossible, however much the whole-hoggers might claim that tariff reform was above party loyalty, to undo the association with the Unionist party.

As Conservative leader Balfour thus stepped naturally into the place that Chamberlain had vacated. Tariff reform became Unionist party policy during the course of 1907, and particularly after the Birmingham speech, but it was a tariff reform which Balfour had defined both in nature and objectives. As *The Times* acutely remarked, tariff reform was adopted 'because time and circumstance have made it the most potent engine for carrying out the traditional aims and policy of the party'.[116] It had met the conditions which Balfour had laid down for its acceptability in 1903 and become 'practical politics'. But by the same process, the 'traditional aims and policy' of the Conservative party had become the policy of tariff reformers, a development which twisted tariff reform away from its radical imperialist origins, and into the defence of limited class interests. If 'time and circumstance' changed yet again, and tariff reform ceased to be compatible with the traditional policies of the party, it would be left high and dry.

7

The Central Coalition

The chief victims of the reaction to socialism and the changes in Unionist policies during 1907 were the Unionist free traders. With their parliamentary representation reduced to a mere handful by the general election of 1906, and already divided by their attitude towards Balfour, they became increasingly isolated from the main body of the party, and thus increasingly defenceless against tariff reform attacks. Yet, whilst able to perceive the gradual movement of Balfour and the party towards moderate tariff reform, they remained totally unable to relate this to their own situation. In retrospect their behaviour appears suicidal. In continuing to insist on their free trade views and to vote against the party on fiscal questions, they attracted the virulent opposition of the whole-hoggers, especially after the spring of 1907. By their intransigence, they alienated Balfour at the very time when they most needed his protection. But the Unionist free traders still believed that they occupied a strong position as representing the forces of 'moderation' in the country, and as the 'centre' wing of the Unionist party able to work with the moderates of either major party. This was particularly true of their relationship with the Liberal League, where mutual opposition to socialism appeared to offer a sound foundation for co-operation on a wider front than in 1903–4, and perhaps even for the establishment of a new centre party on the basis of class interests.

Signs of the pressure from tariff reformers, to which the Unionist free traders were henceforth to be increasingly subjected, were visible by the beginning of 1907, as part and parcel of the general revival of tariff reform activity. Lord Robert Cecil interpreted Austen Chamberlain's letter in *Outlook* and a speech by Maxse at Stevenage, 'dotting Austen's i's', a copy of which he forwarded to Balfour, as foreshadowing a new purge'.[1] By April, Austen Chamberlain had sounded the signal for attack. 'Austen's last speech has fluttered the dovecotes', Sandars informed Balfour:

His impertinence in inviting Unionists like the Duke of Devonshire to leave the party is bitterly resented . . . Hood is much concerned at Austen's performance and thinks something must be done about it . . . but what good. Austen has thought out his game and his speech, and is not likely to water down his speeches because they are disagreeable to those he wishes to offend. It is all part of a policy—Percival Hughes now comes to me with the complaint that everywhere the Liberal Unionists—posing as Liberal Unionists but in reality being T.R. Leaguers—are, with the encouragement of Austen and Co., trying to squeeze out, or else to capture our local Conservative Associations . . .[2]

The tariff reformers knew what they were doing. 'I rather think', Steel-Maitland grimly told Ridley, 'there is a method now for eliminating almost any wobblers from by-elections.'[3]

But the attack was slow in developing, and the Unionist free traders were inclined to take comfort from the hostile reaction of Balfourites to tariff reform aggression. Devonshire found 'signs that the dictation of the TR's is beginning to be resented by the Party', and was consequently opposed to any counter-attack, since 'any aggressive action on our part would only pull them together'.[4] Elliot tended to agree: 'The party position is a very strange one. I know that Walter Long and others strongly disapproved of Austen Chamberlain's speech about the Duke. For the moment, I think *our* value is rising in the market...'[5]

For most of the year, therefore, the Unionist free traders were more alarmed at the drift of party policy than about their own perilous electoral position.[6] Elliot, for example, condemned Balfour's speech at the Albert Hall early in May, which so pleased Austen Chamberlain, and wanted the U.F.T.C. to 'publish a statement of our position as to the Fiscal question' as a response to the Colonial Conference,[7] but no action appears to have been taken. Unionist free traders disagreed with equal intensity with the emphasis which both Balfour and the tariff reform wing of the party placed upon the need for greater revenue. 'I am not yet convinced', Lord Hugh Cecil told Balfour, 'that much more expenditure is necessary, or even safe—whatever your revenue system; for somehow or other the community must pay, and cannot safely pay more than a certain amount . . .' He demanded 'an express rejection' of the corn tax as 'the first and indispensable preliminary for conciliating any Free Trader',[8] and remained 'fully resolved to destroy Tariff Reform and believe in my ability to do it'.[9]

Behind these menacing tones lay Cecil's conviction that Balfour could be bullied into dropping tariff reform even in mid-1907, if the Unionist free traders appeared likely to desert the Unionist party altogether. He also offered what he thought was an attractive inducement, the possibility of picking up supporters from the 'moderate Liberals'.[10] 'Two things about you amaze me,' he told Balfour:

First, you steadily disregard what I believe to be one of the great canons of political tactics—namely, that a secession from a party is much more formidable on the side nearest its opponents than on the more remote side, and that because the near side can easily join the opponents, but the far side have nowhere to go . . . A central party is always more important than an extreme wing. For it holds the balance.

Secondly, your tactics are disastrous . . . I cannot doubt that the only hope is to try for a coalition with the moderate Liberals—Grey, Haldane, etc. So only shall we again get a strong and healthy party. But for this, Tariff Reform must either be dropped altogether, or reduced to a minimum—But you are unresponsive to Rosebery—who would, I think, be very ready to coalesce at a favourable opportunity.[11]

In general, however, Balfour's adoption of tariff reform, although more apparent than real, had discredited his leadership and the Cecilian policy of compromise. Elliot objected strongly to 'Hugh Cecil's way of talking of Balfour as our leader, and *almost* expressing satisfaction with his attitude', and together with other Liberal Unionist free traders welcomed polarization for the impetus it would give towards independent action.[12]

After the publication of the Valentine letters, Strachey thus recommended that the Unionist free traders, while remaining within the Unionist party, should actively oppose tariff reform in the country. By doing so, he predicted that they would become the beneficiaries of 'the forces of reaction' which would in the next five years hit both major parties and enable them to recapture the Unionist party. Five years of opposition and Chamberlain's tactics of 'coquetting with the Labour party and the Trades Unions, and endeavouring to show them that his party is by nature allied to their own, and . . . dwelling on the fact that the Nationalists are in reality a protectionist party . . . will, I believe, give a good many disinterested Tariff Reformers an excuse for abandoning his cause'.

Similar defections were expected from the Liberal party, and the Unionist free trade group, 'composed of men of moderate views', would become the rallying point of these disaffected moderates and thus again become worthy of consideration from the Unionist leadership. After another election 'it may, I think, be confidently said that the majority of the main body of the Unionist party would be ripe for coming to terms with the Unionist free traders and for reconstructing the party on a free trade basis'.[13] This attempt to reconstruct a centre position between whole-hoggers and radicals dominated Unionist free trade thinking, and particularly the thinking of the 'Liberal' Unionist free traders, between the general election of 1906 and the 1909 budget. Nor were such assumptions totally unrealistic. Many Liberals did dissent from the government's increasing radicalism, especially after 1907, and although they ultimately tended to leave politics altogether rather than join the Unionist free traders, the latter course was a possibility for much of the time. The 'middle ground' held as many, or more, attractions after 1906 as it had before, and the dissatisfied were numerous.

The greatest weakness of Strachey's proposed course of action was that it did not indicate how the Unionist free traders might take the vigorous action necessary if they were to stand out as the rallying point. They were caught in a vicious circle in which their very powerlessness prevented them from attracting support which might have made them more powerful, and thus lent some meaning to their independence. The U.F.T.C. meeting on 21 February 1906 immediately revealed this difficulty when it became apparent that independent action at by-elections was impractical because of the lack of political homogeneity amongst the Club's membership. Agreed on free trade and little more, the Club was forced back upon a policy of 'comprehension' and 'inaction', since action would have brought members into open conflict on other issues.[14] 'The outcome of our whole position is that political action in the Constituencies *by the Club* is impossible owing to our difference of opinion on general politics and as to Balfour's leadership. We remain a *protesting* Club of Unionists and no more.' To make their protest 'as vigorous as possible', Elliot hoped that individual members would 'carry the fight a great deal further and operate in the Constituencies wherever they feel they can thereby strengthen the position of both the Union and Free Trade'.[15] But this ignored both the basic aim of the tactics of independent action and its central problem, the need to create an organization which could rival other political organizations, including not only the Tariff Reform League, but the two major parties themselves. The 'middle ground' existed in theory, but it could be made politically important only if the moderates could institutionalize their discontent and act collectively.

Action did not therefore follow upon the upsurge of militancy amongst Unionist free traders after the Valentine letters. Their own paralysis apart, circumstances were not conducive to the continuation of a militant stance. Balfour's silence, which so irritated tariff reformers, was to their advantage, as was the defeat of the tariff reformers on reorganization and the general decline of interest in tariff reform as an issue. In April 1906 Devonshire saw no 'object . . . in trying to raise interest in a question which, if not dead, is at least dormant',[16] and even in February 1907, four days after Balfour's Savoy Hotel speech, still doubted whether anyone would trouble to attend U.F.T.C. meetings 'in the present position of the fiscal question'.[17] Almost the only incident of the year was the eviction of Sir Edward Clarke as free trade Unionist member for the City of London by tariff reformers outraged by his support of the government in the debate on Kitson's amendment. But Clarke was a difficult man to defend. He had accepted tariff reform support during the election and promised to support Balfour in Parliament. His career had been marked by disagreement with his party on many subjects, including the South African war, and Hood described his support of the Liberals as his 'fourth act of disloyalty'.[18] Lord Robert Cecil did urge Clarke to fight,[19] but in general the Unionist free traders did not put themselves out to protect Clarke. His successor, Sir Frederick Banbury, was a reactionary tariff reformer who ultimately turned out to be not unsympathetic to many Unionist free trade attitudes, particularly towards socialism and social reform.

To socialism, indeed, the Unionist free traders reacted strongly. Numbering in their midst many of the most 'conservative' members of the Unionist party, their reaction was fundamentally different from that of the tariff reformers whose radical wing took the initiative. For the majority of the Unionist free traders, 'free trade' involved not merely opposition to customs duties, but to any form of state intervention including collectivist social reforms, and to any concessions to the Labour movement. Strachey, for example, diametrically opposed the tactics which Garvin justified and Balfour followed, wanting instead a strong 'protest in regard to such a matter as the Trades Disputes Bill or the Feeding of Schoolchildren Bill [and] . . . an end put to the education controversy' in order to rally the Nonconformists, 'who are at heart Conservatives', to the anti-socialist side.[20]

Both Strachey and Lord Hugh Cecil were prominent figures in the British Constitutional Association, the object of which 'is, shortly, to combat state Socialism in all its forms, and to do its best to encourage individualism and independence on the old Liberal lines . . .' The 'moving spirit', according to Strachey, was his cousin, Sir William Chance,[21] a leading member of the Liberal League, and 'the leading people in the Association with the exception of Hugh Cecil, are not Tories, but either Unionist free traders, or anti-Socialist Liberals'.[22] In 1907 the B.C.A. made a conscious effort to broaden this anti-socialist front. Cecil, in March, wrote to the secretary, Beasley, to urge the recruitment of tariff reformers lest the Association appeared too much of a free trade organization, and suggested Sir Howard Vincent and Sir Frederick Banbury as likely prospects: 'No doubt some tariff reformers are largely Socialistic in sympathy, but this is not so with them all . . . I am very anxious to draw in the old-fashioned Conservatives all over the country, who must be, I think, the backbone of our army.'[23]

Strachey approved, partly as a means to show that the B.C.A. had no Liberal bias, but also 'to do all we can to wean the Tariff Reformers from any idea of an alliance with the Socialists such as Milner seemed to foreshadow in his speech, and which Chamberlain certainly contemplated'. This re-education of the tariff reformers could be achieved by getting them to work 'against specific schemes of Socialism, like Old Age Pensions . . . No doubt theoretically, Socialism and Protection have a common basis, but very few people realise this . . .'[24] Banbury agreed to join. 'I am sure', commented Lord Hugh, 'he will be useful to us as giving the impression of monied respectability to our Association',[25] and Strachey was consequently able to inform Devonshire in August that the B.C.A. included both tariff reformers and free traders, and officially pursued a neutral policy on the fiscal controversy.[26] This neutrality, however, was little more than superficial. The B.C.A. was in reality as opposed to tariff reform as it was to socialism, because both had a common basis in collectivism and were thus evils of the same kind. Strachey wrote to Rosebery:

I cannot help thinking that the effect of the anti-socialist campaign on the Tariff Reformers must in the end be to make them feel very doubtful as to their fiscal views. Protection and Socialism are really joined at the base. Both involve State servitude, one by forbidding free exchange and free competition in commodities, and the other by interfering in the exchange of human services.[27]

The menace of socialism, far from forcing the Unionist party into a defensive unity, further accentuated existing differences. What to the tariff reformers was an ideological and political struggle between two rival forms of collectivism, was to the Unionist free traders a conflict between collectivism and individualism in which tariff reform and socialism were ranged on the same side. Ideological differences mirrored a different conception of the electoral base of anti-socialism, and thus of the programme on which to oppose it. Whilst tariff reformers, especially the more radical, sought to revitalize the Tory Democracy, and criticized the infusion of the middle classes into the party and the negative influence they had on the party's policies, the 'moderates' of the B.C.A. sought 'monied respectability'. In persuading Rosebery to take the chair at the foundation of the West Surrey branch of the B.C.A., Strachey expected that such a district, 'full of people who ought to be educated and intelligent and in a position of independence, should be on our side . . .' To its leaders, the B.C.A. was the last bastion of genuine anti-socialism. Strachey condemned both a 'ridiculous leader' in the *Morning Post*, 'saying that the only way for Tories to combat Socialism was to go in for a Socialistic programme', and the belief that 'the Liberals will draw back, even at the eleventh hour, and fight Socialism . . . They are far too committed.'[28] In such views, as the membership of the B.C.A. indicated, the Unionist free traders had the support of a fair number of 'old-fashioned Liberals'.

Out of sympathy with both major parties, pressure for an alliance of 'moderates', the reaction of which Strachey had spoken in 1906, became acute during 1907. For Strachey, as for Hewins and Balfour, Asquith's budget promising old-age pensions meant that the government had sabotaged the free trade system. 'My real quarrel with the present government', he wrote in July, 'is that they are pledged to old age pensions. This pledge is, in my opinion, the most deadly blow that has ever been aimed at Free Trade, and for that reason I can no longer regard the ministry as the bulwark of the cause which I hold dear.'[29] By the end of 1907 such alienation was general, even amongst those Unionist free traders who had actively supported the Liberals in 1906 and had been most consistently hostile to involvement with Balfour. In September, Devonshire found it 'not easy to say much for free trade without helping the Government which is the last thing I wish to do'.[30] Even Elliot, in October, noted that he was 'in entire disagreement with much of the Government's policy'. But he added: 'and in consequence

I am becoming more inclined to look to moderate Liberals, and indeed, moderate men of all parties, to save the situation'.[31] Moderate Liberals were, by this time, also becoming alienated from both parties, and in particular the socialist policies of their own. The nucleus of their opposition was the Liberal League, and it was Rosebery who took the initiative in denouncing the government from amongst its nominal supporters.

The Liberal Imperialists, like their fellow wanderers in the wilderness, had found themselves at something of a loss after the general election of 1906. The League's vice-presidents had joined the new Liberal government, and in the face of an overwhelming Liberal majority which made Campbell-Bannerman the most successful Liberal leader in history and immune from any criticism, there was no clear role for the League to play and little inclination to take the risk of looking for one. The League had, to all intents and purposes, lost its reason for existing and faced a bleak future. Its members could, and did, argue that the League's programme, or at least part of it, had been adopted by the government. They could equally claim that in view of the complexion of the cabinet, the League had taken over the party. But in either case the League would have exhausted its purpose, and the logical conclusion was to dissolve. Its members, however, were unwilling to take this final step, seeing no future for returned rebels in a party whose official organization had always been hostile to the League as a rival to itself. The League, or so its members felt, could still fulfil a defensive function. Nevertheless, after 1906 the League was an organization in search of a policy, and its more implacable members tended to snatch at straws wherever they could be found.

One such was the belief, common in 'moderate' and Unionist circles, that the radical wing would tear itself to pieces once it confronted the problems of government. 'There are', Perks wrote as early as March 1906, 'already evident traces of the coalition character of the Cabinet and the party.'[32] On 3 April he reported that Asquith was concerned at the assertiveness of Labour, and wanted the League kept fully organized as the nucleus of a middle party,[33] and was himself convinced that there was 'a division in the Cabinet upon social legislation, and more especially as to the relations of the Government to the Keir Hardie section of the Labour Party . . . With reference to the League, I feel certain that our policy should be to wait the inevitable course of events—namely the cleavage which is bound to come.'[34] Like the Unionist free traders, the Liberal League during 1906 waited to become the beneficiary of an anticipated reaction against excessive concessions to Labour. The same assumptions gave rise to the same expectations, the same impotence produced the same inactivity.

Nevertheless, the collapse of the Liberal government would not of itself solve the problems of the Liberal League. The Unionist free traders had at least the definite objective of converting their party back to free trade. The League lacked any similar coherent aim applicable to the post-1906 situation. It was significant that in this context Perks should single out Labour as the potential cause of division within the party. The League represented the wealthier right wing of the Liberal party, whose members had been increasingly alarmed at the direction of Liberal policies whilst in opposition, and who clung to Rosebery as one of their own who had sufficient stature to make their fears heard if he chose. For such men, the League still served as a sanctuary in a party into which they no longer quite fitted, but which they were not yet ready to leave.

But whilst the League thus lay in the doldrums, Rosebery had been reconsidering his own position and the newer developments of Liberalism, in particular the land reform proposals of the government as they applied to Scotland. In March he finally decided to speak out and chose the meeting of the League's council as his forum.[35] Far from revitalizing the League, however, Rosebery's attack on the government was greeted by the majority of the League with bewilderment, and by a minority with outright hostility.[36] Edwin Montagu went so far as to accuse Rosebery of reneging on the League's original purpose in a severely critical letter which effectively announced his resignation from the League,[37] and further resignations, of Clegg and Fuller, followed. Rosebery was bitter at this hostile response: 'the chain that galls the League', he wrote to Allard, 'also chafes the President, and before September we shall have to consider whether the League shall be continued'.[38]

Rosebery was in two minds after the League's reaction to his criticism of the government, for the speech was not a spontaneous outburst, but the product of serious reflection about the nature of the liberalism he wished to support, and of the action he and his organization should take in order to ensure that the Liberal party remained true to that type of liberalism. To Rosebery:

the Chesterfield speech on which the League was based, and any subsequent speeches, were declarations of moderate Liberalism . . . Therefore, if these

Leaguers agree with the present majority in the House of Commons, which is largely Socialistic, or anti-Imperial, they are abjuring the League, not the League departing from its principles . . .

Now that we find ourselves between the Devil of Socialism and the deep sea of Protection, the League seems to me more necessary in some form or another than ever before.[39]

He had clearly expected his speech to be welcomed. 'I am positive', Allard replied, 'that it would be a blunder to disband the League, and a bigger blunder still for the League to part with its President.'[40] But this was no solution. Meanwhile, if there had been no more withdrawals, there had been no fresh recruits attracted by the new policy.[41]

Allard replied at greater length on 28 May, and began a discussion on the future of the League which lasted until the end of the year. He maintained that the League should remain as it was, with more frequent meetings, but the essential point of his letter and the memorandum which accompanied it, was to emphasize to Rosebery the difficulties which his opposition to the government caused his followers who had to bear in mind party discipline, or hoped for political careers. However perceptive the speeches, there were some things better left unsaid: 'a discreet bearing best becomes Leaguers'. Yet Allard sympathized with the contents of Rosebery's message, 'that the Socialistic force had to be faced squarely'.[42]

The positions taken up by Allard and Rosebery changed little during the course of the year. Rosebery, anxious to speak out, increasingly frustrated by the failure of his nominal followers to appreciate his policy, but ever-hopeful of converting them and thus never finally cutting loose and dissolving the League; Allard, sympathetic to Rosebery's attitude in theory, yet beseeching consideration for men of less independence and less aloofness, each letter an exercise in political tactics, particularly in view of the limited and regional nature of Rosebery's obsession. Allard continually tried to point out that the relative significance of the Scottish Land Bill diminished when seen through the eyes of a London politician, rather than those of a lowland landowner,[43] to the point where Rosebery became exasperated.[44]

The Scottish Land Bill added a personal intensity to the tensions which beset the 'moderate' position, not only within moderate organizations, but even within the moderate individuals who composed them. The real issue between Rosebery and Allard, as it was the fundamental issue for all the many factions of Edwardian politics, was the conflict between principles—the creed to which they adhered, be it tariff reform, Unionism, free trade, moderate Liberalism, radicalism, or socialism, and party loyalty and their personal ambition. In November, Rosebery and Allard at last turned to the discussion of these fundamentals, provoked by a statement by Rosebery that he was outside political parties, and owed no allegiance to the Liberal party. Allard admitted that the government might, on occasions, be at fault, as on Scottish land and the House of Lords, but thought that it deserved 'general support . . . it is after all, a Liberal government'.[45] Rosebery, quite legitimately, asked what was Liberal about the government:

I still hold that 'liberal' is the noblest word in the English language. But the noblest word may be prostituted, and I cannot resist the uncomfortable feeling that, whether owing to old age or to being outside [?] political society, I may not be able to follow the newer developments of what is called Liberalism. The new Liberalism is in reality largely directed against Liberty, the old Liberalism was meant to preserve it . . . I give credit for much to the Government . . . But I maintain my independence of thought and action . . . If the League fetters me in this, for which I have sacrificed everything in public life, I must withdraw from the League. My views on Socialism do not necessarily bring me into conflict with the Government, perhaps my views as to a Second Chamber do. But I regard that question as so important that I cannot restrain the expression of my views even at the risk of displeasing the ministry.[46]

The question of the annual meeting of the Council made the resolution of these differences, and some decision on future action, essential. Allard, on 15 November, forwarded to Rosebery the suggestion that the Council should meet in January, as the Council had always met early in the year. But relations had deteriorated to the point where he also felt obliged to ask not only if he should go ahead and arrange the meeting, but also whether Rosebery would attend. Allard himself opposed a meeting as 'dangerous and anyhow impolitic under the circumstances'.[47] Rosebery issued a circular to elicit the opinion of members, but was himself despondent and inclined towards dissolution,[48] and even the ever-optimistic Perks regarded this as the best solution. But Perks went on to suggest a new organization, since:

there will soon be a very distinct cleavage in the Liberal ranks; or a rearrangement of parties. The Nonconformists are in a state of veiled rebellion. The Temperance people will soon follow suit. Parliament will dissolve with Wales dissatisfied. The commercial classes, represented by Wood of Leicester and Cox of Liverpool, are beginning to see what the Labour party's real aim is ...[49]

As a result, a special subcommittee was appointed to investigate the future of the League.

But the mood and circumstances of the League had changed markedly since Rosebery spoke of the socialist danger in March. Leaguers remained afraid of their own impotence, and of bringing down against them the wrath of the huge government majority, but their underlying sympathy with Rosebery grew step by step with the growth of socialism itself during the year. Developments within the League thus mirrored developments within the tariff reform and Unionist free trade ranks for similar reasons. The Jarrow and Colne Valley by-elections were again the focal points. Jarrow demonstrated to Allard the advance of socialism against inept opposition,[50] and he saw the political outlook in the North of England as ominous for the Liberal party.[51] 'The dread of Socialism', he continued on 16 September, 'is much greater since the Trades Union Congress',[52] and the Kirkdale by-election caused another crisis of conscience.[53]

Allard's position in 1907 was not untypical of many of the League members or of 'moderate Liberalism'. They were alarmed at the rise of socialism, and at certain actions of their government, either in legislation or in electoral arrangements with Labour, which appeared to concede too much. But they did not, because of that, become Conservatives overnight, nor indeed could they do so as long as the Unionist party retained tariff reform as part of its programme. 'How are we to effectively crusade against Socialism,' asked Durham, 'when our allies in that cause will be our opponents in fiscal principles—I think Protection would be an immense impetus to Socialism in a few years time.'[54] Durham was closer to the Unionists than many Leaguers. Allard, above all, was concerned to keep the Liberal party straight on the path of moderation, a central alternative itself to both Conservatism and protection on the one hand, and socialism on the other, without attacking the government.

As an anti-socialist, anti-protectionist group approaching the middle ground of politics from the Liberal side, the League found sympathizers in the Unionist free traders. Even its idea of the electoral basis of this free trade-*laissez-faire* centre resembled the view taken by the Unionist free traders.[55] The way was open for the Unionist free traders and the

League to unite in defence of the frightened middle classes. The Unionist free traders were quick to realize the opportunity offered by Rosebery's anti-collectivist move. These were, or appeared to be, the discontented Liberal moderates whom they hoped to rally to themselves. By July, Strachey was in contact with Rosebery with a view to luring him into the B.C.A. The B.C.A., he argued, was 'entirely in the spirit of the old Liberalism and the old Whig principles for which you stand'.[56] He visited Rosebery with Lord Hugh Cecil and found him not unsympathetic to some union of 'moderate men' of both sides.[57] Elliot, who had talked to Rosebery earlier, was doubtful, in the long run justifiably, of both the chance of a successful coalition and of Rosebery's strength of purpose,[58] but Strachey persisted with the object of using the B.C.A. as the initial basis of the new party, headed by Rosebery and Devonshire working together, as had been mooted in 1903. He also looked for support from Cromer, who had recently returned from Egypt. Devonshire also had some sympathy with the general idea of rallying men against 'what I think must be alarming a good many people now, viz. the increasing growth and strength of Socialism', but he was less than impressed with the B.C.A.[59]

Strachey was successful in bringing the Duke and Rosebery together, but the meeting was unproductive, largely because Rosebery drew back. Devonshire reported that Rosebery 'thinks that people are not yet sufficiently alarmed to make any organisation successful. This is probably true, and any premature action might do more harm than good. But it is a serious state of things, and I do not know what more proofs are required that Socialism will, before very long, have to be fought.'[60] Devonshire indeed was far more committed to the idea of an anti-socialist campaign than Rosebery, and would probably have taken the lead had Rosebery been more enthusiastic. But Rosebery's decision was final, at least temporarily: 'I am strongly of the opinion, as I told the Duke, that there is nothing at the moment to be done in the way of organising against Socialism as the time is not ripe.'[61]

This was always the difficulty with Rosebery, as Elliot had forseen. When it came to taking decisive action which involved organization and spade-work, the time was never ripe. The Unionist free traders were not over-concerned. They still maintained their faith in the future reaction to their benefit, and were complacent about tariff reform progress. 'My impression', wrote Lord George Hamilton in September, 'is that tariff reform has reached the high water mark. It has captured the overwhelming mass of the Unionist party; but there it stops.'[62] The same optimism prevailed at the end of November when Strachey found indications that the tariff reformers were getting uncomfortable: 'what we Unionist free traders have to do is wait'.[63]

For the Unionist free traders, however, the time for such a dilatory approach was fast running out. In the autumn of 1907 they felt, for the first time since the general election, the repercussions of the tariff reform methods for eliminating 'wobblers'. These were no more than the capture of the local associations which Sandars had reported to Balfour as early as April, backed up by the threat of running independent tariff reformers against any candidate whose attitude on the fiscal question was unsatisfactory. The front line of this attack was the 'Confederacy',[64] a 'secret society' formed with this express purpose out of the meeting of whole-hoggers at the Isthmian Club at the end of 1906. By the autumn of 1907 the Confederates were no more than the most active element in a general revival of tariff reform activity. But as a secret society they attracted considerable publicity which, although generally hostile, was itself useful in adding a degree of myth to the reality of work in the constituencies. The Confederacy also acted as a safety valve for both the Tariff Reform League and the Balfourites at a time when their growing rapprochement entailed respectability on the part of the former. It enabled Balfour to denounce proscription without directly attacking the Tariff Reform League, and the Tariff Reform League to dissociate itself from proscription without impeding the progress of tariff reform at the local level.

This pattern was illustrated clearly on the first discovery of the Confederacy, when its attempts to force the Unionist candidate for South Nottingham, Lord Henry Bentinck, into a declaration in favour of tariff reform drew down upon it the wrath of the Duke of Portland, the head of the Bentinck family. Portland, as an influential Nottinghamshire landowner who gave valuable support to both the Unionist party and the Tariff Reform League, had direct access to the party leadership, and complained to Balfour, who passed the matter on to Austen Chamberlain with the comment that he had 'a very vague idea as to who the Confederates are' and expressed his disapproval of their conduct.[65] Austen Chamberlain apologized for 'the trouble in Nottingham' and in turn passed the problem on to Ridley and Goulding of the T.R.L. but himself pleaded or feigned ignorance.[66] Ridley laid down the official League line on these affairs, but similarly, knew nothing:

The League, of course, maintains its absolute right to do what it likes in the way of educating electors, but we have always endeavoured, especially in the last two years, to act with circumspection and not unduly force people who do not want to be hurried, and on these principles we personally assured the Duke of Portland in July that the League had not interfered with Henry Bentinck, and further would not interfere. To that agreement we have strictly adhered.

But we told him that we cannot be responsible for what other people may do: and as a matter of fact, I believe that there has been interference in that constituency on the part of a body called the Confederates. I don't know who these people are: but have reason to believe they came into existence mainly because the T.R.L. was not militant enough for some of its more ardent spirits. It is obvious that we cannot control these people.[67]

Balfour forwarded these repudiations to Portland and washed his hands of the business.[68]

This was not quite the whole story. Sandars, who was not yet quite up with the state of play, and who had been sent a copy of Balfour's letter to Austen Chamberlain by Short, sent back the exasperated comment, 'of course Mr. Balfour knows who the "Confederates" are', and identified both Goulding and Ridley, to whom Chamberlain had appealed to put things right, as Confederates themselves.[69] Such knowledge was, however, politically inconvenient in the new atmosphere of *détente* between Balfour and the tariff reformers. With no one on whom to pin responsibility the right protestations could be made, honour satisfied all round, and yet no one offended. The Confederates went their way undeterred.

Under these circumstances the Unionist free traders had to fend for themselves. Yet they were, in general, slow to realize what the events in Nottingham involved for the future, and when they did react, they reacted as small fragmented groups, exploring various, and often incompatible, possibilities, not as a united movement. During the autumn, indeed, whilst the Confederates mined away at the few electoral supports that remained to them, Unionist free trade thinking did not go below the level of negotiations with the party leadership. Lord Robert Cecil aired within the limited confines of the Cecilian brotherhood the idea of 'driving a wedge between the Walters and the Austens' but found Lord Hugh opposed because 'the olive branch would be mistaken for a white flag', and Salisbury 'a good deal impressed' with this objection.[70] The idea was thus temporarily shelved, only to be revived by Lord Hugh when the pressure became greater. Elliot toyed with the idea 'that a demand by us that Balfour should agree to hang up the subject of tariff reform 'til after a Royal Commission appointed by him has reported, would be good tactics'[71] but failed to say why he held this opinion, which had long since been tried and found wanting.

Nevertheless, the first occasion in the crisis upon which independent Unionist free trade action was considered was in support of this far-fetched idea. On the basis of Elliot's royal commission proposal, Strachey drew up a 'Plan of Campaign', to 'let the main body of the Unionist party and the world in general know that it is our intention, being dissatisfied alike with the Irish and Socialist policy of the Ministry and with the Tariff Reform proposals of the Unionists, to run candidates of our own in all constituencies in which adherents of full-blown Tariff Reform views are standing.' The Unionist free trade candidate was to be withdrawn if the official Unionist agreed not to support tariff reform until a royal commission had been appointed. Strachey admitted that the plan was 'to some extent a case of bluff on our part',[72] and the aim was not to get a Unionist free trader into Parliament, but only to make 'aggression the alternative to a Royal Commission truce'.[73] Strachey optimistically thought that if one tariff reformer would give the undertaking required, they might get a hundred.[74]

A plan to change the policy of the party by intimidation without changing its personnel in Parliament was clearly unrealistic, but perhaps because neither of them was in the House, neither Strachey nor Elliot stooped to consider the problems of existing Unionist free trade M.P.s. Lord Robert Cecil at least tackled this aspect of the problem squarely. By December, he was in touch with Walter Long through the mediation of another moderate Unionist free trade M.P., Philip Magnus. Long, honestly enough, told the Unionist free traders what their problem was: 'the Unionist free traders . . . refuse to recognise that in these days the constituencies really select their own candidates, and then blame the leaders as being responsible for that which is really done by the constituencies themselves'.[75] But he offered his services as mediator 'to do anything in my power to help to bring about reunion—I am afraid my power is very slight'.[76] Lord Robert's activity was stimulated by the considerable extension of Confederate activity by the turn of the year, and in particular by threats against himself and his close associate, G. S. Bowles in Norwood.

Bowles had already had some trouble in his constituency in the summer of 1907, but this had been temporarily smoothed over by a letter from Balfour to the chairman of his association, Hunt.[77] Confronted by further disputes, Bowles therefore turned immediately to the central party and saw Percival Hughes of the Central Office as early as 13 December. Central Office opinion had, however, hardened in the course of the year. From Hughes, Bowles got nothing but a lecture on tariff reform theory and the need for party unity.[78] Bowles indeed gathered from Hood that the Central Office would be at best neutral if a tariff reform candidate was started against him in Norwood, even if his local association remained loyal.[79] Hood further added to Bowles's difficulties by informing him on 23 December that he would only have official support if he accepted official party policy, i.e. the Birmingham programme.[80] Further correspondence took the matter no further, and by the beginning of January Bowles was in touch with the T.R.L. branch chairman, Campbell, with whom he discussed his position on 6 January.[81]

Campbell, a 'kindly, reasonable silly old man', had been stirred into action by the Confederates, whom he met at the Constitutional Club, and although he would not step out of line, was far more concerned with local unity than the purity of Bowles's fiscal convictions. Thus, while withdrawing from the platform of a public meeting Bowles was to address, he told Bowles that a letter of support from Balfour would give him the lever he needed to control the local extremists. Both Bowles and Cecil thought the opportunity offered by a sympathetic local tariff reformer to get Balfour to support a sitting Unionist free trader against tariff reform opposition 'too good to lose'.[82] Much of the pressure, which Cecil, and to a lesser extent Bowles, tried to bring to bear upon Long, Balfour, and the Central Office, stemmed from this. Lord Robert complained on 17 January about the development of the Confederate movement,[83] and again on 31st, to say that 'the position of those Unionists who are unable to accept tariff Reform, seems to me to be becoming rather acute'.[84] But his letters were unproductive. Bowles was 'thrown over' by his local association, the chairman stating that 'the action of the meeting was in entire accordance with the wishes of the Central Office'.[85]

In these circumstances, the resources of the U.F.T.C. were marshalled to solve the first problem which stood in the way of any attempts to induce the leadership to condemn the Confederacy—the discovery of those responsible. Brunker sent some details gleaned from Bagley, Secretary of the T.R.L., to Cecil,[86] and he passed these on swiftly to Balfour, naming Remnant, Winterton, Goulding, Burgoyne, 'and of course Leo Maxse . . . Their plan is to run candidates against any-one they consider to be a Unionist free trader . . . and I am proud to say that from sources I hear that I am regarded as the chief culprit and that there is to be a man out against me within a month . . .' Lord Robert assumed that Austen Chamberlain was also involved, and added that the Unionist free traders would not take this lying down.[87]

By the beginning of 1908, therefore, aggressive attitudes were com-mon to all sections of the U.F.T.C. under pressure. Lord Robert Cecil had indeed contemplated reprisals, at least as a threat, in December 1907, early in his exchanges with Long, but the letter to Magnus was marked 'Not Sent',[88] as though his nerve failed him. Early in January Salisbury revived the idea with a specific suggestion that someone in Worcester should put a piece in the local paper saying that, because of unfair attacks on the Unionist free traders by tariff reformers like Goulding, the Unionist free traders of the city were considering putting up a free trade candidate at the forthcoming by-election.[89] The rumour was spread. Bowles reported that Watson of the *Yorkshire Post* was much excited by the idea, and even came up with a man, Ormsby-Gore who, said Bowles, had a great personal dislike of Goulding.[90] Brunker reported to Elliot on 16 January that 'Unless Balfour repudiates the "Confederates" tomorrow, I should say it is extremely probable that open war will break out between us and the tariff reformers',[91] and Cromer thought likewise.[92]

But again, the thoughts were of blackmail against the leadership, not the practical elimination of a tariff reformer in the constituencies. Cromer, like Strachey, thought of aggression because 'I think that the best way to . . . a compromise is rather to show our teeth.'[93] A real live candidate was, in these circumstances, more than the Unionist free traders could cope with. Brunker hastily dissuaded Ormsby-Gore from fighting Worcester because the local Unionist free traders were already petrified and intended to support Goulding, so that Ormsby-Gore stood to win only a handful of Liberal votes which would make the U.F.T.C. a laughing stock.[94] The lesson from this for those Union-ist free traders who continued to believe that they represented a silent majority of moderates, that those moderates, if they existed, needed organization and leadership at both the local and national level, was, however, lost upon them.[95]

Despite the evidence of Worcester, Cromer thus made an attempt to extort concessions from Lansdowne by threats at the end of January. Seeing compromise on doctrine, and therefore real unity, as impossible, Cromer sought an agreement which would secure Unionist free trade seats. This, he wrote, was urgent because the Executive Committee of the U.F.T.C. was about to consider a resolution that a subcommittee be appointed to select constituencies to be contested. He proposed that tariff reformers should not challenge sitting Unionist free traders, and that Unionist free traders in turn should not put up candidates where it was clear that tariff reformers were in the majority. Where the fiscal nature of the seat was in doubt, the seat would be referred to arbitration. Cromer could not, however, promise Unionist free trade support for tariff reformers in tariff reform constituencies, nor even that they would support the official party policy without specific pledges against food and raw material taxes, and against protection.[96] Even so, Elliot, who had worked closely with Cromer in the plan, and whose memorandum formed the basis of Cromer's letter, felt that Cromer was giving away too much with his proposed terms about seats.[97] He too had learned nothing from Worcester. But there was no hope of Cromer's proposals being accepted. Lansdowne replied that the constituencies must have the last word: 'it is virtually impossible for either side to restrict the activity of its most restless supporters'.[98] As Cromer commented, the reply, 'though very courteous . . . does not help towards a settlement'.[99]

The weakness in all these attempts to secure concessions was that the threats themselves were hollow. Enough of the Unionist free traders had no real intention of running candidates against the Unionist party to ensure that, if the attempt was made, it would destroy the Club. The threat might have been effective if the assumption that the centre of the party was merely waiting for an opportunity to negotiate a truce on equal or favourable terms had been well-founded. But the Balfourites had moved towards tariff reform even faster than Balfour himself during 1907, not only because of tariff reform pressure, but also because tariff reform arguments, especially the need for greater revenue from indirect taxation, seemed reasonable to them in both national and electoral terms. They were far from convinced that they could not win without the help of the Unionist free traders, or that the Birmingham programme entailed the ruin of the party. Even Long, perhaps the most sympathetic of the Balfourite leaders, made few concessions in responding to Lord Robert Cecil's complaints. 'There is', he wrote on 18 January, 'no doubt whatever that the Constituencies in an ever increasing degree are determined to have tariff reform candidates and with this, it is quite clear, no leader can interfere . . .'[100] Lord Robert's confession that he could not support the Birmingham policy finally alienated him completely.

Long had in fact done more than his letters to Lord Robert suggested. Late in December he had written to Balfour expressing the wish that there should be no fiscal amendment to the Address, and discussing the problems raised by his correspondence with Magnus and Cecil.[101] But after the Birmingham speech, with almost complete harmony established between the Balfourites and the whole-hoggers, neither Balfour nor the Central Office were prepared to show consideration for anyone who could not accept this basic programme.

All these men [wrote Hood] jib at the taxation of corn and meat. The wit of man cannot devise a formula which will satisfy Bonar Law and his friends and these other gentry . . . they persist in certain reservations, which, if persisted in, will make it impossible for us to continue to support them. I cannot use our Central Office to return to Parliament a group of men who, when we get a majority, will either refuse to support, or will oppose, the chief measure on which a majority has been secured.

I have far less difficulty with the Tariff Reformers (proper), they are quite willing to give Cecil and co. time to come into line. But they will become more and more restive if time goes on, and these laggards refuse to accept the official party policy as laid down by its recognised chief.

Most important of all, Hood saw through the Unionist free traders' bluff and recognized their impotence. Their attempts to blackmail the Balfourites by threatened reprisals in the constituencies were, therefore, doomed from the outset. 'I don't think there is much chance of the Free Fooders running men in opposition to Tariff Reform candidates', Hood wrote: 'Their following is very small and they have nothing to offer. If there is a split . . . we shall, of course, lose some good men whom we can ill spare, but they *now* have little influence.'[102] The way back to the Unionist fold, at least without pulling the Unionist free trade flag part way down, was blocked.

The breakdown naturally strengthened the hands of the militants when the Unionist free traders again came to consider independent action early in February. Elliot finally decided to act alone and speak at a free trade meeting in Manchester where a by-election was expected because of rumours of Churchill's promotion. Action in North-west Manchester had already been suggested to Strachey by E. Leigh Oliver, a local Unionist free trader, in December. At that time, the idea circulated was for Strachey to stand as a third candidate to force the official Unionist candidate, Joynson-Hicks, into free trade pledges along the lines of Strachey's 'Plan of Campaign'.[103] Oliver thought Hicks was desperate for free trade support, really a free trader at heart, and 'will agree to any terms'. He consequently opened negotiations with Hicks on the basis of a division of the Manchester seats between free traders and tariff reformers which he thought Hicks would accept.[104]

Elliot's decision put Unionist free trade determination to the test. Hitherto, despite the threats of extreme action, those who had made the threats knew full well that they were bluffing. When the question of attendance at free trade meetings organized primarily by Liberals had been considered in December, the general feeling had been that recent developments in Liberal policy towards old age pensions and the House of Lords made participation dangerous to the unity of the Club.[105] Lord Robert Cecil still felt this way about the Manchester meeting and thought Elliot's proposal 'as destructive of the existence within the party of Unionist free traders as any action which the Confederacy itself has taken . . .'[106] Both Lord Hugh and Lord Robert objected to Elliot going to Manchester because it endangered the policy of co-operation with the 'moderates' within the Unionist party in which they still believed, and because they saw Liberal social policies as a greater menace than even tariff reform. 'Free Trade', wrote Lord Hugh, 'seems to me to be in no danger at this moment, and the present Government requires to be restrained much more than the T.R.L.'[107] But the behaviour of Balfour and the Central Office threw doubts upon the basic assumption of this argument, and the 'Liberal' Unionist free traders remained unconvinced, and supported Elliot.[108] The dangers of division consequently reappeared: 'it is obvious', Cromer wrote, 'that unless great care is taken, we shall have a split amongst ourselves, which would be most unfortunate'.[109]

In the case of NW Manchester Elliot was also premature. The negotiations which E. L. Oliver had opened locally with Hicks, and of which he had informed Strachey, were progressing well, and it appeared that Hicks would willingly give satisfactory pledges on the fiscal question in return for Unionist free trade support. Strachey, after interviewing Hicks with Lord Robert Cecil and Tootal Broadhurst, another local Unionist free trader, found Hicks far more sound on free trade than he had supposed, with 'no enthusiasm for tariff reform, or any intellectual convictions, so far as I could see, contrary to the free trade view'. Hicks agreed to consider the fiscal question closed by the election of 1906 and to fight 'on the education question and opposition to Socialism—a matter in regard to which he is very strong'. In return for Unionist free trade support, Hicks also agreed to use his influence to secure an allocation of Lancashire seats to Unionist free traders along the lines of Oliver's suggestion and the proposals Cromer had put to Lansdowne. While both local and national negotiations continued, the Unionist free traders put great hopes in this plan, and anticipated that 'if we could get 50 to 60 seats allocated to us, and could carry some 30 or so of them, the danger of tariff reform would be over'.[110]

The breakdown of Cromer's negotiations with Lansdowne virtually put an end to this hope.[111] Nevertheless, Broadhurst thought the Unionist free traders had to support Hicks even without the arrangement on seats since, if he lost on the pledges he had promised to give, the tariff reformers would argue that the party could only win on a tariff reform platform.[112] Brunker had in any case prepared a breakdown of Lancashire seats for use by the Executive Committee[113] and a subcommittee of Elliot, Lord Robert Cecil, Strachey, Mortimer, Broadhurst, and Darwin was set up to carry the matter on. 'I hope', wrote Darwin, 'we shall seriously consider what we can do in the way of fighting.'[114]

To this point things were still going fairly well for the Unionist free traders. Action had been taken in support of a candidate free trade enough to satisfy the militants, yet still official enough not to frighten off the Tories. It was too good to last. No sooner had Broadhurst told Hicks that they would support him, than Hicks informed him that 'Acland Hood had sent for him—sworn that they would not recognise him if he fought on the lines settled by us . . . So, of course, all our understanding is off . . . Apparently now the official leaders of the party have joined the Confederacy . . . we cannot take this lying down.'[115] In these changed circumstances, Unionist free trade opinion swung round to support Churchill, and although both Cromer and Cecil made representations to the leadership about Hood's intervention, they did so without expecting, or getting, satisfaction.[116]

The incident marked a clear defeat for the moderate policy of working within the Unionist party. For a time the Unionist free traders thought of running Broadhurst as a third candidate but this scheme had little support.[117] Broadhurst himself was reluctant and ultimately nothing was done. Hesitancy characterized the Unionist free traders on this occasion as so often in the past few months. Lord Hugh Cecil felt 'that we ought to avoid a rupture at the present time for any less cause than an attack on sitting members who are Unionist free traders . . .',[118] and even Strachey was for once in agreement that there was 'nothing to be done for the moment but wait'.[119] But as Darwin pointed out, 'we may wait too long for a good tactical reason for striking. After a little the reasons given for firing the first shot get forgotten. What remains is how the shot tells.'[120] In the case of NW Manchester the shot was a blank. Hicks won by a narrow margin over Churchill despite opposition from the Unionist free traders,[121] and thus exposed how weak the Unionist free traders were even in allegedly free trade Lancashire.

Within a week of hearing of the Central Office's action in NW Manchester, Lord Robert Cecil also heard that a tariff reformer was to be run against him in East Marylebone. He was still at this time attempting, through Long, to negotiate terms for himself, Bowles in Norwood, and Abel Smith in East Herts., 'where Winterton has attacked'.[122] He suggested that the Unionist free traders should undertake to resign if they found themselves unable to support a Unionist budget in the next Parliament, but Balfour found 'difficulties (which he fears are impossible)' in the proposed concordat.[123] Lord Robert was able to induce his own local association to accept this pledge, and thus to neutralize his opposition temporarily, but in Norwood the terms were rejected[124] and Lord Robert fought on for the sake of his friends. In March he refused to accept the official whip in support of Goulding's fiscal amendment to the Address, an amendment 'moved and seconded by Confederates'.[125] In April he made his support of Hicks, which Hicks and his local Unionist supporters had requested, conditional upon official help for Unionist free traders.[126] By April, therefore, with the 'Liberal' Unionist free traders advocating co-operation with the Liberal party, and with even 'Conservative' Unionist free traders refusing the party whip or to speak for party candidates, a split had clearly opened up between the Unionist free traders and the official party. 'I do not see how we can possibly continue to act together,'[127] Long wrote to

Lord Robert Cecil. 'I regret the action of the Manchester Free Traders more than I can say; all round here among people who are by no means advanced tariff reformers, it has roused the bitterest feelings.'[128]

The great difficulty of the Unionist free traders in pursuing the Cecilian policy of retaining a foothold for free trade within the Unionist party was the willingness of the leadership to accept such a split as inevitable and the loss to themselves as slight. Balfour, while justifying his policy of non-intervention in constituency affairs, placed most of the blame for their troubles on the free traders themselves and suggested that they might from their behaviour be seeking 'an excuse for leaving the party and joining themselves to some fresh political organisation—perhaps with Rosebery and the secessionists of 1903 at their head . . .[129]', a comment that was not without insight. Strachey's immediate reaction to Hicks's capitulation to the Central Office was 'to think that a Centre Party is our only chance of salvation', although he added that it was 'a consummation not to be hurried'.[130]

An effort along these lines had indeed already been made. Throughout the crisis of the winter of 1907–8, the Unionist free traders had kept in close contact with the Liberal League, and kept alive the idea of a moderate, anti-socialist, anti-protectionist coalition. Lord Hugh Cecil in December had discussed the idea of a free trade newspaper with Rosebery and the general question of 'Centralism' with Edgar Vincent and Farquhar.[131] In February, as the pressure began to tell, negotiations were started in earnest not with Rosebery alone but with representatives of the League, although Rosebery was kept fully informed by both sides. The shift in the League's position during 1907, as it came to accept Rosebery's anti-socialist position and his hostility to the government, gave some foundation to the negotiations for the middle ground because of the similarity of the ideological positions of the two 'central' groups. The new mood indicated by Perks in November, condemning the timid and envisaging a new organization, was reflected in a memorandum which J. H. Tritton drew up to serve as the basis for the report of the subcommittee on the future of the League. The past was written off as successfully concluded, the aims of the Chesterfield speech fulfilled, and their continuation guaranteed by the presence of influential Leaguers in the government. But 'there have arisen questions of the most serious import in domestic politics—the menace of socialism—the menace of collectivism—the menace of universal pauperisation . . . the menace of Irish separation, and protection to which the Tories are committed'. In view of this the League needed a restatement of policy and measures to broaden its basis to 'include those on both sides who shrink from extremes', so that it could become 'the scaffolding of a new organisation'. Tritton thought that Rosebery should circulate members with details of the proposed new step to eliminate the problems of dissent, and that there would be some resignations. Typical of the new mood of the League, however, he did not fear these since they would clear the air.[132]

The subcommittee adopted Tritton's memorandum, but both the draft report submitted by Perks to Rosebery,[133] and Perks's covering letter, revealed the degree to which the reassessment of the League's position was influenced by the negotiations with the Unionist free traders which had been opened by F. W. Maude, and which did, indeed, mean as much to the League in its parlous state as to the U.F.T.C. The subcommittee decided that what the League really needed was not reorganization, but 'an infusion of new life' and that 'in view of any arrangement being made with the Unionist free traders', any proposals for constitutional change within the League were premature. It nevertheless did reach some conclusions:

1. Whatever fusions, alliances or reorganization may take place we will not change the name Liberal League.
2. It is essential to the success of the League that you [Rosebery] continue its President and the director of its policy.
3. That a full meeting of the Council should be called at the earliest possible date at which you should formulate (as you did in 1902 at Chesterfield) the policy of the League—dealing especially with Free Trade, Anti-Socialism, Irish Affairs and the Defence of the Empire.
4. If a satisfactory alliance can be made with the Unionist Free Traders upon such a platform we believe it would greatly strengthen the middle group to which most of our men belong.

    There was a strong feeling in the Committee that the sooner you declare our new programme, especially the anti-socialist part of it, the better. No political party has so far raised that flag and we all think that it would rally to our side an enormous section of the commercial and middle classes, especially if such a declaration of policy were to synchronise with an alliance with the Unionist Free Traders.[134]

The keynote of the subcommittee's report was thus optimism, in the hope of an alliance which would give the League the new blood it needed, and even Rosebery was temporarily enthusiastic.[135]

But the committee had allowed itself to some extent to be misled by Maude's wishful thinking. According to Perks, it believed that Maude had seen both Strachey and Elliot who wanted to 'fuse' the two organizations to support a programme of free trade, anti-socialism, and opposition 'to an independent Irish parliament or executive', and that Cromer favoured both the fusion and the retention of the name Liberal League.[136] Maude's own account envisaged even grander plans. To Rosebery Maude discounted the idea which the subcommittee proposed, of a League invigorated by the adhesion of the Unionist free traders, because he thought the League's association with the government meant that it would only find support 'on the extreme right wing of the Liberal party'. He talked instead of a 'new departure' and 'a great Central party', composed of 'the anti-socialist Free Trade employers of labour, the City Free Traders and the Whig Free Trade forces which are behind the Duke of Devonshire . . .' Maude also told Rosebery that before talking to the Unionist free traders he had told Haldane what he proposed to do, and had received a favourable response. On the other hand it appears that he had not seen Elliot but only Strachey, although he was going to see Elliot. From Strachey he learned that 'Lord Cromer is very bitten with the idea of a Central Party under your leadership', and would be willing to discuss the subject with Rosebery and serve under him.[137] On the basis of Maude's report the subcommittee deputed Freeman-Thomas, Maude, Cory, and Tritton to confer with Unionist free trade representatives in informal talks.

Strachey also wrote to Rosebery on 21 February on the subject of fusion, and although enthusiastic laid down conditions which doomed the talks to failure from the start:

I agree, provided that we can get the Unionist Free Traders as a body to enter such a party (we must stick together) and that the Unionist principle is maintained and provided also that you are willing to lead such a party and to lead it strongly not only against the Tariff Reformers but also against the extreme Liberals and Socialists.

I understood the idea to be the foundation of a Real Centre Party with Anti-Home Rule, Anti-Socialism, Anti-Protection and Anti-Little Englandism as its main platform . . . I also understand that if we Unionist Free Traders join it would be a new party and not the Liberal League . . . We must have a new name like *Centre or National Party* which makes it clear we have not 'joined the Liberals'. The mass of our group are not old Liberal Unionists but Conservatives.

On this understanding of the arrangement the Unionist free traders were inclined to be favourable. Strachey confirmed what Maude had written about Cromer, provided Rosebery came forward as the leader of a real centre party, and had found Balfour of Burleigh and Elliot 'sympathetic', Lord George Hamilton 'encouraging', but Lord Robert Cecil 'cautious', reactions which, with the exception of Hamilton, were to be expected. Strachey also offered the services of the *Spectator* if the new party materialized. 'In a sense the readers of the "Spectator" form already a kind of Centre Party and I think I may say without egotism that they would very largely follow my lead.'[138]

The arrangements were that four from each side should meet in Strachey's flat to exchange ideas. On 25 February, Maude reported the collapse of this exchange:

What 'upset the applecart' was Hugh Cecil's belief that Balfour can still be won back to the Free Trade camp.

Labouring under that delusion he and the Tory Free Traders were averse to tainting themselves with even moderate Liberalism. And the Free fooders don't like to separate themselves from their Tory colleagues. At some future date when it is too late for much good to be done, they admit they will probably have to seek alliance with the Liberal League.

But for the moment they will do nothing but advise us to strengthen our organisation.[139]

Given that the Unionist free traders felt that they 'must stick together' and act as a group or not at all, the unwillingness of the Conservative wing to make concessions to the moderate Liberals was in itself enough to kill the scheme. But even without this there was so much confusion and self-deception on both sides about the real purpose of the talks that they had little chance of success. Neither group could escape from its traditional party affiliations and attitudes, however much it disagreed with its party's majority.

The refusal of the Conservative free traders was an extreme example of this, but even Strachey, though he appeared a supporter of a new central party, was distinctly anti-Liberal. He sought from the negotiations less a new coalition with the League on an equal basis than more support for the Unionist free traders within the Unionist party to 'restore the Unionist party and purge it of the worst, i.e. the Birmingham type, of Tariff Reformer. This is worth doing. The Unionist party (I mean the main body) would surely be tempted to throw over Austin and Bonnar Law [*sic*] if it could get a strong centre group *in exchange*.'[140]

Cecil also thought of exploiting the opportunity in this way, and informed Long that 'Advances are being made to some of us by people on the other side . . . some of us think they should be entertained. Much depends on what our position in the party is to be . . . some think that unless we are to be assured of effective protection from within the party, we ought to seek for it outside, or at any rate accept it if it is offered to us.'[141] It was the old policy of blackmail over again.

But the League was no more flexible than the Unionist free traders. The Unionist free traders reasonably insisted that it should be 'perfectly clear from our first public action that we are founding a new centre party and not joining any section of the Liberal party. The new centre party if it ever comes must involve quite as great or an even greater breach with the existing Liberal party as our breach with the Tariff Reformers.'[142] But the League subcommittee had already made this impossible by its refusal to change either the name or the nature of the League. Both sides went to the meeting talking of a new central coalition but consciously or unconsciously seeking no more than new supporters for their existing organizations. Under these circumstances it was not surprising that Strachey felt that 'when we came to go into details it did not seem there was much we could do'. Rosebery was urged to make a 'strongly anti-socialist speech . . . warning the Government of the terrible danger of committing the country to a vast scheme of socialistic expenditure',[143] and Lord Hugh Cecil suggested 'that perhaps a correspondence might be started in the Spectator on the idea of a Central party', to which Strachey agreed.[144] The 'Centre Party' thus became, artificially, a staple item of *Spectator* journalism for the rest of the year.

Both Strachey and Maude from their respective sides also pressed Rosebery to give the required lead. Maude accepted Rosebery's policy of speaking only at a crisis, but claimed that the present, when 'we are threatened in the near future with a choice of Protection, Socialism, anti-militarism and other abominations' was such a crisis. He also wanted negotiations with the Unionist free traders to continue and for the League to broaden its programme to collect the Liberals as they defected.[145] Strachey did not, and could not, go as far. Whilst urging Rosebery to deliver a critique of excessive party loyalty in times of crisis,[146] he also agreed with Rosebery that 'a real occasion for action . . . has not yet arisen'.[147] It had been clear from the first that the only hope for such negotiations was a bold approach towards the creation of a brand new party such as Maude envisaged. But Maude was in advance of his colleagues both in this and in his realization that even if the League and the Unionist free traders were right in their assumption that a great body of moderate opinion existed, it must be 'organised and led' if it was to be effective.

Internal divisions had much to do with this hesitancy. Since October 1903 Balfour had handled the Unionist free traders gently, at first for his majority and subsequently because he was playing down tariff reform as a divisive question. The Conservative Unionist free traders responded to such treatment even in 1908. Lord Robert Cecil was almost apologetic to Long for Unionist free trade failure to support Hicks in NW Manchester even though he stressed their difficulties.[148] But Long too was playing a Balfourite game. In practice he could do nothing and would do very little, but his professions of sympathy prevented the realities of their situation from being clearly understood by the Unionist free traders. When Lord Robert met Long in February 1908 he came away with the impression that 'he feels most profoundly that the loss of the Unionist free traders would be fatal at any rate to the Unionist party as he understands it, and he made no secret of his own opinion that in some way or another peace should be made'.[140] Yet Long had by this time withdrawn his objections to a fiscal amendment[150] and had written to Balfour 'our Tariff views are gaining ground, why can't we leave the electors to deal with the Free Traders and never mention their names ourselves'.[151]

Behind the 'moderation' of the Conservative free traders lay their strong desire to remain within the Unionist party for other than fiscal reasons. The difficulty of the U.F.T.C., as Lord Robert Cecil commented, was that

> fundamentally we are not quite agreed as to the necessities of the political situation. To me, the greatest necessity of all is to preserve, if possible, a foothold for Free Trade within the Unionist party. For, if not, I and others who think like me, will be driven to imperil either free trade or other causes such as religious education, the House of Lords, and even the Union, which seem to us of equal importance.[152]

The difference within the Unionist free trade ranks which Balfour exploited began in differences about the priority they gave, and the danger they attached, to free trade in the context of other issues. Their differing opinions of Balfour derived in the first instance from these basic differences rather than from anything Balfour did or said. Like the tariff reformers and the Balfourites when they were considering election results, the Unionist free traders saw what they expected or wanted to see in Balfour's speeches. To the 'Liberal' Unionist free trader, H. Shaw Stewart, Balfour at Birmingham 'seems to me to have capitulated horse foot and artillery—he only keeps his commissariat and they will take that from him when it suits them. It really is a question as to how much longer we can call ourselves members of the Unionist party . . .'[153] Elliot naturally concurred as did Strachey who derived a perverse pleasure from seeing the tariff reformers saddled with Balfour as leader.[154] On the other hand, the Conservative free traders were almost satisfied with the Birmingham speech.[155] 'Really,' Bowles commented, 'the more one looks at it, the more Free Trade it appears.'[156]

This attitude was sufficient to hold the Conservative free traders, and thus the U.F.T.C. as a whole, back from decisive action during the most critical moments of the autumn and winter of 1907–8. For the Unionist free traders, the talks with the Liberal League were unfortunately timed. Within a fortnight after the strength of traditional party loyalties had brought about their collapse, Central Office intervention in NW Manchester and intensified tariff reform pressure in their constituencies produced a degree of alienation which, if still not sufficient to induce Conservative free traders to be quit of the Unionist party altogether, might have led to a broader, more flexible approach to the question of co-operation with the League and not have slammed the door so decisively. Strachey wrote early in March:

It looks to me as if Balfour and the official Unionists had come to the conclusion that we are not worth purchasing at any price however small, and that they mean to put themselves completely in the hands of the Tariff Reformers. If so, there is nothing for it but a Centre Party . . . Balfour's silence over the Goulding amendment and the Joynson-Hicks incident makes it look as if the occasion or crisis for the formation of a Centre Party might come to us before it comes to the Roseberyite Liberals. I should be very sorry for this as I think it would be very much better for us if the matter were precipitated by a crisis in the Liberal party.[157]

In fact, the 'occasion or crisis' had already come and been missed. The summer saw a considerable lessening of tariff reform pressure, although the Unionist free traders could take no credit for this. With one major party committed to 'protection' and the other to socialism, and neither prepared to make concessions to backsliders on these issues, the dilemma which had faced the 'moderates' in 1907 remained unresolved in 1908, and the Unionist free traders had exhausted all possible solutions. 'As to the attitude of the Club,' Cromer wrote to Elliot, 'as a body we really have no alternative. We must stick to our old lines and wait for better times . . .'[158] But the old lines had already proved inadequate. 'For the life of me', their harassed secretary commented at the end of April, 'I do not know what we are to put in the report this year. We certainly have a few more members, but our position does not appear to be very bright at present.'[159]

8

The Devil and the Deep Blue Sea

With the breakdown of negotiations for a centre party hopes for a clear political future all but disappeared both for the Liberal League and the U.F.T.C. Temporarily, however, Rosebery's misjudgement, from his point of view, of the nature of the reconstructed Liberal government under Asquith took the pressure off the League. 'I regard the government as a new one,' he wrote to Strachey: 'it has one of the Vice-presidents of the League at the head of it and I am anxious to support it as far as possible.'[1] Strachey had no such illusions and would not 'trust to Asquith to maintain the true Liberal or Whig position. Unless I am mistaken, he has been got hold of by the Lloyd George and Winston people with their Socialistic schemes.'[2] Under Asquith, as Strachey feared, the promotion of Lloyd George and Churchill gave government policy a sharp turn to the left. Part of this was the result of financial pressure. Asquith, who thought that he had made provision for old-age pensions, finally introduced in his budget of 1908,[3] had miscalculated both arithmetically and politically, and by the time of Lloyd George's first budget in 1909 considerable sums were needed to cover the deficit, and this in turn needed new sources of revenue. But Strachey was also correct in regarding Lloyd George and Churchill as committed collectivists. By the end of 1908, Churchill was urging on Asquith the merits of a policy of 'Social Organisation' for reasons which had nothing to do with the exigencies of finance, and wanted to 'thrust a big slice of Bismarckianism over the whole underside of our industrial system'.[4]

The Unionist free traders thus remained alive to the difficulties of their central position. The slackening of Confederate activity gave them time for reflection but as they licked their wounds no new solutions sprang to mind. During the year some toyed again with the idea of independent candidates. Oliver made overtures to Strachey with a view to his standing in NW Manchester but Strachey was unwilling even though he still felt 'very strongly that the Uft. party ought to run candidates of their own'.[5] Elliot had also been invited to stand, and Brunker had by this time secured some seven or eight Unionist free traders prepared to stand independently.[6] The problem was what to do with them in view of recent Liberal policies. 'Under ordinary circumstances', Cromer told Elliot, 'I should have been glad to see you stand for N. W. Manchester . . . But . . . the old age pensions business has introduced an entirely new element into the situation. We can still fight Protection and Colonial Preference but it seems to me that free trade . . . is in the process of being killed dead by Free Traders.'[7] Elliot did not entirely accept this criticism of Liberal policy but he too recognized that the divisions within the Club upon the attitude to be taken to the two major parties precluded action as a Club.[8]

It had taken a long time and all the experience of their impotence in the spring for the Unionist free traders to learn that independent action was not practicable. The effect was to bring home acutely the dilemma of choice between the two major parties which the delusion of independent strength had hitherto masked. At the end of 1908, therefore, in view of the difficulties the Club faced in determining a collective policy, and in view of the prospect of a general election within the next year, Cromer circulated a memorandum on the position of the Club as he saw it and invited comments. Cromer's analysis of the situation was not strikingly original in that he identified the main cause of Unionist free trade difficulties, and the damage to free trade itself, as the great increase in expenditure incurred by the government as a result of increased commitments to defence, of which he approved, and to old-age pensions. In the short run, Cromer himself felt that 'as a choice of evils some increase of direct is preferable to an increase of indirect taxation', despite the risk that

the investing classes will be severely hit . . . thus running counter to what is, to my mind, the dominating necessity of restoring confidence in the minds of the capitalist class.

But from the point of view of practical politics, the case is very different . . . if, as will almost certainly be the case, the Government proposes a heavy increase of direct taxation, my conviction is that a very large number of waverers will be finally converted to Tariff Reform, that the fate of the Government will be sealed and that the cause of Free Trade will receive so heavy a blow that, although it will still be possible to fight against Protection pure and simple, and also against Colonial Preference, resistance to the imposition of indirect taxes for the purpose of increasing the revenue will be well nigh hopeless . . . I regard it as almost certain that a very large number of shaky and even perhaps some rather strong Free Traders will practically combine with the Tariff Reformers rather than bear any fresh burthens in the shape of direct taxation . . .

The Liberal Free Traders appear to me to forget that Free Trade does not consist merely in throwing our ports open to foreign imports. It is a whole economic system, of which the freedom from taxation of foreign imports constitutes, indeed, a very important part, but which also comprises many other principles none of which can be violated without, in a greater or lesser degree, undermining the foundations of the whole edifice.

Cromer stressed that free trade was the only point of contact between the Unionist free traders and the Liberals, and that they differed on the Lords and Ireland as well as on 'State Socialism', although on this last subject 'it is an open question from which quarter the greatest danger is to be apprehended—the Liberals or the Tariff Reformers'. Because of these differences, however, he concluded by advising Unionist free traders 'on no account to vote for a Liberal candidate at the next General Election', advice which he proposed to announce publicly at a general meeting of the Club. Although intended only to elicit opinions, Cromer threatened to resign if the views contained in his memorandum were not accepted.[9]

His assessment of the situation in which the Unionist free traders found themselves was hardly disputed by the members of the Club whom he contacted. The dilemma was real enough and had been foreseen for nearly two years. But only Strachey and Leonard Darwin agreed, even in general terms, with the suggestion that Unionist free traders should consequently support Unionist candidates in a general election. From all the others, the opinion was that it was impossible for the Club, as a Club, to act collectively because the result would be disintegration. The best that could be done was to allow individuals to judge circumstances and candidates and vote accordingly. Hugh Cecil went so far as to question the utility of the Club itself and justified its continued existence only on the dubious grounds 'that it may become more serviceable in the future; and whatever may be thought about the usefulness of its life, there can be no doubt that its death would be highly mischievous'. In effect, as Elliot had argued in the middle of the year, internal disagreement was so great that the Club was paralyzed.

As the political situation developed into a confrontation between the two major parties along party lines over the question of taxation, this paralysis was bound to deepen. For the time being, the Unionist free traders were still prepared to wait and see. But they realized also that the next budget could mark the end of this temporizing and force them to make the awful choice of evils which they had struggled to avoid. 'I am quite clear', Cromer concluded from the replies to his memorandum, 'that for the moment we had better—as a Club—do nothing . . . it is not at all certain that after the next Budget the moment to speak out will not have arrived . . . I confess I think that there are unanswerable objections to continuing this negative attitude right up to the next General Election.'[10]

But the Unionist free traders could not, like the Liberal League, fall back comfortably upon inaction. With the beginning of 1909 the tariff reformers launched their fiercest attack to that date in another attempt to unite the party upon the Birmingham policy before the election took place. The attack began with the publication in the *Morning Post* of 18 January of a black list of M.P.s hostile to, or suspected of being hostile to, the official programme, although signs that something was afoot were apparent in an earlier article on 'The Confederacy' in the *National Review*.[11] In reality, both articles appear to have been aimed at intimidation rather than a purge pure and simple as had been the intention in 1908. Negotiations between Goulding and Law on the one hand and Cecil and Bowles on the other, for settlements in the key constituencies of East Marylebone and Norwood, had been going on before the publication of the *Morning Post* article and continued after it. At the same time Croft and Abel Smith were attempting to reach a similar compromise in East Herts. on what Smith considered acceptable terms.[12] But both sets of negotiations collapsed and the Unionist free traders had to consider the threats of the *Morning Post* at their face value and defend themselves as best they could. No help, as they knew, could be expected from the official Unionist leadership. In November 1908 Hood had reaffirmed the Central Office's attitude in even harsher terms:

The situation is this—the leader of the Party states his adherence to a certain policy in which he is keenly supported by the great majority of the Party— You and your friends do not agree with that policy—what you ask is that the Leader of the Party is to denounce by name in public those who accept his policy and are doing their utmost to support him in order to shield those who refuse to accept his policy.[13]

'Third' candidates seemed to be the most practical alternative if the Unionist free traders were to survive. Lord Robert Cecil called an emergency meeting of the Executive of the U.F.T.C. on 21 January when there was, according to Brunker, general agreement even from the 'Conservative' element that they would have to fight. A full meeting of the Club was called for 13 February. The Executive meeting also agreed to make overtures to the official Liberals to seek a free run against tariff reformers with Liberal support. Brunker was assured by Wallace Carter of the Free Trade Union that the F.T.U. would support this, and that the Liberal whips would discourage local Liberal associations from running candidates against Unionist free traders. Lord Robert Cecil was to write to Asquith for confirmation of this assurance[14] and the Unionist free traders set about raising a campaign fund of their own.[15] There were the usual problems about independent action. Some of the 'Conservatives' still had doubts about fighting too strongly against their own (former) party. Cromer, despite writing to Elliot on 25 January that 'we must evidently fight'[16] still thought it 'difficult to know what to do . . . in electoral as in other matters, it is extremely difficult to adopt a combative policy and yet to fight a very little. Hence a real dilemma.'[17]

It seemed, however, that difficulties notwithstanding the Unionist free traders had finally overcome their doubts. Brunker noted that the press was, in general, hostile to the Confederacy and got in touch with all the black-listed M.P.s to meet the U.F.T.C. Committee to discuss joint action. He also thought that he had secured contributions from Salisbury and W. F. D. Smith for the campaign fund.[18] By early February some progress had been made in regard to candidates and constituencies, when Brunker reported that Abel Smith had been rejected by his constituency association but that both he and Bowles had hopes that the Liberals would give them a clear run; that Cross was standing in Glasgow where the Liberal had withdrawn; that Lambton had Labour as well as tariff reform opposition but had secured the support of the local Liberals; that Lord Robert Cecil was still fighting against rejection; that Lord Hugh Cecil was secretly intriguing for the official nomination for Oxford University; that an independent candidate had been secured for Norwich; that plans to oppose Law in Dulwich were progressing well; that there were hopes of getting free runs from the Liberals in some seats in Lancashire and Scotland; and that Broadhurst was prepared to organize Manchester where the local leaders wanted a candidate, preferably Elliot, to run against Hicks. Brunker confirmed, as this breakdown suggested, that the official Liberals were sympathetic to the Unionist free traders and added that the Unionist free traders intended to run candidates in some constituencies to split the Unionist vote and let the Liberal in. 'The new position', he wrote, 'will strike you as an extraordinary bouleversement. But it is "up to us" now to fight. If only we can raise the standard and get the support we have long believed to exist in the country, we may get a nucleus in Parliament which will turn the tide.' The main difficulty was credibility after so many years of inaction, but Brunker believed that if a few thousand pounds were promised to the fund all would be well, and a surprise announcement of this would create an impact and remove doubts.[19]

Many of the hopes Brunker expressed were indeed fulfilled. Co-operation with the Liberals, in the F.T.U. if not in the whips' office, appeared to be working, although some heart-searching was caused by the F.T.U. demand that the Unionist free traders appear at their 'non-party' meetings.[20] Lambton was not rejected by his constituency association and 'quite routed the Confederates', although he felt this situation would not last;[21] Lord Salisbury came up with £500,[22] and W. F. D. Smith was 'very much inclined' to assist.[23] On 23 February Brunker reported that the campaign fund stood at over £1,300.[24] But there were more failures than successes in the end: Claud Lambton refused to stand as a free trader;[25] Percy Thornton wrote to say he was retiring from Parliament;[26] H. S. King, while prepared to help in individual cases, was not prepared to help in a general campaign against tariff reformers;[27] in Manchester, Broadhurst found there was no chance of a free run in the North-west constituency, or in any other Manchester constituency, after all,[28] and 'was plainly funking the prospect of any fighting and very doubtful if his Manchester Free Trade friends would rise to it'.[29]

But worst of all, many of the M.P.s black-listed by the *Morning Post* took the first available opportunity to explain their position in loyalist terms and some expressed their adherence to the Birmingham programme without qualifications.[30] As Col. Robert Williams explained, he would rather resign than split the party if opposed by a tariff reformer because 'it is much more important to keep out a Radical . . .'[31] This was what the Confederates really wanted—to browbeat the majority of the laggards on tariff reform into public acceptance of the party policy, and to isolate the hard core who might then be fought when the occasion arose. Thus although local difficulties continued, especially in Norwood, East Herts., and Marylebone, the all-out onslaught apparently foreshadowed in the whole-hogger press in January never occurred. Late in February Brunker even had to inquire if anything yet had happened since the attacks on Bowles and Smith seemed to 'hang fire'.[32]

Independent action by the Unionist free traders thus seemed to have neither the support to be successful nor to be justified by circumstances, and the agitation died away with the attacks which had produced it. The idea of independent candidates was still voiced from time to time. Notice was given of a resolution at the general meeting of the Club that tariff reform seats should be attacked in retaliation for attacks on Unionist free trade seats,[33] and Balfour of Burleigh thought 'we may have to consider . . . the policy of starting candidates of our own whenever we are strong enough . . .',[34] but he was out of touch and could not attend the meeting. Elliot, and one or two of the more 'Liberal' members, were always in favour of such schemes. But such occasions were rare and the Club never regained the unity of purpose that it found in January and February. In June, Cromer wanted to let reporters attend the U.F.T.C. meeting to 'enable all Tariff Reformers to see that some of our more ardent spirits are for adopting an aggressive policy and that they are being kept in hand more or less by the leaders'.[35] The old pattern of division and paralysis had reasserted itself.

Any hope of united action was totally destroyed by the budget of 1909. The Unionist free traders had expected for some time that the Liberals would find the money to pay for their 'extravagance' in 'predatory taxation', and Lloyd George's budget came as no surprise. Nevertheless, it confronted them squarely with the dilemma upon which they had been impaled for the past two years: 'we have to choose between proposals of this nature and Tariff Reform. This, from our point of view is really the crux of the whole situation.'[36] In deciding their future policy the Unionist free traders were divided along familiar lines by the budget. On the 'Conservative' side Beach unequivocally preferred tariff reform, and advised his son 'to give his assent to the definition of it laid down by Balfour'.[37] Lord Robert Cecil, despite the continuation of Confederate attacks, objected to Unionist free trade participation in 'non-party' free trade meetings and thought the less said about Unionist free trade electioneering the better. Cromer similarly wished to avoid fighting the Unionist party in view of the changed situation, 'for the more I see of the political situation, the more I am inclined to think that Free Trade versus Protection is falling into the background and that the real fight before long will be Socialist versus anti-Socialist'.[38]

At the annual meeting of the U.F.T.C. on 22 June, Cromer carried out the policy foreshadowed in his memorandum and attacked the government's financial policy.[39] But not all Unionist free trade reaction to the budget was as hostile as that of the 'Conservative' wing, and Cromer's attempts to identify the Club with opposition to the government threatened to tear it apart. Disgruntled 'Liberal' free traders complained that Cromer had gone too far, introduced issues foreign to the main purpose of the Club, and threatened to resign if he continued in this way.[40] Elliot disagreed both with his policy and with his assessment of the current issues in politics:

The difference between the two parties is not between supporting and attacking Socialism; and I doubt whether it will become so quite yet . . . After the general election there will be a new situation, and I am sure that if the Club disperses very many amongst them would prefer to join E. Grey and other moderate Liberals rather than fling in their lot with any Protectionist party.[41]

Cromer, however, pointed out the critical weakness in Elliot's desire for independent action, that there would be a rupture of the Club:

In fact the real issue which, if it is not decided now, will have to be decided before long, is whether it is worth while to keep the Club going at all . . . The moment may, and very probably will, come when the various individual members of the Club will have to decide, each for himself, not so much on the question of Free Trade versus Tariff Reform, as on the relative importance of Free Trade as compared to other subjects.[42]

Either way the members of the Club would have to choose. 'To put it briefly,' as Balfour of Burleigh had written in January using the same metaphor as Rosebery in framing the League's choice in the previous year, 'we are between the Devil and the Deep Sea. Shall we go to the Devil of Protection with our friends, or the Deep Sea of Socialism with our political adversaries?'[43]

Until the end of 1907 the fiscal controversy had been relatively

uncluttered by the demands of other conflicting principles, and individual free traders determined their actions according to the pressures
of party loyalty, their tactics by their impression of Balfour. But during
1908 other questions arose which were to the Unionist free traders as
much questions of principle as the defence of free trade. The choice the
Unionist free traders had to make, although they were only dimly aware
of it until Lloyd George's budget made decision imperative, was no
longer between principle and party, or between different tactics
designed to defend a single principle, but one of priorities between
principles which could not be jointly defended in the existing political
system. They could not prevent single-chamber government, socialism,
Home Rule, and protection but had to decide which was the lesser evil.
Such a decision was never devoid of tactical considerations, since the
proximity or ₁remoteness of the evil feared was as important as its
degree of wickedness. In making their choices, individual free traders
had to assess not merely their political priorities and the degree to which
these were respectively threatened by the policies of the major parties,
but the probable outcome of the next election. 'For myself,' wrote
Strachey, 'I have three political enmities—Home Rule, Protection and
Socialism—and I mean to fight the one which is the greatest danger of
the moment. To my mind, at the moment Socialism is the greatest
danger.'[44] Lord Hugh Cecil reached the same conclusion: 'to vote for
tariff reform is better than voting for . . . the Budget', both because the
budget was in itself a greater evil than tariff reform and because the
danger from it was more immediate. 'The case therefore of the Unionist
free traders is not that they are between the devil and the deep sea, but
between the devil who is very close and a sea which is shallow and
remote.'[45]

Strachey apart, the superimposition of the constitutional upon the
fiscal controversy did not significantly alter the already existing
alignments within the U.F.T.C. The direction of Liberal policies
towards socialism had already raised the subject in another guise, for
attacks by Liberals upon the Lords since 1907 had usually been associated with their socialist intentions. By the same reasoning, the Lords
were the last bulwark of private property. The conflict over the powers
of the House of Lords, which dominated politics once the Lords had
decided to reject the budget in the autumn of 1909, was as much a social
as a constitutional conflict. The question of rejection did however place
even greater pressure upon the anti-socialist, anti-Liberal section of the

Unionist free traders, many of whom had doubts about the wisdom of such action, if only on tactical grounds.[46] But although it was, as Cromer thought, unwise, and although a vote against the budget implied a vote for tariff reform and a 'serious constitutional gamble' with great risks of losing, the alternative was 'to put ourselves on the wrong side at the outset of the great fight between Socialism and private property— for that is what it will come to'.[47] Cromer proposed to do the best he could to avoid rejection, but 'if it comes, I shall vote with Lansdowne and speak on his behalf. The question will have passed beyond the Free Trade versus Tariff Reform issue. It will be Socialism against anti-Socialism and the government by one Chamber against the two Chamber system.'[48]

The rejection of the budget shattered the precarious unity which the U.F.T.C. had hitherto preserved by inactivity. Cromer and Elliot agreed that rejection was inadvisable, but Elliot persisted in his belief that tariff reform remained the greater and the more immediate threat, and thus continued to oppose the official Unionist party which Cromer supported.[49] 'We are', wrote Brunker, 'paralysed by the Budget. How long the Club will continue to exist is another matter . . .'[50] This was the general feeling among Club members. In Manchester Tootal Broadhurst, although he agreed with Cecil in supporting the Unionist candidate, Hicks, at the next election, took refuge in inaction.[51] 'I am afraid', thought Cromer, 'that it will be difficult, if not impossible to keep the Club together much longer . . .'[52] But the same general feeling was also in favour of continuing the existence of the Club despite its divisions. Caught in a situation where any choice between the two major parties involved the betrayal of lifelong principles in one direction or another, the Unionist free traders found hope of a kind, as they had before, in the prospect of some new central coalition emerging after the election. Elliot, Cromer, and Lord Hugh Cecil, despite their differences, all believed that there might soon be a 'rearrangement of parties' and that the Club would then serve as the nucleus of a moderate centre party 'in the very general muddle of parties and politics that may be before us'.[53]

Such hopes were based partly on the hostile reaction of Rosebery and the Liberal League to the budget, partly on the belief that the cabinet itself was deeply divided particularly on the land taxes.[54] Rosebery, in theory, condemned the budget outright as 'essentially and exclusively socialist, and calculated to bleed the House of Lords to death without replacing it',[55] and with such statements before them the Unionist free traders believed that 'there are still plenty of people in the Liberal party who hate Jacobinism . . .'[56] even if they were somewhat timid. There was some foundation for their opinion. Monkbretton, for example, had some hopes that a Unionist free trade association in the City 'even if only a dozen . . . may develop into something later' because of Liberal opposition to the budget,[57] and Brunker noted that Sir Felix Schuster was 'violently opposed' to the budget.[58] From the Liberal League Perks and Tennant set about organizing a dinner to Rosebery which Rosebery agreed to attend, and invited Unionist free trade co-operation in this anti-budget demonstration. Cromer declined, but advised Perks and Tennant to continue and to organize the discontented Liberals.[59] There were signs also of cross-party organization in the raising of a fund to allow Harold Cox, the one Liberal for whom Cromer was prepared to make an exception, to stand as an anti-budget Liberal at Preston.[60]

But the League, like the U.F.T.C., was too much divided by the dilemma posed by the budget to take effective collective action. At a special meeting of the League Executive Committee in June 'the prevailing feeling was that a decision taken at that meeting would be a huge mistake'. Rosebery urged the League to seek a fresh foundation in opposition to socialism and in the support of a second chamber,[61] but few of those present agreed that the budget was socialistic, and 'More than one speaker commented upon the disappointment caused by Lord Rosebery's attitude.' As a result, Paulton felt that it would 'not be advisable to call the further meeting until the Land Clauses of the budget have been disposed of in the House of Commons' and disallowed three resolutions from Agar-Robartes urging a firm stand against these clauses because the ensuing discussion would have shattered the League as the U.F.T.C. had been shattered.[62] 'It makes me wonder', Perks commented after the meeting, 'what use the League can be. I think you were right and I was wrong when I urged the continued existence of the League . . .'[63]

Much still turned on the role that Rosebery was prepared to play in opposing the budget. If he was willing to lead, some of the League waverers might rally to him, but they, like Elliot, had begun to doubt whether Rosebery would ever again take effective political action. Encouragement for him to come forward came from outside as well as inside the League. Lord Wemyss, President of the oldest of the many anti-socialist bodies, the Liberty and Property Defence League, urged Rosebery to come out against collectivism from either the right or the left. 'All we want', wrote Wemyss, 'is to be left alone—and . . . that we should be safe in the possession of our property . . . At present there is no resistance anywhere, on principle, on either side of politics to *Socialist* proposals . . . The so-called Conservatives plant the seedlings that the Labour Socialists falsely called Liberals manure and propagate.'[64] Lansdowne also sought Rosebery's support[65] and Lord Hugh Cecil aired the hope that the King would refuse to dissolve upon the rejection of the budget and call instead upon Rosebery to form a central ministry.[66] Rosebery, however, was uncertain of his political future,[67] and did nothing to assist the development of the central position which he was urged to lead. Without him the League was paralysed by its disunity, and sought refuge like the U.F.T.C. in doing nothing but maintaining its existence to watch future developments. At the October meeting there was still a majority in favour of keeping up the League in the belief 'that within the next year or two there will be an imperative call for some organisation to rally Central independent opinion against Lloyd Georgism', and the League should be kept as a nucleus for this.[68]

In the heat of the election campaign, however, the divisions within both moderate organizations widened to the point where it seemed unlikely that either would remain in existence, still less become the nucleus of a larger movement. Cromer, Strachey, and Lord Hugh Cecil all publicly urged 'in the strongest possible terms that the Unionist free traders should rally to their party at the general election and vote for tariff reformers on the principle of the lesser evil'.[69] But whilst Strachey bent the editorials of the *Spectator* to this end, Elliot, Hobhouse, and others used its correspondence columns in the opposite sense to advise support for the Liberals.[70] Lord Hugh Cecil thought them 'quite mad'.[71] The split was complete.

Nevertheless, the Unionist free traders felt some satisfaction out of the deadlock between the two major parties produced by the election of January 1910. Strachey thought that

both the things I hate, the Liberal policy since the plunge into old age pensions extravagance . . . and also the policy of taxing people highly not because they are rich but because they own a particular form of property, and Tariff Reform, have had a knock. I take the situation to be that the teeth and claws of the Liberal tiger have been cut and that the Liberal party have been

rendered incapable of doing much harm, while at the same time Tariff Reform
has been defeated. This suits me to a 'T' and I threw up my hat . . .[72]

In this situation the question of a centre party was once again canvassed
on the basis of submitting tariff reform to a royal commission. The
initiative was taken by Cox and Strachey[73] with the support of Cromer[74]
and Lord Hugh Cecil,[75] and the scheme was based upon the co-
operation of, and possibly amalgamation with, the Liberal League.
Added stimulus was given by Redmond's declaration that the Irish
wanted guarantees that the powers of the Lords would be dealt with
as a prelude to the introduction of a Home Rule Bill before they would
support the budget. In their rejoicing at the drawn election the Unionist
free traders had forgotten that one consequence of this would be
renewed dependence of the government upon the Irish party. This, as
Cromer noted, introduced 'a new and very important element into the
political situation . . . It rather points in the direction of the formation
of a Central Party being forced upon everybody by the necessities of
the situation.' But, he added ominously, 'events will have to develop
a good deal further before the matter can be considered'.[76] It rapidly
became clear that in practice the U.F.T.C. no longer retained sufficient identity to hold itself together. The 'Liberal' wing of the Club
no longer had any sympathy with the 'Conservative' wing or even
with the 'moderate Liberals'. 'The only question', thought the 'Liberal'
Pollock, 'about the Unionist Free Trade Club, to my mind, is what kind
of funeral we are to order.'[77]

Nor were the 'Conservatives' prepared, at this critical juncture, to
take upon themselves the burden of associating with a new central
party. Their free trade views Cromer declared, were as fervent as
ever, but

from the moment when the present government incurred a huge expenditure
for old age pensions and at the same time took off the sugar duties . . . the
imposition of indirect taxes for revenue purposes was almost inevitable . . . if
we do not put forward the Free Trade argument very strongly just at the
present moment, it is because we think that the dominating issue is the
question of the future and composition of the Second Chamber. If once
the Second Chamber is remodelled in the sense apparently intended by the
Radical party, not only shall we have Home Rule . . . but also the last bastion
against Socialism will be broken down.[78]

In these days of priorities they were therefore prepared to campaign in harness with the tariff reform enemy 'and if they chose to put a 1/- or even a 2/- duty on corn, and promised to go no further than that, I should be inclined, albeit reluctantly, to support them in order to save the country from the greater dangers of letting the extreme socialists in'.[79] The 'Conservative' free traders thus yielded the last and most precious citadel of free trade, opposition to food taxes.

The Unionist free traders in 1910 finally decided to go their separate ways because 'the divisions between the two wings of the Club— Conservative and Radical—are so great as to paralyse any action',[80] and the Executive decided, at its meeting on 22 February, that the Club should dissolve. 'The differences of opinion within the Club', ran the circular announcing the Committee's decision to the members, 'are solely due to the relative importance which individual members attach to free trade as compared with other questions which, since the formation of the Club, have been forced to the forefront of political controversy.' Both groups then set about organizing their supporters into new free trade bodies. The 'Conservatives', Darwin, Cromer, and Hamilton, founded a Constitutional Free Trade Association to keep together those free traders who regarded the Lords issue, the Union, and Socialism as of greater urgency than free trade itself, and who would therefore support the Unionist party despite fiscal differences.[81] The 'Liberals' responded with a circular of 16 March declaring that the immediate issue was free trade against protection as it always had been, that this 'ought not to be left dependent on the results of Parliamentary struggles on constitutional and other questions', and advocated membership of the Free Trade Union.[82]

By default the initiative for the formation of a central party devolved upon secondary institutions, such as the British Constitutional Association, which began negotiations with the Middle Classes Defence Organisation with a view to amalgamation to form the Centre Party Union.[83] Cromer was not enthusiastic about the chances of success, and did not 'believe in the formation of a Centre Party, if by that term is implied a party standing outside the existing parties of the State . . .'[84] Nevertheless he still wanted 'to work up to this result' and therefore sent in his subscription.[85] Prospects again seemed initially good. Onslow, inquiring if Strachey was connected with Cromer in promoting a 'league of moderate men', noted that he had 'been approached by one or two Liberals (one an ex-minister) supporting the formation of such a League',[86] and Cox had been from the first in touch with

Rosebery and his 'moderate Liberals'.[87] He found the League in its usual state of confusion. In February the Executive Committee meeting was postponed, but Perks at least still knew of a body of opinion in favour of continued existence.[88] A meeting early in March decided to seek the advice of the vice-presidents, and Perks reported that 'a motion to end the League, if proposed today, would have been lost by about 12 to 8'.[89] The advice the deputation—of Maude, Napier, Freeman-Thomas, and Perks—received from the vice-presidents was also encouraging for the advocates of a centre party. Offering the vice-presidents three courses of action, to dissolve, to mark time, or to strengthen the League 'by trying to rally round it the moderate men of Liberalism and use the League as a rampart against Socialism and against Home Rule, but especially in favour of a reformed and efficient Second Chamber', Perks found both Haldane and Grey fearful of a split within the government over the House of Lords and therefore desirous of a strengthened League.[90] In April therefore, negotiations opened between the League and Cromer and Cox to investigate the question of amalgamating the various 'moderate' organizations,[91] and even Rosebery seemed momentarily interested.[92] But their meeting was unproductive. 'It is clear', Rosebery reported to Strachey, 'that there is no likelihood of amalgamation between the three bodies as I had hoped and therefore the whole question falls to the ground.'[93] At the end of April, with no more avenues left to explore, its funds exhausted, and its members apathetic, the Liberal League dissolved.[94]

The polarization of politics caused by the budget destroyed not only the central organizations, the U.F.T.C. and the Liberal League, but the central position itself. The C.P.U. briefly continued to press on. Cox was 'in hope of getting into touch with the various Ratepayers Defence Associations throughout the Kingdom. They might form a useful nucleus in each town',[95] and attempts were made in May to extend the C.P.U.'s activities.[96] But traditional party loyalties, particularly at this crisis point, damaged the C.P.U. as they had damaged the U.F.T.C. and the League. Thus Cromer thought there were 'a large number of people who would, I think, be quite prepared to help in organising the moderate vote but who would not care about joining this particular union . . . for it will be regarded by moderate Unionists, and perhaps also to some extent by moderate Liberals as an invitation to leave their own parties altogether . . . This most of them would not be prepared to do.'[97] Perks, while donating money, had no intention of committing himself to further lost causes.[98] Instead, the 'moderates', at least at the parliamentary level, tended to withdraw altogether.

Driven on by events, the 'moderates' found no time to organize themselves or their thoughts before they were forced to make the unpleasant but crucial choice between the two major parties. It was not until their dilemma was forced upon them that they fully realized their exposed position. Then also they realized the missed opportunities of 1908 when they had correctly anticipated the problem they would have to face unless they secured a base independent of existing party alignments.[99]

9

Construction

For the same reasons as it caused discomfiture to the U.F.T.C. and the League, the 'extravagance' of the government played into the hands of the tariff reformers. 'Extravagance' could not be avoided, and the political conflict increasingly appeared as a struggle between alternative forms of collectivism, rather then between collectivism and individualism. The tariff reform answer to Liberal collectivism was not opposition, but extension:

Asquith has *already* introduced old age pensions . . . he has put money by for them by his last Budget . . . we are precipitately but irrevocably committed . . . a universal scheme is now the only alternative to such a partial plan as the ministerial project which simply subsidises one part of the people out of the pockets of another part. The middle classes must be brought in. Whoever contributes to old age pensions must be entitled to draw them.[1]

As political attitudes polarized around the means by which such measures could be financed, so the grip which the tariff reformers had gained upon the Unionist party during 1907 strengthened. 'Tariff Reform', Winterton told Joseph Chamberlain early in 1908, 'is very much the fashion just at present in the most orthodox party circles. It is amusing (though one has to keep one's amusement to oneself) to see how eager are those who two years ago were the most doubtful of Balfourites, to proclaim their belief today in the "whole hog" policy . . .'[2] The continued economic depression, while increasing the financial difficulties of the government,[3] also assisted tariff reformers as falling trade levels and rising unemployment apparently bore out their criticisms of the free trade system. 'Unemployment', declared Law, 'is the question of the hour.' Tariff reformers had been waiting for just such a fall off in trade to 'force the evils of the present system to the notice of the working classes'.[4]

But although the tariff reform solution to unemployment formed the basis of tariff reform propaganda in *Monthly Notes* and in public speeches, the movement's parliamentary leaders found some difficulty in raising the topic in the House, and incurred severe criticism from their impatient followers as a result.[5] The Labour party had moved in and virtually pre-empted the field, so that any tariff reform action on the subject involved co-operation with those whom they were more frequently condemning as dangerous socialists. Early in 1908, Ramsay MacDonald's amendment to the Address criticizing the government for its failure to deal with unemployment confronted the Unionists with this tactical problem. As an issue upon which there was an open rift between the Labour and Liberal parties, the debate offered an opportunity to damage, and possibly even to defeat, the government, since the amendment was lost by only 49 votes whilst the bulk of the Unionist party, following the front-bench lead, abstained. Tariff reform enthusiasts, as represented by the *Morning Post* and the *National Review*,[6] condemned this course, and some 30 Unionists voted with the Labour party. But the Unionist front bench had abstained from 'definite and deliberate' policy, in order to avoid public association with the Labour party and Socialism,[7] and this was to be the pattern of the future.

In March, confronted with a Labour party 'Unemployment Bill, the principal clause of which embodied the right to work . . .', the Unionists again 'of course . . . supported the Government'.[8] In the autumn, the problem arose again when the Speaker gave precedence to a Labour amendment on unemployment, and again the effect upon the Unionist party was divisive. 'I think it was possible', Collings wrote to Joseph Chamberlain afterwards, 'for the Unionist party to have put down an amendment . . . which would have raised the question of tariff reform . . . As it was, I voted all through with the Labour party.'[9] Something of the frustration which these tactical difficulties created can be gauged from the force with which Austen Chamberlain insisted upon a tariff reform unemployment amendment in February 1909, over the heads of his fellow tariff reformers in the shadow cabinet, Chaplin and Arnold-Forster, in order to forestall the Labour party. Hewins appears to have been instrumental in converting Balfour to this line of attack, and Austen Chamberlain got his way, although, once again, 'the pitch is a little queered by a Labour amendment which has got precedence'.[10]

Chamberlain's frustration was wholly justified. Unemployment was an issue upon which the tariff reformers had campaigned from the first. It was by far the most important of Joseph Chamberlain's related social reform proposals that he had urged in his tariff reform crusade between 1903 and 1906, and was the one constructive domestic proposal upon which harmony could easily be achieved with Balfour since it involved no further legislation beyond the tariff itself, and no special financing. Moreover, the tariff reform case for protection of this kind was easily defensible, with a nationalist as well as an economic appeal.[11]

The stumbling block of Unionism, radical or conservative, throughout the Edwardian period was its relationship with organized labour, as distinct from the various vague appeals to 'the working classes' or Tory Democracy. Nevertheless, by treading cautiously after 1906, and particularly by dodging the issues raised by the Trades Disputes Act, the Unionist party had hitherto avoided any direct confrontation with organized labour. But socialism and the existence of the Labour party prevented the tariff reformers from capitalizing on the unemployment question as they might otherwise have done. By the time unemployment had emerged as the critical question with the onset of a depression, politics had polarized too far for the Unionist party to seek an accommodation with the Labour party. The alternative was to oppose organized labour, as in March 1908, when the Unionists supported the government, or abstention as a compromise accepting the fact that abstention might appear feeble in a party which was on most other occasions proclaiming that it had a solution for unemployment and the government had not.

The rise in unemployment during 1908 was thus not only an opportunity for the whole-hoggers, but also a test of their attitude to organized labour. Their unwillingness to associate with the Labour party, despite a certain identity of interests both in theory and in practice, bode ill for the 'constructive policy' which at some time would have to develop a coherent labour policy in greater detail than the simple imposition of tariffs. Nevertheless, in 1908 the Unionists still believed that unemployment and the depression were working to their advantage. Law declared that unemployment had been the decisive issue at the Newcastle by-election, and would have a decisive influence on all future by-elections. A run of by-election successes during the year[12] appeared to bear out this analysis, and naturally confirmed tariff reformers in their belief in constructive politics and in the hold their policy had over the party.

Given the difficulties of the government, the despondency of its supporters, and the gradual acceptance of tariff reform in preference to socialism by the Unionist free traders, the whole-hoggers had reason for satisfaction. But such developments brought comfort to the general body of the party. There was nothing specifically to please the whole-hoggers who, despite the appearance of capturing the Unionist party, were really being absorbed into the Balfourite morass. The programme which they and the Unionist party accepted was Balfour's Birmingham programme, and whatever that programme might foreshadow in the way of fiscal reform, if only for revenue, it said virtually nothing about the details of either a tariff or a social policy. Rather it restricted any social policy within the tight conservative limits of a commitment to free enterprise and individual initiative.

The developments sketched in Austen Chamberlain's outline of a constructive policy in October 1907 went far further, and were the beginning, not the end, of a process by which no sooner had timid Balfourites caught up with the whole-hoggers than new ideas left them behind again. Arthur Lee took up the question of a more detailed social policy at the end of October, inviting Austen Chamberlain, Milner, Garvin, and 'possibly Ridley' to dine, 'with a view to arriving at a general broad agreement as to the outline of a "programme of a constructive policy" for the Unionist party . . .' Lee expected little from Balfour at Birmingham. 'In other words there will be another "un-authorised programme" of some kind or another.'[13] At Chamberlain's suggestion, Fabian Ware, editor of the *Morning Post*, was added to the group.[14]

Almost a year later, such an 'unauthorised programme' finally appeared in the *Morning Post*:

the Unionist party should by now have gained not only a clear idea of the main principles upon which it will proceed, but also of the nature of the practical reforms to which it must first address itself . . .

The basis of all Unionist policy is Union. All national questions, whether domestic or Imperial, should be treated in relation to this fundamental principle, implying the union of classes within the State, national union of Great Britain and Ireland, Imperial union of the self-governing nations and dependencies under the Crown.

Of the questions now before the country, Tariff Reform necessarily comes first. As the only means of protecting employment, of increasing production, and of equitably providing additional revenue for national defence and social reform, it is essential to the union of classes; as the only means of redressing the fiscal and economic grievances suffered by Ireland under the existing system it is essential to the national union of Great Britain and Ireland; as the only means of meeting the proposal unanimously put forward by the self-governing Dominions for promoting closer Imperial relations, it is essential to the union of the Empire.

Tariff reform was defined as 'placing moderate duties' on all imports for revenue, and 'for safeguarding home industries', with preferential remission for the colonies. 'Generally speaking, the amount of the duty should vary with the value in the article imported of the labour which might have been employed upon it in this country', but the duties, taken as a whole, should not increase the cost of living. In the sophistication of its arguments, and in the attempt to develop a whole new theory of 'Unionism' by applying the principle of 'union' not only to Ireland, but to the whole range of Unionist policies, tariff reform had come a long way since Joseph Chamberlain's campaign of 1903. There, however, the 'unauthorised programme' tactfully stopped its discussion of tariffs, avoiding the anticipation of future revenue, and thus the sort of details which Balfour wished to avoid.

Some details of the meaning of 'Unionism' in addition to tariff reform were, however, discussed; defence, on which the programme advocated a two-power standard for the Navy and a 'citizen army' based on 'universal service'; Ireland, where 'the primary duty of the Government' was to enforce 'respect for the existing law', combined with 'some positive constructive policy of rehabilitation . . .' based upon tariff reform; the House of Lords, whose powers as a revising chamber were upheld, provided the House modified 'its own constitution in such a way as to increase its fitness to perform the onerous duties now devolving upon it'; and old-age pensions, to which more space was devoted than to any other topic, and which was described as 'the most important question now before the country . . . in the field of social reform'. The government scheme was condemned as inadequate, both because it was not universal, and because no proper provision had been made for financing it, but the tariff reformers did not, unlike the Unionist free traders, condemn the government's extravagance out of hand. Instead they proposed a rival scheme of their own, treating old-age pensions as

part of the bigger question of State insurance against the incapacity to work, from whatever cause the incapacity may arise. That question should be considered and dealt with in relation to other questions of national organisation, and it is probable that its solution will be found in a contributory system. Such a system would carry with it the incidental advantage of effecting the registration of our industrial population which is a condition essential to the solution of unemployment, and other pressing social problems. This new pension which, as in Germany, might be called the infirmity pension, would, as in that country, gradually replace the existing incomplete, illogical and arbitrary distribution of State pensions.

The similarity between these ideas and Churchill's 'slice of Bismarkianism' revealed how narrow was the gap between 'right' and 'left' wing radicalism in their common pursuit of collectivist social policies, in comparison with the gulf between the 'socialist' and 'individualist' wings of either major party. The tariff reformers also accepted the principle of Wage Boards and the minimum wage in industries 'in which voluntary and effective organisation of workers has not been found practicable'. There were, however, some distinctions which marked off the collectivist right from the collectivist left, most notably in the field of agrarian reform. The 'unauthorised programme' condemned the tenancy provisions of the Liberal Smallholdings Act of 1907 in favour of the traditional Unionist policy of occupying ownerships, created with the assistance of state credit 'on the lines of Mr Jesse Collings' Bill', with simplified land transfer, agricultural cooperation, 'state assistance in such matters as the dissemination of technical information . . . A thoroughgoing reform of local taxation, transferring existing charges to the Exchequer', and 'legislation for the proper regulation of motor traffic'. Even the 'Taxation of Land Values' as advocated by the Henry Georgite group of the Liberal party was not, as yet, condemned outright, but considered as a worthwhile experiment on urban land, 'enabling such municipalities as may see fit to assess and rate separately the value of sites and the value of dwellings'. Two currently controversial, but from the whole-hogger point of view anachronistic, subjects, education and licensing, concluded the programme.

In many ways the whole-hoggers who composed it went out of their way not to offend their more timorous associates in the Unionist party, particularly on the commitment of anticipated revenue to specific schemes of social reform. Their ideas harmonized easily with old Conservative interests on the related issues of National Service and agrarian reform, even when they saw these questions from the state-building rather than the paternalist point of view. But at other times

the programme was distinctly radical; on the taxation of land values
and in their policy for state insurance, the whole-hoggers came
dangerously close to that state socialism which they condemned in the
government and in the Labour party. Equally, the view that the only
limiting factor on a legislative minimum wage was the sufficient power
of the trade unions to look after their own was a dangerously radical
argument.[15]

But the practical difficulties confronting any constructive policy were
sufficient in themselves to ensure that these details were unimportant.
Even apart from Balfour's own aversion to programmes in opposition,
the small group which drew up this 'unauthorised programme' did not
fully agree amongst themselves, either upon the programme or upon
tactics. The original draft of the programme came from Richard Jebb,
and was considered and modified by Milner, Amery, Hills, and Ware
after lunch in the light of two long letters from Law and Austen
Chamberlain.[16] Law, apart from wishing to modify occasional details,
and to 'introduce a paragraph in favour of the cultivation of beet-
root . . .' in the section about Ireland, disagreed completely on the
wisdom of committing the party to universal service, and thought the
taxation of land values 'would be better left out altogether'.[17] The
others could not agree, and had 'conceded down to our irreducible
minimum. Lord Milner is very strong on both these points . . .'[18] Under
the circumstances, however, the tactical disagreement was more important. Law was 'very doubtful whether this is the proper time to
issue an unauthorised programme of this kind, and my personal
inclination would be against it',[19] but he was again overruled by the
others, and publication went ahead.[20]

Law's reservations were a tribute to the success with which Balfour
had begun to capture the tariff reform movement and to harness it to
his own cause, with all the loss of momentum that that entailed.
Earlier in the year, Law excused his refusal to discuss the subject of
food duties in the House of Commons to a highly critical Maxse
because he now believed 'that Balfour does mean the same thing that
we mean, and if I am right in that view, it would not be either wise or
right for me to say anything which he would disapprove of'.[21] It was a
classic example of what Maxse, from the extremist position, termed the
'sleeping sickness' which Balfour's leadership induced in even the most
enthusiastic of tariff reformers.[22]

But Balfour was in fact making some progress. Milner reported in

December that 'things are moving', and that he was, with Balfour's knowledge, to meet Austen Chamberlain, Law, and Hewins 'with a view to starting our Tariff Construction. This is very confidential.'[23] Collings told Chamberlain that at Cardiff Balfour 'spoke very well. Like a pioneer, not a convert.'[24] But Balfour remained cautious as ever, even in working out the details of a policy to which he had, in principle, committed himself. Milner's committee was designed, at least in part, to apply more pressure, for 'nothing will be done, till Balfour takes the matter himself in hand, but this committee will oblige him to do that'.[25] But if Balfour would do little for what was intended to be the first budget of the next Unionist government, he would do even less for policies to which the party was not committed and for which there was less urgency. Collings, for example, was permanently alienated by Balfour's unwillingness to press his land reform proposals. Balfour willingly accepted Collings's ideas in theory,[26] but he would not urge the subject in public as part of Unionist official policy.[27]

Unemployment and the land question were the two subjects upon which the tariff reformers most wanted to make progress with Balfour. On the former, success was easily obtained. Balfour had no difficulty in accepting Austen Chamberlain's proposed amendment in February 1909, regretting that the government had made no proposals for 'increasing the demand for labour by a reform of our fiscal system . . .', particularly since Hewins, Hood, and Sandars were all in favour of it.[28] But such a vague proposal took the constructive policy no further than Joseph Chamberlain in 1903. Progress on other aspects, especially the land question, was more difficult. Unionists were giving the subject prominence even before Lloyd George's land taxes, with particular reference to the evolution of an agricultural policy. This was a long-standing aspect of Birmingham radicalism, and Collings's special relationship with the Chamberlain family kept the subject to the fore in any discussion of the domestic side of tariff reform.

Equally important, however, was the upsurge of farming militancy which alarmed both the Liberal minister of agriculture, Carrington, and his Unionist predecessor in that office, Onslow.[29] Farmers were generally considered to be Conservative voters, and ones who might be expected to support a tariff if they regarded it, as Chaplin regarded it, as an instalment of agricultural protection. If this was not so, however, and both Balfour and Chamberlain denied protectionist intentions, then the farmers stood to lose by a programme which placed duties on manufacturing products alone. Even apart from convincing the labourers of the harmlessness of food duties, the need to win rural support on the basis of the expectations which tariff reform aroused, but which its leaders felt obliged to denounce, constituted a major difficulty in campaigning in rural areas.

The agricultural committee of the Tariff Commission proposed a 1*s*. duty on colonial corn, which the Glasgow programme had let in free, and gave to the optimistic the impression that agricultural protection was not ruled out completely, even if the initial level of this protection was at too low a level to be effective. But the real purpose behind the committee's proposal was to raise revenue which could be spent on increasing the rating relief given to agriculture and in developing the industry. Chamberlain himself, unable to exploit the protectionist argument, had based his case to agriculture on the secondary benefits to be derived from greater revenue, and the mainstream of tariff reform thinking continued along these lines. In the absence of a definite statement from Balfour as the official party leader, however, it was not enough. Balfour himself was not especially sympathetic to agriculture, believing its potential for further development to be severely limited in contrast to the 'practically unlimited' possibilities of industry, 'so that if this country is to increase its wealth and population, the increase must in the main be looked for in other regions than agriculture'.[30] He showed little sympathy with Onslow, who took his fears about the farmers to Balfour in the first instance,[31] or with Collings, despite his professions of agreement with Collings's purpose.

Austen Chamberlain showed far greater interest. Early in February, he sent Maxse 'an attempt to put Tariff Reform to an agricultural audience', with the aim of getting his ideas turned into an article 'called Tariff Reform and Agriculture', or 'an agricultural policy . . . I should say that such a thing if well done would be very useful. There has, as far as I know, been no attempt at any rate on the part of any prominent Unionist, to formulate a policy for agriculturalists in the light of the present position.'[32] Speaking at Shrewsbury, he discussed the agricultural situation at length, and was, according to Collings, following this up by pressing Balfour to include the policy of occupying owner-ship in the official party programme.[33] 'I am *very glad* you came out so strongly on the agricultural programme,' wrote Milner, 'I am sure that is right.'[34] By March, Onslow had taken his problems to Austen

Chamberlain in a memorandum containing 'Suggestions for an Agricultural Policy', which included dealing with the rating problem by taking national services off the rates and paying for them out of national taxation; giving 'greater facilities . . . for the creation of occupying ownerships by advances at a low rate of interest . . .'; using the Board of Agriculture to stimulate experiments with new crops; greater assistance to farmers in general by a small staff of peripatetic organizers especially to aid in the formation of co-operative societies and credit banks; specialist rural education; 'the provision of cottages in rural districts' to reduce rural depopulation; and special measures for the aged rural poor.

Onslow did not involve tariff reform directly, but his proposals involved considerable sums of money on rating relief, schools and teacher training, and an extensive use of state credit. As a policy it depended, as did most Unionist schemes of social reform, on a considerable increase of funds available at the national level to meet these new responsibilities.[35] Tariff reformer though he was, Austen Chamberlain, as the former Unionist Chancellor of the Exchequer, realized that this was the major difficulty. Onslow in fact envisaged the next Unionist government as having sufficient surplus revenue to be able to reduce income tax, and thus to institute 'a national rate for national services', in effect a levy on top of the income tax.[36] He was, however, driven to admit that his ideas were not within the range of practical politics.[37]

Nevertheless, both Onslow and Austen Chamberlain felt that something had to be done for agriculture. The stumbling block was Balfour. Having secured his assent to tariffs for the purpose of revenue, the tariff reformers were bent upon constructing a detailed programme of social reform, particularly agricultural reform, based upon that revenue. Balfour wanted far more information on the revenue a tariff might produce, and disliked intensely pledging the party to specific commitments which were vulnerable to Liberal attack and which the party might not be able to keep when it took office. He would not be moved from the Birmingham policy to accept any of the constructive domestic policies which the tariff reformers sought to elaborate upon that foundation.

These schemes, drawn up and debated by men who did not have the authority to make them official party policy, were thrown dramatically into the background by the budget of 1909. The budget, with Lloyd

George's land taxes, raised another aspect of the land question, the taxation of land values for which a strong and vocal body of Liberal opinion had agitated for years. To many Unionists the land taxes inaugurated the fear of the 'Single Tax' as proposed by Henry George, and thus the gradual nationalization of the land by fiscal means without compensation. Even when they did not themselves share the fears they sought to arouse, the propaganda value of the taxes was too great to be lost in the prevailing atmosphere of anti-socialism. Captain Pretyman, who organized the Land Union to lead the fight against these clauses of the budget, had 'great hopes of putting the Government in a hole over the land tax clauses . . . We want to keep the whole Budget behind that obstacle.'[38] The budget was the fulfilment of tariff reform predictions that the free trade system would collapse under the strain of finding the revenue necessary for social reform and defence, and that it was bound to lead to socialism. As such they, like the Unionist free traders, expected the tariff reform cause to profit from it by the recruitment of the frightened rich.

But there were problems in making tariff reform the first line of defence of the propertied classes, for their interests could be defended negatively against socialism, without offering an alternative source of revenue. Initially, opposition to the budget appeared to be taking this course. Whilst Balfour and Lansdowne said little in public to give a lead to the party in order to avoid committing themselves prematurely to any policy, the rich protested loudly, but without emphasizing the Unionist alternative programme. The Budget Protest League was even instructed by its President, Walter Long, to avoid the subject of tariff reform. Such tactics, however, appeared during the summer to be ineffective. Four by-elections in Cleveland, High Peak, Mid-Derby, and Dumfries Burghs recorded a swing to the Unionists of less than half of that of the previous twelve months.[39] Chamberlain attributed these set-backs to 'the fact that our friends took for their principal issue other things than those we are engaged to fight on',[40] and Ridley thought that 'Walter Long and the Budget Protest League have half spoilt a very favourable situation.'[41] The tariff reformers remained convinced that 'by far the best weapon, indeed the only effective and permanently successful weapon with which to destroy Lloyd Georgeism, is our alternative policy of Tariff Reform . . .'[42]

A striking speech by Lloyd George at Limehouse on 30 July, taking advantage of the ineptitude of the Unionists in making the controversy appear as a war between the rich and the poor, drove home the weakness of the negative approach.[43] 'N.W. Staffordshire', thought Garvin, 'shows that unless we can put fire . . . and definitive thought and real determination into a big social policy, we shall make no headway.'[44] Winterton told Maxse that a friend recently touring the Midlands and North found local Unionist leaders unanimous that they should 'choose any battleground rather than that of coronets and landowners against the Budget . . .',[45] and Onslow reported that 'the last meeting of the Central Chamber [of Agriculture] . . . couldn't carry a resolution against the Budget, so many being of the opinion that it was favourable to the rural classes'.[46] By August, the whole-hoggers were concerned lest the popularity of the budget might induce the party leadership, which still had not spoken out, to abandon the idea of rejection in the Lords.[47]

But even before this, the whole-hoggers had begun to take the initiative again. Maxse sought from Law an answer 'to Asquith's continued challenge for an "alternative Budget", as much harm has been done by giving it the go-by',[48] and Garvin's comment on NW Staffordshire was accompanied by a promise to write an article on 'Free Trade as a Socialist Policy',[49] agreeing later in the month to write a monthly fiscal article: 'henceforth there ought not to be the slightest regard to party exigencies'.[50]

A revolt, however, was unnecessary. Balfour, for reasons of his own but urged on by Garvin both privately and publicly, concluded early in August both that the budget should be rejected, and that the basis for Unionist opposition should be the alternative policy of tariff reform.[51] In August Asquith was due to speak at the Bingley Hall, Birmingham, the citadel of tariff reform, and Balfour had arranged to follow him there to state the Unionist case. Throughout the summer Balfour also had maintained close communications with Hewins, with whom he discussed the financial proposals of the budget and a tariff reform alternative.[52] Hewins provided a detailed analysis of Asquith's Bingley Hall speech, and emphasized that Asquith's argument that capital taken by taxation did not disappear but was re-employed for social reform was 'that with which I have been familiar for the last 20 years amongst what I should call extreme socialists who desire the nationalisation of the means of production. This principle admitted, further schemes of confiscation would be certain to be introduced to meet the deficit which is inevitable under the social schemes which they have introduced and are contemplating . . .' Hewins also sketched the tariff reform alternative, singling out Asquith's omission of the three 'most vital factors' in the financial situation; 'the alteration in the relative productivity of the different states of the world . . . the relative stagnation of British industry . . . [and] the continuous increase of unemployment of British working men . . .' Asquith, that is took no account of the need to increase the sources of the wealth which the government intended to 'plunder'. Hewins restated the economic necessity of tariff reform to revive Britain's agriculture and industry and to reduce unemployment, and reassured Balfour that 'so far as the technical aspects of the question are concerned . . . if a Unionist Government were returned to power, they could at once proceed to introduce a tariff which would satisfy the four conditions laid down in the Birmingham resolution . . .'[53]

Thus fortified, intellectually and politically, Balfour spoke on 22 September. The keynote of his speech, 'the keynote of the coming campaign', was the choice between tariff reform and socialism, the theme with which he began and ended. In so doing, however, he emphasized the novelty of both issues to shift the dispute away from the divisive question of protection against free trade.[54] From his point of view, a fight on the issue of tariff reform against socialism rather than tariff reform against free trade was the more desirable because it would make possible the reunification of his divided party. This was the corollary of the disintegration of the Unionist free traders. With the exception of the few 'Liberal' Unionist free traders headed by Elliot, Balfour was able to lead a united party into the general election of January 1910, a party, moreover, united behind tariff reform, if only as the lesser of two evils. The Balfourites expected the development and welcomed it. 'I said', wrote Sandars, 'that the two wings of the party are bound to come together as soon as Joe leaves us. When the public issue is Socialism—as it will be—the division of our forces will be without meaning.'[55]

The tariff reformers were naturally exultant at the Bingley Hall speech. Balfour did not commit the party completely to the rejection of the budget by the Lords, but the tone of the meeting made it clear that this was his intention. After the Bingley Hall speech it was generally and correctly assumed that the Lords would reject the budget, and that an election would follow. The Lords did so on 30 November. The Unionists, whole-hoggers included, had the election they had sought since 1906.

The decision to reject the budget and to fight on the platform of tariff reform against socialism marked the final stage in the transformation of tariff reform from an imperial to a domestic policy. It had always been a defensive policy, but Chamberlain had advocated tariff reform to preserve and develop the integrity of the Empire against foreign rivals. Under Balfour's leadership from 1907 onwards, it had become no more than another means to raise revenue, the last line of defence of the propertied classes against higher direct taxation. However much they deceived themselves by their enthusiasm for the opportunity to destroy the government and install a Unionist ministry committed to tariff reform—and the whole-hoggers did deceive themselves—it was this domestic role that tariff reform performed in the general election of January 1910.

Theoretically there were two clear and distinct major issues in the election of January 1910: the constitutional question raised by the rejection by the House of Lords of a Finance Bill passed in the Commons, and the alternative methods of increased direct or indirect taxation as the means to raise revenue for national services. The first, clearly, was a Liberal issue which the Unionists sought to play down. But if one of the major 'Liberal strategic considerations ... was ... to bring home the gravity and paramount importance of the constitutional issue',[56] this was done not by arid lectures on constitutional law, but by pillorying the Lords as an intolerable hereditary chamber and as selfish affluent parasites. There were indeed constitutional authorities prepared to defend the legitimacy of the Lords' action in rejecting the budget. It was the socio-economic position of the Lords, not their constitutional function, which made them vulnerable. Their public image had been undermined by decades of radical criticism on these grounds, and the violent reaction of the injured interests to the introduction of the budget, and the peers' performance in the fiscal debates in the Lords, did nothing to restore the balance.[57] 'People talk', declared Northumberland, 'as if Dukes eat banknotes, and as if by changing our diet to bread and butter, we should have banknotes at disposal.'[58] From attacking the Lords on these lines it was a short step to the condemnation of tariff reform for its defence of vested interests, undermining its alleged democratic appeal on economic and social questions;[59] in effect, to outflank Balfour, return the debate to that between free trade and protection, and damn protection as before as a class policy. In this there was the danger, as some of the more astute tariff reformers saw, that 'the popularity of Tariff Reform itself will suffer . . . whatever we may say now, the fight in the minds of 9 out of 10 working men will be . . . "Coronets and landowners against the people's Budget" '.[60]

Efforts by tariff reformers to keep tariff reform distinct from the Lords question could not prevent the policy from being seen for the class policy that it was. However much tariff reform was advocated on other grounds, imperial unity, protection, employment, these were not the reasons why the Unionist party had begun to rally around tariff reform in 1907, nor why the Balfourites made it the theme of the Unionist electoral campaign. Balfour in particular always fled towards the revenue aspect of the tariff reform policy, rather than its wider implications as the 'line that brought all wobblers in'.[61] By the end of 1909, whole-hoggers, even those like Garvin who were loyal to Balfour, began to feel doubts about his failure to make more of tariff reform than its revenue aspect.[62] Subsequently Balfour became more satisfactory on tariff reform, and tariff reform more prominent an issue in the election. At York on 12 January, Balfour promised not only import duties over a wide fiscal field, but was specific about imposing food duties and protective tariffs against foreign manufactured imports.[63]

Nevertheless, this marked no more than a further stage in the public acceptance by Balfour of what had been since the beginning the basic tariff reform programme. It was not a constructive policy such as the tariff reformers had come to understand by that phrase since 1907, with a programme of social reform linked to tariff reform as a domestic package. 'Nothing but hammering again tariff reform and social reform . . . will do our business thoroughly',[64] Garvin thought in November, and the social reform aspect was as vital as the tariff itself:

In the last three weeks I have seen the Socialists face to face for the first time for many years. I am amazed. It is not a new party. It is a new religion. . . . Nothing but a much greater constructive programme than we started with three years ago will save us now . . . unless there is a complete reformation soon in our methods and spirit, the vast social movements of the future will sweep right past us. We want unity, unity, unity, and then we want to revitalise the party. We shall have plenty of time in opposition to settle the Balfour question, and everything else.[65]

The Unionists' difficulty was that they had, by and large, no agreed social policy worthy of the name to add to tariff reform. The outlines of a constructive policy as stated by some whole-hoggers in 1908 had met with no response from the official party leadership. Some lesser figures had their individual proposals, particularly on agriculture, and Balfour himself paid lip-service to such ideas as the extension of occupying ownership, but he neither brought forward a positive proposal, nor supported those in his party who did. 'Hammering' upon social reform, in the constituencies in 1910, produced a rather hollow sound.

The election results revealed the failure of tariff reform to make an impact where it was essential that it should succeed, in the working-class districts of the industrial North.[66] Tariff reform in 1910 was the Unionist answer to Liberal socialism, the programme by which the Tory Democracy was to be won back to its rightful allegiance. Thus Austen Chamberlain did not fear a new register, traditionally regarded as favourable to the Liberals because it enfranchized more lower-class voters, because 'the class of voter who usually makes a new register unfavourable to us, will on this occasion vote for tariff reform and more work'.[67] In fact, they appear not to have done so. The Unionists did well in the South and in rural areas, as Wyndham and others predicted, but they failed to make any impression on the industrial North or in the Celtic fringes. 'This sharp . . . division along geographical lines is the most significant feature of the 1910 results.'[68]

This was partly the result of traditional loyalties disturbed by excessive feelings against the government in 1906 reasserting themselves.[69] But behind the geographical polarization lay the question of class. Those areas which maintained, or returned to, the traditional Unionist allegiance were predominantly either middle-class areas in themselves, or areas where middle- and upper-class influence still predominated, as in the English counties. In those areas which had voted Unionist until 1906, but failed to return to their Unionist allegiance in 1910, particularly Lancashire and parts of London, the dominating factor was class.[70] Scotland, the third main region which failed to return to the pre-1906 position, Blewett explains as less a feature of class polarization than as the 'traditional identification of local nationalism with Liberalism'.[71] But class played a vital part in Scotland also. The Lords were hated there particularly for their social and economic position, and their activities as landlords. Henry Seton-Kerr saw the chief reason for the Unionist failure in Scotland as the hostility of the working classes to the alleged tyranny of the House of Lords, the opposition to food duties, and class hostility. Scotland, he thought, could never be won back by the landed and capitalist classes, but only by trained professional campaigners from the working classes, with the landowners kept well in the background.[72] Arthur Steel-Maitland, shortly to assume general responsibility for Conservative party organization, confirmed both this view of the Scottish situation, and the way in which the socio-economic position of the Lords rather than their constitutional activities had damaged the Unionist party by presenting it as the party of privilege: 'the force of feeling against the House of Lords is largely due to the confusion which has been fostered in the minds of the ordinary voters between Lords, i.e. peers, and their own immediate landlords, to whom they pay their rent'.[73]

As a policy to win the working classes back to the Unionist party, therefore, tariff reform failed in the general election of 1910. Although the Unionists gained considerably, and reduced the government to dependence upon Irish and Labour votes, they had gained not because tariff reform had succeeded in reversing the long-term trend towards class polarization, but because the increased strength of this had swung many of the propertied classes to their side. Some of the losses in the North could be, and were, attributed to defective organization. But this could be remedied. Unionists were well aware that their real problem in the North was class antagonism, and reports from Lancashire echoed those from Scotland.[74] The difficulty was what to do about this situation, whether to press forward with further collectivist social reforms paid for from the revenue from tariff reform in the hope that these would overcome the prejudice against food duties without alienating the propertied classes by increased taxation, or to fall back towards negative conservatism by removing what was unpopular in the Unionist programme, i.e. food duties.

The rejection of the budget to force an election had been in the nature of a gamble, untypical of Balfour's normally cautious leadership. Success would have confirmed his position and solved the difficulties of policy which the Unionists faced. Failure left Balfour more vulnerable, and the position of the party more precarious, than ever. For, as correspondents after the election did not fail to point out, the gamble in 1909 involved not only tariff reform, but the veto powers of the House of Lords and all that such powers defended, the Union, the established Church, especially in Wales, and private property itself. The Unionists had always, rightly, believed that it would take two elections to destroy the Lords' powers, and had entered lightly upon the first. Now that they had lost it, all their cherished causes hung upon the second, yet their policies as they stood were demonstrably inadequate. Some change was clearly necessary if they were not to lose all.

The Lesser Evil

Political activity during 1910 was dominated by the awareness that a second general election was imminent. It was dominated also, for much of the summer and autumn, by the party truce and the Constitutional Conference occasioned by the death, early in May, of King Edward. The Conference first met in June, and did not break up until November when it was clear that a compromise solution to the constitutional conflict created by the Lords' rejection of the 1909 budget was impossible. The Unionist leaders were thus subject to contradictory pressures. With the failure of January just passed, and another election in the offing, it was essential that they reassess their policies in the light of recent experience and do so quickly. But any reassessment involved changes that would either alienate one or other section of the party, or run directly counter to their own beliefs. With a compromise apparently sought by a government in a difficult position, the Unionist leaders found it difficult to convince themselves of the need to tackle this unpleasant task which might be unnecessary. Discussions on policy thus came in spasms as the immediacy of another election waxed and waned, with some activity inevitably following the January defeat, another burst when the Conference seemed like breaking down in September, and excessively rapid changes with a minimum of discussion after the final failure of the Conference, continuing until the eve of the December election itself.

In many ways, the verdict of January left tariff reform the most vulnerable of all Unionist policies. The Union, the House of Lords, the Church, had been Conservative causes for generations, and were associated with the great period of Unionism after 1886. By contrast, tariff reform was a novelty, associated with a period of dismal failure, which had, moreover, failed in January to fulfil the promises made by its supporters. Why it had failed, however, was a far more complex question, and one which, given the aggression and dominance of the whole-hoggers, served to conceal the real weakness of tariff reform within the party until the end of the year.

The overlapping between tariff reform and the socio-economic position of the Lords as election issues made the January defeat susceptible of two separate analyses: the first, that the problem confronting the party was class antagonism, in which tariff reform had proved unsuccessful not because it was protectionist, or advocated food duties, but because it had become involved in a wider class conflict implicit in the existence of the Labour party, the policies of the Liberals, and the struggle over the Lords; and the second, that the Unionists had failed to take advantage of class conflict to win sufficient support from the frightened middle classes because these classes were more afraid of protection than they were of the budget. From these analyses came two widely differing conclusions as to future action. In the former case, to overcome the class distrust of 'Conservatism' on the part of the voters, the Unionist programme had to be made more radical and more constructive; in the latter, tariff reform, and especially food duties, had to be played down or abandoned because they lost the support of those classes who would otherwise have voted against the budget. At stake was the position of tariff reform in the Unionist programme, and the nature of 'Unionism'.

Austen Chamberlain stated the tariff reform case. 'Tariff Reform was our trump card. Where we won, we won on and by Tariff Reform. Even where we lost, it was the only subject in our repertoire about which people really cared.' He admitted the difficulty with food duties but argued that this could be, and had been, overcome when the question was faced 'boldly'. The reasons for the defeat, in Austen's view, were that the association with the House of Lords and with Conservatism had held tariff reform back, and the difficulties created by the existence of a third party since 'Many men . . . voted on this occasion as the Labour party told them, i.e. for the Liberals . . . the existence of the third party deprives us of the full benefit of the 'swing of the pendulum', introduces a new element into politics, and confronts us with a new difficulty.'[1]

The removal of the incubus, as they saw it, of traditional Conservatism was thus a primary objective of the whole-hoggers after January 1910, particularly the reform of the House of Lords. There was clearly considerable support for this from the constituency associations, and however attached the more Conservative members of the party might be to the existing body, few were prepared to defend it on tactical grounds. Support for the powers of the Lords as a second chamber remained unabated but sympathy with its hereditary composition, never very strong in radical imperialist circles, was at a low ebb after January. Some of the more radical even saw it as a threat not only to the Liberal programme but to their own 'progressive legislation'.[2] Even Sandars, following Garvin's lead, was now prepared to urge reform of the Lords on his reluctant master:[3]

The House of Lords, as we know it, is an institution which the Unionist candidates cannot hope to defend with any measure of success and if the issue before the country should be the House of Lords as it is, or no House of Lords, there is no doubt but that the verdict will be against a Second Chamber. Evidence comes to hand day by day and week by week from Scotland, from the North of England, Lancashire and other parts, that unless the Unionist leaders are ready with a bold and positive scheme of House of Lords reform, there is little hope for the Unionist candidates in the constituencies.

Speed was essential if the new policy was to have credibility. Otherwise, 'it will come very much like our Land policy in Scotland, as an afterthought to help candidates in distress'.[4]

The difficulty in bringing the Unionist reform policy forward boldly was that the party did not have, and could not agree upon, any such policy. Reform proposals dealing with the composition of the Lords ran head first into the unwillingness of Balfour and Lansdowne and their supporters in the Lords to consider the subject seriously. They were aware of the tactical necessities of the case, but could not bring themselves to act. 'As you know,' Balfour had written to Lansdowne in December in a masterpiece of understatement, 'this is not a subject on which I am an enthusiastic advocate of change.'[5] At a meeting on 3 March, one of many discussions on the subject but 'remarkable for the presence of Rosebery at our councils', Balfour's opinion was that of the majority:

I dislike the whole thing. I would like to leave things as they are if we could. I don't believe you can make a better House. But that is not the question. The question is: Can you make a Second Chamber strong enough to stand and resist assault? Can you make such changes as will enable our men to fight with success in Yorkshire, Lancashire and Scotland . . . I don't think you can in our democratic days, unless you admit an elective element . . .[6]

The minority was hostile to any change.

With the Unionists thus paralysed, the field was pre-empted by Rosebery who pressed ahead with his own reform scheme, but 'when Rosebery came to his suggestions for introducing the elective element, and to the abolition of the hereditary principle, the sympathy, if any, was very cold . . .'[7] Confronted with the need to make a decision on specific proposals, Lansdowne took refuge in the referendum as a means of solving the deadlock between the two Houses, thus sidestepping composition reform altogether, although he continued to write as if it was an addition to, and not a substitute for, composition reform. Nevertheless, he was not an enthusiastic supporter of this plan either, and his concerns were purely tactical.[8] This further complication only served as a further excuse for delay. Aware that the government had difficulties with the Irish, whose support it needed on the budget, aware also that there was dissension in the cabinet on the government's resolutions dealing with the powers of the Lords,[9] the Unionist leaders could not bring themselves to commit the party to a change they disliked so much. It was not until almost the end of the year, when the Constitutional Conference had failed and the election was almost upon them, that they finally bowed to tactical necessity, and produced a reform scheme which savoured not a little of panic and lacked credibility as a result.[10]

The Unionist leaders considered little but the House of Lords in the early months of 1910. On their own the tariff reformers, as they had done in 1908, ranged further afield, calling for a lead on Poor Law reform, and considering what could be done about the popularity of Lloyd George's land taxes in urban constituencies. The whole-hogger leaders, unlike their supporters, were generally agreed that the urban landlord was a ram which could be sacrificed without qualms. The most constructive proposal to emerge from the early months was the tariff reform solution to this problem, to retain the principle of the land taxes as 'a reform of rating, not as in the Budget . . . a new National tax'. The purpose of this proposal, however, was less to reform rating for its own sake than to outflank the Liberals, since allocating this revenue to the municipalities denied it to the Treasury, and forestalled nationalization by fiscal means by any future radical or socialist Chancellor.[11]

Tactics were the main consideration. There is nothing to suggest that the whole-hoggers would have considered this aspect of a constructive policy if their hands had not been forced by the Liberal initiative. Nor were they making much of a sacrifice if they believed that little revenue would result from their scheme. Lansdowne too approved of the idea, not because it was an attack on the problems of urban land speculation, but for defensive considerations, to 'show the public that the urban landowners are not actuated by purely selfish considerations, and are ready to bear their full share of local taxation'.[12] Tactically, the scheme had merits. Freed from the necessity of raising revenue by tariff reform, the Unionists could afford to give away more money to the localities than the Liberals. From a broader point of view, however, it represented yet another defensive use of tariff reform in the domestic arena. It was the revenue from tariff reform which made such a rating reform proposal possible. Moreover, the scheme involved the retention of the land taxes, or the principle upon which they were based, even if the revenue now went to another source. But the land taxes had assumed a symbolic significance during the struggle against the budget, and there were strong forces working within the Unionist party for a commitment to repeal the taxes when the party next gained office, which made it improbable that these rating proposals would secure a very widespread acceptance.

Progress on land reform, and in particular land purchase, which the tariff reformers had forgotten, but which Lansdowne added as a question 'upon which Balfour had always laid great stress',[13] similarly ran into difficulties, despite the long discussions before 1909, and the existence of numerous bills prepared by back-benchers like Collings. A committee had been set up by Balfour, but it immediately fell into dispute over the merits of the state or independent land banks as the lending agency. The chief product of its discussion was a bitter feud between the protagonists of these rival schemes, Collings and Sir Gilbert Parker.[14] Lord Onslow, as another agricultural expert, caused even greater confusion when he expressed the belief 'that the Radicals are right when they say that there is no "land hunger" in England',[15] and cast doubts upon the whole policy.

Neither Balfour nor Lansdowne nor the whole-hoggers were at this stage distraught with anxiety. All believed that the government was in greater difficulties than themselves, and might well fail to hold its coalition together long enough to pass its own projects. In the case of Lansdowne and Balfour also, the changes which they might have to make to party policy were changes they disliked, and had no desire to pronounce upon unless they were forced to do so by the most dire necessity. Their hesitation in that respect was reinforced by the alternative view of the defeat in January and the change of issue which that defeat entailed. The passage of the budget had become inevitable. The next election would not be on economic questions, taxation, unemployment, trade, or social reform, but on the Lords pure and simple. The central issue of politics thus became the old Conservative cause of resistance to Radical demands for change. The enemy was, despite the new issues raised by collectivism, barely distinguishable from that of the Gladstonian era, which had been responsible for the disestablishment of the Irish Church, had challenged the Union, threatened the Lords, and was permanently opposed to the greatness of the Empire. In defence of these institutions, the Unionist party could again reunite on a negative 'Conservative' programme.

The weakness of the 'conversion' to tariff reform of some parts of Balfour's faction was revealed soon after the defeat. Even before the election, Conservative free traders, while prepared to support tariff reform in opposition to the greater evil of socialism, expressed the fear that tariff reform might prevent the party from gaining the full benefit of the Lords' action in defence of property.[16] After January, such fears were more widely expressed and carried more weight because of the issues now at risk. Salisbury, from a Balfourite standpoint, persuasively argued for the postponement of the preferential side of tariff reform on the grounds that the failure in the North had been due to the unpopularity of the food duties. Without them he felt that the Unionists would have had a majority, even if they had stood by all the other aspects of the full tariff reform programme. They would then, as Salisbury temptingly pointed out to Chamberlain, have had a 10 per cent all-round duty to prove the success of tariff reform, from which base they could have appealed for a new mandate to pass food taxation. On the other hand the loss of the election had had disastrous consequences. If the next election was lost the constitution would collapse. 'The Lords will go, and then the Church, the Union, the barrier against Socialism, and possibly even the Empire.'[17] His brothers, Lord Hugh and Lord Robert Cecil, took the bull by the horns and suggested to Joseph Chamberlain himself that he should propose the postponement of food taxes for the next election, in order that the struggle could be concentrated on Home Rule:

It would not be necessary to abandon this tax altogether in order to make it electorally unimportant . . . such a declaration of postponement would be

perfectly consistent with a continued advocacy of the tax on its merits, and
with the general principles which are involved in its imposition. There would,
in fact, be no sacrifice of principle at all in a pledge not to deal with the
subject during the next Parliament . . .[18]

The balance of strength between the factions in the party had not yet
changed so much as to make this a practical proposal, particularly as
the tariff reformers could explain the last defeat in a different way. As
Law commented:

The Unionist party is now committed to the whole policy of Preference,
including food duties, and there is a large section of the Party . . . which
regards Preference not as a political opinion, but as something almost sacred.
If therefore Mr Balfour, Mr Chamberlain, and Mr Austen Chamberlain were
to propose to postpone this part of the proposal, even then there would, in
my opinion, be a wholesale revolt among the rank and file . . . this consideration is in itself absolutely decisive.[19]

Nevertheless, the tariff reformers went backwards. One aspect of the
food duties, the 1*s*. duty on colonial corn proposed by the agricultural
committee of the Tariff Commission in its report in 1906, came under
severe criticism and was vulnerable. It had not formed part of Joseph
Chamberlain's original tariff reform proposals, and was, if not contradictory, at least out of place in the Unionist propaganda on behalf
of preference which had shifted its emphasis away from the compensatory reduction of other duties to the 'lines adopted by Mr Balfour
in his recent speeches . . . that the proposal of Preference by widening
the area of supply of wheat, will diminish the danger of higher
prices'.[20] After the election even the whole-hoggers were doubtful of
this item in their programme. Mary Maxse of the Women's Tariff
Reform Association found Chamberlain's old policy of the compensatory reduction of other food duties 'does not go down in the least . . .
The only way to fight this question is to point out that food is growing
dearer under Free Trade, and that only by enlarging Imperial supplies
can we have cheaper food in the future. The "free British loaf" is a cry
which will catch on.' She was consequently 'strongly against 1/- on
Colonial corn'.[21] H. A. Gwynne, editor of the *Standard*, advocated its
removal in a memorandum to Balfour[22] and in his paper, and at the
meeting of whole-hogger leaders on 8 March Austen Chamberlain
himself took this line.[23] Sandars, who as usual reported all this to
Balfour, inevitably went off to find Hewins, and found, as he feared,[24]

that Hewins was 'much concerned about the proposed abandonment of the 1/- duty on colonial corn', because of the effect on the tariff reformers' agricultural policy. Hewins recommended leaving well alone until they came to consider the details of tariff reform when in office.[25]

Austen Chamberlain's opinion that the abolition of the duty would not be resented by the farmers, a view which Gwynne shared, was also challenged. G. L. Courthope informed Austen in February that 'there is a great revival of political activity among agriculturalists all over the country, and there is no doubt that agricultural matters will be forced to the front in the House in the next few years . . . I am sure that it is worth an effort to show that our leading men sympathise with the farmers actively.'[26] The abolition of the 1s. duty was hardly a propitious beginning in this direction, and Chaplin deprecated any reduction in the duties already proposed 'or there will be the greatest risk of exciting and alarming the farmers in the counties which have been for so many years the best supporters of Unionist candidates and members'.[27]

The discussion threatened to leave the Unionist party in a dilemma, with the risk of strongholds in the counties being weakened to gain votes in the towns, particularly since its agricultural policy was still in disarray. But in practice, with so many members already pledged against the duty, and with confusion threatening to emerge on this point as it had on so many others, Balfour had no difficulty in deciding to announce the abandonment of the duty, which he did by letter on 16 April.[28] In itself, it was not a great modification of the tariff reform programme, and in no way undermined the arguments for food duties and preference generally. But it was none the less a concession to Balfourite 'practical politics' and inevitably fostered rumours that the food duties themselves were about to be abandoned. Worst of all, it was a concession brought about by the doubts of the tariff reformers themselves, and could not but give heart to their opponents. As the only major change to come out of the debates on party policy in the early months of 1910, the party could hardly claim to have laid the foundations for a great constructive policy appealing to the democracy.

The Constitutional Conference temporarily put an end to these debates on policy. Its effect, however, was to increase the frustration of the party, without, in the end, bringing the compensation of an honourable compromise. The rank and file of both parties viewed the Conference with extreme suspicion from the start.[29] The 'first principles' of the situation were, according to Willoughby de Broke:

The Radicals cannot, or will not, govern on the same Double Chamber system that prevails in any other country worthy of the name.

(2) They cannot destroy this system without coercing the king to make 500 Peers

(3) They have now realised that this is a physical and a moral impossibility, and probably not ultimately efficacious as you are by no means certain of your Peer, *once he is created.*

Now what I want to know is why we cannot leave them in this position and tell them to get out of it the best way they can . . . it seems to me that they hope to improve their complexion by the Conference. I really can't see what we are going to get out of it.[30]

The reaction of the radical right to the Constitutional Conference revealed clearly for the first time the attitude which was to govern the Unionist party's political behaviour in the last years of pre-war politics, but which had all along been the force behind whole-hogging, and the explanation of the hold which tariff reform had upon some sections of the party. Tariff reform appeared to offer a way to prevent the apparent slide of Britain into decadence, impotence, and anarchy. It was, and Chamberlain presented it as, an aggressive response to the insecurity felt on a wide spectrum of the political right. The counterpart was contempt for those who either did not realize the danger, or who lacked the courage to prevent it. In 1903 the mood was muted because Joseph Chamberlain only prophesied disaster. In 1910 collapse was just around the corner. The Conference was, or threatened to be, a sell-out to those who were primarily responsible, and whose avowed aim was to bring about this collapse. There should, the right argued, be 'no compromise with dynamite. It can't be done . . .'[31]

Frustration, as always, focused upon Balfour.[32] There were, declared the *Morning Post* in an article on 'Unionist Somnolence', a wide range of subjects on which the party leaders needed to declare themselves— their opposition to 'the principle which underlies all late Radical Finance, of taxing capital as income and spending it as such'; the imperial side of tariff reform; occupying ownership, both as a 'necessary corollary of Tariff Reform', and 'the basis of any plan for the social amelioration of the agricultural population and for resuscitating the prosperity of our rural industries'; the Osborne judgement; the navy;

the army; and Ireland.[33] Threatened revolt and constant pressure were, as usual, the tariff reformers' approach to the problems of an apparently recalcitrant leadership,[34] but the summer passed with no public pronouncements to reduce their frustration.

By the autumn, however, continued silence had become impossible. Austen Chamberlain believed a speech was necessary to 'remove the suspicion that the Conference is a "put up job" between the leaders to silence their followers and damp down all activity'.[35] Hood had his speakers and vans ready for the autumn campaign, and needed a speech from Balfour to indicate the line they should take, 'especially on the question of the land and the Imperial Conference',[36] and fears for the future of the Conference reinforced the pressure to take the initiative.[37] Even Long, generally hostile both to the advanced tariff reformers and to constructive politics, pressed for a lead to end the 'grumbling among our people', and forecast a renewed outbreak of unauthorized programmes if no lead was given. Long suggested that Balfour should reaffirm the party's commitment to tariff reform, take up 'Land Purchase' as 'the only policy which will stop Socialism, by giving us a strong Conservative element in all the country districts', and declare the official policy on the Osborne judgement, the payment of members, the land taxes, and defence. 'A few plain strong words on these subjects will, I firmly believe, rally the party . . .'[38]

By the time Long wrote, the party was already in the throes of a discussion on these subjects. Balfour was committed to speaking in Edinburgh early in October, and although still hesitant, could not back down. Attention was focused on the needs of the industrial North. Balfour regarded Lancashire 'as the very key and centre of the next electoral battlefield',[39] and for once the whole-hoggers agreed with him, although their solution to the problem was 'not new arguments but a new personality'. In August Goulding was trying to persuade Law to leave his safe seat in Dulwich to contest a Manchester seat at the next election,[40] a move which Garvin thought 'would electrify our people there, and his speeches would spread the clear doctrine day by day'.[41] Shortly afterwards Law agreed, with some reservations, to go.[42]

But the question remained, what 'clear doctrine' was the new personality to expound, especially upon the urban and working-class issues of the land taxes and the Osborne judgement. Sandars thought some reference to the payment of members by Balfour in his Edinburgh

speech was imperative. The party would 'not tolerate the idea of legislative reversal' of the Osborne judgement, but

the alternative policy of Payment of Members, *while not agreeable perhaps to us
who naturally prefer the existing order of things,* was one which sooner or later
was bound to come as part of our Parliamentary system . . . The case it seems
to me is eminently one for tactics. It is good to stand by the Osborne Judgement. It will be prudent, I think, to be at least sympathetic in the question of
Payment of Members.[43]

Ironically, it was Balfour's free trade cousin, Lord Robert Cecil, whose
arguments swung him to this view:

because while his prejudices were of course strongly in favour of the existing
system, he had been forced to the conclusion that it was hopeless fighting the
Trades Unions if their organisation was used for political purposes, and that
the only way to prevent the misuse of their power was to make working men
members of Parliament independent of Trade Union funds . . .

Balfour still saw the Unionist difficulty in Lancashire as due almost
entirely to trade union influence and class politics, as did the tariff
reformers, and thought recovery was impossible 'unless the Trades
Unions can be induced to revert to their proper and undisputed
functions in connection with their trade interests'.[44]

There was general support, as Sandars assumed, for the maintenance
of the Osborne judgement over a wide spectrum of party opinion. But
the alternative policy of the payment of members was hopelessly
divisive. Lansdowne disliked it,[45] Long and Wyndham were hostile,[46]
and Austen Chamberlain rejected it even as 'the lesser evil'.[47] Amongst
the whole-hoggers, Maxse was dogmatically opposed,[48] and Willoughby
de Broke expressed similar views.[49] On the other hand Goulding,[50]
F. E. Smith,[51] and Gwynne[52] all favoured the idea, as did Law:

The Unionist party is unanimous in the determination to uphold that judgement; but that being so, we as a Party, are faced with one of two alternatives:
Either we must be prepared to support some real alternative by which Labour
representation can be secured; or we must take up the attitude that we are for
practical purposes opposed to it. The last alternative is impossible; and so far
I have seen no method is suggested which seems to me feasible, except
payment of members.

Its first effect, in my belief, would be that members of Trades Unions
would not see the fun of subscribing for political purposes, and that therefore
the political influence of the Trades Unions would be destroyed.[53]

The debate on the Osborne judgement was central to the strategy of the party at the next election, central indeed to the definition of its relationship with the working classes in the future. Despite the opposition of many whole-hoggers to the payment of members, if the party on this occasion rejected this proposal the credibility of the Unionist party as a radical party, and of tariff reform as a working man's question, would be severely undermined. Opposition to both the reversal of the Osborne judgement and to the payment of members which, as Law pointed out, was *de facto* opposition to working-class representation, ran counter not only to the analysis which the tariff reformers put forward of the party's position after the January defeat, but also to their view of the party's role in British politics as a national party, and to the ideology of national and imperial unity. The more radical of the whole-hoggers indeed wished to push forward with direct working-class participation in the form of Conservative working-men's candidates, a scheme which Law linked directly to the payment of members, since he believed that only if such candidates were independently financed would they gain the confidence of their fellows.[54]

The idea of distinct Conservative working-class candidates was an old one, dating back at least to the mid-1880s and the extension of the franchise, when Salisbury had considered the idea favourably, but it had been rejected by the Conservative Chief Agent, Captain Middleton.[55] In 1909, the *Standard* had launched a campaign to run working-class candidates and raised £6,074, but the four candidates run by the Central Office were sent to impossible constituencies.[56] Such candidates were, nevertheless, the logical corollary to Joseph Chamberlain's presentation of tariff reform as a working-man's question, and his attempt to win trade union and working-class support. His failure to win over the leaders of organized labour—the T.U.C. in 1903 condemned tariff reform as a 'malignant disease'—led, in April 1904, to the formation of the 'organised Labour Branch of the Tariff Reform League', which eventually became the Trade Union Tariff Reform Association.[57] Despite its widespread propaganda activities, this organization had not made much progress before 1909, and was regarded with some scepticism by the League itself. Hewins, when consulted by Balfour about the Association in 1908, felt that in some places 'they are doing very good work', but in general he was unimpressed.[58]

Early in 1909, however, the organization was taken in hand by
Amery, supported by Milner who had always been strongly in favour
of Unionist working-class M.P.s. Amery described the T.U.T.R.A. as
a 'body of Trades Unionists pure and simple, organised originally and
still financed by Medhurst, at one time connected with the T.R.L. but
now entirely separate . . .', and thought that as a result of the Osborne
judgement it might develop into 'a real Unionist Labour party . . .' He
wanted to set up a committee to organize the Association and get some
of its members into the House of Commons, so that it would 'at the
end of a few years stand entirely on its own feet and compete effectively
with the existing Labour party . . .'[59] Hills[60] was prepared to act as
Treasurer, and thus resuscitated the T.U.T.R.A. participated in the
summer of 1909 in the general tariff reform onslaught on Lancashire.
James Reid, Unionist candidate for Greenock in 1906, directed the
campaign with some effect, so that by September a local district council
could be established, and by the end of the year, with at least 20
branches, it was a transformed organization. 'It is', Amery told Maxse,
in asking him to say a few words about the T.U.T.R.A. in a speech he
was to make in Manchester, 'a really useful and effective body full of
business. It has pretty well 10,000 members and if it had the encouragement of a larger revenue and the presence of one or two of its members
in the House of Commons, would grow very rapidly.'[61]

In 1910 Wolmer again took up the question of securing the working
classes and trade unions in the Unionist interest, with specific reference
to the class difficulty in Lancashire, which he hoped to overcome by
making the organization more democratic, and allowing the working
men to choose the candidates themselves from among their own class.
Convinced that it was not 'tariff reform . . . that has lost Lancashire'
but 'class feeling'[62] Wolmer was optimistic that, given this democratization, much could be achieved. 'If Trade Unionists are ever going to
desert their Socialist leaders, they will do so on the Tariff question, so
this seems to be a great opportunity.'[63] Wolmer himself set about
organizing Conservative trade unions in Lancashire, but cautiously
refused the assistance of the T.R.L. and the Central Office, keeping the
organization in the hands of the trade unionists themselves.[64]

This movement, together with the whole question of Conservative
working-class candidates, could be put at risk by a failure of the party
leaders to express sufficient sympathy with working-class aspirations.
'The Conservative working men', Salisbury wrote, 'are, I am informed,

in a very tight place, and are looking most anxiously to an assurance of the support of the Conservative party against the Socialists and anti-Osbornites.'[65] But Willoughby de Broke and Law had both put their finger on the fundamental difficulty in dealing with the payment of members, the 'grave danger of a party split on it'.[66] The divisions were essentially about tactics, however wide the implications of the choice. With the exception of Gwynne, Amery, Wolmer, and their radical fringe, even the advocates of payment of members argued for it only on tactical grounds, and against their principles, as 'the necessary alternative to a reversal of the Osborne judgement . . .'[67] Balfour, with whom the final decision rested, similarly disliked it, but thought 'it might possibly strengthen our hands in upholding the judgement . . .'[68] With the whole-hoggers divided there would never be sufficient pressure upon Balfour to make him act. The Constitutional Conference was still in session, and if compromise seemed unlikely, it was still possible; tactical exigencies were not yet urgent; the arguments used by Lansdowne, Austen Chamberlain, and others expressed Balfour's own feelings. The Conservative working men looked in vain for relief to a timid leadership, for Balfour made no announcement, and 'the party entered the election opposed both to reversal, and to the payment of members.'[69]

By implication the leadership was also opposed to working-class representation. This did not prevent the *Standard* launching another campaign to run working-class candidates, and six working-class Unionists stood, without success, in December.[70] The debate, however, demonstrated the contradictions in the idea the tariff reformers held of the Unionist party. However authoritarian their radicalism, they still campaigned for tariff reform as a radical policy, as the basis of a constructive social programme, and sought working-class support. But whilst they were prepared to offer economic benefits to the working classes, or policies which they thought would bring economic benefits, they were not prepared to share political power. Their radicalism was economic, not political; it was still the philosophy of ransom, and employment, higher wages, and social legislation were all part of the ransom the Unionists were willing to pay to retain the monopoly of power. Chamberlain's failure to win the support of organized labour for his tariff reform proposals, and the development after 1900 of a political consciousness among trade unionists which found expression at the general election of 1906, created a dilemma for radical Unionists.

Increasingly, however much they might seek to avoid confrontation, the resolution of that dilemma found them in opposition to labour aspirations. In the final analysis, despite the claims to radicalism and constructive policies, they were not prepared to make those concessions which might undermine organized labour from below or exploit its internal disagreement.

The party could achieve no greater unity or clarity on its policy on the land taxes, although here the divisions of opinion were more between the leadership and the backbenches than within the leadership itself, with the Land Union, under the leadership of Captain Pretyman, pressing for a commitment to complete repeal. The bait again was the offer of success in the North: 'the Land Union', Pretyman told Austen Chamberlain, 'has met with a lot of support and we are really making great headway. Particularly in Lancashire. We are also hopeful of doing good work in Scotland where there is so much to be gained.'[71] His proposals, however, frightened Austen Chamberlain, whose smoothing congratulations 'on the success which has attended your work with the Land Union', did not disguise his hostility to such far-reaching commitments.[72] Chamberlain also did not really believe Pretyman's assertions about the Land Union's success in urban areas, having heard from urban members as to the electoral danger of a root-and-branch attack upon the land taxes, and warned Balfour of this new danger.[73] But remaining uncommitted was Balfour's favourite political position, and he had no difficulty on this occasion in seconding Austen Chamberlain's views. He had already written to Croft in June to say that he could not commit himself to the policy he would adopt towards the land taxes if and when returned to office.[74]

Nevertheless the Land Union, following well-established precedents, kept up the pressure. Pretyman caustically replied to Austen Chamberlain that before they worried about what they would do when in office they first had to 'get in . . . I am assured that the repeal of the Land Taxes is our trump card.'[75] 'There can be no doubt', he wrote again on 28 October, 'that Lloyd George will shortly announce a policy of rating reform based upon Land Values, and we must have our alternative to put before the country . . .'[76] The Land Union's alternative was nothing if not comprehensive, including the repeal of part one of the 1909 budget; the amendment of the licensing clauses of part two; the removal from local rates of all national services, 'e.g. Poor Law, Education, Main Roads . . .'; a general graduated 'rating tax' to raise some £25 to £30 million to be levied on all incomes including wages; the revision of the methods of assessing rates; the levy of a 'contribution' from urban building land; and the reform of the financial administration of the Poor Law and education.[77]

Behind many of these reforms lay the desire to reduce expenditure, particularly local expenditure and local rates, and thus meet some long-standing grievances associated with the land question, particularly the grievances of the farmers. It was also the type of detailed programme which Balfour abhorred, and which no shadow chancellor would wish to be tied to before taking office. But linked to the repeal of the land taxes it widened the appeal of the Land Union considerably, and thus the force of its pressure for official recognition. Balfour, his back to the wall, had appealed to Austen Chamberlain in October for some formula to send to his increasing band of correspondents seeking a public promise to repeal the land taxes when next in office.[78] The Central Office and candidates were also finding difficulty in dealing with the influence of the Land Union, and were similarly being pressed embarrassingly hard for a definite line.[79]

But this pressure had to be resisted. Pretyman's contention that the policy of repeal was popular in Lancashire and the North was dismissed by the leadership, both whole-hogger and Balfourite.[80] In fact, the question of the land taxes, like the food duties required for preference, trapped the Unionists in the familiar dilemma of a conflict of interest between the urban and rural electorates.

In rural districts [wrote Hood] the feeling is strongly in favour of Repeal, partly owing to the large number of small owners of land and cottage property, partly from a fear that the so-called exemption of agricultural land is illusory . . .

In the urban districts, especially in the North, our members and candidates are not inclined to advocate repeal. In many of the industrial towns there are very large ground landlords and our men fear they will have to fight the battle of these owners in places where the taxes are popular.[81]

Again, at the risk of alienating the Land Union, Balfour temporized, and the party entered the December election officially accepting the 1909 budget and the verdict of January.

The failure of the leaders to meet the demands of their followers for a lead was in many respects more the result of lack of agreement than lack of effort, combined with the difficulty of making aggressive campaigning speeches whilst discussions continued with the Liberals for a compromise settlement. But in consequence, whole-hogger criticism of what little they did say was damning. In the opinion of the *Morning Post*, Austen Chamberlain's speech at Birmingham on 23 September proposed no more than the policy accepted by all active Unionists six months earlier:

Generalities have ceased to be of the slightest use; what is needed is a concrete and alternative constructive programme based on the general sentiments of the Unionist Party, and opposed to the destructive proposals of Radicalism. What is wanted is not a declaration that if you preach Tariff Reform you will win, but an outline of the future Tariff. The demand in the agricultural districts is not for a reaffirmation of the principles of small private ownership but for a scheme which will carry those principles into practice. The need of the great masses of Tory working men in the industrial cities is not vague professions of belief in a Tory social policy, it is the production of that policy . . . [82]

By these standards, Balfour's statement at Edinburgh also fell far short of what was wanted. The speech, thought the *Morning Post*, 'resembles far more such impartial summaries of political feeling as appear in publications like the "Annual Register", than a fighting proclamation . . . On no single issue touched on by the leader of the Opposition has a definite lead been given.'[83]

Under these circumstances, as the paper commented, Unionist divergencies were bound to continue and become more numerous. A warning of what the leadership could expect had been given the previous day, with the announcement that back-bench discontent had crystallized with the formation of a group of 'wealthy and active' members of both Houses, led by Croft and Willoughby de Broke, to pressurize the party leaders for greater activity, and for a change in party policy from one of defence to the elaboration of a definite programme.[84] This, the 'Reveille' movement, was launched at a dinner presided over by Malmesbury,[85] and had decided Confederate and anti-Balfourite overtones.[86] As a movement, Reveille was always more an expression of frustration on the part of back-benchers with the inactivity caused by the constitutional truce than a rebellion in favour of a particular programme, and the *Morning Post* found its constructive proposals disappointing.[87]

Nevertheless, the Reveille manifesto, particularly in its concern for the inter-relation of its various proposals, marked a further stage in the creation of a distinctive ideology of constructive 'Unionism', based on, but extending, tariff reform itself. It claimed to offer

a coherent and united plan of action. In a single word it may be described as a National Policy. Tariff Reform is an essential element of that policy but it is far from the whole of it . . . Tariff Reform is only a means to an end, and that end is the promotion of national security and prosperity . . . the Reveille programme makes no distinction between foreign and home politics. A national policy regards them as inseparable.

In this respect, as the *Morning Post* itself commented, the most original of its proposals was the definite linking of industrial insurance to protection, an extension of Joseph Chamberlain's initial argument that the products of labour had to be protected to make the protection of labour effective:

With Tariff Reform to induce the greater investment of capital here, insurance, and other measures of social reform, become practical under the conditions of a rising market for labour. By insurance, and by the increase of . . . small owners of the land, the ends which the Socialists have in view will be attained by practical instead of fatal methods. Destitution will gradually be abolished but without the loss of industrial initiative . . . So we shall avoid the ruin of a Right to Work Bill. State credit will assist in the purchase of land by smaller owners. So we shall avoid the risk of State ownership of the land.

Domestic reform alone, however, would not, according to the Reveille manifesto, bring security and prosperity. 'When all that has been done that is possible to develop the force and security of our island people, there remains the fact that only by gathering together the several nations of the Empire can we cope in the international balance of power with the newly organised continental states.' Defence dominated all other aspects of Reveille's policy, with the navy as the most important consideration, but defence as an all-embracing question. The single principle on which, according to the *Morning Post*, the manifesto rested

may be defined by the statement that it is the business of the State to conserve and foster the dynamic energies of the people. This end can only be attained by a conjoined and inter-related scheme which embraces the whole field of national life from foreign policy to the Navy and Army, from the military forces to the defensive development of national industries on which the support of armaments depends, and from the industrial security behind the

Tariff to social advance and prosperity within the area the Tariff protects . . .
it is in the application of these doctrines to the Empire as a whole that every
single state and individual within it must look both for safety and progress.[88]

Ideology apart, however, the attack upon the Constitutional Conference and upon the policy of compromise made by the Reveille
movement revealed serious divisions within the whole-hogger ranks
upon tactics. Garvin, for example, as one of the principal advocates of
the Conference and of compromise politics which, by the autumn of
1910 had gone so far as to include a federal solution to the Irish
question, was provoked by the Reveille manifesto into a violent attack
upon his former associates,[89] and F. S. Oliver, who as 'Pacificus' had
also supported 'federalism' in a series of influential letters to *The Times*,
wrote to defend himself against accusations of 'opportunism'.[90]

But by October the Reveille group and the opponents of compromise in general had a case against the Constitutional Conference and
against their own leaders. The Conference had reached deadlock and
all but broken up by the end of July over the impossibility of finding
a compromise solution to Ireland. In allowing the discussions to drag
on—discussions which by October had little to do with the Conference
itself—the Unionist leaders allowed the Liberals to widen the area of
Unionist disagreement. In October Lloyd George made overtures for
the formation of a 'National Government' based upon a memorandum
he had drawn up in August. He stressed, in almost whole-hogger terms,
the difficulties, internal and external, confronting the country and the
need for national unity at a time of crisis caused by 'the rapid rise of
great foreign competitors . . .' Joseph Chamberlain could not have
put the position better. A national government could, according to
Lloyd George, deal with the measures which were necessary for this
re-equipment programme, but which no single party could take up
because of their unpopularity. 'The questions which call for immediate
attention . . . are first of all questions which come under the category of
Social Reform.' These he listed as housing, drink, insurance against
accident, illness, death and implicitly, unemployment, defence, including
the 'question of compulsory training', local government, trade, the
land, imperial policy, involving 'schemes for uniting together the
Empire, and utilising and concentrating its resources for defence as for
commerce'; a just settlement to the Irish question; and foreign policy.
On specific remedies, however, the memorandum was vague in the
extreme.[91]

The memorandum itself played little part in the discussions which followed from Lloyd George's proposals, for apparently he never showed it to the Unionist leaders but only gave them verbally a rough indication of its contents.[92] Using F. E. Smith initially as an intermediary Lloyd George opened talks with Balfour early in October, and the other Unionist negotiators at the Constitutional Conference, Cawdor, Lansdowne, and Austen Chamberlain were informed by the middle of the month, as was Law. Garvin was also told of the scheme. From Lloyd George the Unionists gained the idea that his proposals were highly favourable to the furtherance of their own policies. Austen Chamberlain was thus impressed by the apparent concessions of greater expenditure on the navy, the establishment of a system of national service, and action on preference, and was prepared 'to give the most attentive and even friendly consideration to these proposals' even though they depended 'on agreement for a settlement of the Irish question on the lines of what I understand Lloyd George calls Federal Home Rule for the United Kingdom and what I should call Provincial Councils'.[93]

But deliberately or not, Lloyd George created confusion as to his purposes. Even apart from giving F. E. Smith the false impression that his Irish devolution proposals had been discussed by the Constitutional Conference, and that the Conference was in danger of breaking up because of Unionist intransigence, against which both Balfour and Austen Chamberlain protested, he was obscure also on his intentions toward tariff reform. Austen Chamberlain understood that:

in addition to giving a preference to the Colonies on the existing rate of duty, Lloyd George was ready to consent to the appointment of a Commission which should be required to report within six months on what further duties it was desirable in the interests of the Empire to impose, and he was prepared to bind himself to accept and act upon the report of such a Commission.[94]

But according to Balfour, Lloyd George, who 'talked about a Commission of Enquiry into Fiscal relations . . ., *said nothing about reporting in six months etc* . . . Defence, Education, Licensing were the things on which he laid stress, and on none of these, of course, any more than on the others, had he precise suggestions to make.'[95]

Balfour himself was cautious and sceptical from the start. 'I did not take up a *non possumus* attitude', he told Austen Chamberlain, 'but I saw no object in a detailed discussion about the pattern of the wall-papers which are to adorn this new political structure when the foundations have not been laid!'[96] But the scheme ultimately collapsed because Balfour would not take the risk of splitting his own party, or, in Lloyd George's terms, shedding a few extremists on the Irish proposals. By October 1910 a coalition of the 'collectivist centre', which might have stood against a coalition of the 'individualist centre' formed from the alliance of the Liberal League and the U.F.T.C. was impossible. Probably it always had been. Yet the subjects upon which Lloyd George laid stress in his August memorandum were sufficiently cross-party for his proposals to appear credible, such was the confusion of Edwardian politics. Lloyd George's own motives are also more intelligible in the light of this confusion created by the existence of a wide range of cross-party issues, for at first sight he had little to gain and risked much in the coalition idea. It was this, in part, which aroused Unionist interest. 'If it succeeds,' wrote F. E. Smith, 'it means a national party, and well directed power for ten years . . . If it fails, L. G. and W[inston] are ruined: we are not, and might have ten years on our own . . .'[97]

Possibly Lloyd George was 'impelled by a statesmanlike desire to solve . . . national difficulties', as Alfred Gollin argues.[98] But it is equally arguable that he was impelled by an attack of nerves. Gwynne reported to Sandars in September that Lloyd George was restless, and that this stemmed from his worry about the land taxes.[99] At the same time his insurance proposals seemed to be foundering against the opposition of the insurance companies,[100] whilst the prospective failure of the Constitutional Conference threatened a revival of constitutional conflict which would, at least in the short run, block those social reform proposals by which the Liberal party had been apparently reinvigorated since the doldrums of 1908. Some of his senior cabinet colleagues to whom he sent his memorandum certainly found the future outlook bleak. Crewe thought 'we have got not far from the end of our tether as regards the carrying on of large reforms',[101] and Grey believed that 'If the Conference breaks up without agreement, I foresee the break-up of the Liberal party, and a time of political instability, perhaps of chaos, to the great detriment of the country.'[102]

Both Crewe and Grey, therefore, viewed Lloyd George's proposals with some approval. But Lloyd George's technique, which ensured something of a favourable reception for his scheme on both sides, also made the ultimate achievement of a coalition difficult, if not impossible.

According to Searle, 'Lloyd George hoped to bring the two parties together by writing in a liberal sense to his colleagues and talking in a conservative sense to his opponents.'[103] This procedure was self-defeating if Lloyd George seriously expected a coalition to emerge from his proposals. As Searle himself admits, 'This cunning stratagem, however, would obviously misfire, should Asquith and Balfour meet for the comparing of notes . . .',[104] which is precisely what they would do if brought together. Asquith maintained afterwards that 'he had known all about [these] proposals from the first', and the available evidence supports his claim.[105] But he nevertheless remained unconcerned and amused as negotiations proceeded which, if successful, involved for him the same fate as he had earlier reserved for Campbell-Bannerman, banishment to the House of Lords. His attitude however is intelligible if Lloyd George did not seriously expect a coalition to result from his scheme, as is Lloyd George's note to Balfour of 2 November that he had just seen Asquith who thought it 'undesirable *at this stage* to take part in the negotiations. But he asked me to say that all I did was with his full concurrence.'[106] Lloyd George did not need to 'invent' this message to prevent Asquith and Balfour from meeting if Asquith knew that Lloyd George did not expect a coalition. Under the circumstances, a meeting with Balfour would indeed have been an embarrassment. As it was, Asquith could, without danger to himself, enjoy a ringside seat at a game of political intrigue played by two grand masters of the art. In October 1910 a plot by Lloyd George, with Asquith's connivance, to undo the Unionists was more likely than a plot between Lloyd George, Balfour, and an assortment of Unionist lesser lights to remove Asquith and half of his cabinet.

Asquith therefore watched as Lloyd George flew his coalition kite to exploit the divisions of the Unionists over policy, and to deepen their indecision. The issues which Lloyd George raised were sufficiently cross-party to appear areas of compromise. Many of the younger Unionists, particularly those attracted into the Unionist party by Chamberlain's tariff reform campaign, were not traditional Conservatives, and were, as the policy discussions within the party during 1910 revealed, prepared to go a long way in a 'liberal' or collectivist direction. Their priorities too were not those of traditional conservatism. For them, economic, social, and imperial issues all took precedence over traditional causes such as the Lords, and even the Union. In 1910 many of the younger intellectuals of the party 'less involved in the

controversies of '86 and '93' than the party hierarchy, agreed with
Garvin that a 'new phase of the Irish question' had opened, and were
prepared to accept a 'federal' solution to the Home Rule problem.[107]
In their view the international repercussions of the Irish problem,
prejudicing as it did relations with both America and the colonies
because of their sympathies with Ireland, made its rapid solution
essential. Garvin's unwitting role in supporting federal proposals in
the *Observer* was not, as he believed, to prepare public opinion for 'the
bigger scheme', but to widen the area of Unionist dissension.

The vital point about Lloyd George's 'bigger scheme', however, is
that it appeared, at least as explained by Lloyd George, credible to
sections of both parties. The experienced hands in the Unionist party,
Balfour and Austen Chamberlain, remained sceptical, but those less
experienced in political intrigue—Garvin and F. E. Smith—felt that
the coalition was worth working for.[108] Balfour's close questioning of
Garvin's federal proposals for Ireland[109] revealed the hollowness of
such aspirations, and his refusal to countenance any change in Unionist
Irish policy kept that debate within tolerable limits. But during the
course of 1910 virtually all Unionist policies were thrown into the
melting pot—Ireland, the House of Lords, its attitude to organized
labour, and even tariff reform. The Unionist party spent 1910 tearing
itself to pieces, unable to decide either its policies on major questions in
isolation, or the priorities between those policies should it be forced to
choose. But time was on the side of the Liberals.

Discussions on Lloyd George's coalition proposals came to an end
on 3 November, and the Constitutional Conference was abandoned on
the 10th. Almost immediately, as soon as it had received guarantees
from the King that he would, if necessary, create sufficient peers to
ensure the passage of its Parliament Bill in the Lords if it won the next
election, the government announced the dissolution. The election
found the Unionists completely unprepared, and forced them into the
hurried announcement of policies they had hoped to avoid. Briefly at
least, however, 'constructive' proposals still held sway over 'negative'
conservatism. Tactical pressures overcame Unionist reluctance to
tamper with the ancient constitution. Rosebery's resolutions on the
composition of the House of Lords were passed after a brief discussion
on 17 November, and the Unionist reform policy was announced and
debated on the 23rd and 24th. Balfour's speech to the National Union
Conference at Nottingham, although not neglecting the dangers of

Home Rule and Socialism, similarly emphasized the constructive side of Unionism, particularly tariff reform, and delighted the whole-hogger activists. 'At last,' declared the *Morning Post*, 'the party has been given the responsible lead for which it has so long been waiting.'[110] Temporarily criticism was forgotten, and the party again rallied behind its leaders; the Reveille revolt subsided.[111]

In reality, however, Balfour and the Unionist party had little to offer, and Balfour at least had little intention of developing the constructive programme as the campaign went on. He felt, on the contrary, that the party had already said enough about such details, and although 'entirely in favour of a "constructive" policy . . .' still believed that the 'greatest electoral victories that have occurred in my time, e.g. the Disraeli victory in '74 and C.B.'s in 1906, were due not to construction but criticism . . .'[112] Despite the favourable start to the election campaign for the whole-hoggers, the auguries for continued success were not good. October and early November was the high point of their influence, and thus the high point of the acceptance of constructive politics. Their decline was as much due to their own divisions as to the strength of their opponents. Since 1908 the whole-hoggers had been considering their own 'unauthorised programme' but each succeeding development of that programme had revealed conflicts of opinion both on policy and tactics, and these divisions persisted during 1910. The constitutional truce found Austen Chamberlain participating in, and Garvin and F. E. Smith fervently supporting, an attempt at compromise which was anathema to a wide range of whole-hogger opinion, as represented by the Reveille movement. On land taxes the more advanced radicals of the tariff reform movement, whilst at one with the leadership, were at loggerheads with the back-bench activists of the Land Union. The payment of members scattered them in all directions. In so far as 1910 was a year of lost opportunities for the Unionist party, it was the whole-hoggers who had lost most. The December election was the final blow which destroyed the tariff reform movement. Under pressure because so much was at stake, quarrelling amongst themselves on the various additions to their basic programme, tariff reformers finally quarrelled about tariff reform itself.

The key factor in this was the removal of Bonar Law to Manchester. Strongly urged by whole-hoggers as a means of bringing the big guns of tariff reform to bear on Lancashire and capturing it for tariff reform, they neglected the influence of a Lancashire environment on Law himself. Law, however, did not, and pointed out that 'in N.W. Manchester, there must be a considerable number of businessmen who are not in favour of Tariff Reform, but who would now vote for a Unionist candidate, though they might not support me'. Yet if he were defeated, as Law admitted, 'I should injure the party and not advance its interests.'[113] He might thus be forced by Lancashire conditions to minimize rather than emphasize tariff reform, with disastrous consequences on the national campaign. His doubts were shared by others in the whole-hogger camp. Even before the end of the Constitutional Conference, pressure had begun from sections of the whole-hoggers for the postponement of food duties in order to make the rest of tariff reform more palatable to the industrial North. The divisions within the whole-hoggers, moreover, tended to fall along already established lines, with Garvin leading the retreat on this subject as he had led the movement for compromise throughout the year.[114]

Inevitably, however, such proposals would have to overcome the opposition of Highbury, or at least convince Balfour that he need not fear the reaction from that quarter. Food duties, Austen Chamberlain told him on learning of this defection, 'were necessary to any effectual Colonial preference . . . I told him . . . that if he now took Preference off his flag, he could never put it back again.' In November 1910, however, the debate was no longer about imperial policy, but electoral tactics.

From his own account Austen had a sympathetic interview with Balfour, who having 'come slowly to the Food Duties . . . didn't like to go back on them'.[115] But pressure within the party, particularly whole-hogger pressure, continued to build up in favour of a change of policy. On 16 November, Austen reported to Highbury:

Just now we are all flooded with letters from 'ardent' but wobbly Tariff Reformers begging us . . . to run away from them today that we may live to fight for them again, etc., etc. . . . Here is G[arvin] . . . explaining that we would thus keep the counties because they would believe that they would get agricultural protection after all, and win the towns because they would believe that they wouldn't.[116]

As both Austen Chamberlain's and Garvin's promises to Balfour revealed, the Unionists had still found no easy solution to the geographical–social–economic polarization evident in the January election results. At this stage Austen could still report that Balfour 'stands firm, and will nail the flag to the mast tomorrow'. But by the 21st, Balfour was beginning to weaken.[117]

Two factors were vital in Balfour's final capitulation to the demands for change: the emergence to prominence of the referendum and the 'conversion' of Bonar Law in Lancashire. Attention had been focused on the referendum during the Constitutional Conference, and in particular by Lansdowne's resolutions giving the Unionist alternative to the Parliament Bill on 23 November. 'Correspondence pours in', Sandars wrote to Garvin: 'will Mr Balfour say that Tariff Reform will be referred by Referendum to the people?'[118] Law's conversion occurred at about the same time, whilst he was campaigning in the North. On 26 November, Garvin received a telegram from the editor of the *Textile Mercury*, E. E. Marsden, that 'Lancashire can be won only if Balfour announces that Tariff on passing would be submitted for confirmation by Referendum . . .', and that Garvin should advocate this in his edition of the 27th. Garvin, without time for consultation, rewrote the leader for his London edition, and informed Sandars of his reasons for this. Sandars in turn promised his support in winning Balfour over.[119]

Marsden's telegram was in fact slightly misleading in citing Law's approval for the idea of advocating the referendum on tariff reform in the *Observer*. Law wrote to Balfour on 26 November, that he thought the proposal 'would destroy the whole of the attack on the referendum as part of the proposals in regard to the relations between the two Houses which have been put forward by Lansdowne, and . . . that it would make certain of securing the votes all over the country of people who still believe in Free Trade, but are Unionist otherwise . . .' On these grounds 'there was much to recommend it . . .', but Law was cautious, and feared that he might not have given sufficient thought to the possible objections.[120] He also sent a copy of this letter to Austen Chamberlain. Balfour, on whom in the last resort everything depended and who had to speak on the 29th, also forwarded Law's letter to Chamberlain, terming the referendum for tariff reform 'Bonar Law's suggestion'. He was, although he wrapped his opinion up in a cautious discussion of the arguments for and against, generally favourable to the idea.[121]

Chamberlain naturally telegraphed his opposition. But even his dissent was not complete. Instead, he prepared a compromise formula that Balfour should propose making the referendum offer on tariff reform conditional upon Asquith accepting the referendum for the resolution of deadlocks between the Lords and the Commons, thus abandoning the Parliament Bill.[122] Law also clarified his letter of the 26th in response to a request from Sandars,[123] but his position remained ambivalent. He too, like Austen Chamberlain, thought that any commitment should be conditional, although his reasoning and his conditions differed from Austen Chamberlain's:

> All wealthy Unionists, even strong tariff reformers, would say such declaration would mean victory but I find all working class audiences only interested in Tariff Reform and declaration would do no good with them and might damp enthusiasm of best workers . . . Would there be any use in saying if government undertake in event of their obtaining majority not to pass Home Rule without Referendum, we should give same undertaking regarding Tariff Reform.[124]

Neither this nor Austen Chamberlain's views influenced Balfour, who had by this time become convinced that the change was probably desirable, and in any case unavoidable. At the Albert Hall, on 29 November, he declared that he had 'not the least objection to submit the principles of Tariff Reform to Referendum'. Although he challenged the Liberals to respond on Home Rule, his statement was, as it stood, unconditional. Balfour explained his action the following day, and again on 13 December, to Austen Chamberlain, by laying stress on the need to meet the Liberal challenge that the referendum, as a measure affecting the constitutional dispute alone, would only apply to Liberal measures, since no constitutional conflict would arise when the Unionists had a majority in the Commons: 'all the colleagues I have been able to see were strongly in favour of the course . . .'[125] In fact, Balfour consulted few of his colleagues and made little effort to find them. The decision in the last resort was his and Lansdowne's, perhaps because he feared that he would not have been able to get his way if his colleagues had been consulted more fully.[126]

But it was not Balfour and Lansdowne who killed the food duties in the December 1910 election even though theirs was, as the party leaders, the final decision. Garvin, Law, and the 'wobbly' tariff reformers had already undermined the party before Balfour spoke at the Albert Hall. The 'referenders' themselves did not see their attitude as marking a retreat from tariff reform. Garvin savagely criticized Austen Chamberlain for 'the fossilised rigidity of his attitude', and regarded the decision to refer tariff reform as inevitable, partly because he agreed with Balfour that it was the only possible response to the Liberal challenge, partly to meet the tactical dilemma posed by Lancashire. But 'this doesn't touch the principle of the food tax. Doesn't mean any reversal of it. Doesn't demand any reference to it. The referendum is a heaven born solution.'[127]

The disagreement between referenders and whole-hoggers was tactical, as were so many of the Unionist disagreements in 1910. But on the tactical question it meant that the referenders were prepared to accept the free trade analysis of the outcome of the January election, and thus differed radically from Austen Chamberlain. It meant also, given Law's assessment that in Lancashire tariff reform was the only subject to attract the working classes, that the referenders and Balfour preferred to rely on middle-class votes. This in itself was ominous for the future of tariff reform within the Unionist party. But so too was the referenders' argument that principle could be separated from immediate policy for tactical reasons. It provided, whenever tariff reform appeared detrimental to the party's chances, a way out for the 'wobbly' tariff reformers who could remain 'ardent' believers, yet sabotage the full policy in good faith. The expedient was to have considerable repercussions in the next full-scale food duties crisis in 1912–13.

The change of policy indicated also how far tariff reform had declined from a great imperial ideal worthy of sacrifice to a tactical expedient, even in the eyes of its alleged supporters. It was the culmination of the process set in motion in 1907 by which tariff reform became a domestic policy in defence of the traditional establishment. By 1910 the Unionist party, leaders and followers, had become obsessed with tactics to the point where it became difficult, even for them, to see what precisely they were attempting to defend. In practice tactics meant concessions, the adoption of policies in which, except for a small minority of whole-hoggers, they did not believe but which might win a few votes. Fundamentally no one wished to yield anything of the positions already taken up. All choices became the lesser evil, and as to which was the lesser evil opinions differed. But since all positions were equally sacrosanct, so all were equally flexible. The composition of the Lords, the reduction of its powers, federal Home Rule, the payment of members, and various schemes of social reform were all considered as possible sacrifices. Lacking in clear leadership for most of the year the various factions were left to argue amongst themselves as to the priority of Unionist causes, which should be sacrificed, which defended, which offered the best, and which the least, chance of winning the next election. It was only after the Conference that the leaders were both able and forced to lead, and that priorities were finally defined.

For the bulk of the party, even for the bulk of the whole-hoggers, tariff reform did not and could not command the same loyalty as the Constitution and the Union. By December the Unionist leaders had announced on behalf of their party their willingness to sacrifice the composition of the Lords, preference, and part at least of the Lords' powers, in order to preserve the essence of those powers and thus, they hoped, the Union. By the nature of the concessions they had made, and even more by the concessions they had not made, the party leaders in November and December 1910 turned their backs upon constructive politics. They thus rejected both the tariff reform analysis of the causes of defeat in January, and the direction in which tariff reform sought to appeal. The referendum was aimed at the middle classes of Lancashire, the 'moderates' whom the Unionist free traders claimed to represent. The working classes, to whom tariff reform was alleged to appeal, were in practice given up as lost.

This carried still wider implications. Chamberlain had aimed tariff reform and his policies for Unionism since 1886 at the working classes to avoid the development of 'class politics'. Radical Unionism was explicitly opposed to class conflict, and the unity of classes at home was as important as the unity of the Empire overseas. In 1910 the Unionist leaders turned their backs upon this view of Unionism also. In 1909 and in the January 1910 election they had sought to conceal the class nature of their policies beneath the cloak of tariff reform as a working-class policy. When this failed tariff reform was rejected, and the Unionists openly accepted their class position. In the wings disillusioned radical imperialists, the men who had been responsible for the constructive Unionist programme of 1908 and the Reveille manifesto, awaited the results of this latest example of Balfourite betrayal.

I I

Balfour's Resignation

If the Unionists had won the general election of December 1910, thus
confirming Balfour's judgement, the tariff reformers would have been
crushed. Defeat ensured that reconciliation would be temporary. On
1 December, despite his 'great disappointment', Austen Chamberlain
came into line with the referendum pledge,[1] and Balfour went out of his
way to make this acceptance possible.[2] But as the results of the election
came in, so discontent grew. Complaints from Rowland Hunt[3] and
Richard Jebb,[4] both notorious extremists known for their hostility
to Balfour and the party establishment, carried little weight.

But when Sir Joseph Lawrence added his voice,[5] it became clear
that discontent was more broadly based. Maxse wrote to Edward
Goulding on 10 December:

our mutual friend has done more harm to Tariff Reform during the last two
months than he did good in the previous five years . . . I calculate that
Balfour's Albert Hall speech, which I understand was the result of an
intrigue, . . . cost us 40–50 seats. It is unpardonable. Balfour must go, or
Tariff Reform will go—that is the alternative.[6]

Balfour's tactics had failed the crucial test. His speech was 'nothing
less than a crime. It has not, as you see, been attended by any degree of
success which alone justified it.'[7] From 5 to 9 December Austen
Chamberlain grimly compiled a memorandum on the effects of the
referendum pledge. 'Was it worthwhile?' he concluded; 'What
evidence is there that we have gained any real strength in the constituencies by this new policy?' 'It encouraged people everywhere to
put Tariff Reform in the background and the House of Lords in the
forefront,' he wrote to Lansdowne on the 18th, 'and that played straight
into the hands of the Government.'[8]

Chamberlain's main concern was that the pledge should not become
a permanent part of the party's policy. With this in mind, in his last

speech of the campaign at Buxton on 15 December, he stressed that
the pledge was good 'for this election only'. This was going no further
than Garvin had intended when he first urged the proposal, no further
even than the Cecils when they had urged his father to postpone food
duties back in March. But those who had adopted the referendum
programme had done so because they had accepted the tactical arguments of the free traders. Both Balfour[9] and Lansdowne[10] rejected
Austen Chamberlain's claim that on the evidence of the election results
the referendum pledge had been a mistake. Because of this, Balfour's
pledge had, by the end of the campaign, taken on a degree of permanence, and Chamberlain's Buxton speech was much resented.[11] 'A
perfect epidemic of internal difference seems to have broken out now
that the Elections are over', commented Maurice Woods. 'It was almost
the same last January.'[12] The Unionists were still divided on tactics.

The position of the referenders was, however, difficult to maintain.
Ideally they wanted 'to stick to the Tariff policy . . . to prove . . . that
the Referendum is the greatest help the policy ever had, and to preach
steadfast loyalty to the man who had the courage and wisdom to see
the salvation of his Party and the salvation of the great policy in a
frank adoption of the Referendum'.[13] But just as the dropping of the
1*s.* duty on colonial corn in April 1910 had given rise to speculation
that the food duties were about to be dropped altogether, so the
referendum announcement gave new heart to those agitating for the
complete abandonment of preference. The referendum pledge thus
followed Balfour's other statements on tariff reform in becoming not
a decided party policy but a middle position, and the referenders were
forced on to the defensive on both fronts. 'There is going to be another
fight between the wholehoggers and the backers of the referendum,'
complained R. D. Blumenfeld, editor of the Balfourite *Daily Express:*

The Daily Mail is plainly going straight for the dropping of Food Taxes. The
T.R.L. is going to organise a campaign to relegate the Referendum question
to the limbo of things forgotten . . . I can't do it. If it had not been for Mr.
Balfour's speech at the Albert Hall, we should have lost 30 or more seats, and
the Coalition would have been placed in complete possession of the field . . .
But the dropping of Food Taxes and Preference is another question. I don't
see what becomes of Tariff Reform with that slice hewn off.[14]

Garvin found himself in the same difficulties, damned by his former
friends but hardly in agreement with his old enemies. He denounced

Austen Chamberlain's speech in far stronger terms than Blumenfeld, as 'a calamity and an outrage . . . arrogant as well as stupid',[15] and was alarmed to see F. E. Smith inclined to follow 'Austen's disastrous lead'. But he nevertheless felt bound to excuse himself to the whole-hoggers, and to throw the blame for his advocacy of the referendum on Bonar Law. Much of his anger against Fabian Ware similarly stemmed from the fact that although he had told Ware that he supported the referendum because of Law, Ware had taken no notice, and had not altered the line of the *Morning Post*.[16] At the same time, Garvin was also threatened from the anti-preferentialist side. The owner of the *Observer*, Lord Northcliffe, also owned the *Daily Mail*, through which he had been hinting since September that the negotiations for a Reciprocity Agreement between Canada and the United States might make preference untenable.[17]

At the end of January 1911, when the terms of the treaty became known, the *Daily Mail* came out openly against food duties and Northcliffe naturally sought the support of Garvin and the *Observer*. Garvin, like Blumenfield, could not go that far. The referendum, he argued, offered 'something like a "conscience clause" to reasonable objectors', but it 'was meant to expedite Tariff Reform' and not result in 'the indefinite postponement of the policy which has been and remains the "first constructive plank" in the Unionist programme'.[18] Garvin therefore 'never dreamed of dropping Imperial Preference altogether'.[19] He had to find a new proprietor. The permanence of the referendum became submerged in this wider conflict. One immediate result of Garvin's defence of preference was the healing of the breach with Austen Chamberlain, but his discomfort revealed the difficulty of the referenders' position. They could not prevent the dispute from being widened once a breach had been made in the policy of tariff reform. But once that conflict had been widened, their own position became irrelevant and they were forced to choose sides. Their alternative was silence, and this was a luxury which only Balfour, and his essentially uncommitted following, could afford.

Both the pledge and tariff reform itself were in any case swept aside by other considerations soon after the December election. There was, as F. E. Smith pragmatically observed, no sense in 'squabbling at this stage about the referendum . . . The fact is we have lost the election and they have won; it is "up to them" to show whether they are able and willing so to modify the constitutional position as to leave an opening for the referendum.'[20] After the election it was the constitutional aspect of the referendum, as embodied in Lansdowne's proposals for the reform of the House of Lords, which most interested Unionist leaders. They were unaware that the government had secured its guarantees prior to the election, and were sustained by reports of ministerial divisions. Moreover, they continued to believe that in the last resort the government either would not, or could not, create the 500 or so peers necessary to pass its bill. As a result, the Unionists continued to act as if they, and not the government, were masters of the situation. Sandars confidently expected that

if Lansdowne steadily presents his scheme . . . if the country is then made aware of our sincerity in the matter, and of the fair chance which, under it, Radical measures will have of becoming law with the assent of the people, there will grow up, as the date of the coronation approaches, a general feeling against a policy that is so destructive and grotesque, and in the end the Government will seek a basis of compromise. They will try to come to terms . . . Out of reasonable amendments, some compromise will be shaped.[21]

He thus agreed with Garvin that 'compromise and agreement are more likely to be accomplished if we are stern—if we seem to be prepared to face the creation of Peers than if we shrink from the violent alternative'. But there were other, more pressing reasons for defiance than this:

it starts our Party on good fighting lines. . . . an important consideration. Owing to Alick's [Hood] neglect of our young men and the enforced truce policy following the King's death, these good fellows fell an easy prey to the Maxses and Morning Post manipulators—If they are looked after in the new Session and encouraged to take their part in a stout fight, it will be an excellent thing for the political vitality of our forces.[22]

Thus, although the hypothesis that the government had already obtained guarantees for the creation of peers was considered, and although the party leaders were well aware that forcing the creation of peers would result in a radical House of Lords which would rapidly pass all the measures they disliked, including Home Rule, they preferred to take a hard line, and encourage their followers in this.

The 'young men' were indeed still restive as a result of the passive policy of the previous year. In January Steel-Maitland, cautiously loyal, put to Sandars a scheme to harness some of this energy for party purposes by conducting 'an irregular warfare on the flank, so that it can either be made use of or disowned as occasion chooses'. He wrote to ensure that there would be no misunderstandings, and that the leaders did not interpret this as a revolt.[23] Sandars was prepared to accept the idea, and suggested some harmless topics that the group could 'get up'.[24] But in reality Steel-Maitland was covering his own flank, and the movement was, if not dangerous to the leadership because of its youth and inexperience, implicitly hostile to it, and to its views. 'Being', wrote Charles Bathurst, 'like our mutual friend Lord Milner, a thoroughgoing democrat, the extreme Tory views of some of those who rule the destinies of our Party make me not a little anxious about the future.'[25]

Steel-Maitland's 'irregulars' were another manifestation of the extreme radical unionists who had criticized and pressurized Balfour since the very beginning of the tariff reform movement. Their idea of action was not to learn side-issues from Blue books to gain experience, but an amendment to the Address on Lords reform proposing the exclusion of the hereditary principle from any aspect of the reconstituted second chamber.[26] Milner commented:

> The party direction, if such a thing exists, is too hidebound to cut itself clean adrift from the 'hereditary principle'. But the younger Unionists in the House of Commons who have survived two elections with the incubus of the Lords on their backs, can afford to make a demonstration on that line . . . and if it is a successful one, the party as a whole may take the hint.[27]

Lansdowne, as one of the hidebound, found this tendency disturbing: 'A great many most worthy peers are plumping against heredity, even in homeopathic doses . . .', he wrote to Sandars;[28] and to Balfour, 'Our people are, as you know, hopelessly divided as to House of Lords reform . . .'[29]

The democrats were easily identifiable as a group, 'B.L., F.E., Wyndham and colleagues of that type',[30] because the factions fell along familiar lines. In general, the radical reformers of the House of Lords in the spring of 1911 were the old whole-hoggers, advocates of a constructive policy and opponents of the attempted compromise of 1910. With certain exceptions, most notably Bonar Law, they were equally to become the Diehards in the autumn. The essence of their position in 1911 was the paramount importance of maintaining, and even increasing, the powers of the second chamber. In comparison with this, its composition was a secondary issue. 'The British Constitution in all its integrity is the only thing that Conservative electors

understand and respect,' wrote Willoughby de Broke. 'Some reform
of the *Composition* of the House of Lords is now expected; but no
diminution of its *functions*.'[31] Democratization of the House of Lords
was, as usual, linked with plans for a wider programme of reforms to
appeal to the democracy. Steel-Maitland thus wanted Northcliffe to
give general instructions to his editors

> to emphasise the need that the Unionist Party should take up certain social
> reforms with a real wish to get them carried . . .
> We shall never get support for our Imperial policy if we are barren in
> social reforms that can be carried and are . . . wholly in accord with Unionist
> principles. The immediate result of our barrenness is the Canadian Reciprocity
> Agreement.
> They are thoroughly desirable in themselves, quite apart from their being
> alternative to Socialistic measures which some people dread.[32]

As before, they were also against any compromise or 'surrender' to the
government. 'The Peers ought to stand by their amendments to the
Parliament Bill no matter what happens.'[33]

What happened was not an election, which was widely rumoured in
June, but Asquith's revelation early in July that an election was unnecessary because the government already had the guarantees it
needed to enact its proposals, and Balfour's consequent recommendation that the peers should not prevent the passage of the Parliament
Bill. Even before this, however, 'the group who profess to want an
extreme course—just those you would expect,'[34] had begun to suspect
their leaders of weakness, and Balfour of deliberately obstructing
a determined opposition to the bill.[35] 'It remains', Ormsby-Gore wrote,
'for the backwoods peers to save the country.'[36]

The organization of these peers was taken in hand by Willoughby
de Broke: 'we are getting a move on at last,' he reported to Maxse in
June. 'We have a body of 35 to 40 already who have already signed or
who are prepared to sign a resolution urging Lord Lansdowne to be
firm . . .'[37] This was at the time when the Diehards still saw their
choice as between accepting the bill or forcing an election, a perilous
course in view of the two previous defeats. Asquith's statement that
the government already had its guarantees thus strengthened rather
than weakened the Diehards in their convictions. 'The apprehension
of an election being removed,' F. E. Smith told Balfour, 'I confess the
arguments for resistance à outrance coûte que coûte appear to me
overwhelming . . .'[38]

The effect of knowledge of the government's guarantees, and the adoption of a 'surrender' policy by Balfour, was to give the Diehard movement leaders. The shadow cabinet met on 7 July to consider the new situation and was deeply divided. The majority favoured 'surrender', but the Diehards included Selborne, Salisbury, Halsbury, Austen Chamberlain, Wyndham, Carson, F. E. Smith, and the new chief whip, Lord Balcarres. The aged Halsbury became the symbolic head of the rebels, but the real organization remained in the hands of the 'young men', particularly Smith, Amery, and Willoughby de Broke.[39]

In the event it was not enough. Lansdowne's policy of abstention, and the votes of 37 Unionist peers in the government lobby, were sufficient to overcome the resistance and ensure the passage of the Parliament Bill without the creation of peers. In the intervening weeks, however, the schism had developed into one of exceptional bitterness, and the passage of the bill by Unionist 'rats' made this acute. 'Feeling runs very high against the 35,' Sandars wrote to Balfour. 'Only one dared to show his nose in the Carlton after the division and he . . . had to leave shortly . . . The criticism of Lansdowne is very keen.'[40] Balcarres wrote in a similar vein, and as chief whip was fearful for the future.[41] In the days that followed the discontent grew. Sandars reported on 14 August that resentment was high because of a belief that the passage of the bill had all along been fixed by the two front benches. Steel-Maitland had believed that 'any attempt to get the local associations of the party to record approval of what had been done, or to pass a vote of confidence in the leaders was foredoomed to fail . . .', and was reinforced by Eddy Talbot.[42]

Inevitably this discontent focused on Balfour. 'Surrender' confirmed all the suspicions that had been built up from his apparently half-hearted leadership that he was too friendly with the Liberal leaders, and even that he was in collusion with them. Moreover, his compromising had, in the long run, failed. He had led the party to three successive defeats in ten years, and however successful the blocking of Liberal legislation until 1908, the budget had passed, the Lords' veto had been destroyed, and the Union was now in serious danger. As early as June Maxse had warned Sandars that 'men who surrender over the Parliament Bill, which as Asquith has himself told us, involves Home Rule, are equally capable of surrendering Home Rule.'[43]

But the most perceptive comment on Balfour's action in this crisis, and on his leadership as a whole, came from Collings. 'In this crisis he has left his place as leader, and 'qui quitte sa place la perd' should apply . . .'[44] Just as the whole-hoggers and Diehards confused a constructive policy with aggressive tactics, so Balfour confused a refusal to commit himself to details of policy with an abdication of leadership. This was particularly true after the rejection of the 1909 budget. Having committed the party to a course which was bound to lead to conflict between the two Houses if the Unionists lost the election of January 1910, Balfour had no contingency plans for this event, and never made any. Much of the confusion which overtook the party in 1911 was due to Balfour's vacillation after January. Both the referendum on tariff reform and 'surrender' were examples of this. Both had been the subject of discussion for months before Balfour made his decision, and in both cases the party was ill-prepared for the sudden change in policy.[45]

For his decisions themselves, especially his surrender in 1911, Balfour had sound reasons. 'I regard the policy which its advocates call "fighting to the last" as essentially theatrical,' he wrote. 'It does nothing, it can do nothing . . . we are the victims of a revolution.' The best the party could do, he thought, was to exploit the two sessions' delay to which measures rejected by the Lords were subject under the terms of the Parliament Act. The alternative was a radical House of Lords, 'a mere annexe of the present House of Commons', which would pass Home Rule in a single session.[46] But the party had never been confronted by its leaders with its real impotence. Liberal threats in July to create peers were seen as bluff by disbelieving Diehards reared on a doctrine of defiance. Always amenable to pressure, Balfour's erratic behaviour under the confused pressures after January 1910 finally destroyed his credibility as leader.

The decision of the Diehards to stay together after the immediate cause of their formation had passed reflected this lack of confidence.[47] By October they had created the Halsbury Club, which, while not overtly hostile to the party leaders, was designed to ensure that in future they would not be 'stampeded' by other influences 'as they were last August by Curzon'. The Diehards, as Wyndham explained their position to Austen Chamberlain:

regarded Lansdowne's scheme of Lords' Reform as dead and the Albert Hall pledge for a Referendum on Tariff Reform as void and expired after the events of this summer. They had come to the conclusion that a purely elected Second

Chamber was the only one to which we could now persuade the country to give effective and sufficient powers . . . They wished to speak more plainly about national dangers and National Defence; to give a more definite form to the Unionist programme of Social Reform; and in all things to take a more vigorous fighting line . . . [48]

Neither Chamberlain nor the other party leaders who formed the Halsbury Club sought Balfour's replacement as leader. 'My position', Chamberlain wrote, 'had been from the first that there could be no question about Balfour's leadership as long as he was willing to lead. The leading spirits of the Halsbury Club knew my views and shared them.'[49] The Club even took on, in their eyes, a positively loyalist aspect. Chamberlain saw in it a means 'to retain the Diehards . . . in the party and prevent them throwing up their positions in the local associations etc., in disgust, as they were doing . . . and to prevent the wilder ones running amuck as Leo Maxse did'.[50] The Club itself never represented a dangerous threat to Balfour's position. Its members were too divided, both on policy and on the alternative to Balfour if Balfour left. 'I am convinced', Steel-Maitland wrote to Balfour, 'that it is not hostile, but that it is muddle-headed.' He offered to join the Club to 'get a hold of it', if Balfour thought this desirable,[51] but Balfour never took the Club seriously.[52]

But despite the views of the Halsbury leaders, the leadership question was wide open. Chamberlain miscalculated on his ability to restrain the wilder elements, on the impression the Club would create, and on Balfour's own mood. The breakdown in relations between leader and followers had left its mark upon Balfour as well as the party. 'Balfour', Balcarres told Chamberlain, 'was very restless under the criticisms made upon him and might go in a few months.'[53] Even before the crucial vote in the Lords, Balfour had left for the Continent. 'Politics have been to me quite unusually odious,' he wrote to Lady Elcho from Paris. 'As you know I am very easy going and not given to brooding over my wrongs. But last Friday and Saturday I could think of nothing else.'[54] Rumours of Balfour's disenchantment were circulating even before the party split asunder, and rendered Balfour's position intolerable.[55]

Maxse did his best to maintain Balfour's unease. In the spring of 1911, after a lengthy period following the Birmingham speech in which his criticism of Balfour had been muted and interspersed with praise, Maxse resumed his attacks upon Balfour in the *National Review*.

After the 'surrender' in July, he launched an all out campaign to oust Balfour from the leadership under the slogan B.M.G.—'Balfour Must Go'. The press campaign was the more dangerous because it was linked to a resolution which Maxse had put down for debate at the Annual Meeting of the National Union at Leeds in November, which, by commending the action of the Diehard peers, was in effect a censure motion on Balfour. At this meeting of constituency delegates Maxse could hope for considerable support. It was amongst the leaders of the party associations in the country rather than in the parliamentary party that the surrender was most deeply resented.[56] Malmesbury informed Austen Chamberlain:

from every direction and from every sort of constituency comes the same complaint, the same unhappy story of people resigning their posts on local committees or cancelling their subscriptions to the party funds (local or central or both) due to the apathy and discontent out of the present situation.[57]

The most extreme action was taken by the Unionist candidate for South Bedfordshire who 'has taken a strong line repudiating the leadership of Balfour and Co. He is backed up by the Duke.'[58]

The leaders of the constituency organizations were the natural audience for the views Maxse put forward in the *National Review*. As early as 1904, Balfour had remarked that the local leaders were in the main whole-hoggers, in advance of both the parliamentary party and the electorate.[59] To them, and not to the parliamentary party, Maxse directed his attacks in the autumn of 1911. In the *National Review* for September, he emphasized the distinction between the party in Parliament and the party in the country, and urged the latter 'to seek its own salvation . . . any attempt to replace our heads under the Balfourian yoke is doomed to failure. B.M.G.'[60] He returned to this theme again in November, alleging that the parliamentary party was determined to 'scuttle' with Balfour through a mistaken sense of loyalty to persons not principles. In both cases, the message was clear. The Unionist rank and file should revolt, bring their M.P.s to heel, and censure Balfour's conduct.[61] It was an impressive campaign, and combined with the resolution before the National Union Conference, not without effect. 'You will know better than most what is best done at the National Union,' Midleton wrote to Balcarres, 'but assuredly, if the leaders are to remain, Maxse must somehow be defeated or modified.'[62]

Midleton was reassured a few days later by Steel-Maitland, whom he found alive to the danger, and inclined 'to talk plainly to Balfour'.[63] As chief organizer, Steel-Maitland was in close contact with the party agents and local associations, and was deeply impressed by the discontent which prevailed in those circles:

There are many danger points in the autumn especially the Leeds meeting on November 16th. I think that, as a rule, people who apprehend resolutions of this kind, generally overrate the possibility of their being successful. There is, however, no doubt whatever as to the discontent which is abroad. It is not only a few individuals but there is considerable feeling among the rank and file as well in the constituencies. I have heard this from workers well-disposed and ill-disposed, from every one of our Central Office agents, who have been quite united upon the point . . . and it is corroborated from the press and other sources. My real fear is that, from the point of view of the country, even should he [Balfour] be successful to the extent of getting back to power at the next election, we shall have the same troubles over again if we are not careful, and we shall do no good as regards the real objects for which it is alone worth while getting back to power.[64]

But Steel-Maitland was more inclined to blame Balfour than his critics for this situation.[65] In the middle of September he made an uninvited and unexpected visit to Whittinghame[66] where Balfour was brooding after his return, and on the 20th drew up a memorandum which probably embodied the substance of his message. The difficulty which Steel-Maitland and Balcarres faced was their responsibility for the coming autumn campaign, and the need for an authoritative statement from Balfour before that began. Superficially, Steel-Maitland's memorandum was directed to this problem, and discussed the methods by which Balfour might make his views known to his followers. In essence, it amounted to a complete condemnation of Balfour's leadership, and above all, his indecisiveness.[67] Steel-Maitland told Balcarres:

What is most needed is that his party should feel he is taking a real grip of them . . . Ergo, let him make an important speech early . . . provided he is clear . . . if he can meet his House of Commons members and talk to them straight and simply, it would do a lot of good. If he can't talk to them straight and simply enough, he had better not.[68]

Steel-Maitland's criticisms were crucial in inducing Balfour to make up his mind to resign. At the end of September he summoned Balcarres and Steel-Maitland to Whittinghame for the week-end, and informed them that he intended to announce his resignation at Edinburgh on 21

October. A letter from Long, which confirmed the reports of discontent and again criticized his leadership and urged changes, arrived during the week-end and hardened his resolve. But the vacillation which had characterized his leadership in its last two years extended to his own resignation. Asked if his decision was final, Balfour confessed that it was not, and under pressure from Balcarres he agreed to defer his announcement until the Leeds meeting in November.[69]

In the light of Maxse's resolution, Balcarres's choice of venue for the announcement was curious, since the usual procedure at the National Union Conference was for the leader to speak on the evening of the the first day, in which case Balfour would announce his resignation immediately after the debate on Maxse's resolution, and convey the impression he most wished to avoid, that he had been driven out by the Diehards. Nothing would do more to perpetuate the party split. The Central Office, however, was apparently taking action to ensure that Maxse's resolution would be excluded, if not completely, then at least from the first day of the Conference. J. T. Middlemore was informed by a Birmingham correspondent that Steel-Maitland, who 'has great influence here, especially among Conservatives', was exerting his influence against the resolution,[70] and Maxse himself got wind of an intrigue against him. He wrote to Croft on 18 October:

I don't precisely know what form the intrigues of the Central Office are now taking. I am told they intend to try and fill up the first day, (Nov. 16th)— which is the only day that counts—with 'sawdust' about organisation etc. Then in the evening we are to be electrified by a Rule Britannia speech pumped into AB and pumped out by him, and under the influence of this, the Conference will be asked to pass a vote of unabashed confidence in our great and glorious leader. There should be a sufficient body of stalwarts at the Conference to stop all this rot, and to insist that the resolution shall come on the first day, and if, on a show of hands, we manage to carry it, which if all the Associations were fairly represented, we probably should, or at any rate to be a large minority—nothing but good will accrue. Time is pressing however, as there is a lot of thimble-rigging going on by the Central Office, and a great many Associations have already chosen, or are about to choose, their nominees . . .

Maxse wrote in order to promote his counter-measures, urging anyone who could 'exercise any influence either in the selection of delegates to attend the National Union Conference, or on the delegates themselves' to do whatever they could 'in order that the resolution may have a good show . . . If I could get a substantial number of nominations given to me, I would undertake to fill them with good men and true.'[71] He also sent out a circular letter to M.P.s whom he thought might be sympathetic to his cause, bearing the same message.[72]

Reaction from those whom Maxse approached was mixed. P. A. Clive refused 'to assist . . . in "rigging" the Conference',[73] and Mark Sykes, even though he still considered the passage of the Parliament Bill an 'egregious blunder', nevertheless did not wish 'to throw such a bombshell into the Conference . . .'[74] Mostly, the opponents, while sympathizing with the reasons for Maxse's action, disagreed with it on tactical grounds,[75] or, like Mark Sykes, were concerned for the future: 'The real business we have in hand is to point out that there is *no* constitution at this present moment. A fact which even our people are forgetting—and which, if they do forget it finally, England is doomed to Bureaucracy first, then Mob Rule, then Dictatorship— wranglings on past errors will not avert these dangers.'[76]

Maxse's supporters also had difficulties. Leconfield, who promised to try and 'round up some names', found that the Horsham Association had already decided not to send delegates to the Conference since it was too far from their businesses, and 'hitherto these Conferences have been quite abortive'.[77] Jesse Collings[78] and J. T. Middlemore[79] both sent word of their support from Birmingham, but when Middlemore inquired what might be done he was told that as a Liberal Unionist he had no official standing with either the local or national Conservative organizations. But there was also some effective support from this area. The agent for South Wolverhampton was told by Col. Hickman 'to try to get the full contingent of delegates from that division to attend and vote for Mr. Maxse's resolution . . .';[80] Prothero promised to do all he could in Bedfordshire,[81] and Charles Craig reported that 'Our Irish Association will be at Leeds in full force and you may rest assured they will back you up in a Forward policy.'[82]

Maxse's chances of complete success were nevertheless limited. Middlemore's Birmingham correspondent thought that if local feeling was typical, Maxse would get a majority 'on the merits of the question', but not 'if the opposition represents that the resolution implies a vote of censure on Mr Balfour' which would compel his resignation.[83] But Maxse did not have to win. Provided he achieved a substantial minority, which would show that the party was divided upon Balfour's leadership, he would achieve his object.

In prolonging and increasing discontent, Maxse was assisted, despite
the views of its leaders, by the formation of the Halsbury Club, which
was, from the first, in a false position. In the face of the Club's leaders'
loyalty to Balfour, the real malcontents soon despaired of it as an
effective anti-Balfourite agency. H. A. Gwynne asked Maxse:

Do you know what our friends of the Halsbury Club are going to do? I don't.
It seems to me that they are neither flesh nor fowl nor good red herring. The
ostensible reason for the establishment of the Club was to make a protest
against the leadership of AJB. Each member now seems to be vieing with
the other in proclaiming from the rooftops his intense loyalty . . . at the
present moment our leader seems to have got the Halsbury Club in the hollow
of his hand and he is going to make them feel the weight of his hand.[84]

The paralysed condition of the Club was fully revealed at a meeting on
6 November, when Austen Chamberlain attempted to carry a resolution
of confidence in Balfour. He was met by an anti-Balfour amendment
and was only successful in forcing through his vote after both he and
Halsbury had threatened to resign, and after F. E. Smith had promised
the anti-Balfourites 'that there would be satisfaction within a week or
so'. The meeting demonstrated the latent depths of feeling against
Balfour among the rank and file, but it demonstrated equally that they
could never use the Club to give collective expression to their opinions
without dooming it to self-destruction.

   To the party faithful, however, the Club gave the impression that
Austen Chamberlain and other influential Unionist leaders were
heading an anti-Balfourite movement.

I am quite sure [wrote Long] the leaders of the Halsbury Club do not mean
to be disloyal . . . to AJB, but they desire to drive him along the road they
have selected, and this comes to the same thing! Meantime in the country, to
my knowledge, the Club is being used as a centre for a determined attack on
him and Lansdowne; and this seems to me to be the real and serious danger.[85]

Even Alfred Lyttelton, despite his high rank in the party, thought that
Austen Chamberlain would be unable to join in a declaration of loyalty
to Balfour because of his membership of the Club.[86]

   The ill-feeling against Balfour that derived from the divisions of
July and August was thus maintained and heightened throughout the
autumn. During October, as resolutions of censure continued to come
in from the associations, Balfour became increasingly determined to
resign. On 23 October Sandars noted that he talked of nothing else,[87]

and on 30 October Balfour began telling his closest associates of his decision. It had become clear also that the Leeds meeting, divided by Maxse's resolution which focused all the diffuse discontent in the local party leadership, was not the best occasion for the announcement. Despite the long months during which the decision had matured, Balfour's resignation was eventually sprung upon the party. He cancelled an engagement to attend a dinner for his colleague, Hayes Fisher,[88] and spoke to a specially and hurriedly convened meeting of the Executive Committee of his constituency association in the City. Lack of notice ensured that the meeting was small.

For political reasons he resigned alone, and the reasons he gave, his age, his declining health, his long years in office, were personal. At the same time Lansdowne was persuaded, against his will, to remain as leader in the Lords. In both cases the reasoning was the same—to avoid the impression that the party leaders had been forced out by the Diehards, and thus to facilitate the reunion of the party. Balfour's apparent weakness in July, the Diehard movement, and Maxse's agitation had all shifted attention temporarily from the question of policy and made the leadership itself the main source of controversy within the party. It was this which gave Balfour's resignation political meaning, this indeed which rendered it politically necessary if he were not to undo the work of the previous eight years during which the unity of the party had been his main, almost his sole, concern. By his resignation, Balfour removed the leadership at least from the area of dispute.

Briefly, the troubles threatened to break out again when Austen Chamberlain and Walter Long both presented themselves as rival candidates for the succession. But since neither was acceptable to the opposing faction, both withdrew in favour of Bonar Law who was elected as a compromise candidate, a whole-hogger who had supported the referendum, supported 'surrender', and never joined the Diehards. With Law's election, Balfour achieved his immediate purpose. The rivalry between Chamberlain and Long demonstrated that Law was the only possible leader who could unite all sections of the party, and the leadership was correspondingly strengthened.

But Law's election was still, to a great extent, a whole-hogger victory. Law owed his political reputation almost exclusively to his abilities as a tariff reform leader. He had been associated with the most extreme elements of the tariff reform movement, including the Confederates, and with the demand for a constructive policy. He was thought to be, and expected to be, sound on tariff reform above all else. From the first he took a positive attitude. His speech to the National Union as the new leader satisfied the extremists, even Maxse, who wrote to praise his emphasis on the 'wages aspect' of tariff reform.[89] Law drove home the constructive message with a letter to George Balfour, the candidate, for use in the Govan by-election in December, again emphasizing tariff reform as the essential foundation to economic recovery, and hence to higher wages and social reform.[90] On 17 January he assured Austen Chamberlain that he would make no changes in tariff policy without his consent. 'You and I stand too much together on this question for us to have any difference about it.'[91]

At the same time, Law set about repairing the breach with the young activists which had opened up under the none too tactful Hood. Comyn Platt wrote to Steel-Maitland:

During the last two months practically every member of the Unionist government, as also the Whips in both Houses of Parliament, have visited the 1900 Club, with the result that the younger members of the Party have been brought into the closest touch with the leaders and other prominent men . . . The fact that the younger members of the Party are thus given an opportunity of meeting ex-ministers has given the greatest satisfaction to those who are fighting constituencies.[92]

Law and his officials were rewarded at the end of November by the disbanding of the Diehard vigilantes: 'the "Reveille" . . . have unanimously decided to bank fires and funds and to cease any independent action in the country . . . we agreed to do this as a mark of our esteem and confidence in yourself'.[93] On the surface, Law gave every impression of being, from the Diehard and whole-hogger point of view, a great improvement on Balfour as leader.

Nevertheless, in one respect Law was suspect as a whole-hogger by 1911. He firmly believed that the food duties were an electoral handicap, and did not share Austen Chamberlain's conviction that Unionist victories in 1910 were won by the positive appeal of tariff reform. Rather, he took the free food view that they were won by the general reaction of the propertied classes against the government. The logic of this position had led him to support the referendum in 1910, and theoretically led to the continuance of Balfour's pledge, despite Balfour's resignation. His attitude was tested immediately upon his election as leader. Balfour's resignation had removed the leadership from the arena, but it did not remove the conflicting pressures which had led to that resignation. As soon as he heard of Balfour's resignation Chamberlain repudiated the referendum pledge, and on Law's election he drew Law's attention to this.[94] But on 13 November Derby wrote from Lancashire 'that Tariff Reform as at present advocated will not do for us here, and that by hook or by crook we have got to make some such alteration as will prevent our opponents having the very taking cry that we are taxing the people's food . . .'[95] Others wrote to Law in the same sense. 'He is', commented Chamberlain, 'beset by letters asking him to abandon food taxes altogether . . .'[96]

In the short run Law's nerve held and he remained true to his whole-hogger principles. 'I think', he replied to Derby, 'there is nothing for us but to go straight forward with the programme as it is.'[97] But Chamberlain was right to be suspicious and to take decisive action. In the new year, under continuing free food pressure, Law began to show signs of weakening and Chamberlain lamented that Law had not committed himself publicly to the abandonment of the referendum pledge at Leeds. Law went so far as to ask Chamberlain 'whether I should mind his saying in the course of the Tariff Reform debate . . . that we should submit a Tariff Reform budget to the Referendum if even now Asquith consented to take the same course with Home Rule'.[98] Chamberlain naturally demurred, and Law gave way under a thinly veiled threat of a tariff reform revolt. Lansdowne too came unconvincingly to the conclusion that they had better return to the original tariff reform programme, and that they were, in the altered circumstances, free from any pledges made before the December election.[99]

The decision to abandon the referendum was taken in principle at a meeting of the shadow cabinet at the end of February. It was taken reluctantly and without conviction, for the prevailing mood remained that food duties were a handicap. But as Law explained, any modification of the full tariff reform programme or continuation of the referendum pledge would 'split our party from top to bottom'.[100] The full programme was thus reinstated and Chamberlain satisfied. Initially Law intended 'not to make any definite statement on the subject at the present time,' but under pressure from Austen Chamberlain and from Steel-Maitland, who 'was constantly being asked for directions by candidates', he gave way on this point also, and promised 'to find some formula that would make the position clear'.[101] In the event he delayed his announcement until the end of the year.

In choosing between the tariff reformers and the free fooders, Law and his shadow cabinet, despite their tactical reservations, chose the former because they appeared to be the stronger faction within the party. The free fooders were trapped by the polarization of politics as they had been since 1909, and had 'no choice between supporting a Tariff Reform party and supporting the methods of the present Government'.[102] The Halsbury Club was a recent confirmation of this. Dominated by whole-hoggers, committed to a constructive policy which included the abandonment of the referendum pledge, its membership demonstrated the willingness of the Unionist free traders to subordinate their fiscal convictions to the need for unity against greater evils. Lord Hugh Cecil had pressed Austen Chamberlain in October 1911 to postpone food duties as 'a frightful handicap in obtaining the necessary popular support',[103] but when Chamberlain refused both he and Lord Robert came into line, and Chamberlain was assured that 'neither Bob nor Hugh Cecil would give any more trouble about tariff reform'.[104] Nor was the nature of the anti-Balfourite agitation, as a condemnation of his weakness on tariff reform as well as on the Parliament Bill, lost upon the new leadership. The Diehards demanded above all a fighting uncompromising lead. Threatened with the prospect of a tariff reform revolt, Law could hardly begin his career as leader with what would have been, with his reputation, a retreat.

The whole-hoggers had good reason to be elated in the spring of 1912. In all respects they appeared to have triumphed over the set-backs they had suffered in the last year of Balfour's leadership. The Halsbury Club was determined on a forward policy; the shadow cabinet accepted the need to restore the full programme of tariff reform to pride of place in the party platform without tactical reservations, and perhaps most important of all, Balfour's resignation removed almost the last of the Balfourite 'old guard' from key positions in the party hierarchy. With the installation of Bonar Law as leader and Steel-Maitland at the Central Office, whole-hoggers, supporters of a constructive policy, now controlled the central party machine. Law's opening statements set the tone of the new regime. He emphasized tariff reform as the solution to the industrial questions of unemployment and low wages, as the road to imperial federation, and as the essential prerequisite of the party's constructive alternative to Home Rule and the economic development of Ireland, particularly of Irish agriculture. The 'constructionists' were not unnaturally delighted, and in this benign atmosphere tariff reform even recovered some of its crusading fervour. After a speech by Law at Glasgow in May, Amery wrote:

What the country wants to rally it our way . . . is a big ideal clearly held up before them, and Imperial Unity is the only big ideal of our age. We can fill it in with every detail, above all the detail of a prosperous and harmonious people living in a true social order, but the framework of the big ideal must be there all the time to hold it all together.[105]

But the assurance with which the radical imperialists wrote of their ideals and of their eventual success concealed deep anxiety about the immediate future. In 1912 the enemy was at the gates, even in possession of the imperial citadel. A Home Rule government was about to begin the dismemberment of the Empire, unchecked by an emasculated House of Lords; in an economic climate of rising prices and falling real wages, new theories and a rapidly rising trade union membership led to industrial unrest on a hitherto unprecedented scale, and seemed to presage class war and socialist revolution. Lloyd George, spurred on by past successes and by the radicals in his own party, was soon to launch a new onslaught on the landed interest, the heart of Tory England. In this hostile atmosphere the task the radical right set itself was not just to urge a sympathetic public to seize its opportunity, but to reeducate public opinion from scratch.

I am convinced in my own mind [wrote Willoughby de Broke] that in addition to the victory over Home Rule and Disestablishment, and the consequent introduction of Tariff Reform and the Restoration of the Constitution, that we also ought to found a school of thought that will stand by us in future hours of need, and create a strong permanent body of followers who will rely on you to vindicate National or Tory principles

. . . I am quite certain that there are millions of people who are now ready to receive an appeal to the old British conception of Justice, Unity and Freedom; and that the Unionist Party wants a doctrine, and a reaffirmation of nationalist principles. To get people to *think* rightly will do much; even more than passing laws. The renewal of the right spirit is now of supreme importance. It is because we have lost sight of first principles that we have got into all this trouble; the public mind is looking for a leader of thought . . .[106]

He was to be bitterly disappointed. The next year was to reveal both the limitations of the constructive Unionist ideal itself, and the exposed position it occupied within the Unionist party.

Reaction

The triumph of the whole-hoggers in the spring of 1912 was largely illusory, and rested on the insecure basis of the confusion between constructive policies and aggressive actions which characterized the Unionist party for the whole of its period in opposition. In rejecting Balfour's style of leadership the Diehards temporarily associated retreat from the full policy of tariff reform with the retreat from an all-out defence of the constitution. But the identification was short-lived, and did not survive Balfour's resignation. In the long run, the Diehard movement, uniting as it did men who differed widely and violently on the fiscal question, was the Unionist party's first adjustment to the change of issues which had taken place in politics.

After the election of January 1910, the defence of the constitution, the Union, and the established Church replaced tariff reform and socialism as the dividing line between parties around which politics revolved. The Diehards were united by their opposition to these recent revivals of Gladstonian liberalism, and by their desire for action even if this meant no more than shouting down Asquith in the Commons and threatening civil war in Ulster from the platform. But it was an essentially negative unity. The Diehards were against the policies of the government. On a constructive alternative to those policies there was complete disagreement. Lord Hugh Cecil, for example, was totally hostile, both from policy and tactics, to constructive politics.[1] Milner on the other hand, an enthusiastic supporter of a constructive and democratic policy, went too far and found that his sympathy with a federal solution to the Irish problem precluded complete co-operation.[2] As Balcarres commented of the Halsbury Club: 'You aren't agreed about Reform of the House of Lords or Tariffs or anything.'[3] Despite the apparent dominance of the Diehards, the failure of the party in January 1910 was the failure of tariff reform and constructive politics. Tariff reformers as well as free traders demanded the referendum in

December. These doubts, and the essentially negative nature of the Unionist position in the new political situation, transferred the advantage to the free traders and bode ill for the Tory Democrats like Willoughby de Broke, who appealed for new inspiration.

Nowhere was this more true than in the party's attitude to labour. It was one of the basic tenets of Tory Democracy, on which tariff reform and the constructive policy was built, that there was a special relationship between their party and the working classes. Opposition to socialism was not necessarily opposition to labour. But in practice the party was hesitant, its discomfort increasing with the growth of labour's political independence. After the failures of 1910, and their counterpart the success of the socialists in capturing organized labour, the Unionist party began to lose faith both in constructive policies themselves and in the possibility of a rapprochement with labour.

The sudden upsurge of trade union militancy after 1910 confirmed these doubts. Preoccupied with the Parliament Bill and its own internal disputes, the party at large had taken little notice of the industrial discontent of 1911. In March 1912, however, a major coal strike led to industrial paralysis on such a scale that the government felt obliged to intervene, and forced the Unionists to define their attitude. It revealed that the party was on the high road to reaction.[4] The Unionist rank and file took an unsophisticated view of the troubles, and advocated an unsophisticated solution. Tullibardine informed Law:

It is entirely a leaders-engineered strike . . . If the men were sure of proper protection, many of them would break away from the strike and go back to work . . . A ballot for strikes under proper control, and after the men had seen their wives, would make a good deal of difference . . . the whole of the traders and their dependents of all classes of politics are strongly against the miners and are openly cursing them.[5]

Charles Bathurst, radical unionist though he was, held the same opinion of the strike in the Forest of Dean, and urged the abolition of 'peaceful picketing' to enable 'men who are now longing to get back to work to do so without intervention from the extreme socialist section and with the support (if required) of police and military protection'.[6] Another radical, Collings, agreed. 'There is one thing the Government . . . ought to do, that is to repeal the miserable clause in the 1906 Trades Disputes Act allowing so called peaceful picketing.'[7]

Broadly speaking, the Unionist rank and file subscribed to the view that the strike was a socialist conspiracy, maintained by the intimidation of the bulk of the men who would otherwise return willingly to work, and could thus be solved by a combination of legislation to repeal the right of picketing and the deployment of superior force. The Unionist rank and file's reaction to the coal strike threw into doubt the tactics upon which the constructive policy rested, and which the party had followed at least since 1903, the avoidance of confrontation with organized labour. The conspiracy thesis tended to indicate that such tactics were unnecessary, and even short-sighted. If the unions were dominated by a small group of agitators, and their militancy achieved by intimidation, then the avoidance of confrontation would achieve nothing, whilst confrontation and the destruction of the political power of the unions would not result in the alienation of the working classes at large, who were not willing partners to militancy. On the contrary, from their reaction the Unionists would be the natural beneficiaries:

the prospect of recovering the freedom which has been filched from the men by the Trade Union leaders, would cause a great transfer of votes to our party, while there can be no doubt that the prospect of fewer strikes and freedom from Trade Union pressure would appeal with success to employers, to tradespeople, and to the vast majority of the middle classes . . . [8]

Tactically that is, the Unionist party had a better chance of winning the next election, even of winning back the working-class vote, by a policy of confrontation and negative anti-socialism. It was a conclusion which harmonized with the mood of the party on other more important issues such as Home Rule, and one which removed almost the last prop of constructive Unionism.

The Unionist leadership was both more committed to constructive policies and better informed, officially and unofficially,[9] of the real situation and the government's problems in reconciling the industrial conflict. G. R. Askwith in particular made it clear to Law that the miners' leaders were fully supported by their followers, and that the leaders would have difficulty in persuading them to accept the government's proposed legislation.[10] The information was given for a purpose —to strengthen Law in the conviction that he should do his utmost to restrain the reactionaries in his own party lest the government be defeated by an unholy alliance of county members and the Labour party. Law, as Askwith recognized, 'had more than a difficult task in preventing unwise interference during this crisis . . .',[11] and the government's messages produced at least some of the desired response. Law admitted that the question of the coal strike was 'a very difficult one for this or any other Government', and informed Carson that 'the situation can only be dealt with by a Government which has the support of a majority in the House of Commons; if, after testing this by a division on the second reading, the Government retain their majority, we shall take no further steps to interfere with them in carrying out their policy'.[12]

But Law also sympathized to some extent with the views of his followers, and believed that the government should have made it 'perfectly clear that they will give protection at all costs, by soldiers, or if possible by special constables, to any man who is willing to work'.[13] Unionist attitudes, even amongst the leadership, increasingly centered around the protection of 'free labour'.[14] Any plan to protect non-strikers was strike-breaking by force and involved confrontation with the unions not merely as a policy, but physically at the picket lines. Its practicality as a policy relied heavily on the assumption that the militants were indeed an isolated minority, an illusion of which Law at least had been disabused, but in which he and his front-bench colleagues apparently still half-believed. But Law also shared his supporters' suspicions of the government's motives. 'The Government', he told Carson, 'have simply been manœuvring to gain time till they make sure of the Labour vote.'[15] However great their attachment to constructive politics, the party leadership could no more compromise with militant trade unionism than its straightforwardly reactionary supporters.

But there was more to this attitude than a concern for industrial liberty. Fundamentally, the Unionist party was not prepared to tolerate labour as an independent force, particularly an independent political force. It had never been prepared to repeal the Osborne judgement, and part of the tactical argument in favour of the payment of members was that it would make Labour M.P.s independent of the unions. Even so, despite the dangers of being stigmatized as the party of the rich, the Unionists had not been able to bring themselves to support the payment of members in the general election of December 1910. When the government, therefore, took up the question in 1911, they were relieved of the embarrassment which their divided attitude created, and might have left the question alone. Their unwillingness to do so demonstrated the force of the reaction that the party was undergoing. In April 1911 Collings reported to Joseph Chamberlain that 'A committee . . . is being formed to oppose the payment of members',[16] and Balfour, considering the possibility that payment might be effected by a vote in supply needing annual renewal, inclined 'towards the policy of dropping the Vote if, and when, we get the power'.[17] Radical Unionists took a dim view of this reaction. 'It is interpreted as an advertisement of the fact that the Tory party consists entirely of plutocrats.'[18]

But the party was no longer ashamed of appearing as the party of the rich, and no longer interested in tactical concessions to avoid that public image. 'I may tell you in all confidence', wrote Law when he had become leader, 'that in my view payment of members ought to be abolished.'[19] The shadow cabinet accepted this view in August 1913, although Steel-Maitland persuaded Law to postpone any announcement for the old tactical reasons. 'It would only be raising a new subject of interest when it is not at the moment to our interest to draw red herrings, and though the predominant opinion is against payment, the cry of the rich party not letting the poor man in is a very awkward one to meet unless we have devised a solution.'[20] Law, however, felt that 'a declaration that we would not continue payment of members would help us',[21] and he made no effort to devise the solution Steel-Maitland wanted. He, and the party with him, were counting on winning by the reaction against the government, organized labour, and socialism, and being known as the party of property would not hinder such tactics. He therefore reaffirmed his intention, 'before the election, to state that we will not continue the payment of members'.[22] The party, under Law's leadership, did not devise and did not want a constructive social policy towards industrial labour. In Willoughby de Broke's words, 'All right thinking people are sick of paid demagogues, don't you think?'[23]

The Unionist response to the threat of a new Liberal initiative on the land question was initially more promising from the constructive point of view. The party had early warning that Lloyd George intended to launch a new radical crusade in that direction. Lloyd George's unofficial Land Enquiry Committee was established in June 1912 as a prelude to the campaign, but hesitancy within the Liberal leadership slowed down progress. It was not until February 1913 that Lloyd George announced, 'the P.M. has now unleashed me', and not until the autumn of that year that he unleashed himself, with speeches at Bedford and Swindon.[24] The Unionist party had ample time in which to prepare its answer, whatever it was to be, to the 'Land Campaign'.

Nor was activity lacking. F. E. Smith's fears of the campaigning abilities of Lloyd George, and the dangers his new campaign might hold for Unionist electoral prospects were widely shared. If confirmation were needed, either of Liberal intentions or of their dangers, the two by-elections at North-west Norfolk in May 1912 and Hanley in July, provided both. Both were won by out-and-out land reformers, E. G. Hemmerde and R. L. Outhwaite, campaigning almost exclusively on the land issue. Collings used the opportunity of the NW Norfolk election and the rumour 'that Lloyd George was going to attack the counties' to tell Law that the farm labourers 'cannot be got to believe that the Unionists intend to carry out their land purchase scheme . . .' because 'the Unionist leader—that is yourself—has given no definite promise as regards England,' and to urge him to make some statement.[25] In July, Collings's Rural League began to canvass Unionist landowners for support for Collings's Land Purchase projects, again stressing the dangers of Lloyd George's campaign and the need for a positive alternative:[26] 'the radicals (confound them) are always much more ready with a policy than we are,' wrote Malmesbury, 'all we have ever had in the past is the great Negative policy of "Anti-xxx!"'[27]

Collings and Malmesbury were answered almost immediately when Lansdowne addressed the annual meeting of the Rural League, and pledged official Unionist support for the main items of League policy—the use of state credit to create owner-occupied smallholdings and to assist sitting tenants to buy their holdings; state aid to improve rural housing; and an agricultural curriculum for rural schools. To this Hewins unofficially added that 'a well-balanced scheme of Tariff Reform was essential to the success of a system of cultivating ownerships and to agriculture in general; and that fact must be proclaimed concurrently with Land Reform'. This, too, was Rural League policy. At the end of the month Bonar Law, speaking at Blenheim, endorsed Lansdowne's statement, and although the details were still undefined in places, particularly housing, Collings felt secure enough to declare that the League's programme 'was in the front rank of Unionist policy'.[28]

In the heady summer of 1912 it appeared that the Unionist leaders were prepared to go even further still, and work out the details. Steel-Maitland 'got the leaders of the Party to get the Land Question put into the hands of Lord Milner and another man to think out',[29] and practical preparations were made to deal with Lloyd George in the autumn.[30] Lloyd George did not go on the rampage that autumn, but Milner continued his work, and completed his investigations into the details of an alternative policy by the end of the year.[31] Steel-Maitland reported to Law on 27 January 1913 that he was preparing a letter to accompany Milner's land memorandum, with a view to immediate action. 'It would not get votes, but would give us a good hit against Lloyd George if we got in first.'[32]

In January, however, Milner's memorandum was overtaken and overshadowed by another far more important development in Unionist policy, which threw doubts not only upon the party's agricultural programmes for England and Ireland, both of which were inevitably tariff orientated, but upon tariff reform itself. The shadow cabinet, which in February decided reluctantly to abandon the referendum pledge, had met amidst repeated requests for some sort of pledge, the referendum, a second election, anything which would prevent the food duties from being an issue at the next general election. The most forceful argument concerned priorities, and had been stated by Salisbury as early as February 1910, but it had gained added force after the second defeat in December. 'I should not dwell so much on the matter if the tariff question stood by itself,' wrote James F. Hope in opposition to the food duties, 'it is the magnitude of the other issues involved that staggers me. Already, it is the food bogey (and nothing else) that has crippled the Constitution, and if it again drags us down next election, the Union will go with us, and God knows what else.'[33] Salisbury could, and did, reiterate his old arguments.[34] His brothers sent another long memorandum to Joseph Chamberlain,[35] and a copy to Law.[36]

Most important of all, however, was a letter from Derby reversing the reluctant assent he had given at the shadow cabinet. Admitting that 'to drop them now would probably split the Party absolutely', Derby still felt:

when we come to introduce them, if we ever do . . . the danger of a split is just as great, and . . . I do not think that I should be able to support them. The question to my mind therefore is if one could suggest some means by which we could decently bury them, and the only suggestion I myself can make is this, that you should say that if we came in, Preferential treatment of the Colonies should be taken quite apart from any taxation for Revenue purposes. That it should form the subject of an Enquiry which should try and ascertain if there was no preferential treatment which would meet the case of the Colonies *other than a tax on food* . . . If there was, then that would be adopted in preference to the food taxes, but if food taxes had to be adopted, it should be made subject for the referendum.[37]

This was to be the basis of Derby's policy throughout the year. But having gained their point, the Chamberlains were not thinking in terms of concessions,[38] and in the light of the letters from the leading rival protagonists it became increasingly clear that any statement upon the subject would cause a split in one direction or the other. Like Balfour before him, Law found refuge in silence.

The controversy, however, would not be stilled. A twelve-page letter from Lord Hugh Cecil descended upon Law in July, when he had 'just heard' that Law was about to make his announcement.[39] R. A. Yerburgh wrote in August that it would be impossible to win without the referendum pledge,[40] and letters continued to arrive from the North-west, not to suggest 'dropping the question', but to 'do or say something to mollify the fears (real fears) of the so-called free traders'.[41] In September Derby's patience ran out, but Balcarres managed to soothe Derby for the moment.[42] Increasingly, however, as the summer wore on the free traders got the better of the argument, and the most devout whole-hoggers began to show signs of unease against the free food claim that they were jeopardizing the Union by their inflexibility.

The T.R.L. itself was divided, with the central organization out of harmony with its branches in the North, where the local men wished to play down tariff reform.[43] 'I see speech after speech by many leaders or prominent speakers on our side without even the bare mention of our positive policy', complained Lawrence; 'could not a third, at all events, of every speech, wind up with an exposition of the counter policy we offer to the electors.'[44] Lack of interest in tariff reform, and hence the work of the T.R.L., was already making itself felt at the end of 1911, when the League, supposedly a rich organization, began to run short of funds. A fresh appeal obtained '£700 of outstanding subscriptions . . . but only £17 of fresh money', and the response to the invitation to the Annual Conference was so poor that the meeting had to be packed.[45] In June 1912 Lawrence noted that Sir Alexander Henderson, the Treasurer of the T.R.L., was prepared to 'beg for the party' but would not 'put us on to wealthy people, any more than he will tap them for subscriptions to the T.R.L. . . .'[46] In the same month the T.R.L. was driven to tap its own Executive Committee for funds.[47] League work in the constituencies suffered similarly.[48] The decline in activity, the decline in funds, the conflict between the central League and the branches, were all further indications of the loss of faith in a constructive policy with a positive appeal to the electorate.

By the autumn, Lansdowne had become convinced, under continued

questioning about the referendum pledge, 'that an explicit statement upon this point is inevitable . . .' Lansdowne had prepared a
draft letter, by which he intended to announce that the party was no
longer bound to the pledge, but ultimately the much-delayed statement
was made on 14 November in his speech at the Albert Hall. Free trade
reaction was at first muted. Strachey took the expected free trade line
on 15 November, 'that while maintaining my free trade principles I
shall say the very least I can, and certainly say nothing which can be
used to persuade anyone to support Liberals against Unionists'.[50]
Whole-hogger exultation, however, unleashed free trade resentment.

Early in December the torrent of letters, mostly from the North,
objecting to the Albert Hall declaration and demanding either the
postponement of food duties or the referendum, began in earnest.
Their arguments were familiar: the declaration would prevent any
further seats being won in the North, jeopardize the otherwise good
chance of a Unionist victory at the next election, and thus constituted
a betrayal by the party of its other causes. At the same time resentment
at being neglected and misunderstood added an element of bitterness
to the northern revolt. 'It appears to me,' wrote Alfred Cluttall from
Blackburn, 'that your people in London do not seem to understand
Lancashire.'[51] Long found the same discontent on his 'long unsatisfactory visit to Yorkshire . . . The same complaint that sufficient steps
were not taken to ascertain the views of the leaders on the spot and the
probable effect of the policy'.[52] In an attempt to meet these free trade
attacks, Law did take up one neglected point in Lansdowne's Albert
Hall speech which Lansdowne drew to his attention on 15 December—
that they would in any case do nothing in the way of imposing food
duties until the views of the Dominions were known. The precise
position of the party, Lansdowne pointed out and Law stated in his
speech at Ashton-under-Lyme on 16 December, was that if the colonies
wanted 'a moderate duty on foreign wheat sufficient to bring into our
markets the great unlimited granaries of Canada and Australia, we shall
not be deterred from examining their proposal by the mere statement
that it will involve the taxation of food . . .'[53] It was not, on the surface,
a change of policy, but it was an indication of the way the winds were
blowing. To those shrewd enough to see, it was more. 'If there is
anything certain in politics,' Sandars commented, 'it is after Bonar
Law's speech there will be no food taxes.'[54]

Nevertheless, the Ashton policy was not enough to arrest the revolt in the North, joined now by free traders like Strachey who might otherwise have accepted the Albert Hall statement.[55] F. E. Smith telegraphed a warning on 18 December, and explained by letter that 'Things in Lancashire are on the verge of a smash.' Smith feared that at a meeting of the Lancashire Conservative Association to be held on the 21st, 'a resolution will be passed . . . that the food duties recommended (if such be the case) . . . should not become law without an election . . . You know I am not an alarmist and have good nerves, but unless the position is promptly dealt with we are going straight on the rocks.'[56] At this stage Percy Wodehouse, deputy chairman of the Manchester Conservative Association, still thought the discontent might be contained, though he had to promise the dissentient members of his own Association that Law would give them an interview in January.[57] But the most important single feature in the Lancashire situation was the attitude of Derby, 'a growing power in Lancashire'.[58] Derby still felt in December 'very strongly that before a food tax can be imposed there must be some way of securing the approval of the country to it and I am in hopes that you will find a way out . . .' Derby urged Law 'to devise a scheme' which would carry out the suggestion that he had made in March, that preference could be given immediately on imports other than food, but that food duties would have to be put to the electorate in some way.[59]

Much of the anxiety which the meeting of the Lancashire Conservative Association created stemmed from the knowledge that Derby was to attend and speak, and the fear that he would publicly denounce the Albert Hall policy. After a short and uncontroversial speech by Derby, the meeting was in fact held in private. It revealed, as Derby wrote, that things were very critical:

I would not let them come to a vote but if they had I have not the least doubt that they would practically unanimously have passed a vote asking that the question of preferential treatment with the Colonies should be postponed and not be a subject for discussion at the next General Election . . . They were very desirous of coming to some definite conclusion but I have prevented that and suggested an adjournment . . . but they would not hear of one later than the 11th of January when I do not think we can possibly avoid some definite resolutions . . . You were good enough to say that you would attend a dinner of Lancashire Members in London. Instead of that if I had a luncheon on the 10th for the members and candidates and for a few of the influential political leaders of the county, could you possibly come up for it?[60]

The outcome of the meeting, as Derby had handled it, left the question open, and put considerable pressure upon Law.[61] This Derby intensified by his suggested luncheon, in Lancashire not London, and including 'influential political leaders' as well as members and candidates who were far more amenable to parliamentary leadership.

Derby's account of his actions at the Lancashire meeting on 21 December implied that he had been carried along by the tide of opinion, and had rescued the situation by his suggested adjournment. Wodehouse, however, gave a different account, not of what Derby did, but of how it was done and of the impression created upon the meeting. The proposal 'that the meeting should be adjourned for three weeks' was thus apparently made not because the majority at the meeting pressed for a vote which would have been hostile to the official policy, but in Derby's opening speech before any other opinions had been expressed:

> There were many expressions of opinion: at first in favour of the restoration of the Referendum . . . What later seemed to me to find most favor was the suggestion that we could win if the programme for the next Parliament was Reformed House of Lords, Amended Insurance Act, Housing, Taxation of Foreign manufactures and Conference with Colonies as to terms of Imperial Preference; these to be settled if they included no Food Tax, but if they did, the proposals, and what was to be given in return, to be submitted to the next General Election . . .[62]

During the course of the meeting, under Derby's leadership, those present had gradually worked their way round to a proposal that was a fairly precise version of Derby's 'way out'.

This policy was one source of Derby's strength. Law himself was contemptuous of the opposition because 'while the great bulk of our members are agreed in desiring to get rid of the food duties, none of them have any clear idea as to what the policy of the party would then be'.[63] But precisely because of this, all those who feared the food duties would rally to Derby who could provide such an alternative lead. There had indeed been suggestions from within Lancashire that 'if circumstances compel a change of leadership, it is your Lordship who would be most welcome',[64] but it is possible that Derby had other plans for that eventuality. He bitterly resented Balfour's resignation and the 'cursed rebels' who in his view compelled it. 'Still, I can't help feeling that six months from now, when Balfour is taking, as he must do, *the* leading part in the fight against Home Rule, the party will want him back . . .'[65] On 22 December he virtually invited Balfour to return to lead the Lancashire revolt 'with a policy that did not include food taxes . . . If you did, I believe the country would rally to you in a marvellous way . . .'[66]

In London, the party leaders were justifiably suspicious of Derby, and less justifiably inclined to underestimate the resentment in Lancashire as a result. In preparation for the meeting of 11 January, Derby had put specific questions to the associations asking whether the abandonment of the referendum was harmful, whether the election could be won with food duties, and whether any preferential arrangement with the colonies should be the subject of a second election. 'Derby', wrote Law, 'is the sole cause of all the trouble, as I suspected.'[67] Law therefore rejected the proposed luncheon, and left Derby to face the consequences of his actions, which Law expected would be 'a complete split'.[68] Seeing the Lancashire revolt in this light, Law also thought that Balcarres should attend the Lancashire meeting as a Lancashire member 'and tell them to ignore policy and simply to pass a vote of confidence in the Party Leaders'.[69]

By the end of December, therefore, the leaders and the Lancashire rebels were on a collision course. 'On January 11', Derby told Long, 'we shall pass a resolution calling on Bonar Law to give us some guarantee that there should be some appeal to the country before Food Taxes are imposed. It would be useless to try to stop them. Moreover I entirely agree with them . . . A split seems to me inevitable, unless the food taxers give way.'[70] Law was equally obstinate. 'There is really no question of going back on the policy which we have announced', he told J. P. Croal, editor of the *Scotsman* on 1 January. 'That I cannot do . . .'[71] Wielded by Law, the threat of resignation was a considerable weapon: '*if Bonar Law goes*', thought Balfour, '*the Party, as far as I can see, is doomed*'.[72]

Derby was well aware of Law's threat and had been since at least 20 December, and was well aware also of the consequences. But he was none the less far less impressed by the dangers than the other free fooders, and although he expressed his regret, preferred 'followers without a leader rather than a leader without followers . . . and if I saw at the present moment any man in the House of Commons who was likely to make even a decent leader, I should not hesitate to come out strongly against food taxes in the country'.[73] As it was, Derby hesitated but he did not retreat. Law's hard line towards Lancashire was, at best, based on a partial misunderstanding of the real situation. He attributed too much of the revolt to Derby's intrigues, and too little to rank-and-file resentment. Derby had no need to foment revolt in Lancashire, only to channel discontent as he had done towards his own ideas. But by the time Balcarres told Law of the real position,[74] Law had already taken up his intractable attitude. Moreover, Law was still convinced, as he had been in the spring, that any backsliding from the position he had taken up on tariff reform, first as an individual and then as leader, would precipitate a tariff reform revolt of even greater proportions than the free trade revolt with which he was now confronted. There were indications in December that the free traders would, as they had in the past, give way for the sake of unity.[75] Derby alone, by giving a lead to the Lancashire rebels, called the whole-hoggers' bluff.

The controversy in the first week in January thus became a test of nerves between the free fooders and the whole-hoggers. But by the end of 1912 the nerve of the whole-hoggers, with the exception of some leaders, had cracked. This was especially true of those who represented northern constituencies like G. R. Lane Fox, or Mark Sykes, who wrote from their Yorkshire fastnesses that 'we shall not make any progress in the West Riding while the food taxes occupy so prominent a place in the party programme'. They reasoned, as the free fooders had reasoned, that the risk was too great, but they had also lost faith in a programme which had 'already sacrificed the House of Lords', and threatened 'to sacrifice Ireland, the Church, and other valuable causes for food taxes which are not apparently wanted by Canada, and certainly are the only trump card that the Radicals hold against us'.[76] Goulding, the most active of the vice-presidents of the Tariff Reform League, wrote to Law on 20 December offering, if it would be of any use, to get the rank-and-file tariff reformers to sign a petition to Law asking for the reinstatement of the referendum.[77] By 29 December Ridley reported that the affairs of the League had reached a crisis point and that the 'funkers' had taken the chance to scuttle.[78]

Their position was made easier by the nature of the free food campaign: 'all that is asked for', Lord Robert Cecil urged on Law on 4 January, 'is a temporary postponement—not of the whole policy, but of one part of it—If the rest of tariff reform is established and is successful, surely it will be then far easier to complete it?'[79] Derby, too, argued that his policy involved only a change of method, not a change of principle. The party remained committed to preference, and would indeed enact this immediately provided that it did not involve food duties. Under the circumstances, the argument was readily seized upon by tariff reform wobblers. Astor told Austen Chamberlain:

The first effects of industrial protection in England should be to our party advantage. The Colonies might be induced to offer better terms, which, with our proposals to protect agriculture, should appeal to both urban and rural voters. If, in addition to this we could put forward some social proposals . . . we ought to stand a good chance of winning the Election, and carrying food taxes by the verdict of the people . . .[80]

The wobblers retreated with clear consciences.

Law had for some time shared their opinion as to the tactical disadvantages of food taxes, but he may well have been surprised by the extent of the tariff reform defection.[81] On 7 January, when he drew up a memorandum on their position for Lansdowne, he still felt that the leaders would have to resign if the pressure for modification of the party programme became irresistible.[82] But the attitude of the tariff reformers was decisive for Law. As soon as he was convinced that there would be no serious split from that side he began looking for a way out. By 8 January this had been found in a suggestion by Carson, supported by Balcarres, that a Memorial should be drawn up, and signed by as many members as possible, requesting Law and Lansdowne to stay as leaders, but that if food duties were required for preference, these should not be imposed until after a second general election. The Memorial went easy on the tariff reform conscience, reaffirming the party's commitment to preference, and arguing that the change involved no abandonment of the principle, but only a modification of procedure made in order to unite the party at a time of exceptional crisis. The leaders accepted this Memorial on 13 January, and at Edinburgh Law announced a policy which was, to all intents and purposes, that devised by Derby.[83]

In the last stages of this crisis even those tariff reformers who still believed in food duties put up little resistance. In December, Austen Chamberlain continued to maintain that the food duties were no handicap if tackled bravely, and counselled Law 'to stand firm [and] the party will rally to you'.[84] But with the defection of his followers and the suggestion of the Memorial to Law he washed his hands of the affair, and 'would do nothing to dissuade men from signing'.[85] His colleagues in the Tariff Reform League had similarly given up hope.

There were several reasons for this; they felt powerless when the rank and file of their movement deserted them; they were trapped in the same conflict of priorities; and after the Ashton speech they felt they had nothing to defend. The emphasis which Law placed on proposing food duties only to meet the demands of the colonies was sufficient in their eyes to ruin the policy of preference. As Ridley explained:

even if Bonar Law stands boldly to what he has said and campaigns for it his Ashton speech bears the interpretation of throwing the onus of an unpopular tax on the Dominion Governments. How can we get out of that? . . .

For myself I have no heart for Protection without Preference, and though I must support *anyone* against the present Government, I will feel unable to take any part, however humble, in an administration that could not deal with Preference.[86]

Milner recorded in his diary for 1 January that there had been an 'awful upset' in the party and the food duties could not be saved. 'I had a call from Page Croft,' he wrote on the 2nd, 'much perturbed about the political situation. I gave him the best advice I could, but I fear it was cold comfort as I see that the policy in which we both believe has, through altered circumstances, become impracticable.'[87] 'I met Goulding', Lawrence reported to Austen Chamberlain on the 5th, 'and I gathered from him the hopeless position of matters and his own belief that "we are done"—that is over the food duties. They have no friends, or very few.'[88]

Not all whole-hoggers were as defeatist as this. Richard Jebb, extremist to the last and one who put tariff reform before the Unionist party or anything else, felt that Chamberlain could, with his few followers, form the nucleus of a new breakaway group within the party.[89] The advice, however, was unrealistic. The real problem for the tariff reformers was contained in Ridley's remark that he had to support anyone against the government. Any moves they made had to be made from within the party, and any new programme one which made the best of the Ashton and Edinburgh speeches.

This, however, was difficult, especially in regard to agriculture. Contrary to Astor's belief, the party had no 'proposals to protect agriculture', and had never had any. After the Ashton speech it had the reverse. Tapping 'the unlimited granaries of Canada and Australia' as an argument to win over the urban working classes ran the risk of alienating the rural areas which had stood firm in 1910. 'I find very considerable perturbation amongst the rank and file of the Unionist party,' Herbert Williams informed Law, 'as to the new policy with regard to the taxes on foodstuffs . . . great difficulty in reconciling the point of view that the proposed food duties were justifiable from a domestic point of view, with the new view that they are only justified if the Dominions ask for them.'[90] 'B.L.'s speech', commented Garvin, 'was dangerous enough for the Counties, without helping us much in the towns . . . but repudiation of the food duties . . . will leave us perfectly helpless in the Counties against Lloyd George . . .'[91] The difficulty was, however, in no sense a new one. Law's defence of the Ashton policy was sound and familiar:

I have always said that the Food Duties were not proposed by us for the sake of Protection, but solely for the sake of Preference; and obviously if they are not necessary for Preference, then they would not be imposed. This is not only the view which I have always advocated, but so far as I can remember, it was the view invariably taken by Mr Chamberlain himself.[92]

Apart from throwing the burden of demanding food duties upon the colonies, the Ashton speech was perfectly in line with contemporary tariff reform thinking about food taxation and food prices. As recently as October, *Monthly Notes* had disclaimed any protective intentions on behalf of tariff reformers, arguing that agricultural prosperity depended on 'the whole agricultural policy of the Unionist Party, and the larger and more profitable markets which increased industrial prosperity under Tariff Reform must bring'. Tariff reform in fact, far from being expected to raise food prices in the eyes of its advocates, was expected to reduce them by stimulating the production of food in the colonies. The thinking behind this was urban, to proclaim that tariff reform would 'enable our working classes to obtain the necessaries of life at their lowest prices', but it left the farmers high and dry.

The argument that tariff reform would permit an increase in the scale of food production in the Dominions and thus reduce food prices had been expounded by Garvin in the summer of 1903 in a series of articles on tariff reform in the *Daily Telegraph*, even before Joseph Chamberlain began his tariff reform campaign. Chamberlain, however, instinctively but in the long run wisely, judged that it would be better political tactics to accept the arguments of free trade economics that the duties would raise prices, rather than rely upon any novel economic arguments. He defended his policies by arguing that the competition of the untaxed supply of foodstuffs from the colonies would force the foreigner to pay most, or all, of the duty, in order to keep his share of the British market, and by promising the compensatory reduction of duties on other items of food taxed. The policy recommended by the Tariff Commission in 1906, which neither officially replaced Chamberlain's Glasgow programme nor was incorporated into Balfour's Birmingham programme, of a 1*s*. duty on colonial corn to raise revenue for the promotion of domestic agriculture by non-fiscal means, to some extent made nonsense of the first part of Chamberlain's argument. But the 1*s*. levy was a recognition by the Tariff Commission, staffed by more logical economists than the political leadership of the tariff reform movement, of the difficulties which the preferential policy directed at encouraging colonial agriculture created for British farmers and therefore for Unionist county members. The Tariff Commission and *Monthly Notes* thus placed greater emphasis not on incidental protection, but on non-fiscal supplementary policies for agriculture.

At Edinburgh, when he announced the postponement of food duties until after a second election, Law also tried to take this line, arguing that any increase in the farmers' cost for agricultural machinery as a result of import duties on manufactured goods, would be offset by the benefits they would gain from a steadier market, and promising rating relief, assistance to tenant farmers when estates were sold above their heads, attention to rural housing, and inevitably 'that which would be the greatest of all possible blessings to this country—to establish small-holders throughout the land'. The programme, such as it was, had a hollow ring to it. Collings had spent the previous decade arguing that smallholdings could not flourish without the protection of a tariff. But of greater importance, any non-fiscal agricultural programme had received a severe blow, if not a fatal one, by Balfour's repudiation of the 1*s*. levy on colonial corn in 1910. *Monthly Notes* bravely tried to reassure the farming community that the change announced at Edinburgh was procedural only, and 'does not mean the abandonment of the duties or any alteration of the Unionist agricultural policy', but it was forced to concede that 'it does mean that some other means of financing non-fiscal agricultural policies will have to be found'.

The tariff reform leaders, as distinct from Hewins and the Tariff Commission, had always had an ambivalent attitude to the 1*s*. revenue duty, and saw it disappear without resistance and without regret. The Ashton speech, and subsequently the Edinburgh policy, forced them to recognize what they had hitherto concealed, as much from themselves as from the public, that they really did expect tariff reform to give some incidental protection to British agriculture, and that this protection was the *sine qua non* of their land policy for both Great Britain and Ireland. It was this that lay behind Collings's insistence that tariff reform and land reform were interrelated, and behind the demands of Milner and his circle for a constructive social policy for Ireland as a Unionist alternative to Home Rule. The Ashton speech, Amery thought:

> would seem to preclude all protection of any sort to British agriculture . . . It seems to me essential to make clear that 'food' in the Ashton speech only referred to wheat and meat, in the ordinary sense of the food of the masses, and that we are not precluded from protective as well as preferential duties on barley and oats, fruit, hops, poultry, and, I should like to add, dairy products. This is all the more vital in my view of the Irish situation. If Home Rule is to be killed for good and all by the defeat of this Bill, it must be by a really rapid economic development in Ireland following our return to power . . . Whatever the Ashton speech was meant to convey, we must somehow or other get out of the hole in which we will be left if nothing is to be done for agriculture. I would sooner, if need be, drop the wheat and meat preference outright and promise to devote a million or two millions a year to subsidise the freight rates on Imperial wheat and meat than say that we are frankly giving up all idea of helping agriculture in this country.[93]

The essential points to be salvaged from the wreck which Law's Ashton speech made of tariff reform were thus 'Imperial preference, and as much agricultural protection as is essential both to our smallholdings policy and to our general policy in Ireland'.[94] But Amery's proposal to achieve this, that the Unionists should pledge themselves to impose no duties on specific items of food that were the main diet of the poor until after a referendum, differed from the policy adopted by Law only in that it defined 'food' within certain narrow limits. Duties on wheat remained the core of the problem for both preference and protection, and for this Amery's proposal held no solution.

The alternative to tariffs was subsidies, in some form or another, to compensate for the protection and preference lost. Lawrence floated the idea of direct subsidies after finding 'the Chairmen of two or three local Conservative Associations . . . in despair over the situation . . . I said there were "bounties" and at their request I developed that idea in my speech and it gave immense satisfaction.'[95] But although Lawrence himself rapidly developed some enthusiasm for the idea, he did so more because of the desperate need of the tariff reformers for an alternative policy, than because of the intrinsic value of the policy itself.[96] The 'bounty' idea did not find sufficient support. 'I doubt the bounty idea will help us,' wrote G. A. Williamson. 'The cry at once would be that the offer of such a bounty would help the landowner',[97] and Leverton Harris agreed. 'Bounties would lead us into the depths of dismay.'[98]

With no alternative available, however, the tariff reformers were already in the depths of dismay. At the League headquarters Bagley was being asked what it all meant, and 'divisional councils all demand meetings to pass resolutions of the most contradictory character. It means chaos.'[99] Chaplin urged Austen Chamberlain to 'take some decided line or the T.R. League will tumble to pieces'.[100] But the leaders had no more idea of how to deal with the crisis than the divisional councils. The General Purposes Committee of the League decided that for the present its policy would remain unchanged, and that its speakers 'should be given some formula which would enable them to speak for the policy of the party while still supporting the policy of the League; so that we should not be ordered out of every constituency when food taxes are mentioned'. But Ridley stressed the great 'difficulties that face us in advocating the full policy when every party candidate will be banning the "food taxes". And I really don't know that I have the heart for it now . . .'[101]

The situation was considered by the tariff reform leaders on 26 January, when it was arranged that Hewins should devise the formula for their speakers, leaflets would be written by Lloyd, Amery, and Wyndham, 'who all had ideas', and that Austen Chamberlain should draft a resolution 'suitable for a declaration of opinion and policy by the Committee of the T.R. League'.[102] But the League had little policy and absolutely no freedom of action left. Excluding an independent role, attacking both Unionists and Liberals alike, there was nothing to be done except 'gain time', reduce the scale of their activities, and 'make the best of a bad job'.[103] 'Funds are all right for the present', Ridley reported to Austen Chamberlain, 'but . . . uncertain for the future, and Henderson is in favour of shutting down as much as possible.' He agreed with Chamberlain that they could not proceed on Confederate lines, but all else was confusion:

(1) the party that can be stampeded away from part of the policy can be stampeded from the rest: and I have no doubt the attempt will be made: especially as the present position will prove untenable.

(2) if we stick to our present full policy, someone will start a League with only the party policy on its programme.

(3) if we take up the party policy, someone will start a League for the whole policy.

(4) if we do neither we shan't know what to say.

(5) if we dissolve the League we shall do serious harm to the Unionist Party. And yet many men feel, like me, that the present programme isn't worth fighting for.

What a mess![104]

The compromise ultimately adopted, to continue to advocate the full policy but also to support any candidate who accepted Law's Edinburgh policy, successfully reconciled the members' Unionism with their tariff reform principles. It was nevertheless an indication of the degree to which the League, and tariff reform itself, had become subordinated to the party since 1907, that the League's members should consider League policy from the viewpoint of constructive Unionism in general. But the search by Amery, Lawrence, and others for an alternative agricultural policy to deal with the difficulties created by the Ashton speech exceeded, and even denied, the proper function of the League. That remained tariff reform, including food duties for the sake of imperial preference, as laid down by Joseph Chamberlain in 1903. The T.R.L. could not now advocate an alternative to tariff reform.

The party leaders found themselves faced with the same difficulties. Having rejected the full tariff reform programme and with bounties deemed politically impossible, they were forced to rely for their social policy in general, and for their land policy in particular, upon non-fiscal measures. Milner's Land Memorandum, around which discussion at the leadership level centred during the first half of 1913, was largely concerned with the details of land purchase schemes of the kind advocated by Collings and endorsed by Lansdowne in June 1912. Within these limits Milner produced a far-reaching plan of rural reconstruction, but the memorandum introduced few new ideas.[105] From it Lansdowne concluded no more than that 'we must not only reiterate our profession of faith in the policy of small ownerships created by means of state assistance, but . . . be more specific in regard to the extent to which we are prepared to go',[106] and this he did at Matlock on 21 June.[107]

But the land question itself was rapidly changing, and the controversy between ownership and tenancy, which had been the main distinction

between Unionist and Liberal land policies in the past, was rapidly
declining in importance as the investigations of Lloyd George's Land
Enquiry Committee and the increasing militancy of agricultural
labourers focused attention on their poor working and living conditions, and on the low wages which lay behind these conditions.
'Things are travelling fast in rural districts,' wrote Prothero in his
comments on Milner's memorandum, 'and the weak point in the
Unionist programme is the length of time that is needed for its effective
development.' He predicted, accurately, that the Liberals would take
up the question of a minimum wage, if only as the necessary pre-
condition to solving the problem of rural housing to which they were
already committed. 'Against such a policy, the Unionist programme,
slow as it must inevitably be, both in action and effect, would have no
chance.'[108]

The Unionists agreed with the government on the nature of the
problem. 'The real solution to the rural housing question', Selborne
told Law, 'depends on raising the earnings of the agricultural labourer.'[109] The problem was how this was to be achieved. In August
1912 a committee to investigate the land question and devise a Unionist
policy, appointed by Walter Long and presumably therefore unofficial,
reported in favour of a legislative minimum wage tied to prices.[110] In
the reaction of 1913, however, the Unionists were slowly and indeci-
sively turning away from this proposal, as they were turning away from
all forms of state interference. An official committee headed by
Salisbury, which reported in August 1913, did not rule out the legislative minimum wage completely, but concluded only that 'if wages
are raised by legislative action, agriculture should receive a corresponding relief . . .'[111] It was not a policy.

On this question, however, the hand of the leadership was forced by
the radicals on the back-benches. At the end of August Alexander
Thynne sent Talbot a proposal that the larger Unionist landowners
should voluntarily 'give a strong lead on their own estates' by raising
wages in the expectation that 'the best of the country gentlemen would
at once follow suit'. Behind the suggestion, however, was the threat
that if the party did not do something—and Thynne and his supporters
considered Wages Boards the only possible alternative, much as they
disliked it—then 'the establishment of Agricultural Wages Boards . . .
will undoubtedly be advocated from the Tory backbenches by some of
us who in spite of a very deep affection for the Party and loyalty to its

leaders cannot and will not see the agricultural labourers wage remain at its present level.'[112]

'This will be a serious question for us,' Law told Lansdowne, 'because I am quite sure that a great many will take Thynne's line and go for the minimum wage if there is no alternative.'[113] Lansdowne, however, thought the scheme impractical because of the time it would take to organize; impolitic, because 'it would be universally, and rightly, regarded merely as an attempt to seize the position before Lloyd George has had time to occupy it,' and unnecessary because wages were tending to adjust themselves to prices. Lansdowne in fact took a thoroughly negative view:

I have often heard you say, and I believe with absolute truth, that it is better tactics to make capital out of the mistakes of our adversaries than to compete with them by producing rival proposals of our own. I hope, nevertheless, that in the speeches which we shall have to deliver during the autumn we shall . . . make it clear that we are in general sympathy with the demand for a rise in the labourer's wages and for an improvement in the conditions under which he at present lives.[114]

Lansdowne, after he had seen Salisbury, made the meaning of 'sympathy' clearer by telling Law that they both felt that Wages Boards should not be utterly rejected, since the party had already accepted the principle for other industries. But again, it was not a policy.

The result of the inactivity of the leaders in the face of back-bench pressure was another potential split within the party. 'I'm afraid', Pretyman wrote to Law, 'there are great differences in the Party about land policy.'[115] But whilst the radicals, true to the pattern of the past, went ahead and published their own ideas,[116] they met with mounting opposition. 'There is', wrote Pretyman, 'as wide a gap between Leslie Scott, Joynson Hicks and co., and the bulk of the rural Unionists as there is between us and the Radical party. You cannot expect your agricultural followers to accept such a policy as these "social reformers" are putting forward.'[117] Because of the resistance of the radical group, Pretyman, although he preferred 'to fight straight', proposed a compromise: that Law should 'appoint a committee of enquiry to take . . . evidence as a counter to Lloyd George's enquiry. This would tide over the awkward moment . . .'[118] The purpose of the inquiry was manifestly to keep the radicals quiet. But they were also prepared to compromise on these lines, and indeed made the same suggestion that 'an enquiry should be held by the Unionist party in those districts where wages are notoriously low with a view to ascertaining what is the best method of securing an increase without causing that friction between the farmer and the labourer which is the greatest danger attending on hasty legislative action.'[119] This was the 'policy' which Law eventually announced officially at Norwich on 13 November.

Even more than the Edinburgh programme on tariff reform, the compromise was a substitute for a coherent policy devised to sustain party unity. Like the Edinburgh policy it had to be rigidly adhered to if that unity was to survive. Hills thus wrote to Law shortly after the announcement to make clear his understanding that Law intended 'an enquiry to be set up by the Unionist party', and not a royal commission which could not be appointed until the party took office and amounted to shelving the issue. He also demanded that in the meantime the opponents of Wages Boards should be silenced if the split in the party was not to reopen.[120]

Under pressure both from the radicals in his own party[121] and from the Liberals, Law could not close the discussion. In January Salisbury discussed the land question with Lansdowne, and in February sent Law the recommendations of the Land Policy Committee. Inevitably its first proposal was for a 'public and impartial enquiry' into the level of wages. But the Committee recognized that the inquiry was certain to reveal that wages in some areas were too low, and was forced to consider what action the party should take to raise them. Without inspiration from the radical back-benchers the leadership was bankrupt of constructive ideas, and although the Committee did not reject legislation completely, it still hoped that by giving publicity to the low level of wages they could bring about a voluntary increase, and thus avoid legislative interference.[122] Even this was perhaps going too far. Long accepted this recommendation, but he did so largely because he expected wages to be raised voluntarily. In May, fearful that the radical Unionists would again revolt if no lead were given, he was still prepared to suggest no more than an inquiry.[123] As far as the agricultural labourer was concerned, after a year and a half of debate the Unionist party was back where it started.

Much of the tactical difficulty the party found in dealing with the question of agricultural wages, as distinct from its dislike of state intervention in principle in the mood of 1913, was the direct result of the Edinburgh policy itself. Throughout the discussion on land policy the party was obsessed with the need not to alienate the farmers. Long emphasized 'the dangers of estranging or even alarming the landowners and farmers who are the backbone of our party',[124] and the policy he proposed with regard to wages in 1914 was suggested to him by Trustram Eve, secretary of the Farmers' Club.[125] The farmers were already wavering in their allegiance after Law had announced a tariff on manufactured goods only, and were attracted by the proposals for security of tenure which the Liberals put forward in the Land Campaign. On the tariff question indeed there was something of a revolt. Almost immediately after Law had agreed to the postponement of food duties, H. W. Palmer, secretary of the Lincolnshire Farmers' Union, notified Law of his organization's opposition 'to any change in our fiscal policy that excludes Agriculture from its benefits'.[126]

Lincolnshire was traditionally an area of agricultural militancy, and its Farmers' Union was, according to Chaplin, 'the most widely and powerfully organised body of farmers in the country, and there are farmers enough in each constituency to turn the scale in the great majority'.[127] Chaplin may have been deliberately alarmist, for he himself refused to accept the Edinburgh policy because of its neglect of the farmers, and apparently used his great influence with the Lincolnshire farmers to create trouble for the local Unionist party, even to the point of urging the farmers to sponsor their own candidates.[128]

But if Chaplin ever led the farmers' revolt, it rapidly passed beyond his control into the hands of Bernard Gilbert's Farmers Tariff Union. By the autumn this opposition had become openly hostile to the Unionist party as long as it adhered to the Edinburgh policy, which Gilbert regarded as more detrimental to agriculture than no tariffs at all.[129] Gilbert, moreover, had the sympathy of some of the agricultural experts in the Unionist party itself. Christopher Turnor, one of Milner's agricultural advisers, commended one of Gilbert's pamphlets to John Baird, and compared it favourably to the public defence of the Edinburgh policy to agricultural audiences:[130]

The farmers are getting more and more angry with the Unionist leaders and what they consider the persistent way in which they are ignoring the interests of the farmers. In fact, I know for certain that quite an important group of men, who really are Unionists, are about to start an organisation for the purpose of inducing farmers throughout the country to vote against the Unionists at the next election . . . the farmers are beginning to feel (and personally I think rightly) that though they have suffered under free trade, they have at all events been upon the same footing as all other industries; but that now their position will only be made worse by any measure of protection being granted to any of the other industries, and it is quite useless to try and throw dust in their eyes.[131]

Hewins too considered that it was 'practically impossible to reply' to Gilbert's pamphlet

upon the broad principle which is raised namely that in any readjustment of the tariff, Agriculture should be treated on equal terms with manufactures. The fundamental, historic principle upon which all tariffs that I am acquainted with, have been framed, is to safeguard the position of Agriculture, and I do not see how, in the light of the evidence available, it is possible to maintain that a purely urban policy of industrial protection would be of advantage to British agriculture.[132]

Not surprisingly, Steel-Maitland, as Chief Organiser, was becoming alarmed at the prospects of the party in rural areas.[133]

Law appears to have taken up Turnor's suggestion that he discuss the farmers' problems with Colin Campbell and G. A. Bellwood of the National Farmers' Union 'to nip this movement in the bud', although the results were not entirely those that Turnor anticipated. 'Our recollection', Bellwood wrote to Law after the meeting, 'is that you undertook, when returned to power, and Tariff Reform without direct benefits to agriculture was carried, to make good the Farmers' loss by relief in local rates . . .'[134] The difficulty with these promises, particularly in respect of rates, was, in Turnor's view, revenue. 'The duty on the proposed taxable articles would be comparatively small and I cannot imagine the townspeople allowing any of that duty to go into the pockets of the farmers . . .'[135]

The Edinburgh policy was, in practice, almost impossible to defend. Technically, the Unionists might argue that the change was only procedural, that the farmers would ultimately get their tariff, and that in the meantime the tariff on manufactured products would create a more prosperous home market for agricultural produce. They could also offer non-fiscal assistance, such as security of tenure and land purchase. But it was all unconvincing, and Hewins predicted that, as a result of Gilbert's pamphlet, 'many of our supporters will be persuaded to abstain, and the sort of things they will say to their employes [sic] will be like 1906 over again, and drive the labourers into the arms of the

Liberals', if they were not already there as a result of Liberal proposals for an agricultural minimum wage:

> In these circumstances, it seems to me that only two courses are open to you; (1) To explain fearlessly that the arrangement confirmed by Mr Bonar Law at Norwich is a purely temporary one, leading up to a full tariff policy . . . In that case you will unquestionably win the enthusiastic support of the farming classes.
>
> (2) To realise that the policy which is being announced involves the loss of the farmers' vote in many constituencies . . . and to meet this, as far as it can be met, by evolving a policy which is likely to win to our side the votes of the agricultural labourers.[136]

Hewins's recommendations were quite unrealistic. Law could not make much of the argument that the Edinburgh policy was intended to, and would, lead up to the full policy of tariff reform including food taxes without destroying its effectiveness in urban areas. The party was still caught, as in 1910, in a conflict of interests between town and country, and the policy it adopted to overcome this smacked not a little of duplicity. As Austen Chamberlain had commented on similar proposals in 1910, 'we would thus keep the counties because they would believe that they would get agricultural protection after all, and win the towns because *they* would believe that they wouldn't'.[137] Nor could the party evolve a policy which would appeal to the labourers more than Liberal policy without alienating the farmers completely. Law made the best of a bad job in defending the Edinburgh policy to the farmers, but he fully realized that the policy was not just unappealing in rural areas but a positive liability. 'I agree with you', he wrote to a farming correspondent, 'that it would be much better for farmers if there were a tariff on the articles they produce as well as on manufactured articles.'[138] But unable to promise protection Law had to placate the farmers as best he could, and this deprived him of any chance of making positive proposals to the labourers. In the last resort the party was forced to choose between farmers and labourers on class lines, as employers and employees, because it could not make proposals for the agricultural industry as a whole.[139] Instinctively, Law recognized this:

> The real question . . . which I think farmers ought to consider is not whether they would gain more by having a tariff on their produce as well as on manufactured goods; but whether, on the whole, taking advantages and

disadvantages together, they are likely to fare better under a Unionist Government which has always been interested in agriculture, or under a Radical Government which has never moved a finger to help it, and which, as I am sure you will agree, is only taking up the question now in the hope of gaining votes, and gaining them not so much from the farmers as from the labourers.[140]

Exploitation of the farmers' hostility as employers to Liberal proposals to better the condition of their employees by state intervention was part of the retreat of the party in 1912 and 1913 not only from the full policy of tariff reform, but from the constructive policies it engendered and sustained. As early as February 1913 Austen Chamberlain commented on Law's tendency to shun defining an alternative constructive policy because he was 'convinced that if we are united we can win on the faults of our opponents'.[141] Individual tariff reformers continued occasionally to ask Law to reconsider his Edinburgh pledge, usually because of the difficulties it created with the farmers, but Law was under equal or greater pressure from the other side to drop food duties and even tariff reform altogether. Consequently he refused to meet a deputation from the Tariff Reform League, and urged concentration on Ireland, since 'such a deputation with an account of it in the papers afterwards would simply be playing into the hands of our enemies'.[142] Neither Law nor the majority of the party had any confidence in tariff reform or the constructive approach. Many of the radicals themselves apparently shared this view. Steel-Maitland himself issued the instructions to Unionist speakers to ignore Lloyd George and concentrate upon Ireland.[143] 'To my mind,' wrote Milner, the most constructive of them all, 'there is only one road of salvation for Unionists now, and it is to shout "Ulster, Ulster", all the time . . . No running after Lloyd George, no mention of tariff reform . . .'[144]

Radical Unionism

By 1913 tariff reformers were a small minority even within the Unionist party. At the beginning of January when they tried to organize resistance against the demand to postpone food taxes, Balcarres noted that no one put their numbers above forty and some estimates were as low as fifteen to twenty.[1] Jebb, while urging independent action, was fully prepared to accept *The Times*'s estimate of seventeen.[2] Even so, their influence within the party was disproportionate to their numbers. They were, by and large, a closely knit group, the same names recurring through the Confederacy, the Diehards, the Unionist Social Reform Committee, and the various unofficial working parties on agriculture; they had a clear idea of what policies they wanted and bombarded the leadership with memorandums arguing their case and threatening revolt if these demands were not met; they were, in the main, able and energetic—all the leaders of the Conservative party between Balfour's resignation and the Second World War came originally from the tariff reform wing of the party, and moreover from the extreme end of that wing.

After 1912, however, they were able to create difficulties for the leadership but not to force the acceptance of their policies. Their own leaders, caught in the dilemma between yielding on tariff reform and endangering the Union, were completely demoralized and inclined to withdraw from politics, if not altogether, at least temporarily. Milner, Steel-Maitland, and Willoughby de Broke accepted and agreed with the official party line of concentration upon Ulster; Wyndham withdrew, at first to his estates and subsequently to Paris, as did Fabian Ware who had lost the editorship of the *Morning Post* in 1911; Chaplin was too old and Joseph Chamberlain was too ill; his son, like Ridley, saw no alternative but to follow whither Bonar Law led: 'I should like to get the Government out', he told Steel-Maitland, 'but I have no desire to see our Party in . . . I am thoroughly discouraged by the mismanagement (as I think it) of our affairs, and I do my public work without pleasure or satisfaction.'³

In all probability the tariff reformers, the whole-hoggers, had always been a small minority within the party.⁴ Tariff reform was acceptable as a policy to defeat the government and socialism, but its acceptance by the bulk of the party was tactical, dependent upon the fulfilment of the promises of electoral victory. Reaction followed defeat in 1910 not only against tariff reform but against constructive Unionism as a whole. In combating this reaction the radical Unionists were undermined by their own misconception of their constructive alternative. Steel-Maitland, for example, retained his suspicion of the negative approach even whilst, officially, he urged concentration upon Ireland. 'Many of our people', he told Glazebrook, 'even now are blind to the real state of feeling. We cannot outbid the Liberals or the Socialists, but we ought to realise that the bulk of the population are alive to their own interests and have an exaggerated belief that these can be bettered by legislation to an extent that no one would have dreamed of 15 years ago.' With this view of the situation, however, Steel-Maitland could not advocate constructive policies with confidence. His suggestion that 'even if we cannot outbid, we ought to show that we sympathise',⁵ was no answer to Lloyd George.

But strictly speaking constructive policies based on tariff reform were not attempts to 'outbid' the Liberals. It was not a question of greater or lesser promises made within the same frame of reference to solve commonly agreed problems, but of two alternative, different, approaches to society and economics which not only advocated different solutions but identified different problems. There were similarities; both policies rested on underconsumptionist arguments and both were collectivist in their acceptance of state interference. But the differences were greater. The Liberal party found the revenue for social reform in higher direct taxation, in effect using taxation to redistribute wealth, and creating a larger market for industry from the greater consuming power which resulted. Tariff reform envisaged a larger market in the Empire and in a more prosperous home market, both defended by tariffs, deriving the revenue for interventionist social policies from these indirect taxes. On this basis tariff reform did not question just the policies of the Liberal government, still less attempt to outbid them, but disputed the very principles on which they were based and denied their effectiveness. Tariff reformers from Joseph Chamberlain to the Reveille movement always argued that social reform legislation would be ineffective without tariffs. The same was true of any legislative attempt to increase wages as a solution to industrial unrest after 1911.[6] On tariff reform arguments, Liberal proposals were indeed counter-productive since they would price British goods out of the market or lead to greater ruthlessness on the part of employers in dismissing inefficient labour. Either way, the consequences would be greater unemployment and greater social distress.

Agriculture presented special difficulties and tariff reformers never overcame the contradiction between fostering development in the colonies and the protection of British agriculture. Despite its generally preferentialist line, even *Monthly Notes* at times slipped into protectionist arguments.[7] This contradiction was more apparent in theory than in practice because of the variety of agricultural produce, which allowed not only incidental protection of the staples, wheat and meat, from preferential and revenue duties, but also direct protection of lesser crops. But the essential feature of tariff reform policy, for agriculture as for industry, was to increase productivity:

No policy can be sound which simply concerns itself, as the Liberal policy apparently does, with re-arranging the relationship and financial interests of existing classes under existing conditions. The Liberal policy makes little, if any, attempt to stimulate production, while it actively discourages the employment of more capital on the land by making the position of the present holder or of the prospective investor precarious and unremunerative.[8]

The tariff reformers and the 'new Liberals' were advancing what amounted to rival ideologies with the tariff reformers emphasizing increased production and the Liberals redistribution as alternative means of solving the problems of social distress and economic stagnation, and, in the case of the tariff reformers, international impotence.

The tariff reformers' difficulty was that they could not get the debate conducted in these terms. Chamberlain's failure, and the failure of the tariff reform movement, was the failure to escape from the legacy of the past. Neither tariff reformers nor 'new Liberals' were free traders in the sense that men like Cromer and Strachey understood the term. But because it was familiar, because it had assumed the proportions of a faith, both tariff reformers and Liberals related their propaganda to free trade, the latter willingly, the former because they felt obliged to. Much of the confusion of Edwardian politics stemmed from the fact that there were not two but three competing ideologies with the consequent fragmentation of political groupings. But in carrying on the debate within the framework of free trade ideas as a revival of the controversy between free trade and protection, the tariff reformers were at a great disadvantage because of the automatic association of protection with the defence of vested interests. Tariff reformers, particularly the radicals, did not intend this but rather the opposite. 'So-called free trade', wrote Rowland Hunt, 'is represented by, and advocated in the interests of, rich men with great financial interests or investments abroad, against Tariff and Preference which are in the interests of our working people, their full employment and good wages.'9 But the weight of contemporary opinion, even of contemporary economists, was against them.

The attitude of many of the whole-hoggers themselves lent substance to the belief that tariff reform was no more than an attempt to revive protection for the benefit of a particular wealthy class, partly because many of them did understand tariff reform to mean protection, partly because of the elements in that doctrine they chose to emphasize. The attraction of tariff reform was not simply, nor even primarily in many cases, its economic content, but its 'moral' or 'cultural' side, what Chamberlain in 1903 had termed the 'character of the race'. In the years immediately before the war, whole-hoggers became particularly concerned at the want of moral fibre in the country and especially in their own party. They assumed the heart of the country to be sound, but thought that it was being destroyed by a combination of Liberals and socialists while a torpid and apathetic Unionist party looked helplessly on. Selborne was struck by the condition of the Unionist party after his return from South Africa in 1910. 'I saw a want of faith, a vacillation, an opportunism which disgusted me . . .'10 'How', asked Amery, 'are we ever going to carry through a policy of reconstruction bold enough, broad enough, and strong enough to see us through the next generation with men who run away at the slightest provocation?'11 Tariff reformers were first and foremost idealists who sought to imbue their fellow-countrymen with their own sense of purpose, to arrest the decline of the country before it was too late.

For their inspiration, however, these tariff reform ideologues turned to the past, to the 'traditions of the country'.12 Chamberlain had drawn on the record of Tory Democracy, and in its last stages tariff reform became associated with an aggressive revival of this doctrine.

'We must drive a wedge between Ramsay Macdonald and Co and the working classes whose only chance is Toryism,' wrote Willoughby de Broke. 'Toryism means Progress. The Radical–Labour leaders do not represent the people. The Tory party must survey the whole problem of Physical and Mental Regeneration and get back to their rightful and hereditary place as the friends of the people, and the only National Party.'[13] Their identification with this particular tradition of the past was deliberate, as was the rejection of other traditions. The cause of the party's lack of moral courage was, according to Selborne, 'the disastrous leadership of the Duke of Wellington and Sir Robert Peel which taught the party to conform to the motives of its opponents and to turn its back on its most cherished convictions.'[14] Rightly or wrongly, Peel was held responsible for the sell-out of the land in the 1840s, the creation of Liberal Toryism, the absorption of the urban middle classes into the Conservative party, the acceptance of free trade and the neglect, and consequent alienation, of the working classes.[15]

In contrast, the Tory Democrats of the 1900s asserted essentially rural convictions and traditions. The resentment of the radical Unionists was a reaction against the increasing domination of the party by wealthy, or at least comfortable, urban interests and their self-satisfied, negative defence of the *status quo*. Their real enemy was the 'Plutocrat', a bogey figure of immense wealth and cosmopolitan financial interests, frequently Jewish, or German, or both, who had no stake in, or loyalty to, the country. The connection of various members of the Liberal government, especially Lloyd George, with wealthy foreigners, the Baron de Forest, Cassel, Brunner, Mond, and others, made this a useful stick with which to beat the government and attack the Land Campaign. Maxse urged 'a vigorous counter-attack on the multi-millionaires of the Radical party and their hangers-on who divert attention from themselves by attacking the one form of property which they happen not to possess'.[16] But the motives behind the Radical Plutocracy Enquiry which Maxse carried on in the *National Review* were not entirely tactical, and George Wyndham's hostility to 'the Plutocrats who have bought the Government in order to sell the country'[17] was completely sincere. 'I do not think', he wrote, 'that Mond and Chiozza Money are the "Natural Leaders" of the English people.'[18] The rejection of 'financial', as distinct from industrial and landed, property went further than chauvinist attacks tinged with anti-semitism against isolated individuals with foreign sounding names.

Of Lancashire, Wyndham wrote, 'the people are sound and strong. It is the Merchants who live on commissions, and the Oriental Financiers that ruin it.'[19] 'No one', wrote Winterton, 'has attempted, so far as I know, to analyse the type and class of men who are tyrannising over us, nor has anyone pointed out that the Government themselves are a typical Bourgeoisie Government, by birth, tradition and training, which accounts for their fierce hatred of the class above them and their terror of the class below.'[20] Tory Democracy in the 1900s envisaged an alliance of 'Rural England' with the industrial working classes, the two classes which produced, against those who ignored the call of national duty.

However great their concern for industrial stagnation and the living conditions of the working classes, the restoration of 'Rural England' was the primary consideration. Britain was already, in the eyes of the Tory Democrats, over-industrialized. Amery wrote to Law:

The last thing we stand for is to aggravate the existing lop-sided condition of these islands. The redress of the balance in the interests of agriculture, and above all, of Ireland, is now, as before, an integral part of our constructive policy . . . There has been, during the last ten years, a phenomenal increase in the output of manufacturing industry and in the numbers of those who depend on it. The sound balance of agriculture and industry in the world has been upset.[21]

The consequence was greater vulnerability to industrial depression, industrial discontent, socialism, and class conflict. Yet in this respect at least, the Tory Democrats were economic reactionaries. Although they emphasized the need for greater agricultural efficiency, resulting in greater total output, they also envisaged a greater number of people being involved. Economics were not, in this case, the sole or even the primary consideration. The aim was social and political. 'I start', Milner wrote in his Land Memorandum:

from the axiom that it is a political necessity to increase the number of men having property in land, or at any rate some interest other than that of mere wage earners . . . There can be no manner of doubt that the institution of private property is seriously menaced at the present time . . . If the present Social Order is to endure, it is simply necessary, at whatever cost, to effect a great increase in the number of people who have a direct personal interest in the maintenance of private property. There is no bulwark against communism at all equal to that provided by a large number of small property owners, especially small owners of land . . .[22]

The central feature of the restoration of Rural England was the recreation of a conservative peasantry. *Monthly Notes* declared:

The security of the nation depends upon the continuance of a sturdy country-bred race who have the physique and capacity for endurance which their forbears had who fought under Nelson and Wellington. Where can such men be recruited at present? Unemployed starvelings and the anaemic denizens of city slums are totally unfit for the task . . . It is therefore essential to our security as a nation that we should encourage a high spirited and independent race of yeomen, and this race cannot be brought into being except by the adoption of the Unionist policy of small ownerships and Tariff Reform.[23]

Tory Democracy, despite its radicalism in matters affecting the material standard of living, was profoundly conservative socially and politically. It envisaged no great changes in the social order, either in the relationship of classes, the ownership of wealth, or the distribution of political power. In this last respect especially, even many radicals were unwilling to accept change and followed the bulk of the Unionist party into a position which implicitly denied the right of the working classes to an independent political existence. Unionists in theory did not disapprove of trade unions—in places they even tried to organize them on anti-socialist lines—and they actively approved of direct working-class representation in Parliament. But they opposed both the repeal of the Osborne judgement and the payment of members which made this representation possible, they opposed the inviolability of trade union funds, and they sought to destroy the effectiveness of the one weapon the working classes possessed, the strike, by the abolition of peaceful picketing. Nor did they regard such attitudes as contradictory. The working men, the bulk of them, were thought to be sound, hard-working, and patriotic, their apparent discontent and class militancy the result of agitation and intimidation by a small number of socialists. Even the rise of the Labour party and the loss of three elections did not suffice to remove this idealized view of the British working man. But in ignoring the general election results, particularly those of 1910, and in arguing that the trade union leadership and the Labour party did not represent the feelings and aspirations of the working classes, the tariff reformers allowed their ideals to cloud their appreciation of reality.

All these ideas, often with strong emphasis, could be found in Joseph Chamberlain's tariff reform speeches. Chamberlain identified the foreigner as the enemy, warned workers of the mobility of capital and its disregard for national boundaries, stressed duty and sacrifice for the good of the nation, and condemned wealth, consumers, and millionaires. Both Joseph and Austen Chamberlain endorsed Collings's land purchase policies and justified them for political reasons. But the direction which tariff reform took, particularly its close identification with the landed interest, did not correspond to the 'centrist' national policy that Chamberlain intended in 1903. The identification was slow to develop. Chamberlain launched his campaign in urban centres and his Tariff Commission was packed with industrialists as well as land-owners, although it contained no bankers and, ominously, no workers. By 1913, however, changes in tariff reform policy which gave rural interests a special grievance, and the intense interest in the land question in general, both drew attention to the relationship between the landed interest and protection. Moreover, although they might dismiss the Lancashire rebels as 'middlemen',[24] it was obvious after 1910 that tariff reform, far from uniting the nation behind a national policy, had opened up divisions between agricultural and commercial interests which the Unionist party could not afford to ignore. Chamberlain not only failed to overcome the tendency of politics to reflect class by demonstrating that all producers, urban and rural, rich and poor, employer and employed, had common interests in a national economic system, he divided even those classes which favoured the Conservatives along lines of interest. In contrast, the Liberals, by compounding landowners, peers, and landlords were able to present a programme which allowed them to attack a traditional enemy whilst benefiting from a wide spectrum of class hostility, even when the issue was primarily constitutional. Their tactics were not entirely successful, for the defection of the Liberal right headed by the Liberal League indicated that large sections of the propertied classes were alarmed by the 'new Liberalism'. But the party achieved sufficient of a national consensus to win three successive elections, after almost twenty years in the wilderness, and to govern with the aid of Labour and the Irish until the disruption of war completely changed political conditions.

The co-operation of the Labour party with the Liberals was the political expression of Chamberlain's failure to reverse class politics, the co-operation of the Irish, his failure to transform the structure. The Irish, as Milner, Amery, and the radical Unionists realized, had a vested interest in protection, and worked with the Unionist party on land reform and education. But for the Home Rule controversy there was nothing to prevent the Irish party from working with a reforming

Unionist party, and much to incline it in that direction. But the party system turned upon Home Rule in 1886 and despite its frailty still did so in 1914. Tariff reform became the main issue in Edwardian politics in opposition to free trade and socialism in an interlude when the Irish question was dormant. But the Irish question still existed, unsolved, and faced every Unionist who dissented from his party on fiscal matters with a choice of priorities. Every tariff reformer, every Unionist free trader, who thought of breaking up the party, risked destroying its effectiveness in defence of the Union. That, the loyalty of Conservatives to their party and their leader, and their unwillingness to follow a distrusted radical into a redefinition of 'Unionism', were obstacles that Chamberlain never overcame.

Even discounting the loyal, though often bewildered, Balfourites, few tariff reformers or Unionist free traders were prepared to put the fiscal question above the Union and the party. At times they tried to equate them. 'Protection seems to us an evil of the same class as Home Rule,' wrote Lord Hugh Cecil.[25] But it was not a tenable position and Unionist free traders had to choose between them. Because of the emergence of socialism as an issue after 1906, most Unionist free traders had already chosen, as property owners and Unionists, to accept protection and give up free trade, before the revival of interest in Ireland. In turn, the tariff reformers were forced to choose after 1910 and they too chose as property owners and Unionists, and agreed to oppose Home Rule and socialism on the negative basis of the defence of the existing system rather than revolt in favour of an alternative constructive programme.

In the end, the 'Conservative' conception of the 'Conservative and Unionist' party prevailed over the radical interpretation of Unionism. With exceptions in some fields such as the tariff on imported manufactured goods and land purchase, the party adopted a negative and even reactionary attitude to the government's policies. It became unashamedly an employers' party, defending English and Irish landowners, Irish protestants, English farmers, and employers, the holders of power within the existing social structure. As such it appealed to the middle classes for class reasons and gave up the attempt to establish a national unity that transcended class divisions. The disapproval of some Unionist M.P.s of Maxse's Radical Plutocracy Committee typified this class reaction: 'if those who have anything begin to attack each other, they will only be playing into the hands of the Socialists . . . it is really a check on the Radical side to have a capitalist section, which does not therefore want weakening'.[26] Richard Jebb, as one of the extreme radical fringe of the tariff reform movement with no commitment whatever to the Unionist party, saw the reaction as inevitable. He wrote to Croft:

The cause has got to be attached to that of the 'living wage' if it is to become a national creed in this country in our time, which means that, politically it should be attached to the Labour party . . . its present attachment to the Unionist party is a positive obstacle to its progress, for it is idle to think that Conservatism is going to welcome or expedite the social and economic upheaval which is implied in any genuine 'living wage' policy.[27]

Regarded thus, tariff reform, as a genuinely radical policy as distinct from a tactic to defend the *status quo* as Balfour made it in 1907, had never been 'practical politics'. In 1903 the Unionist party was already too much a middle-class Conservative party for a redefinition of its role to be successful. Those who thought otherwise had deceived themselves and deceived their followers, as they finally realized. 'The ultimate cause of the trouble at the Morning Post', Jebb told his former editor, Fabian Ware, 'was that we were running a Radical policy in the name of Conservatism, trying to twist the principles of Conservatism . . . to suit our purpose, which was Liberal Unionist. We did it in good faith, but it was a fraud all the same . . .'[28]

Notes

INTRODUCTION

1 J. L. Garvin and Julian Amery, *The Life of Joseph Chamberlain* (1935–69), i. 532. Vols. 5 and 6 were published in self-contained form as Julian Amery, *Joseph Chamberlain and the Tariff Reform Campaign* (1969).

2 Peter Fraser, *Joseph Chamberlain. Radicalism and Empire, 1868–1914* (1966), 46.

3 For Henry George see Elwood P. Lawrence, *Henry George in the British Isles* (1957).

4 For this quotation and the question of the defence of property in the 1880s, see D. Southgate, *The Passing of the Whigs, 1832–1886* (1962), 355–82.

5 Robert Taylor, *Lord Salisbury* (1975), 83–4.

6 For the Liberty and Property Defence League, see N. Solden, 'Laissez-Faire as Dogma: The Liberty and Property Defence League, 1882–1914', in K. Brown (ed.), *Essays in Anti-Labour History* (1974), 208–33, and E. Bristow, 'The Liberty and Property Defence League and Individualism', *Historical Journal*, xviii, 4 (1975).

7 W. S. Churchill, *Lord Randolph Churchill* (1906), ii. 6–20.

8 P. Fraser, 51.

9 E. Bristow, 763.

10 R. Taylor, 17.

11 Robert Blake, *The Conservative Party from Peel to Churchill* (1972), 181–2.

12 R. Taylor, 16–17.

CHAPTER I. THE WITCHES' CAULDRON

1 For the history of these bodies see: B. H. Brown, *The Tariff Reform Movement in Great Britain, 1881–1895* (1953), and J. E. Tyler, *The Struggle for Imperial Unity* (1938).

2 Churchill to Salisbury, 6 Nov. 1886, W. S. Churchill, *Lord Randolph Churchill*, ii. 223.

3 Salisbury to Churchill, 7 Nov. 1886, ibid. 223–5.

4 Beach to Salisbury, 'Xmas Day' 1886, Lady Victoria Hicks Beach, *The Life of Sir Michael Hicks Beach, Earl St. Aldwyn* (1932), i. 301.

5 Chamberlain to Churchill, 23 Dec. 1886, W. S. Churchill, ii. 252.

6 Balfour to Salisbury, 24 July 1892, B. E. C. Dugdale, *Arthur James Balfour, First Earl of Balfour* (1936), i. 211.

7 W. H. Smith to Salisbury, 3 Feb. 1889; Salisbury to Smith, 5 Feb. 1889, Viscount Chilston, *W. H. Smith* (1965), 295–6.

8 Chamberlain to Balfour, 8 Dec. 1894, K. Young, *Arthur James Balfour* (1963), 167. See also, Chamberlain's memorandum of 13 Nov. 1894, in P. Fraser, *Joseph Chamberlain. Radicalism and Empire*, 152.

9 Chamberlain to Salisbury, 15 Nov. 1894, J. L. Garvin and J. Amery, *The Life of Joseph Chamberlain*, ii. 617.

10 Salisbury to Balfour, 26 July 1892, B. E. C. Dugdale, i. 212–13.

11 Morley to Haldane, 29 Jan. 1888, Haldane Papers, MS. 5903, f. 77.

12 Rosebery to Gladstone, 30 Sept. 1892, in P. Stansky, *Ambitions and Strategies. The Struggle for the Leadership of the Liberal Party in the 1890s* (1964), 12. This discussion of the Liberal party relies heavily upon this study and those of D. A. Hamer, *Liberal Politics in the Age of Gladstone and Rosebery. A Study in Leadership and Policy* (1972), and H. C. G. Matthew, *The Liberal Imperialists. The Ideas and Politics of a post-Gladstonian Elite* (1973).

13 Harcourt to Rosebery, 4 Apr. 1894, P. Stansky, 131–2.

14 Ibid. 135–7.

15 Wemyss Reid to Rosebery, 14 May 1896, R.P. Box 44.

16 P. Stansky, 172.

17 Rosebery to Ripon, 13 Aug. 1895, ibid. 180.

18 Ibid. 258.

19 Ibid. 273–4.

20 Wemyss Reid to Rosebery, 13 Aug. 1901, R. P. Box 45; Perks to Rosebery, 8 Aug. 1901, R. P. Box. 39.

21 H. C. G. Matthew, 67.

22 Ibid. 70.

23 Ibid. 71.

24 Ibid. 68.

25 Ibid. 71–2.

26 Rosebery, ibid. 127. On Ireland the Liberal Imperialist position was confused. Both before and after the Chesterfield speech Asquith, Grey, and Haldane campaigned in favour of a 'step by step' policy. This certainly involved the formal abandonment of the Irish alliance, which had already collapsed in practice, and the postponement of Home Rule into the indefinite future, but implied that Home Rule must ultimately be granted. In its place, temporarily, they advocated 'conciliatory and remedial measures' following the lines of the Unionist Local Government Act of 1898, hoping, perhaps, for the evolution of a bipartisan approach which would remove Ireland from the party controversy. Rosebery, on the other hand, spoke out both at Chesterfield and Liverpool against Home Rule at any time, and apparently misunderstood the 'step by step' policy of his lieutenants. Perks and Fowler, both Nonconformists, followed Rosebery's 'Unionist' line, and although the 'step by step' policy was written into the Liberal League manifesto, Rosebery's dominant role and the identification of Asquith, Grey, and Haldane with his position at this time made them appear Roseberyites on Ireland. See H. C. G. Matthew, ch. VIII, and H. W. McCready, 'Home Rule and the Liberal Party, 1899–1906', *Irish Historical Studies*, 13 (1962–3), 316–48.

27 Asquith, H. C. G. Matthew, 128.

28 Fowler, ibid. 127.

29 Ibid. 139. ' "Sane imperialism" and the "larger patriotism" were deliberately vague phrases . . . But their function was primarily domestic—to offer a concept which could unite the various Liberal factions and attract the centre vote.'

30 Ibid. 137.

31 Rosebery, ibid. 141.

32 Rosebery, Bernard Semmel, *Imperialism and Social Reform. English Social and Imperial Thought, 1895–1914* (1960), 62–3. For the ideas behind 'National Efficiency', see also G. R. Searle, *The Quest for National Efficiency* (1971).

33 Perks to Rosebery, 8 Sept. 1901, R.P. Box 39. For the Webbs see H. C. G. Matthew, 73.
34 Perks to Rosebery, 23 Aug. 1901. R.P. Box 39.
35 Perks to Rosebery, 4 and 20 Mar. 14 and 16 June 1902, R.P. Box 40. For 'ordinary subscriptions' see Allard to Rosebery, 26 Feb. 1906, R.P. Box 106.
36 W. D. Pearson to Perks, 23 Sept. 1904, R.P. Box 41.
37 H. C. G. Matthew, 227n. and 142.
38 Ibid. 140.
39 Ibid. 241–2.
40 Ibid. 246–52.
41 Ibid. 228–35, 238–40.
42 Perks to Rosebery, 24 Feb. 1902, R.P. Box 40.
43 Roy Jenkins, *Asquith* (1964), 133.
44 For the 'Co-efficients', see B. Semmel, 72–82.
45 e.g. C. E. Hobhouse to Rosebery, 2 Feb. 1902, R. P. Box 106.
46 G. R. Searle, 132–8.
47 H. C. G. Matthew, 86. Even Asquith, forgetful of the letter he had written but not sent in 1898, denouncing reunion with the Liberal Unionists as impossible, declared in January 1902 that the 'clean slate' might make it possible for the Liberal Unionists to rejoin the party.
48 Ibid. 163.
49 Hon. A. R. D. Elliot, *The Life of George Joachim Goschen, First Viscount Goschen, 1831–1907* (1911), ii. 139–41, 157–9.
50 Beach to Balfour (1895), Lady Victoria Hicks Beach, ii. 30.
51 Beach's conflict with Chamberlain over expenditure preceded the South African war by some years. See Beach to Salisbury, 1 Nov. 1897 and 11 Jan. 1898, ibid. ii. 47, 65–6.
52 Beach to Salisbury, 27 Jan. 1899, ibid. 90–1.
53 Beach to his wife, 26 Jan. 1899, ibid. 76–7.
54 Beach to Salisbury, 17 Oct. 1899, ibid. 109–10.
55 Beach to his son, 11 Apr. 1901, ibid. 137.
56 Beach to Salisbury, May 1901, ibid. 149.
57 Ibid. 151–2.
58 Beach to Chamberlain, 2 Oct. 1901, ibid. 157–8.
59 Salisbury to Beach, 14 Sept. 1901, ibid. 152–3.
60 Chamberlain to Beach, 30 Sept. 1901, ibid. 154–6.
61 Balfour to Beach, 11 and 13 July 1902, ibid. 172–4.
62 e.g. George Wyndham to his brother, 'Christmas Eve' 1901, J. W. Mackail and Guy Wyndham, *Life and Letters of George Wyndham* (n.d.), ii. 433–4.
63 Grey to Milner, 16 Mar. 1902, H. C. G. Matthew, 144.
64 Churchill to J. Moore-Bayley, 23 Dec. 1901, Randolph S. Churchill, *Winston S Churchill* ii. C(ompanion) V(olume), 104–5.
65 Lord Hugh Cecil to Churchill, 12 Oct. 1902, ibid. 112–13.
66 Churchill to Rosebery, 10 Oct. 1902, ibid. 168.
67 Rosebery to Churchill, 12 Oct. 1902, ibid. 168.
68 Chamberlain to Devonshire, 22 Sept. 1902, and Chamberlain to Balfour, 4 Aug. 1902, J. L. Garvin and J. Amery, v. 97–8.
69 Rosebery to Churchill, 7 Oct. 1902, Randolph S. Churchill, ii. C.V. 166.

CHAPTER 2. THE DIVISION OF THE UNIONISTS

1 The cabinet crisis of 1903 has been studied in considerable depth in Julian Amery, *Joseph Chamberlain and the Tariff Reform Campaign* (1969), A. Gollin, *Balfour's Burden. Arthur Balfour and Imperial Preference* (1965), and R. A. Rempel, *Unionists Divided. Arthur Balfour, Joseph Chamberlain and the Unionist Free Traders* (1972). For the sake of simplicity, reference is made wherever possible to Amery's fundamental study, even though the passages cited may be found elsewhere, particularly in the biographies of the major participants.

2 J. Amery, v. 15-16.

3. For the proceedings of the Colonial Conference, see ibid. 28-55.

4 Ibid. 72-4.

5 Chamberlain to Devonshire, 25 Aug. 1903, ibid. 372-4.

6 Balfour to the King, 21 Oct. 1902, ibid. 117.

7 C. T. Ritchie, Memorandum of 15 Nov. 1902, ibid. 119-21. Middleton was the Conservative Chief Agent.

8 Ibid. 97.

9 Sandars to Balfour, 4 Sept. 1902, B.P. 49761, ff. 26-9.

10 Balfour to the King, 10 Nov. 1902, J. Amery, v. 121.

11 C. T. Ritchie, Memorandum of 21 Feb. 1903, ibid. 153.

12 Ritchie to Beach, 7 May 1903, ibid. 154.

13 Ibid. 155-61.

14 See Ritchie's Memorandum of 15 Nov. 1902. Unless otherwise stated, references to Ritchie's views are from this memorandum.

15 Speech of 16 May 1902, J. Amery, v. 17.

16 Minutes of the Colonial Conference, ibid. 45.

17 Speech at Birmingham, 4 Nov. 1903, C. Boyd (ed.), *Mr. Chamberlain's Speeches* (1914), ii. 241.

18 C. T. Ritchie, Memorandum of 21 Feb. 1903, J. Amery, v. 153; Chamberlain, see his speeches at the Colonial Conference of 1902, ibid. 32-8, and Austen Chamberlain to Joseph Chamberlain, 24 Feb. 1903: 'I am disposed to agree with him [Ritchie] that our military burdens are greater than we can properly bear, or the people will long endure.' Ibid. 154.

19 Ibid. 178-9.

20 Balfour to Devonshire, 29 Aug. 1903, ibid. 179.

21 Chaplin to Chamberlain, 11 May 1903, ibid. 181.

22 Beach to his son, 26 Apr. 1903, ibid. 179.

23 e.g. Ian Malcolm and J. Dickson-Poynder attended the deputation; W. F. D. Smith and G. J. Goschen wrote in support. *The Times*, 16 May 1903.

24 Balfour to the King, 12 May 1903, J. Amery, v. 182.

25 Balfour to Devonshire, 27 Aug. 1903, J. Amery, v. 183; R. A. Rempel, 31.

26 C. Boyd, ii. 125-40.

27 Chamberlain to Halsbury, 18 May 1903, Chamberlain to Sutherland, 19 May 1903, J. Amery, v. 226.

28 Chamberlain to Lovesay, 19 May 1903, ibid. 226-7.

29 Ibid. 227.

30 R. A. Rempel, 33.

31 A. Gollin, 56-9. See R. A. Rempel, 36.

32 Devonshire to Chamberlain, 29 May 1903, J. Amery, v. 238-9.

33 Ibid. 230.

34 Ibid. 235. See Harcourt's comment: 'Of course, after Chamberlain's last speech, the question has become one of protection pure and simple and quite outside

the limits of Colonial preference.' Harcourt to Campbell-Bannerman, 29 May 1903, C.B.P. 41220, f. 108.

35 Devonshire to Balfour, 31 May 1903, J. Amery, v. 240–1.
36 Balfour to Devonshire, 4 June 1903, ibid. 241–2.
37 Ibid. 246–7; K. Young, 213–14.
38 J. Amery, v. 246.
39 Ibid. 258.
40 Harcourt to Campbell-Bannerman, 29 May 1903, R. A. Rempel, 40–1.
41 Beach to his wife, 10 June 1903, J. Amery, v. 251.
42 R. A. Rempel, 45.
43 J. Amery, v. 306–7.
44 Chamberlain to Devonshire, 25 Aug. 1903, ibid. 372–4.
45 Ibid. 265–8.
46 Chamberlain to Devonshire, 25 Aug. 1903, ibid. 372–4.
47 B. Semmel, *Imperialism and Social Reform*, 112–13.
48 Balfour to Devonshire, 30 July 1903, J. Amery, v. 365.
49 R. A. Rempel, 50–1.
50 Balfour to Lady Elcho, 9 Aug. 1903, J. Amery, v. 366.
51 Devonshire to Balfour, 12 Aug. 1903, ibid. 368–9.
52 Sandars to Balfour, 18 Aug. 1903, ibid. 370–1.
53 Balfour to Devonshire, 27 Aug. 1903, ibid. 377–8. See also, R. A. Rempel, 54.
54 Devonshire's memorandum and Devonshire to Balfour, 27 Aug. 1903, J. Amery, v. 378–81.
55 Balfour to Devonshire, 29 Aug. 1903, ibid. 381–2.
56 Balfour to Devonshire, 7 Sept. 1903, ibid. 386–7.
57 Devonshire to Balfour, 9 Sept. 1903, ibid. 388.
58 Chamberlain to Balfour, 9 Sept. 1903, ibid. 391–2.
59 Ritchie to *The Times*, 10 Oct. 1903, ibid. 402.
60 Ibid. 395–417.
61 Balfour to the King, 15 Sept. 1903, ibid. 396–7.
62 Elliot's note, ibid. 401; R. A. Rempel, 58.
63 Balfour to the King, 16 Sept. 1903, J. Amery, v. 411.
64 Balfour to Devonshire, 30 Jan. 1904, ibid. 407.
65 Ritchie to Devonshire, 20 Aug. 1903, ibid. 375–6.
66 R. A. Rempel, 59–61.
67 Devonshire to Chamberlain, 19 Sept. 1903, J. Amery, v. 430.
68 Balfour to Devonshire, 3 Oct. 1903, ibid. 445–6.

CHAPTER 3. CHAMBERLAIN'S TARIFF REFORM

1 Extracts from Chamberlain's speeches in this chapter are from C. Boyd, *Mr. Chamberlain's Speeches*. See also, B. Semmel, *Imperialism and Social Reform*, 83–127.
2 W. Langer, *The Diplomacy of Imperialism* (2nd edn. 1960), 77.
3 Churchill to J. H. Lawton, 1 July 1903, Randolph S. Churchill, *Winston S. Churchill*, ii. C.V. 205–6.
4 Churchill to Col. J. Mitford, 9 July 1903, ibid. ii. C.V. 208.
5 Ibid. ii. 64.
6 Churchill to Col. J. Mitford, 9 July 1903, ibid. ii. C.V. 208.
7 Ibid. ii. C.V. 207–8.
8 Churchill to J. Moore-Bayley, 20 May 1903, ibid. ii. 57.

9. Lord Hugh Cecil to Balfour, 4–6 May 1907, B.P. 49759, ff. 185–7.
10 Churchill to the editor of the *Oldham Chronicle,* 28 Oct. 1902, ibid. ii. C.V. 169.
11 Churchill to *The Times,* 16 July 1903, ibid. 64.
12 J. Amery, *Joseph Chamberlain and the Tariff Reform Campaign,* v. 440–4.
13 Ibid. vi. 483–4; R. A. Rempel, *Unionists Divided,* 67–8.
14 R. A. Rempel, 68.
15 Ibid. 46.
16 Ripon to Campbell-Bannerman, 30 May 1903, C.B.P. 41225, ff. 4–7.
17 H. Gladstone to Campbell-Bannerman, 1 June 1903, C.B.P. 41216, ff. 276–7.
18 Churchill to Rosebery, 27 Oct. 1903, R.P. Box 8.
19 Churchill to Rosebery, 30 Oct. 1903, Randolph S. Churchill, ii. C.V. 246.
20 Beach to Harcourt, 9 Sept. 1903, R. A. Rempel, 62.
21 Randolph S. Churchill, ii. C.V. 195.
22 Beach to his wife, 10 June 1903, Lady Victoria Hicks Beach, *The Life of Sir Michael Hicks Beach,* ii. 192–3.
23 Lord Hugh Cecil to Churchill (30 May 1903), Randolph S. Churchill, ii. C.V. 188–9.
24 Churchill to Campbell-Bannerman, 29 May 1903, ibid. 188.
25 Churchill to Lord Hugh Cecil, 30 May 1903, ibid. 190–2.
26 Campbell-Bannerman to Harcourt, 4 July (1903), J. Amery, v. 264.
27 W. S. Robson to Campbell-Bannerman, 1 July 1903, C.B.P. 41237, ff. 126–8.
28 J. Amery, v. 254.
29 Copy, Tweedmouth to Churchill, 1 July 1903, H.G.P. 46022, ff. 53–4.
30 Harcourt to Campbell-Bannerman, 5 July 1903, C.B.P. 41220, ff. 132–5.
31 Harcourt to Campbell-Bannerman, 7 July 1903, C.B.P. 41220. ff. 136–7.
32 H. Gladstone to Campbell-Bannerman, 18 May 1903, C.B.P. 41216, f. 263. See also, Perks to Rosebery, 12 May 1903, R.P. Box 40.
33 Jesse Herbert to Gladstone, 25 Jan. 1903, H.G.P. 46025, ff. 124–5.
34 See, copy, H. Gladstone to Paulton, 29 Jan. 1903, Paulton to Gladstone, 30 Jan. 1903, copy, Gladstone to Paulton, 31 Jan. 1903, Paulton to Gladstone, 5 Feb. 1903, copy, Gladstone to Paulton, 6 Feb. 1903, H.G.P. 46060, ff. 111–30.
35 W. Crook to Gladstone, 21 Feb. 1903, H.G.P. 46024, ff. 131–7.
36 For the trouble in Rye and the unpopularity of Dr. Hutchinson with both the League and the Whips Office see the correspondence between Hutchinson, Gladstone and Freeman-Thomas in February 1903, H.G.P. 46060, ff. 130–65, and between Crook, Allard, and Gladstone, H.G.P. 46024, ff. 5–17. The chairman of the Rye Association was Captain Ellice, a notorious Leaguer.
37 W. Crook to Gladstone, 8 Oct. 1903, H.G.P. 46024, f. 37.
38 J. Herbert to Gladstone, 12 Mar. 1903, H.G.P. 46025, ff. 139–42.
39 J. Herbert to Gladstone, 29 Oct. 1903, H.G.P. 46026, ff. 11–12. See also, Bass to Allard, 5 June 1903, R.P. Box 106, reporting on his work in Norwich where 'with a few exceptions the most influential members of the party are also members of the League . . . The Liberal candidate, Mr. Louis Tillett is also a strong supporter of Lord Rosebery', and Leicester where 'a branch can be formed at any time'. Allard thought 'The people who criticise the League (of Leicester) are the timid folk who have brought Leicester Liberalism to its knees. Leaguers have raised it and enabled it to face the foe. The Treasurer and the Hon. Secretary of the Leicester Liberal Association are Leaguers as well as the President.' Allard to Rosebery, 2 Nov. 1903, R.P. Box 106.
40 W. Crook to Gladstone, 2 Nov. 1903, H.G.P. 46024, f. 48.
41 W. Crook to Gladstone, 8 Mar. 1904, H.G.P. 46024, ff. 167–8.
42 J. Herbert to Gladstone, 11 Oct. 1904, H.G.P. 46026, ff. 63–4.

43 Copy, Freeman-Thomas to Hutchinson, 16 Jan. 1905, H.G.P. 46062, f. 80; copy, Gladstone to Freeman-Thomas, 28 Feb. 1905, H.G.P. 46062, f. 134.

44 Freeman-Thomas to Gladstone, 1 and 7 Mar. 1905, H.G.P. 46062, ff. 135 and 139.

45 Churchill to Rosebery, 29 May 1903, Randolph S. Churchill, ii. C.V. 185.

46 Lord Hugh Cecil to Churchill, 30 May 1903, ibid. 189.

47 Lord Hugh Cecil to Devonshire, 29 June 1903, J. Amery, v. 263–4.

48 Campbell-Bannerman to Harcourt, 27 Nov. 1903, Campbell-Bannerman to Bryce, 7 Dec. 1903, ibid. vi. 511.

49 For Churchill's continued hopes of a 'Central Party' see Churchill to Rosebery, 13 Aug. 1903, R.P. Box 8, and 9 and 30 Oct. and 25 Nov. 1903, Randolph S. Churchill, ii. C.V. 227, 246, 256.

50 R. A. Rempel, 69–70.

51 Devonshire to James, 7 Oct. 1903, J. Amery, vi. 482.

52 Goschen to Devonshire, 9 Oct. 1903, R. A. Rempel, 69; Lord George Hamilton to Devonshire, 3 Oct. 1903, ibid. 63.

53 Campbell-Bannerman to Harcourt, 27 Nov. 1903, J. Amery, vi. 511.

54 R. A. Rempel, 72–3.

55 Ibid. 72–4. Of Ludlow, Campbell-Bannerman wrote, 'Ludlow is not very enlightening.' Copy, Campbell-Bannerman to Gladstone, 24 Dec. 1903, C.B.P. 41217, f. 58. Herbert Gladstone was less surprised than most by the results. He reported 'wild expectations' in Lewisham, Ludlow, 'and even Dulwich', and thought they might win Ludlow, would do well in Dulwich, and that there might be a revolt of local Tories against Harris there. But he also noted that 'These elections draw a lot of money from me. They have been looked upon as such desperately bad chances that candidates were not to be found who would pay for them.' Gladstone to Campbell-Bannerman, 5 Dec. 1903, C.B.P. 41217, f. 412. Bryce blamed Lewisham on the 'Liberal Imperialism of Cleland. He had none but the Liberal Leaguers round him as agents etc. The anti-Jingo section was alienated and the League sorely discouraged by the result.' Bryce to Campbell-Bannerman, 28 Dec. 1903, C.B.P. 41211, ff. 254–7.

56 Churchill to Rosebery, 9 Oct. 1903, Randolph S. Churchill, ii. C.V. 227.

57 R. A. Rempel, 71–2.

58 Ibid. 79–80.

59 Gladstone to Campbell-Bannerman, 16 Nov. 1903, C.B.P. 41217, ff. 35–6.

60 Campbell-Bannerman to Gladstone, 9 Nov. 1903, H.G.P. 45988, f. 60.

61 J. Amery, vi. 511.

62 Gerald Balfour to Austen Chamberlain, 26 Dec. 1903, R. A. Rempel, op. cit. 81.

63 Gladstone to Campbell-Bannerman, 10 Nov. 1903, C.B.P. 41217, ff. 32–3.

64 Copy, Gladstone to Campbell-Bannerman, 24 June 1903, H.G.P. 45988, f. 45.

65 Gladstone to Campbell-Bannerman, 3 Nov. 1903, C.B.P. 41217, ff. 28–9.

66 Tweedmouth to Campbell-Bannerman, 28 Nov. 1903, C.B.P. 41231, ff. 83–6.

67 Campbell-Bannerman to Gladstone, 3 Dec. 1903, H.G.P. 49588, ff. 66–7). Campbell-Bannerman was prepared to consider cases, particularly, at this time, Dickson-Poynder, after Fuller, a Liberal Leaguer, had raised the 'case' (Campbell-Bannerman to Gladstone, 9 Nov. 1903, H.G.P. 45988, ff. 60–1), and after Asquith had added a voice in favour of supporting him on the grounds that 'if we showed a disposition to do so, he would run as a Liberal' (Asquith to Gladstone, 11 Nov. 1903, H.G.P. 45989, ff. 83–4). See also, Campbell-Bannerman to Bryce, 7 Dec. 1903, C.B.P. 41211, f. 250. Poynder apart, Gladstone saw difficulties with the other 'Liberal' Unionist free traders, Churchill, Guest, and Seely, since 'Oldham, Plymouth and the Isle of Wight are all well occupied by

Liberal candidates . . .' (Gladstone to Campbell-Bannerman, 5 Dec. 1903, C.B.P. 41217, ff. 41–2), as did Campbell-Bannerman (Campbell-Bannerman to Gladstone, 7 Dec. 1903, H.G.P. 45988, ff. 67–8).

68 R. A. Rempel, 77.

69 Gladstone to Campbell-Bannerman, 21 Dec. 1903, R. A. Rempel, 80.

70 Campbell-Bannerman to Gladstone, 22 Dec. 1903, H.G.P. 45988, ff. 21–2. Campbell-Bannerman's gradual advance was none the less marked in contrast to his attitude in the summer, when he had written to Nash: 'I am against everything that would compromise our normal position. If joint meetings are ever held, it must be at their request and on our terms: I would not yield an inch and we are strong enough to take our time.' Copy, Campbell-Bannerman to Nash, 29 Aug. 1903, C.B.P. 41237, f. 156.

71 Spencer to Campbell-Bannerman, 23 Dec. 1903, C.B.P. 41229, ff. 231–5.

72 Copy, James's memorandum, 21 Dec. 1903, C.B.P. 41217, ff. 61–2. The memorandum embodied the substance of a conversation between James and Asquith and was sent by Asquith to Gladstone with permission to send it to Campbell-Bannerman. Asquith also raised with Gladstone Devonshire's letter to Rosebery on co-operation on the Address and on Unionist free trade seats, and the Duke's desire to open negotiations with Spencer (Asquith to Gladstone, 23 Dec. 1903, H.G.P. 45989, ff. 92–5). All this was duly forwarded to Campbell-Bannerman (Gladstone to Campbell-Bannerman, 24 Dec. 1903, C.B.P. 41217, ff. 59–60). Campbell-Bannerman was unimpressed: 'We are to withdraw candidates whenever our local people will allow it in order to save the skins of the Free Traders. In return, the Free Traders are, most of them, to run away or join the enemy on any amendment to the Address.' (Campbell-Bannerman to Gladstone, 26 Dec. 1903, H.G.P. 45988, ff. 77–8.) Asquith agreed with Campbell-Bannerman, and was 'against any open or general declaration of policy . . . each case should be dealt with on its merits and with regard to local conditions and susceptiblities . . . Sooner or later being as they are between the devil and the other thing, the Freefooders will either be squeezed out of existence or come over to us.' Asquith thought there 'might be about a dozen places in which the seat being hopeless for us, we might help them against a protectionist' (Asquith to Campbell-Bannerman, 28 Dec. 1903, C.B.P. 41210, ff. 227–8). Spencer read the memorandum differently, as an offer of a reciprocal agreement with the weakest candidate of either side withdrawing, and without bias was prepared to continue discussions (Spencer to Campbell-Bannerman, 28 Dec. 1903, C.B.P. 41229, ff. 239–40).

73 James to Asquith, 5 Jan. 1904, R. A. Rempel, 81.

74 Ibid. 83.

75 Asquith to Gladstone, 29 Dec. 1903, H.G.P. 45989 ff. 98–9. Gladstone took this up. Gladstone to Campbell-Bannerman, 14 Jan. 1904, C.B.P. 41217, ff. 76–9.

76 Campbell-Bannerman to Bryce, 15 Jan. 1904, C.B.P. 41211, f. 267; Bryce to Campbell-Bannerman, 16 Jan. 1904, C.B.P. 41211, ff. 269–70; R. A. Rempel, 83.

77 Perks to Asquith, 23 Dec. 1903, Asquith Papers, 10, ff. 118–19.

78 The Liberals also agreed to James's suggestion for a conference of the two sides, but 'The question of *political* relations must, of course, be left to the Duke and Lord Spencer. What I had in mind was organisation in the country on the fiscal question alone . . . Cooperation between the Free Trade Union and the Free Food League appears to me to be distinct from the party relations which the Duke and Lord Spencer are considering.' Copy, Gladstone to James, 11 Jan. 1904, H.G.P. 46018, ff. 64–5. See also, copy Gladstone to James, 7 Jan, 1904, H.G.P. 46018, ff. 58–9; James to Gladstone, 9 Jan. 1904, H.G.P. 46018.

ff. 60–3; James to Gladstone, 12 Jan. 1904, H.G.P. 46018, ff. 66–9. In this last letter James threw doubts upon the possibility even of the co-operation of the two Leagues.

79 For all these negotiations, and the final scheme, see R. A. Rempel, 80–4.
80 Campbell-Bannerman to Gladstone, 26 Dec. 1903, J. Amery, vi. 549.
81 R. A. Rempel, 82.
82 Ibid. 84–5.
83 Spencer to Campbell-Bannerman, 27 Dec. 1903, C.B.P. 41229, ff. 237–8.
84 Copy, Balfour to Sandars, 22 Feb. 1904, B.P. 49762, ff. 84–5.
85 Beach to his son, 11 Dec. 1903, Lady Victoria Hicks Beach, ii. 200.

CHAPTER 4. FACTIONS AT PLAY

1 R. A. Rempel, *Unionists divided*, 87.
2 Sandars to Balfour, 18 Feb. 1904, B.P. 49762. f. 66.
3 Sandars to Balfour, 21 Feb. 1904, B.P. 49762, ff. 75–80.
4 Copy, Balfour to Sandars, 22 Feb. 1904, B.P. 49762, ff. 84–5.
5 Sandars to Balfour, 21 Feb. 1904, B.P. 49762, ff. 75–80.
6 J. Amery, *Joseph Chamberlain and the Tariff Reform Campaign*, vi. 558–9; R. A. Rempel, 118–19.
7 Chamberlain to Northcote, 22 Apr. 1904, J. Amery, vi. 562–3.
8 Ibid. vi. 567–8; R. A. Rempel, 119. The figure of 22 Unionist free traders is taken from Rempel. Amery says 'only five Free Fooders went so far as to vote with the Opposition'.
9 J. Amery, vi. 574–90.
10 Ibid. vi. 573–4; R. A. Rempel, 120. The figure of 177 M.P.s is from Rempel. Amery says 'Exactly 200 . . .'
11 J. Amery, vi. 591–6.
12 R. A. Rempel, 121–2.
13 J. Amery, vi. 610–12.
14 Austen Chamberlain's letters of 24 Aug. 1904 and 12 Sept. 1904, together with Balfour's reply of 10 Sept. 1904, are printed in Sir Austen Chamberlain, *Politics from Inside* (1936), 22–34. For Sandars's comments see Sandars to Balfour, 8 Sept. 1904, B.P. 49762, ff. 116–19 and 13 Sept. 1904, ibid. ff. 114–15. Parts are quoted in J. Amery, vi. 619 and 624, and the remark on Oswestry in R. A. Rempel, 122. For Lyttelton's idealism, see Lyttelton to Chamberlain, 12 Mar. 1905 in J. Amery, vi. 676.
15 Sandars to Balfour, 8 Sept. 1904, B.P. 49762, ff. 116–19.
16 Selborne to Balfour, 7 Sept. 1904, B.P. 49708, ff. 12–14.
17 Selborne to Balfour, 17 Sept. 1904, B.P. 49708, ff. 15–16, and Wyndham to Balfour, 28 Sept. 1904, B.P. 49804, ff. 230–4.
18 Copy, Balfour to Selborne, 19 Sept. 1904, B.P. 49708, ff. 19–20.
19 Sandars to Balfour, 8 Sept. 1904, B.P. 49762, ff. 116–19.
20 Austen Chamberlain to Balfour, 12 Sept. 1904, Sir Austen Chamberlain, 32.
21 Copy, Balfour to Selborne, 19 Sept. 1904, B.P. 49708, ff. 19–20.
22 Wyndham to his sister, Mary, 19 Oct. 1904, J. W. Mackail and G. Wyndham, *Life and Letters of George Wyndham*, ii. 482–3.
23 Chamberlain to Chaplin, 27 Sept. 1904, J. Amery, vi. 626–7.
24 Ibid. 635–6.
25 Chamberlain to Lyttelton, 4 Oct. 1904, ibid. 634.

26 Sandars to Balfour, 16 Oct. 1904, B.P. 49762, ff. 162–3.
27 Lyttelton to Chamberlain, 21 Sept. 1904, J. Amery, vi. 628–9.
28 Copy, J. Chamberlain to Leverton Harris, 8 Oct. 1904, J.C.P. 19/7/57.
29 Chaplin to Chamberlain, 28 Oct. 1904, J. Amery, vi. 639.
30 Sandars to Balfour, 9 Oct. 1904, B.P. 49762, f. 156.
31 Sandars to Balfour, 16 Oct. 1904, B.P. 49762, f. 163.
32 Chamberlain to Balfour, 12 Feb. 1905, J. Amery, vi. 654.
33 Balfour to Chamberlain, 18 Feb. 1905, ibid. 655–8.
34 Chamberlain to Balfour, 24 Feb. 1905, ibid. 658–60.
35 Sandars to Balfour, 21 Jan. 1905, B.P. 49763, f. 75.
36 Chamberlain to Maxwell, 25 Feb. 1905, J. Amery, vi. 665–6.
37 Ibid. 673–90.
38 Griffiths Boscawen to Chamberlain, 30 Mar. 1905, ibid. 690–1.
39 Garvin to Maxse, 30 Apr. 1905, M.P. 453. See also Garvin to Maxse, 8 May 1905, M.P. 453.
40 J. Amery, vi. 693–6.
41 Ibid. 697–704.
42 Balfour to Lyttelton, 27 May 1905, ibid. 706.
43 Ibid. 706–9.
44 Wyndham to Balfour, 3 June 1905, J. W. Mackail and G. Wyndham, ii. 507.
45 J. Amery, vi. 709–10.
46 Lord Hugh Cecil to Balfour, 9 Jan. 1905, B.P. 49759, ff. 63–80.
47 Lord Robert Cecil's memorandum of 18 Feb. 1905, B.P. 49737, ff. 129–32; copy, Elliot Papers, MS. 4246, Box 14, F. 86; R. A. Rempel, 141–2.
48 Lord Hugh Cecil to Balfour, 1 Dec. 1904, B.P. 49759, ff. 51–2.
49 Lord Hugh Cecil to Balfour, 5 June 1905, B.P. 49759, ff. 109–12.
50 Lord Hugh Cecil to Balfour, 9 Jan. 1905, B.P. 49759, ff. 63–80.
51 Lord Hugh Cecil to Balfour, 2 Mar. 1905, B.P. 49759, ff. 87–90.
52 Copy, Balfour to Lord Hugh Cecil, 9 Dec. 1904, B.P. 49759, ff. 55–62, part quoted in R. A. Rempel, 143.
53 Copy, Balfour to Lord Hugh Cecil, 6 Dec. 1904, B.P. 49759, ff. 53–4. See also, copy, Balfour to Lord Robert Cecil, 8 Jan. 1906. B.P. 49737, ff. 36–8.
54 Lord Robert Cecil to Sandars, 18 Feb. 1905, B.P. 49737, ff. 27–8.
55 Two memorandums (? March 1905) possibly prefaced by Manners Sutton to Elliot, 18 Mar. 1905, Elliot Papers, MS. 4346, Box 14, F. 86.
56 Lord Robert Cecil to Elliot, 24 Mar. 1905, Elliot Papers, MS. 4246, Box 14, F. 86, part quoted in R. A. Rempel, 136. See also, Lord Robert Cecil to Elliot, 26 Mar. 1905, Elliot Papers, MS. 4246, Box 14, F. 86.
57 Lord Hugh Cecil to Strachey, 12 Jan. 1905, S.P. 4/3/5.
58 Lord Hugh Cecil to Strachey, 6 June 1905, S.P. 4/3/6.
59 Draft copy, Strachey to Lord Hugh Cecil, 3 June 1905, S.P. 4/3/6.
60 R. A. Rempel, 151–2.
61 Chamberlain to Northcote, 13 June 1905, J. Amery, vi. 712.
62 Ibid. 723–7.
63 Lord Hugh Cecil to Balfour, 13 July 1905, B.P. 49759, f. 125.
64 Wyndham to Balfour, 8 July 1905, J. Amery, vi. 727–8.
65 Ibid. 740–3.
66 Hood to Sandars, 7 Nov. (1905), B.P. 49771, f. 112.
67 Wyndham to Balfour, 8 Nov. 1905, J. W. Mackail and G. Wyndham, ii. 517–20.
68 J. Amery, vi. 753.
69 Ibid. 757–60.

70 Hood to Sandars, 28 Aug. (1905), B.P. 49771, ff. 57–60, and 14 Oct. (1905), B.P. 49771, ff. 94–5.
71 Sandars, Memorandum (1905), B.P. 49764, ff. 130–2.
72 Sandars to Balfour, 13 Dec. 1905, B.P. 49764, ff. 123–7.
73 Sandars, Memorandum (1905), B.P. 49764, ff. 130–2.
74 Sandars to Balfour, 13 Dec. 1905, B.P. 49764, ff. 123–7.
75 Chamberlain to Maxse, 21 Dec. 1905, M.P. 453.
76 Sandars, Memorandum (1905), B.P. 49764, ff. 130–2.
77 Balfour to Chamberlain, 2 Nov. 1905, J. Amery, vi. 737–40.
78 Asquith to Gladstone, 22 Oct. 1905, H.G.P. 45989, ff. 131–2, part quoted in H. W. McCready, 'Home Rule and the Liberal Party', 342.
79 Campbell-Bannerman to Gladstone, McCready, 342. The question was still deeply divisive. Elgin thus made reservations before he accepted office since 'any question of Home Rule legislation, as it took shape in the past, or alliance with the Irish party for that end, must be fatal to the usefulness of the Liberal party'. Elgin to Campbell-Bannerman, 7 Dec. 1905, C.B.P. 41214, ff. 13–14.
80 J. Lawson Walton to Gladstone, 18 Mar. 1905, H.G.P. 46062, ff. 168–9.
81 J. Lawson Walton to Gladstone, 28 Nov. 1905, H.G.P. 46063, ff. 132–3.
82 R. A. Hudson to Gladstone, 28 Nov. 1905, H.G.P. 46061, f. 92.
83 Gladstone to Campbell-Bannerman, 27 Nov. 1905, C.B.P. 41217, f. 281. Gladstone thought 'Rosebery evidently wanted to quarrel and chose a point on which he thought he had most to gain and C.B. most to lose.' Copy, Gladstone to Hudson, 28 Nov. 1905, H.G.P. 46061, ff. 94–5.
84 Rosebery to Spender, 1 Dec. 1905, Spender Papers, 46387, f. 61.
85 Copy, Gladstone to Campbell-Bannerman, 30 Nov. 1905, H.G.P. 45988, ff. 204–9. See Rosebery to Spender, 'St. Andrew's Day' 1905, Spender Papers, 46387, ff. 59–60.
86 Copy, Gladstone to Campbell-Bannerman, 30 Nov. 1905, H.G.P. 45988, ff. 204–9; Strachey to Gladstone, 6 Dec. 1905, H.G.P. 46063, ff. 105–6.
87 Rosebery to Spender, 7 Dec. 1905, Spender Papers, 46387, f. 62.
88 Gladstone to Campbell-Bannerman, 30 Nov. 1905, H. W. McCready, 345.
89 Grey to Gladstone, 29 Nov. 1905, H.G.P. 45992, ff. 120–1.
90 For details of the 'Relugas Compact', see the biographies of the participants, especially Haldane. For the intervention of Acland in 1905 and the intrigue and persuasion needed to get Asquith, Grey, and Haldane to join the new Liberal cabinet, see Spender's notes in Spender Papers, 46388, ff. 59–76.

CHAPTER 5. VALENTINE

1 According to R. A. Rempel, *Unionists Divided*, 116: 'The figures usually given for the 157 Unionists returned are: 109 Chamberlainites, 32 Balfourites and 16 Unionist free traders.' Neal Blewett has another version of the 'usual' contemporary figures; 'A classification of the post-electoral strength of the three factions given by *The Times* . . . was; Tariff Reformers, 109, Balfourites, 32, Free Fooders, 11, not classified, 5', and he also notes the 'slightly different figures used by Devonshire, 'Tariff Reformers, 102, Balfourites, 36, Free Fooders, 16, not classified, 3.' Neal Blewett, 'Free Fooders, Balfourites, Wholehoggers. Factionalism within the Unionist party, 1906–10', *Historical Journal,* xii, 1 (1968), 96.
2 R. A. Rempel, 230.

3 N. Blewett, 96; the members are listed on p. 114.
4 E. Sassoon and H. Butcher. But for Sassoon, see N. Blewett, 97 n. 10.
5 R. A. Rempel, 157.
6 Ibid. 228.
7 Ibid.
8 Chamberlain to Maxse, 28 Dec. 1905, M.P. 453.
9 e.g. Lord Robert Cecil to Balfour, 10 and 25 Jan. 1906, B.P. 49737, f. 39 and ff. 40–2.
10 Chamberlain to Mrs. Endicott, 30 Jan. 1906, J. Amery, *Joseph Chamberlain and the Tariff Reform Campaign*, vi. 799.
11. Chamberlain to Balfour, 25 Jan. 1906, ibid. 803–5.
12 Sandars to Balfour, 21 Jan. 1906, B.P. 49764, f. 149.
13 Sandars to Balfour, 27 Jan. (1906), B.P. 49764, ff. 155–8.
14 Mrs. Chamberlain to her mother, 3 Feb. 1906, J. Amery, vi. 813.
15 Chamberlain to Garvin, 5 Feb. 1906, ibid. 814–16.
16 Chamberlain to Ridley, 6 Feb. 1906, ibid. 821–4.
17 Balfour to Chamberlain, 6 Feb. 1906, ibid. 824–6.
18 Chamberlain to Balfour, 7 Feb. 1906, ibid. 826–7.
19 Balfour to Chamberlain, 8 Feb. 1906, ibid. 832–3.
20 Balfour to Lord Hugh Cecil, 14 July 1905, B.P. 49759, f. 126.
21 Chamberlain to Ridley, 8 Feb. 1906, J. Amery, vi. 831–2.
22 Ridley to Law, 5 Jan. 1906, B.L.P. 18/2/10.
23 Ridley to Chamberlain, 12 Feb. 1906, J. Amery, vi. 842–3.
24 Chamberlain to Pike Pease, 7 Feb. 1906, J.C.P. 21/2/78.
25 Garvin to Maxse, 4 Feb. 1906, M.P. 455.
26 Lansdowne to Balfour, 28 Jan. 1906, J. Amery, vi. 808–9.
27 Sandars to Balfour, 21 Jan. 1906, B.P. 49764, ff. 149–51.
28 Sandars to Balfour, 27 Jan. 1906, B.P. 49764, ff. 155–8.
29 Douglas to Balfour, n.d. (1906), B.P. 49772, f. 37.
30 Sandars to Balfour, 27 Jan. 1906, B.P. 49764, ff. 155–8.
31 Copy, Balfour to Cawdor, 7 Feb. 1906, B.P. 49709, f. 26.
32 Cawdor to Balfour, 8 Feb. 1906, B.P. 49709, f. 27.
33 Lansdowne to Balfour, 28 Jan. 1906, J. Amery, vi. 808–9.
34 Salisbury to Selborne, 10 Aug. 1904, Selborne Papers, 5, ff. 88–91.
35 Salisbury to Selborne, 25 Feb. 1906, Selborne Papers, 5, ff. 128–37.
36 Chamberlain to Goulding, 23 Jan. 1906, Wargrave Papers, A/3/2.
37 W. J. Ashley to Maxse, 7 Feb. 1906, M.P. 455. See also, Maxse to Law, 29 Jan. 1906, B.L.P. 18/2/12.
38 Salisbury to Selborne, 12 Feb. 1906, Selborne Papers, 5, ff. 118–27.
39 Pembroke to Douglas, 5 Feb. 1906, Viscount Chilston, *Chief Whip. The Political Life and Times of Aretas Akers-Douglas, First Viscount Chilston,* 334.
40 Ridley to Chamberlain, 22 Jan. 1906, J. Amery, vi. 798.
41 Maxse to Law, 29 Jan. 1906, B.L.P. 18/2/12.
42 Chamberlain to Balfour, 7 Feb. 1906, J. Amery, vi. 827–8.
43 E. B. Iwan-Muller to Maxse, 1 Jan. 1906, M.P. 455.
44 E. B. Iwan-Muller to Maxse, 4 Jan. 1906, M.P. 455.
45 Gilbert Parker to Chamberlain, 8 Feb. 1906, J. Amery, vi. 830.
46 Chamberlain to Balfour, 9 Feb. 1906, ibid. 833–4.
47 Chamberlain to Ridley, 9 Feb. 1906, ibid. 834–5.
48 Chamberlain to Ridley, 10 Feb. 1906, ibid. 838.
49 Chamberlain to Balfour, 10 Feb. 1906, ibid. 835–8.
50 Balfour to Chamberlain, 11 Feb. 1906, ibid. 843.

51 Balfour to Chamberlain, 14 Feb. 1906, Chamberlain to Balfour, 14 Feb. 1906, ibid. 846–7.
52 Lord Hugh Cecil to Devonshire, 16 Feb. 1906, R. A. Rempel, 169.
53 Strachey to Maxse, 16 Feb. 1906, M.P. 455.
54 Salisbury to Selborne, 25 Feb. 1906, Selborne Papers, 5, ff. 128–37.
55 Copy, Balfour to F. Hammond Clarke, 19 Feb. 1906, B.P. 49858, f. 182.
56 W. G. Howard Gretton, 'The Unionist Leadership', *National Review*, Feb. 1907.
57 'The Organisers of Disaster', ibid., Aug. 1906.
58 Sandars to Balfour, 14 May 1906, B.P. 49764, f. 186: 'Joe is very active just now behind the scenes . . . he is working old Harry Chaplin for all he is worth to block the National Union scheme of reorganisation . . .'
59 Ridley to Steel-Maitland, 25 May 1906, Steel-Maitland Papers, G.D. 193/130.
60 *National Review*, June 1906, 554.
61 The Committee had seven members, one of whom was the chief whip, 3 others were to be nominated by him, and 3 by the National Union. In 1906 the nominations of the National Union were the chairman, Imbert-Terry, Lord Granby, and Sir William Plummer, all respected Conservatives but, as Ridley remarked, 'None of these is of any use to us, and I hardly know what to suggest.' Ridley to Steel-Maitland, 25 May 1906, Steel-Maitland Papers, G.D. 193/130.
62 See Sir Frederick Milner's letter of protest to *The Times*, 27 July 1906.
63 Copy, Steel-Maitland to Alfred King, 13 July 1906, Steel-Maitland Papers, G.D. 193/133.
64 For a report of the Conference from which this account is taken, see *National Union Gleanings*, vol. 27, July–Dec. 1906, 151.
65 *National Review*, July 1906.
66 Lawrence to Chamberlain, 27 July 1906, J.C.P. 21/2/58.
67 Lawrence to Chamberlain, 28 July 1906, J.C.P. 21/2/58. See also, Lawrence to Ratcliffe Cousins, 3 Aug. 1906, J.C.P. 21/2/59.
68 W. C. Bridgeman to Balfour, 2 Aug. 1906, B.P. 49764, ff. 195–200.
69 Sandars, 'A Note on Bridgeman's letter', 20 Aug. 1906, B.P. 49764, f. 216.
70 Chamberlain to Northcote, 29 May 1906, J.C.P. 21/2/69.

CHAPTER 6. SOCIALISM

1 *National Review*, Sept. 1906, 27, and Oct. 1906, 203.
2 B. E. C. Dugdale, *Balfour*, i. 438–9.
3 Salisbury to Selborne, 19 Jan. 1906, Selborne Papers, 5, ff. 110–17.
4 Wyndham to his father, 24 Jan. 1906, J. W. Mackail and G. Wyndham, *Life and Letters of George Wyndham*, ii. 540–1.
5 Stanley as reported by Fitzroy, J. Amery, *Joseph Chamberlain and the Tariff Reform Campaign*, vi. 791.
6 Wyndham to his mother, 24 Jan. 1906, J. W. Mackail and G. Wyndham, ii. 539.
7 Ibid. 539.
8 Garvin to Maxse, 4 Apr. 1906, M.P. 455.
9 Balfour to Lansdowne, 13 Apr. 1906, K. Young, *Balfour*, 265.
10 Sandars to Balfour, 22 Jan. 1907, B.P. 49765, ff. 11–16, largely quoted in B. E. C. Dugdale, ii 43–4.
11 J. Parker Smith to Balfour, 28 Jan. 1907, B.P. 49859, ff. 131–6.
12 Wyndham to Philip Hanson, 28 Nov. 1905, J. W. Mackail and G. Wyndham, ii. 527.

13 Wyndham to Sandars, 26 Nov. 1905, ibid. 525.

14 Wyndham to his father, 19 Jan. 1907, ibid. 563–4.

15 *M(onthly) N(otes) on T(ariff) R(eform)*, Nov. 1906, 327.

16 B. R. Wise to Steel-Maitland, n.d. 'Thursday' (1906), Steel-Maitland Papers, G.D. 193/130.

17 Garvin to Maxse, 4 Dec. 1906, M.P. 456.

18 For the Confederacy, see A. Sykes, 'The Confederacy and the Purge of the Unionist Free Traders, 1906–10', *Historical Journal*, xviii, 2 (1975), 349–66.

19 B. R. Wise to Steel-Maitland, 12 Dec. 1906, Steel-Maitland Papers, G.D. 193/133.

20 Garvin to Maxse, 10 Jan. 1907, M.P. 457.

21 *National Review*, Sept. 1906, 28. For Elibank's attack on Labour see ibid. Oct. 1906, 203.

22 Sandars to Balfour, 13 Jan. 1907, B.P. 49765, ff. 5–8.

23 Milner at Manchester, 14 Dec. 1906, in *The Nation and the Empire; Being a Collection of Speeches and Addresses: with an Introduction by Lord Milner, G.C.B.* (1913) 135–52.

24 Milner at Wolverhampton, 17 Dec. 1906, ibid. 161.

25 Filmer to Balfour, 18 Dec. 1906, B.P. 49859, ff. 118–20.

26 Austen Chamberlain to Hewins, 17 Jan. 1907, Hewins Papers.

27 *Outlook*, 5 Jan. 1907.

28 Hood to Short, 14 Jan. (1907), B.P. 49771, ff. 166–7.

29 Sandars to Short, 17 Jan. 1907, B.P. 49765, ff. 9–10.

30 Sandars to Balfour, 22 Jan. 1907, B.P. 49765, ff. 11–16, part quoted in B. E. C. Dugdale, ii. 43–4.

31 Copy, Balfour to Horace (Hutchinson), 5 Nov. 1906, B.P. 49859, f. 109.

32 Copy, Balfour to Sandars, 24 Jan. 1907, B.P. 49765, ff. 23–5, largely quoted in B. E. C. Dugdale, ii. 44.

33 Copy, Balfour to Lord Hugh Cecil, 16 Jan. 1907, B.P. 49759, f. 176.

34 Copy, Balfour to Sandars, 24 Jan. 1907, B. E. C. Dugdale, ii. 44.

35 Garvin to Maxse, 6 Feb. 1907, M.P. 457.

36 Memorandum, 'The Fiscal Question in February, 1907', B.P. 49780, ff. 236–54; Austen Chamberlain to Balfour, 4 Feb. 1907, B.P. 49736, ff. 3–7.

37 Ridley to Austen Chamberlain, 15 Jan. 1907, A.C.P. 7/6/2.

38 Copy, Austen Chamberlain to Ridley, 16 Jan. 1907, A.C.P. 7/6/3,

39 Ridley to Austen Chamberlain, 19 Jan. 1907, A.C.P. 7/6/5; copy, Austen Chamberlain to Ridley, 20 Jan. 1907, A.C.P. 7/6/7.

40 Balfour to Austen Chamberlain, 4 Feb. 1907, 'The Fiscal Question in February 1907', B.P. 49780, ff. 240–2; also B.P. 49736, ff. 8–9.

41 Austen Chamberlain to Balfour, 5 Feb. 1907, 'The Fiscal Question in February 1907', B.P. 49780, ff. 242–3. The shadow cabinet was to meet on Tuesday morning after the King's speech. Balfour to Austen Chamberlain, 4 Feb. 1907, ibid.

42 Balfour to Austen Chamberlain, 9 Feb. 1907, ibid. ff. 244–7; also, B.P. 49736, ff. 12–15.

43 Sir Austen Chamberlain, *Politics from Inside*, 48.

44 Balfour to Austen Chamberlain, 9 Feb. 1907, 'The Fiscal Question in February 1907', B.P. 49780, ff. 244–7.

45 Copy, Hewins to Austen Chamberlain, 9 Feb. 1907, Hewins Papers.

46 'The Fiscal Question in February, 1907', B.P. 49780, f. 248.

47 Chamberlain told the ex-cabinet that Douglas and Long had not been invited to the tariff reform meeting because, as members of the front bench, they might

be embarrassed. However he subsequently admitted that Bonar Law and Arthur Lee, both also on the front bench, had attended the meeting. 'The Fiscal Question in February 1907', B.P. 49780, f. 252.

48 Balfour to Austen Chamberlain, 13 Feb. 1907, ibid. ff. 249-50.

49 Ibid. ff. 250-1.

50 *The Times*, 15 Feb. 1907.

51 See *The Times*, 16 Feb. 1907, letters from Sir Gilbert Parker, J. F. Remnant, J. Hills, A. Lee, and E. Cecil. There are minor discrepancies between the accounts in the 'Fiscal Question' memorandum and *The Times* as to the numbers present, with *The Times* giving a total of 52 and the resolution passed by 41 votes to 4. A list in Austen Chamberlain's papers of the M.P.s summoned to the meeting gives 42 names as in attendance, and also names Mason as one of those summoned rather than deliberately left out, as the 'Fiscal Question' memorandum claims. (I owe this reference to Dr. Neal Blewett.) Austen Chamberlain himself claims 43 were present, and the vote was unanimous, 'the two who left early agreed with the majority'. Sir Austen Chamberlain, 51-2.

52 See Long to Law, 20 Feb. 1907, B.L.P. 18/3/31.

53 'The Fiscal Question in February 1907', B.P. 49780, f. 254; Sir Austen Chamberlain, 52.

54 Austen Chamberlain to Hewins, 3 Dec. 1906, Hewins Papers.

55 Copy, Balfour to Sandars, 24 Jan. 1907, B.P. 49765, ff. 23-5.

56 Austen Chamberlain to Hewins, 23 Dec. 1906, Hewins Papers.

57 Balfour to Hewins, 12 Jan. 1907, copy, Hewins to Austen Chamberlain, 16 Jan. 1907, Austen Chamberlain to Hewins, 17 Jan. 1907, Hewins Papers. Sandars approved of these talks. Sandars to Short, 17 Jan. 1907, B.P. 49765, ff. 9-10.

58 'Notes of my conversation with Mr. Balfour at Whittinghame in January 1907', Hewins Papers.

59 Hewins, 'A memorandum on Food Taxes', 11 Feb. 1907, B.P. 49779, ff. 36-40.

60 *Standard*, 16 Feb. 1907.

61 Sandars to Balfour, 6 Nov. 1907, B.P. 49765, ff. 80-1.

62 For praise of Balfour by a leading whole-hogger, see J. F. Remnant's speech welcoming the appointment of Percival Hughes as Conservative Chief Agent, *The Times*, 22 Feb. 1907.

63 See *National Review*, March 1907. But Maxse's 'Episodes of the Month' made no mention of the Savoy Hotel speech.

64 Copy, Balfour to Lord Hugh Cecil, 26 Mar. 1907, marked 'Not Sent', B.P. 49759, ff. 182-4.

65 *National Review,* Mar. 1907.

66 Sandars to Balfour, 6 Nov. 1907, B.P. 49765, ff. 80-1.

67 Amery to Maxse, 21 Apr. 1907, M.P. 457.

68 Collings to Joseph Chamberlain, 29 May 1907, J.C.P. 22/38.

69 Copy, Joseph Chamberlain to Halsbury, 12 May 1907, J.C.P. 22/87.

70 Milner to Joseph Chamberlain, 14 July 1907, J.C.P. 22/98.

71 Sir Austen Chamberlain, 72.

72 Ibid. 78.

73 Ibid. 79.

74 Ibid. 82-3. Chamberlain noted a few days earlier that 'A. J. B. and Hewins appear to be "as thick as thick". A. J. B. sent for him yesterday afternoon and went through his Albert Hall speech with him in advance, "and I stiffened it up throughout" said Hewins.' Ibid. 80.

75 Ibid. 89.

76 Copy, Joseph Chamberlain to Northcote, 24 May 1907, J.C.P. 22/101.

77 Sir Austen Chamberlain, 86.
78 Hewins to Balfour, 13 May 1907. See also Hewins to Balfour, 2, 10, and 14 May 1907, Balfour Papers, 49779, ff. 81–99.
79 Hewins to Balfour, 14 May 1907, B.P. 49779, ff. 98–9.
80 Sandars to Short, 10 Oct. 1907, B.P. 49765, f. 67.
81 Sandars to Short, 6 Oct. 1907, B.P. 49765, ff. 63–4.
82 Rutland to Balfour, 18 Oct. 1907, B.P. 49859, ff. 173–6.
83 A. Fellowes to Balfour, 24 Oct. 1907, B.P. 49858, ff. 183–5.
84 Sandars to Balfour, 6 Nov. 1907, B.P. 49765, f. 81.
85 F. C. Gardiner to Law, 21 Nov. 1907, B.L.P. 18/3/47.
86 Copy, Austen Chamberlain to Balfour, 24 Oct. 1907, A.C.P. 17/3/23.
87 A. Lee to Austen Chamberlain, 28 Oct. 1907, A.C.P. 17/3/64.
88 See Milner's speech at Tunbridge Wells, 24 Oct. 1907, *The Nation and the Empire*, 195–209.
89 Milner to Maxse, 12 Jan. 1907, M.P. 457.
90 Milner at Tunbridge Wells, 24 Oct. 1907, *The Nation and the Empire*, 196–7.
91 Milner at Rugby, 19 Nov. 1907, ibid. 244–5.
92 Milner to Jebb, 28 Oct. 1907, Jebb Papers.
93 Ware to Jebb, 25 Sept. 1907, Jebb Papers.
94 Milner at Guildford, 29 Oct. 1907, *The Nation and the Empire*, 214–15.
95 Ridley to Balfour, 1 Nov. 1907, B.P. 49859, ff. 190–3.
96 *T.R.L. Speakers' Handbook*, 4th edn. 1907, 176–7, and 3rd edn. 1905, 19.
97 Copy, Balfour to Austen Chamberlain, 23 Oct. 1907, B.P. 49736, ff. 37–8.
98 Copy, Balfour to A. Fellowes, 30 Oct. 1907, B.P. 49859, ff. 188–9.
99 Long to Balfour, 31 Oct. 1907, B.P. 49776, ff. 208–11.
100 Long to Balfour, 10 Nov. 1907, B.P. 49776, ff. 220–1.
101 Long to Douglas, 10 Nov. 1907, and Long to Sandars, 7 Nov. 1907, Viscount Chilston, *Chief Whip. The Political Life and Times of Aretas Akers-Douglas*, 339–40.
102 Sandars to Douglas, 10 Nov. 1907, Viscount Chilston, 341.
103 Long to Balfour, 31 Oct. 1907, B.P. 49776, ff. 208–11.
104 Wyndham to Sandars, 28 Oct. 1907, B.P. 49806, ff. 31–42.
105 Sandars to Short, 28 Oct. 1907, B.P. 49765, ff. 74–7.
106 Ibid.
107 Copy, Balfour to Ridley, 2 Nov. 1907, B.P. 49859, f. 194.
108 Memorandum of Mr. Balfour's Conversation with Mr. Hewins, 1, 2, 4 Nov. (1907), B.P. 49779, ff. 117–28.
109 Sandars to Balfour, 6 Nov. 1907, B.P. 49765, ff. 80–1. Sandars specifically linked the resolutions to the Savoy Hotel speech.
110 For Balfour's speeches and an account of the conference, see *The Times*, 15 and 16 Nov. 1907.
111 *National Review*, Dec. 1907, 510.
112 Joseph Chamberlain to Maxse, 22 Nov. 1907, M.P. 457.
113 Maxse to Joseph Chamberlain, 23 Nov. 1907, J.C.P. 22/96.
114 *The Times*, 15 Nov. 1907.
115 Ridley to Joseph Chamberlain, 22 Jan. 1906, J. Amery, vi. 798.
116 *The Times*, 15 Nov. 1907.

CHAPTER 7. THE CENTRAL COALITION

1 Lord Robert Cecil to Balfour, 17 Jan. 1907, B.P. 49737, ff. 62–4.
2 Sandars to Balfour, 2 Apr. 1907, B.P. 49765, ff. 34–8.

3 Copy, Steel-Maitland to Ridley, 26 Apr. 1907, Steel-Maitland Papers, G.D. 193/135.
4 Devonshire to Elliot, 1 May 1907, Elliot Papers, MS 4246, Box 14, F. 93.
5 Elliot to Strachey, n.d., S.P. 16/1/16.
6 e.g. Lord George Hamilton to Elliot, 5 May 1907, Elliot Papers, MS. 4246, Box 15, F. 100.
7 Elliot to Strachey, 4 May 1907, S.P. 16/1/9. Elliot wanted to make it clear 'that Colonial Preference is not the establishment of reciprocity between us and the Colonies; that at present they are highly favoured by us, not us by them; that Colonial Preference in the electorate is supported as the beginning of Protection; that Colonial Preference *does* involve the taxation of Corn; that we, a free trade country, get more into the markets of protected countries than do other protected countries. All to be seasoned with indisputable statistics.'
8 Lord Hugh Cecil to Balfour, 4–6 May 1907, B.P. 49759, ff. 185–97.
9 Lord Hugh Cecil to Balfour, 27 July 1907, B.P. 49759, ff. 210–17.
10 Lord Hugh Cecil to Balfour, 4–6 May 1907, B.P. 49759, ff. 185–97.
11 Lord Hugh Cecil to Balfour, 27 July 1907, B.P. 49759, ff. 210–17.
12 Elliot to Strachey, 11 July (1907), S.P. 16/1/2. See also, Elliot to Strachey, 24 May (1907), S.P. 16/1/2: 'They could, if they would, have invited our co-operation, but they have not done so. *My own position* is a clear one. Since Balfour and the Party whips have run a candidate against me as not being a Unionist and would do so again if I were a candidate tomorrow, I shall not respond to the Whips' invitations or account myself in any way a follower of Balfour's till they have made their position clear on the Free Trade question.'
13 Strachey, Memorandum of 19 Feb. 1906, Elliot Papers, MS. 4246, Box 15, F. 96.
14 W. R. Malcolm to Elliot, 22 Feb. 1906, Elliot Papers, MS. 4246, Box 15, F. 97.
15 Copy, Elliot to Devonshire, 27 May 1906, Elliot Papers, MS. 4246, Box 13, F. 72: 'I need scarcely say that I should have preferred to draft something more pugnacious . . .'
16 Devonshire to Elliot, 29 Apr. 1906, Elliot Papers, MS. 4246, Box 14, F. 93.
17 Devonshire to Elliot, 18 Feb. 1907, Elliot Papers, MS. 4246, Box 14, F. 93.
18 N. Blewett, 'Free Fooders, Balfourites, Wholehoggers', 116.
19 Copy, Lord Robert Cecil to Clarke, 29 May 1906, R.C.P. 51158, ff. 78–9.
20 Copy, Strachey to Devonshire, 2 Jan. 1907, S.P. 5/3/4. See also, V. Chirol to Maxse, 4 Mar. 1907, M.P. 457.
21 Copy, Strachey to Devonshire, 27 Aug. 1907, S.P. 5/3/5.
22 Copy, Strachey to Rosebery, 9 Aug. 1907, S.P. 12/7/4.
23 Copy, Lord Hugh Cecil to Beasley, 17 Mar. 1907, S.P. 4/3/7.
24 Copy, Strachey to Lord Hugh Cecil, 10 Apr. 1907, S.P. 4/3/7.
25 Lord Hugh Cecil to Strachey, 22 Apr. 1907. S.P. 4/3/7.
26 Copy, Strachey to Devonshire, 27 Aug. 1907, S.P. 5/3/5.
27 Copy, Strachey to Rosebery, 22 July 1907, S.P. 12/7/2.
28 Copy, Strachey to Rosebery, 29 July 1907, S.P. 12/7/3.
29 Copy, Strachey to Devonshire, 2 Jan. 1907, S.P. 5/3/4; copy, Strachey to Margot Asquith, 5 July 1909, S.P. 11/7/16; Elliot to Strachey, 4 May 1907, S.P. 16/1/9.
30 Devonshire to Elliot, 27 Sept. 1907, Elliot papers, MS. 4246, Box 14, F. 93.
31 Copy, Elliot to Balfour of Burleigh, 19 Oct. 1907, Elliot Papers, MS. 4246, Box 15, F. 100.
32 Perks to Rosebery, 23 Mar. 1906, R.P. Box 41.
33 Perks to Rosebery, 3 Apr. 1906, R.P. Box 41.
34 Perks to Rosebery, 30 Apr. 1906, R.P. Box 41. Perks also reported a late revival of the rumour of a Chamberlain–Liberal Imperialist coalition: 'Gilbert

Parker who is very closely in touch with Chamberlain and in his confidence, told me the other day that Chamberlain's idea is to reorganise and reconstruct the Tory Party. Parker says that Chamberlain is relying on the certain help of Milner and Curzon. He [Parker] said that they were hopeful of coming to some terms with the Asquith–Haldane–Grey section.'

35 *The Times*, 27 Mar. 1907.

36 Allard to Rosebery, 27 Mar. 1907, R.P. Box 107; Perks to Rosebery, 27 Mar. 1907, R.P. Box 42.

37 E. Montagu to Rosebery, 27 Mar. 1907, R.P. Box 107. Allard thought it was 'an epistle endorsed by several Liberal League M.P.s in the Eastern counties . . . and was certainly written with a view to publication.' Allard to Rosebery, 28 Mar. 1907, R.P. Box 107.

38 Copy, Rosebery to A(llard), 16 May 1907, R.P. Box 107.

39 Copy, Rosebery to A(llard), 17 May 1907, R.P. Box 107.

40 Allard to Rosebery, 23 May 1907, R.P. Box 107.

41 Sir Walter Foster joined but his reasons appear to have been personal—his failure to obtain office. Allard to Rosebery, 3 May 1907, R.P. Box 107.

42 Allard to Rosebery, 28 May 1907, R.P. Box 107.

43 Allard to Rosebery, 3 Sept. and 15 Nov. 1907, R.P. Box 107.

44 See copies, Rosebery to Allard, 4 Sept. 1907, and 21 Nov. 1907, R.P. Box 107.

45 Allard to Rosebery, 16 Nov. 1907, R.P. Box 107.

46 Copy, Rosebery to Allard, 21 Nov. 1907, R.P. Box 107.

47 Allard to Rosebery, 15 Nov. 1907, R.P. Box 107.

48 Rosebery, Memorandum ('Not Sent'), 25 Nov. 1907, R.P. Box 107. See also, copy, Rosebery to Jones, 6 Jan. 1908, R.P. Box 107: 'My general view is that the League is merely a clog, and a costly clog, that has survived its animating principles. It is now considered by the Government . . . as a superfluous critic, if not a lurking assassin . . . The policy of anti-Socialism and pro-Second Chamber could best be promoted by some other organisation.'

49 Perks to Rosebery, 26 Nov. 1907, R.P. Box 42.

50 Allard to Rosebery, 16 June 1907, R.P. Box 107.

51 Allard to Rosebery, 26 July 1907, R.P. Box 107.

52 Allard to Rosebery, 16 Sept. 1907, R.P. Box 107.

53 Allard to Rosebery, 23 Sept. 1907, R.P. Box 107.

54 D(urham) to Rosebery, 31 July 1907, R.P. Box 82. See Allard to Rosebery, 13 Nov. 1907, R.P. Box 107: 'There is some restiveness at the silence of the Liberal League . . . Lord Durham is not wholly content . . .'

55 B(urghclere) to Rosebery, 5 July 1907, R.P. Box 107.

56 Copy, Strachey to Rosebery, 29 July 1907, S.P. 12/7/3.

57 Strachey to Elliot, 23 July 1907, Elliot Papers, MS. 4246, Box 15, f. 96.

58 Elliot to Strachey, 13 Aug. 1907, S.P. 16/1/5.

59 Devonshire to Strachey, 29 Aug. 1907, S.P. 5/3/5. See Devonshire to Elliot, 3 Sept. 1907, Elliot Papers, MS. 4246, Box 14, F. 93: 'I cannot think that any considerable good will be effected by his British Constitutional Association which he would like me to join, though it may do some little good.'

60 Devonshire to Elliot, 3 Sept. 1907, Elliot Papers, MS. 4246, Box 14, F. 93. See Devonshire to Strachey, 10 Sept. 1907, S.P. 5/3/5.

61 Rosebery to Strachey, 5 Sept. 1907, S.P. 12/7/6.

62 Lord George Hamilton to Elliot, 11 Sept. 1907, Elliot Papers, MS. 4246, Box 15, F. 100.

63 Copy, Strachey to J. Moore-Bayley, 27 Nov. 1907, Elliot Papers, MS. 4246, Box 15, F. 96.

64 The origins of the 'Confederacy' are obscure, but for a discussion see A. Sykes, 'The Confederacy and the Purge of the Unionist Free Traders', 350–1.
65 Copy, Balfour to Austen Chamberlain, 23 Oct. 1907, B.P. 49736, ff. 18–20.
66 Austen Chamberlain to Balfour, 24 Oct. 1907, B.P. 49736, ff. 21–32.
67 Ridley to Balfour, 1 Nov. 1907, B.P. 49859, ff. 190–3.
68 Copy, Balfour to Ridley, 2 Nov. 1907, B.P. 49859, f. 194.
69 Sandars to Short, 28 Oct. 1907, B.P. 49765, ff. 24–7.
70 Salisbury to Lord Robert Cecil, 20 Sept. 1907, R.C.P. 51085, ff. 9–14.
71 Elliot to Strachey, 27 Nov. 1907, S.P. 16/1/20.
72 Strachey to Elliot, 28 Nov. 1907, Elliot Papers, MS. 4246, Box 15, F. 96.
73 Strachey to Elliot, 10 Dec. 1907, Elliot Papers, MS. 4246, Box 15, F. 96.
74 Strachey to Elliot, 21 Dec. 1907, Elliot Papers, MS. 4246, Box 15, F. 96.
75 Copy, Long to Magnus, 14 Dec. 1907, R.C.P. 51158, ff. 139–44.
76 Long to Lord Robert Cecil, 4 Jan. 1907 (*sic* ?1908), R.C.P. 51072, f. 51.
77 See copy, Bowles to Hood, 17 Dec. 1907, R.C.P. 51072, f. 104.
78 Bowles to Lord Robert Cecil, 13 Dec. 1907, R.C.P. 51072, f. 103.
79 Copy, Bowles to Hood, 17 Dec. 1907, R.C.P. 51072, f. 104.
80 Copy, Hood to Bowles, 23 Dec. (1907), R.C.P. 51072, f. 108.
81 Copy, Campbell to Bowles, 3 Jan. 1908, R.C.P. 51072, ff. 117–18.
82 Bowles to Cecil, 6 Jan. 1908, R.C.P. 51072, f. 120. See also, copies, Campbell to Bowles, 8 and 10 Jan. 1908, R.C.P. 51072, ff. 126, 131.
83 Copy, Lord Robert Cecil to Long, 17 Jan. 1908, R.C.P. 51072, ff. 53–5.
84 Copy, Lord Robert Cecil to Long, 31 Jan. 1908, R.C.P. 51072, ff. 60–1.
85 Lord Robert Cecil to Balfour, 13 Jan. 1908, B.P. 49737, ff. 84–5.
86 E. G. Brunker to Lord Robert Cecil, 9 Jan. 1908, R.C.P. 51072, ff. 152–4.
87 Lord Robert Cecil to Balfour, 13 Jan. 1908, B.P. 49737, ff. 84–5.
88 Draft, Lord Robert Cecil to Magnus, 18 Dec. 1907, marked 'Not Sent', R.C.P. 51158, ff. 142–53.
89 Salisbury to Lord Robert Cecil, 6 Jan. 1908, R.C.P. 51085, ff. 15–18.
90 Bowles to Lord Robert Cecil, 10 Jan. 1908, R.C.P. 51072, f. 127.
91 E. G. Brunker to Elliot, 16 Jan. 1908, Elliot Papers, MS. 4246, Box 15, F. 100.
92 Cromer to Elliot, 17 Jan. 1908, Elliot Papers, MS. 4246, Box 15, F. 100.
93 Cromer to Elliot, 10 Jan. 1908, Elliot Papers, MS. 4246, Box 15, F. 100.
94 E. G. Brunker to Elliot, 16 Jan. 1908, Elliot Papers, MS. 4246, Box 15, F. 100.
95 Copy, Strachey to Balfour of Burleigh, 14 Jan. 1908, S.P. 2/5/8.
96 Copy, Cromer to Lansdowne, 27 Jan. 1908, Cromer Papers, F.O. 633/18, ff. 304–12.
97 Copy, Elliot to Cromer, 28 Jan. 1908, Elliot Papers, MS. 4246, Box 15, F. 100.
98 Lansdowne to Cromer, 30 Jan. 1908, Cromer Papers, F.O. 633/18, ff. 22–8.
99 Cromer to Lord Robert Cecil, 31 Jan. 1908, R.C.P. 51072, f. 6.
100 Long to Lord Robert Cecil, 18 Jan. 1908, R.C.P. 51072, ff. 56–7.
101 Long to Balfour, 29 Dec. 1907, B.P. 49776, ff. 229–34.
102 Hood to Sandars, 11 Jan. (1908), B.P. 49771, ff. 170–1.
103 Strachey to Elliot, 21 Dec. 1907, Elliot Papers, MS. 4246, Box 15, F. 96.
104 E. L. Oliver to Strachey, 9 Jan. 1908, S.P. 16/2/3.
105 L. Darwin to Elliot, 10 Dec. 1907, Elliot Papers, MS. 4246, Box 15, F. 100.
106 Lord Robert Cecil to Elliot, 21 Jan. 1908, Elliot Papers, MS. 4246, Box 15, F. 100.
107 Lord Hugh Cecil to Elliot, 18 Jan. 1908, Elliot Papers, MS. 4246, Box 15, F. 100.
108 e.g. F. Pollock to Elliot, 28 Jan. and 1 Feb. 1908, W. Younger to Elliot, 29 Jan. 1908, Elliot Papers, MS. 4246, Box 15, F. 97.
109 Cromer to Elliot, 24 Jan. 1908, Elliot Papers, MS. 4246, Box 15, F. 100.

110 Copy, Strachey to Cromer, 28 Jan. 1908, R.C.P. 51072, ff. 1–5.
111 Copy, Strachey to Broadhurst, 3 Feb. 1908, S.P. 16/2/9.
112 Broadhurst to Strachey, 3 Feb. 1908, S.P. 16/2/9.
113 E. G. Brunker to Lord Robert Cecil, 1 Feb. 1908, R.C.P. 51072, ff. 158–9.
114 L. Darwin to Lord Robert Cecil, 7 Feb. 1908, R.C.P. 51158, ff. 166–7.
115 Copy, Broadhurst to Strachey, 4 Mar. 1908, S.P. 16/2/22. See also, R.C.P. 51158, ff. 184–5, and B.P. 49729, ff. 306–9.
116 Sandars (?) draft letter to Lansdowne, (1908), B.P. 49729, ff. 306–8; Lord Robert Cecil to Strachey, 7 Mar. 1908, S.P. 4/4/1; copy, Cromer to Lansdowne, 10 Mar. 1908, Cromer Papers, F.O. 633/18, ff. 317–19.
117 L. Darwin to Lord Robert Cecil, 20 Mar. 1908, R.C.P. 51158, ff. 199–200.
118 Memorandum, Lord Hugh Cecil to Lord Robert Cecil, 6 Mar. 1908, R.C.P. 51157, f. 7.
119 Strachey to Lord Robert Cecil, 10 Mar. 1908, R.C.P. 51158, f. 189.
120 L. Darwin to Lord Robert Cecil, 16 Mar. 1908, R.C.P. 51158, ff. 196–7.
121 See Broadhurst to Lord Robert Cecil, 14 Apr. 1908, R.C.P. 51158, ff. 224–5; Cromer to Elliot, 16 Apr. 1908, Elliot Papers, MS. 4246, Box 15, F. 102. Churchill apparently did not receive Unionist free trade support either. Because of his refusal to pledge himself against Home Rule, the Unionist free traders abstained. E. G. Brunker to Elliot, 29 Apr. and 1 May 1908, Elliot Papers, MS. 4246, Box 15, F. 102.
122 Lord Robert Cecil to Balfour, 16 Mar. 1908, B.P. 49737, ff. 90–1.
123 W. Short to Lord Robert Cecil, 20 Mar. 1908, R.C.P. 51071, f. 7.
124 Bowles to Lord Robert Cecil, 14 Apr. 1908, R.C.P. 51072, ff. 132–5.
125 Lord Robert Cecil to Balfour, 4 Mar. 1908, B.P. 49737, ff. 88–9.
126 J. Hicks to Lord Robert Cecil, 9 Apr. 1908, T. Broadhurst to Lord Robert Cecil, 10 Apr. 1908, J. Hicks to Lord Robert Cecil 10 and 13 Apr. 1908, The Bishop of Manchester to Lord Robert Cecil, 14 Apr. 1908, draft copy, Lord Robert Cecil to Hicks, 14 Apr. 1908. Broadhurst withdrew his support from Hicks after Hicks 'has failed me'. Broadhurst to Lord Robert Cecil, 14 Apr. 1908, R.C.P. 51158, ff. 211–29; Lord Robert Cecil to Balfour, 14 Apr. 1908, B.P. 49737, ff. 95–6.
127 Long to Lord Robert Cecil, 17 Apr. 1908, R.C.P. 51072, ff. 69–71.
128 Long to Lord Robert Cecil, 24 Apr. 1908, R.C.P. 51072, f. 82.
129 Copy, Balfour to Selborne, 6 Mar. 1908, B.P. 49708, ff. 106–30.
130 Copy, Strachey to Broadhurst, 5 Mar. 1908, S.P. 16/2/22.
131 Lord Hugh Cecil to Rosebery, 2 Dec. 1907, R.P. Box 82.
132 J. H. Tritton, Memorandum, 19 Feb. 1908, R.P. Box 107.
133 Perks, draft report, 21 Feb. 1908, R.C.P. Box 107.
134 Perks to Rosebery, 21 Feb. 1908, R.P. Box 42.
135 Rosebery to Strachey, 24 Feb. 1908, S.P. 12/7/7.
136 Perks to Rosebery, 21 Feb. 1908, R.P. Box 42.
137 F. W. Maude to Rosebery, 21 Feb. 1908, R.P. Box 107.
138 Strachey to Rosebery, 21 Feb. 1908, R.P. Box 107.
139 F. W. Maude to Rosebery, 25 Feb. 1908, R.P. Box 107.
140 Strachey to Lord Robert Cecil, 22 Feb. 1908, R.C.P. 51158, ff. 172–3.
141 Copy, Lord Robert Cecil to Long, 24 Feb. 1908, R.C.P. 51072, ff. 65–6.
142 Strachey to Lord Robert Cecil, 27 Feb. 1908, R.C.P. 51158, f. 174.
143 Copy, Strachey to Rosebery, 25 Feb. 1908, S.P. 12/7/7. See also, Rosebery to Strachey, 27 Feb. 1908, S.P. 12/7/7.
144 Lord Hugh Cecil to Strachey, 25 Feb. 1908; copy, Strachey to Lord Hugh Cecil, 27 Feb. 1908, S.P. 4/3/10.

145 F. W. Maude to Rosebery, 25 Feb. 1908, R.P. Box 107.
146 Copy, Strachey to Rosebery, 25 Feb. 1908, S.P. 12/7/7.
147 Copy, Strachey to Rosebery, 28 Feb. 1908, S.P. 12/7/7.
148 Copy, Lord Robert Cecil to Long, 18 Apr. 1908, R.C.P. 51072, ff. 72–7.
149 Copy, Lord Robert Cecil to Lord Hugh Cecil, 13 Feb. 1908, R.C.P. 51157, ff. 1–6.
150 Long to Balfour, 19 Jan. 1908, B.P. 49777, ff. 1–2.
151 Long to Balfour, 21 Jan. 1908, B.P. 49777, ff. 3–5.
152 Lord Robert Cecil to Elliot, 27 Jan. 1908, Elliot Papers, MS. 4246, Box 15, F. 97.
153 H. Shaw Stewart to Elliot, 18 Nov. 1907, Elliot Papers, MS. 4246, Box 15, F. 97.
154 Copy, Strachey to Lord Hugh Cecil, 19 Nov. 1907, S.P. 4/3/9.
155 Lord George Hamilton to Elliot, 20 Nov. 1907, Elliot Papers, MS. 4246, Box 15, F. 100.
156 Bowles to Lord Robert Cecil, 10 Jan. 1908, R.C.P. 51072, f. 127.
157 Strachey to Lord Robert Cecil, 5 Mar. 1908, R.C.P. 51158, ff. 182–3.
158 Cromer to Elliot, 10 May 1908, Elliot Papers, MS. 4246, Box 15, F. 102.
159 E. G. Brunker to Elliot, 29 Apr. 1908, Elliot Papers, MS. 4246, Box 15, F. 102.

CHAPTER 8. THE DEVIL AND THE DEEP BLUE SEA

1 Rosebery to Strachey, 21 May 1908, S.P. 12/7/11. See also Rosebery to Strachey, 14 Mar. 1908, S.P. 12/7/9.
2 Copy, Strachey to Rosebery, 16 Mar. 1908, S.P. 12/7/8. In May Strachey wrote: 'I, like you, admire Asquith and should have liked, if he had given me any chance, to have treated the Ministry as a new Ministry, and supported it. But all his old firmness seems to have deserted him. It is surrender after surrender. The Budget and Old Age Pensions I regard as a deadly blow to Free Trade and to the character and independence of the working classes, and now comes the monstrous hauling down of the flag to the suffragists because Winston's nerves could not stand the lady with the dinner bell! In addition to that there is Brunner's proposed nationalisation of the railways and all minerals, and large loans for public works without a word of protest from Asquith, and either acquiescence or paens of encouragement in the Liberal press. I am sure you will agree with me that to add a million railway servants and miners under the direct employment of the State, which is what nationalisation means, is utter madness . . .' Strachey to Rosebery, 22 May 1908, S.P. 12/7/11.
3 e.g. Asquith to Strachey, 9 May 1908, S.P. 11/6/6.
4 Churchill to Asquith, 29 Dec. 1908, in Randolph Churchill, *Winston S. Churchill*, ii. C.V. 862–4.
5 Copies, Strachey to Oliver, 9 and 11 June 1908, S.P. 16/2/27. Strachey added: 'I would not stand except as a whole-hearted Free Trader and Anti-Socialist, so I could not stand as a supporter of the present Government for I consider they are not only endangering the Union but also endangering Free Trade and weakening the character of the nation.'
6 Copy, Strachey, to E. G. Brunker, 28 July 1908, S.P. 16/2/34.
7 Cromer to Elliot, 13 July 1908, Elliot Papers, MS. 4246, Box 16, F. 110.
8 Elliot, 'A Note on the Unionist Free Trade Club', 1908, enclosed with Elliot to Cromer, 17 May 1908, Cromer Papers, F.O. 633/18, ff. 51–61.

9 Cromer's Memorandum and replies, Cromer Papers, F.O. 633/18, ff. 99–140.
10 Cromer to Lord Robert Cecil, 7 Jan. 1909, R.C.P. 51072, f. 31.
11 *National Review*, Jan. 1909. Strachey commented: 'It looks as if the wretched Unionist party were going to be re-split by the extreme Tariff Reformers, as if the original split . . . was not bad enough. Really, the world appears to be going mad.' Copy, Strachey to Balfour of Burleigh, 19, Jan. 1909. S.P. 2/5/9.
12 For these negotiations see Goulding to Law, Jan. (1909) B.L.P. 18/5/84–8; Goulding to Lord Robert Cecil, Jan. 1909, R.C.P. 51159, ff. 23–9; Goulding to Croft, n.d., Croft Papers, WA/2; Joseph Chamberlain to Croft, 15 and 26 Dec. 1908, Croft Papers, CH/23, CH/25; Croft to Joseph Chamberlain, 25 Jan. (1909), Croft Papers, CH/24.
13 Hood to Lord Robert Cecil, 17 Nov. (1908), R.C.P. 51158, ff. 260–1. See also, Sandars to Short, 5 Jan. 1909, B. P. 49765, ff. 205–6.
14 Lord Robert Cecil to Asquith, 21 Jan. 1909; copy, Asquith to Lord Robert Cecil, 27 Jan. 1909, Asquith Papers, Box 12, ff. 3–5, 9. Cecil threatened that if the Liberals stood against Unionist free traders and gave them no chance, they might retire altogether. Asquith returned a 'Balfourite' reply, that these matters were settled locally, although he was disposed to discourage Liberal opposition in constituencies which were normally Unionist. Abel Smith also sought Liberal help after the breakdown of negotiations with the local tariff reformers in East Herts. Smith to Lord Robert Cecil, 11 Mar. 1909, R.C.P. 51159, ff. 122–4, and 7 Apr. 1909, R.C.P. 51159, ff. 160–1; Salisbury, 'Note' on Smith and East Herts., n.d., R.C.P. 51085, f. 24; Salisbury to Lord Robert Cecil, 16 Apr. 1909, R.C.P. 51085, f. 28.
15 E. G. Brunker to Elliot, 22 Jan. 1909, Elliot Papers, MS. 4246, Box 15, F. 103. Lord Robert Cecil replied to a Mr. Terrell who had written to him as an 'outcast of the Liberal party' that the general feeling was 'that nothing very decisive could be done just now' about a centre party, but that if the Confederates carried out their threats, Unionist free traders would have to stand independently and, if elected, would form the nucleus of an independent group which might attract others and 'even develop a leader which is at present the great desideratum'. Terrell to Lord Robert Cecil, 20 Jan. 1909; copy, Lord Robert Cecil to Terrell, 22 Jan. 1909, R.C.P. 51159, ff. 7, 12–13. See also, Memorandum by Lord Robert Cecil, n.d., Elliot Papers, MS. 4246, Box 15, F. 103.
16 Cromer to Elliot, 25 Jan. 1909, Elliot Papers, MS. 4246, Box 16, F. 107.
17 Cromer to Lord Robert Cecil, 29 Jan. 1909, R.C.P. 51072, ff. 33–4. Cromer had declined to chair a free trade meeting for Asquith 'as I did not want to associate myself too much with the Liberals. This was before the recent action of the Confederates, but on the whole I do not regret my action.'
18 E. G. Brunker to Elliot, 29 Jan. 1909, Elliot Papers, MS. 4246, Box 15, F. 103.
19 E. G. Brunker to Elliot, 5 Feb. 1909, Elliot Papers, MS. 4246, Box 15, F. 103.
20 See e.g. Balfour of Burleigh to Lord Robert Cecil, 29 Jan. (1909), and 10 Feb. 1909, R.C.P. 51159, ff. 39–40, 76–9; C. E. Mallet to Lord Robert Cecil, 11 Feb. 1909, R.C.P. 51159, ff. 81–2.
21 Copy, Lambton to E. G. Brunker, 7 Feb. 1909, Elliot Papers, MS. 4246, Box 15, F. 103.
22 Salisbury to Lord Robert Cecil, 19 Feb. 1909, R.C.P. 51085, f. 23.
23 W. F. D. Smith to Lord Robert Cecil, 8 Feb. 1909, R.C.P. 51159, ff. 65–6.
24 E. G. Brunker to Lord Robert Cecil, 23 Feb. 1909, R.C.P. 51072, f. 176.
25 Claud Lambton to Lord Robert Cecil, 8 Feb. 1909, R.C.P. 51159, f. 67.
26 P. Thornton to Lord Robert Cecil, 9 Feb. 1909, R.C.P. 51159, ff. 74–5.
27 H. S. King to Lord Robert Cecil, 8 Feb. 1909, R.C.P. 51159, ff. 69–70.

28 Copy, T. Broadhurst to E. G. Brunker, 13 Feb. 1909, Elliot Papers, MS. 4246, Box 15, F. 103.

29 E. G. Brunker to Lord Robert Cecil, 23 Feb. 1909, R.C.P. 51072, f. 176.

30 R. A. Rempel, *Unionists Divided,* 191; *Morning Post,* Jan.–Feb. 1909.

31 R. Williams to Lord Robert Cecil, 4 Feb. 1909, R.C.P. 51159, ff. 51–2.

32 E. G. Brunker to Lord Robert Cecil, 23 Feb. 1909, R.C.P. 51072, f. 176. Two whole-hoggers, Ridley and Gwynne, sent their regrets to Lord Robert Cecil that these negotiations had failed and offered their help. H. A. Gwynne to Lord Robert Cecil, 15 Feb. 1909, Ridley to Lord Robert Cecil, 18 Feb. 1909, R.C.P. 51159, ff. 92, 94–7.

33 E. G. Brunker to Elliot, 10 June 1909, Elliot Papers, MS. 4246, Box 16, F. 105.

34 Copy, Balfour of Burleigh to E. G. Brunker, 25 June 1909, R.C.P. 51072, ff. 197–8.

35 Cromer to Lord Robert Cecil, 26 June 1909, R.C.P. 51072, ff. 43–4.

36 Copy, Cromer to Strachey, 14 May 1909, Cromer Papers, F.O. 633/18, ff. 339–43.

37 Beach to Lord Robert Cecil, 23 May 1909, R.C.P. 51159, ff. 182–4.

38 Cromer to Lord Robert Cecil, 28 May 1909, R.C.P. 51072, ff. 40–1.

39 R. A. Rempel, 194.

40 e.g. Hugh S. R. Elliot to the Secretary of the U.F.T.C., 1 July 1909, S. Le Blanc Smith to (Brunker), 20 June 1909, Elliot Papers, Box 16, F. 104.

41 Elliot to Cromer, 17 July 1909, Cromer Papers, F.O. 633/18, ff. 220–4.

42 Cromer to Elliot, 19 July 1909, Elliot Papers, MS. 4246, Box 16, F. 107.

43 Balfour of Burleigh to Cromer, 9 Jan. 1909, Cromer Papers, F.O. 633/18, f. 129.

44 Copy, Strachey to Bell, 7 July 1909, S.P. 16/3/13.

45 Lord Hugh Cecil to Cromer, 27 Oct. 1909, Cromer Papers, F.O. 633/18, ff. 278–81.

46 e.g. Beach to Balfour, 20 Sept. 1909, Lady Victoria Hicks Beach, *The Life of Sir Michael Hicks Beach,* ii. 259–61; Balfour of Burleigh to Cromer, 23 Aug. 1909, and copy, Balfour of Burleigh to Stanmore, 30 Aug. 1909, Cromer Papers, F.O. 633/18, ff. 241–3, 248–50.

47 Cromer to Elliot, 20 Aug. 1909, Elliot Papers, MS. 4246, Box 16, F. 107.

48 Cromer to Elliot, 27 Sept. 1909, Elliot Papers, MS. 4246, Box 16, F. 107.

49 Elliot to Cromer, 25 Aug. 1909, Cromer Papers, F.O. 633/18, ff. 243–50. See also, Elliot to Cromer, 26 Sept. 1909, ibid., ff. 246–7, and, copy, Elliot to Cromer, 29 Sept. 1909, Elliot Papers, MS. 4246, Box 16, F. 107.

50 E. G. Brunker to Lord Robert Cecil, 6 Sept. 1909, R.C.P. 51072, ff. 201–2.

51 T. Broadhurst to Lord Robert Cecil, 15 Oct. 1909, R.C.P. 51159, ff. 260–1.

52 Cromer to Lord Robert Cecil, 21 Oct. 1909, R.C.P. 51072, f. 49.

53 Copy, Elliot to Cromer, 26 Oct. 1909, Cromer to Elliot, 27 Oct. 1909, Lord Hugh Cecil to Elliot, 30 Oct. 1909, Elliot Papers, MS. 4246, Box 16, F. 107.

54 Cromer to Elliot, 20 Aug. 1909, Elliot Papers, MS. 4246, Box 16, F. 107.

55 Copy, Rosebery to Allard, 19 June 1909, R.P. Box 107. See also, Rosebery to Malcolm, 10 July 1909, R.P. Box 107.

56 Strachey to Cromer, 18 Aug. 1909, Cromer Papers, F.O. 633/18, ff. 232–5.

57 Monkbretton to Lord Robert Cecil, 11 June 1909, R.C.P. 51159, ff. 191–6.

58 E. G. Brunker to Elliot, 28 May 1909, Elliot Papers, MS. 4246, Box 16, F. 105.

59 Copy, Cromer to Lansdowne, 12 Aug. 1909, Cromer Papers, F.O. 633/18, ff. 365–6. See also, copy, Strachey to Tennant, 12 Aug. 1909, S.P. 16/3/18.

60 Copy, Strachey to Cox, 4 Nov. 1909, Perks to Strachey, 30 Nov. 1909, S.P. 16/3/20.

61 Copy, Rosebery to Allard, 19 June 1909, R.P. Box 107.

62 ? Paulton, Memorandum on the general meeting of the Executive Committee of the Liberal League, 28 June 1909 enclosed with Paulton to Rosebery, 29 June 1909; Agar-Robartes to Rosebery, 28 June 1909, R.P. Box 107.

63 Perks to Rosebery, 28 June 1909, R.P. Box 42.

64 Wemyss to Rosebery, 5 Sept. 1909, enclosing F. Millar to Wemyss, 1 Sept. 1909, R.P. Box 83.

65 Lansdowne to Rosebery, 6 Sept. 1909, R.P. Box 107.

66 Lord Hugh Cecil to Rosebery, 8 Oct. 1909, R.P. Box 83.

67 Copy, Rosebery to Northumberland, 3 Sept. 1909, R.P. Box 107.

68 F. W. Maude to Rosebery, 16 Nov. 1909, R.P. Box 107.

69 Copy, Strachey to Balfour, 30 Nov. 1909, S.P. 2/4/20. 'So far as I am personally concerned,' Cromer wrote, 'I shall without the smallest hesitation advise Unionist free traders to vote against the present Government at the next election.' Cromer to Elliot, 11 Dec. 1909, Elliot Papers, MS. 4246, Box 16, F. 107.

70 *Spectator,* Nov.–Dec. 1909.

71 Lord Hugh Cecil to Cromer, 13 Dec. 1909, and n.d. Cromer Papers, F.O. 633/18, ff. 297–8, 301–2.

72 Copy, Strachey to Margot Asquith, 25 Jan. 1910, S.P. 11/7/28. See also, copy, Strachey to Lord Hugh Cecil, 24 Jan. 1910, S.P. 3/4/8.

73 Cox to Cromer, 26 Jan. 1910, Cromer Papers, F.O. 633/19, f. 7.

74 Cox to Cromer, 31 Jan. 1910, Cromer Papers, F.O. 633/19, ff. 9–10.

75 H. Darwin to Cromer, 8 Feb. 1910, Cromer Papers, F.O. 633/19, ff. 13–14.

76 Cromer to Elliot, 11 Feb. 1910, Elliot Papers, MS. 4246, Box 16, F. 110.

77 F. Pollock to Elliot, 9 Feb. 1910, Elliot Papers, MS. 4246, Box 16, F. 110.

78 Copy, Cromer to Mallet, 22 Feb. 1910, Cromer Papers, F.O. 633/19, ff. 154–8.

79 Copy, Cromer to Strachey, 1 Feb. 1910, Cromer Papers, F.O. 633/19, ff. 149–52.

80 Copy, Cromer to T. Broadhurst, 4 Mar. 1910, Cromer Papers, F.O. 633/19, ff. 161–2.

81 Circular letter, 8 Mar. 1910, Elliot Papers, MS. 4246, Box 16, F. 110.

82 Circular letter, 16 Mar. 1910, Elliot Papers, MS. 4246, Box 16, F. 106. See H. Hobhouse to Elliot, 26 Mar. 1910, Elliot Papers, MS. 4246, Box 16, F. 110: 'The split was inevitable and it is just as well that the policy of the Liberal section should go forth to the public.'

83 Cox to Cromer, 21 Feb. 1910, Cromer Papers, F.O. 633/19, ff. 20–1. Strachey supported this. Copy, Strachey to Cox, 3 Mar. 1910, S.P. 4/14/2.

84 Copy, Cromer to Cox, 4 Mar. 1910, Cromer Papers, F.O. 633/19, ff. 160–1.

85 S. T. Whitfield Hayes to Cromer, 15 Mar. 1910, Cromer Papers, F.O. 633/19, ff. 33–4.

86 Onslow to Strachey, 9 Apr. 1910, S.P. 17/1/12.

87 Cox to Rosebery, 2 Feb. 1910, R.P. Box 107.

88 Perks to Rosebery, 17 Feb. 1910, R.P. Box 42.

89 Perks to Rosebery, 3 Mar. 1910, R.P. Box 42.

90 Perks to Rosebery, 5 Mar. 1910, R.P. Box 42.

91 F. Freeman-Thomas to Rosebery, 22 Apr. 1910, R.P. Box 107; H. Cox to Strachey, 21 Apr. 1910, S.P. 4/14/3.

92 Rosebery to Strachey, 25 Apr. 1910, S.P. 12/7/20.

93 Rosebery to Strachey, 29 Apr. 1910, S.P. 12/7/22. See, copy, Strachey to Rosebery, 26 Apr. 1910, S.P. 12/7/21.

94 Perks to Rosebery, 29 Apr. 1910, R.P. Box 42.

95 Cox to Strachey, 21 May 1910, S.P. 4/14/3.

96 Copy, Strachey to Perks, 23 May 1910, S.P. 17/1/17.

97 Copy, Cromer to Strachey, 23 May 1910, Cromer Papers, F.O. 633/19, ff. 170–1.
98 Perks to Strachey, 24 May 1910, S.P. 17/1/18.
99 F. W. Maude to Allard, 24 June 1909, R.P. Box 107. See Maude to Rosebery, 1 May 1910, R.P. Box 107: 'Personally,' Maude wrote of the dissolution of the League, 'I regard it as a national misfortune that with the extreme sections on either side growing daily more . . . unreasonable, it should be given out to the world that the forces of moderation . . . are going to lay down their arms. It means that for some years to come we shall be ruled either by Tariff Reformers, or Lloyd George Radicals. This, whilst up and down the country there are immense forces running to waste, Moderate Liberals, Unionist Free Traders, Individualist Free Churchmen, which, if properly organised and led, might have saved us from the evil results of corruption and fanaticism.'

CHAPTER 9. CONSTRUCTION

1 Garvin to Maxse, 8 Jan. 1908, M.P. 458. See also, Garvin to Maxse, 12 Jan. 1908: 'As to old age pensions, I may be entirely wrong, but I think the Unionist party is committing a fundamental mistake in not recognising that this question is the key of the whole political and financial problem now.'
2 Winterton to Joseph Chamberlain, 27 Mar. 1908, J.C.P. 22/47. Collings commented in May that Hood was 'well to the front on tariff reform'. Collings to Joseph Chamberlain, 25 May 1909, J.C.P. 22/40.
3 Sandars to Balfour, 7 May 1908, B.P. 49765, ff. 152–3.
4 28 Sept. 1908, B.L.P. 20/22.
5 Lawrence to Law, 23 Oct. 1908, B.L.P. 18/4/78.
6 See the account in *National Review*, Mar. 1908, 19–22.
7 Austen Chamberlain to Maxse, 2 Feb. 1908, M.P. 458.
8 Sir Austen Chamberlain, *Politics from Inside*, 98.
9 Collings to Joseph Chamberlain, 27 Oct. 1908, J.C.P. 22/43.
10 Sir Austen Chamberlain, 140–4.
11 Amery to Balfour, Oct. 1908, B.P. 49775, ff. 137–48.
12 Neal Blewett, *The Peers, the Parties and the People. The General Elections of 1910* (1972), 45–7.
13 A. Lee to Austen Chamberlain, 28 Oct. 1907, A.C.P. 17/3/64.
14 A. Lee to Austen Chamberlain, 31 Oct. 1907, A.C.P. 17/3/65.
15 Proof copy, B.L.P. 18/4/75. On the 'programme', Amery wrote to Maxse: 'It has been the result of a series of symposia and interchanges of letters extending over a little more than a year. Milner, Austen, B.L., have been the leading people in it on the political side and through Austen Joe has also been consulted. Among the minor people were Jebb, Ware, Hills and myself. In the end the actual editing of a draft was undertaken by Jebb, and in view of this and of Ware's help, it was eventually decided to let the document appear in the Morning Post rather than to launch it in the Times or send it to the press in general.

As for the document itself, it is not in the nature of an unauthorised programme but rather an attempt to discover and state the chief points on which what we may call the advanced wing of the Unionist party are in general agreement. It is just a basis for discussion and not an attempt to run a policy or to queer a pitch.' Amery to Maxse, 8 Oct. 1908, M.P. 458.

16 Ware to Law, 29 Sept. 1908, B.L.P. 18/4/75. For Austen Chamberlain's comments see A.C.P. 7/7A/2.
17 Copy, Law to Ware, 8 Sept. 1908, B.L.P. 18/8/10.
18 Ware to Law, 29 Sept. 1908, B.L.P. 18/4/75.
19 Copy, Law to Ware, 8 Sept. 1908, B.L.P. 18/8/10.
20 Ware to Law, 29 Sept. 1908, B.L.P. 18/4/75.
21 Law to Maxse, 4 June 1908, M.P. 458. Law wrote to Alfred Deakin: 'Balfour is now definitely fighting on the right side and I think he is going to carry his party almost solidly with him and his leadership on the right side has always seemed to me the only thing necessary to make success assured.' Copy, Law to Deakin, 17 Jan. 1908, B.L.P. 18/8/6.
22 Maxse to Law, 5 June 1908, B.L.P. 18/4/66.
23 Milner to Steel-Maitland, 6 Dec. 1908, Steel-Maitland Papers, G.D. 193/88/3.
24 Collings to Joseph Chamberlain, 22 Nov. 1908, J.C.P. 22/45.
25 Milner to Steel-Maitland, 12 Dec. 1908, Steel-Maitland Papers, G.D. 193/88/3.
26 e.g. copy, Balfour to Collings, 7 May 1908, B.P. 49859, ff. 251–2.
27 Collings to Joseph Chamberlain, 22 Nov. 1908, J.C.P. 22/45.
28 Sir Austen Chamberlain, 142–6.
29 See Sandars to Balfour, 16 Dec. 1908, B.P. 49765, ff. 194–5; Carrington to Ripon, 28 Sept. 1906, Ripon Papers, 43544, ff. 109–10.
30 Copy, Balfour to Collings, 7 May 1908, B.P. 49859, ff. 251–2.
31 Sandars to Balfour, 16 Dec. 1908, B.P. 49765, ff. 194–5.
32 Austen Chamberlain to Maxse, 5 Feb. 1909, M.P. 459.
33 Collings to Joseph Chamberlain, 26 Feb. 1909, J.C.P. 22/46.
34 Milner to Austen Chamberlain, 10 Feb. 1909, A.C.P. 17/3/74.
35 Onslow, 'Suggestions for an Agricultural Policy', A.C.P. 8/1/3, enclosed with Onslow to Austen Chamberlain, 25 Mar. 1909, A.C.P. 8/1/2.
36 Onslow to Austen Chamberlain, 6 and 8 May 1909, A.C.P. 8/1/8 and 9.
37 Onslow to Austen Chamberlain, 9 May (1909), A.C.P. 8/1/10.
38 Pretyman to Maxse, 18 June 1909, M.P. 445.
39 N. Blewett, *The General Elections of 1910*, 73–4, 82.
40 Joseph Chamberlain to Goulding, 27 July 1909, Wargrave Papers, A/3/2.
41 Ridley to Maxse, 15 Aug. 1909, M.P. 460.
42 Maxse to Law, 29 July 1909, B.L.P. 18/5/100.
43 N. Blewett, *The General Elections of 1910*, 75.
44 Garvin to Maxse, 2 Aug. 1909, M.P. 460.
45 Winterton to Maxse, 18 Aug. 1909, M.P. 460.
46 Onslow to Austen Chamberlain, 31 May (1909), A.C.P. 8/1/11.
47 A. Gollin, *The Observer and J. L. Garvin* (1960), 109; N. Blewett, 75; Garvin to Maxse, 20 Aug. 1909, M.P. 460.
48 Maxse to Law, 29 July 1909, B.L.P. 18/5/100. Law did not think that this was possible. Law to Maxse, 30 July 1909, M.P. 460.
49 Garvin to Maxse, 2 Aug. 1909, M.P. 460.
50 Garvin to Maxse, 21 Aug. 1909, M.P. 460.
51 A. Gollin, 112–16.
52 See especially Hewins to Balfour, 1 and 26 July 1909, B.P. 49779, ff. 208–16.
53 Hewins to Balfour, 19 Sept. 1909, B.P. 49779, ff. 221–31.
54 *The Times*, 23 Sept. 1909.
55 Sandars to Balfour, 8 Aug. 1909, B.P. 49765, ff. 228–9.
56 N. Blewett, *The General Elections of 1910*, 108, 112.
57 Ibid. 74–5, 99–100, 114–16.
58 Northumberland to Strachey, 19 Aug. 1909, S.P. 11/5/6.

59 N. Blewett, *The General Elections of 1910*, 121.
60 Winterton to Maxse, 18 Aug. 1909, M.P. 460.
61 Sir Austen Chamberlain, 141.
62 Garvin to Law, 27 Nov. 1909, B.L.P. 18/5/107; Garvin to Goulding, 5 Dec. 1909, Wargrave Papers, A/3/2.
63 See N. Blewett, *The General Elections of 1910*, 121–3, for this and the following paragraph.
64 Garvin to Sandars, 29 Nov. 1909, ibid. 107.
65 Garvin to Goulding, 5 Dec. 1909, Wargrave Papers, A/3/2.
66 Wyndham to his mother, 'Christmas 1909', Guy Wyndham (ed.), *The Letters of George Wyndham* (1915) ii. 369–70.
67 Sir Austen Chamberlain, 184; N. Blewett, *The General Elections of 1910*, 97.
68 N. Blewett, 381.
69 Ibid. 395–8.
70 Ibid. 383, 398, 400–1, 403–9.
71 Ibid. 402.
72 H. Seton-Kerr to Balfour, 5 Feb. 1910, B.P. 49860, ff. 213–17.
73 Copy, Steel-Maitland to Morris Miller, 18 Feb. 1910, Steel-Maitland Papers, G.D. 193/147.
74 N. Blewett, *The General Elections of 1910*, 406–9.

CHAPTER 10. THE LESSER EVIL

1 Austen Chamberlain to Balfour, 29 Jan. 1910, Sir Austen Chamberlain, *Politics from Inside*, 196–200.
2 G. Locker-Lampson to Steel-Maitland, 8 Mar. 1911, Steel-Maitland Papers, G.D. 193/151.
3 Sandars to Balfour, 29 and 31 Jan. 1910, B.P. 49766, ff. 123–4.
4 (?) Sandars, Memorandum, 1 Mar. 1910, B.P. 49766, ff. 147–51.
5 Copy, Balfour to Lansdowne, 29 Dec. 1909, B.P. 49730, ff. 39–40.
6 Sir Austen Chamberlain, 220.
7 Sandars to Balfour, 15 Mar. 1910, B.P. 49766, f. 178.
8 Lansdowne, Note of 23 Mar. 1910, B.P. 49730, f. 67. See also, Lansdowne to Balfour, 27 Mar. 1910, B.P. 49730, ff. 60–80. Curiously, in the light of subsequent events, Austen Chamberlain was opposed to the use of the referendum. See Lansdowne to Balfour, 14 Apr. 1910, B.P. 49730, f. 71.
9 For reports of Liberal difficulties reaching the Unionist leadership see B.P. 49766, ff. 200–32. For the Liberal difficulties themselves see N. Blewett, *The General Elections of 1910*, 145–53.
10 N. Blewett, *The General Elections of 1910*, 171–4.
11 Sir Austen Chamberlain, 228–31.
12 Ibid. 231.
13 Ibid. 230.
14 Collings to Mrs. Chamberlain, 20 Mar. 1910, J.C.P. 22/48. See also, Collings to Blumenfeld, 11 and 16 Apr. 1910, and Blumenfeld to Collings, 12 Apr. 1910, Blumenfeld Papers.
15 Onslow to Austen Chamberlain, 30 Jan. 1910, A.C.P. 8/1/12.
16 A. V. Dicey to Maxse, 25 Sept. 1909, M.P. 460.
17 Salisbury to Austen Chamberlain, 2 Feb. 1910, A.C.P. 8/5/6.
18 Memorandum by Lord Robert Cecil and Lord Hugh Cecil, enclosed with Lord Hugh Cecil to Joseph Chamberlain, 7 Mar. 1910, J.C.P. 22/20.

19 Copy, Law to Salisbury, 4 Feb. 1910, B.L.P. 20/34.
20 Ibid.
21 Mary Maxse to Law, 3 Apr. 1910, B.L.P. 18/6/119.
22 Memorandum by H. A. G(wynne), Jan. 1910, B.P. 49797, ff. 91–5.
23 Sir Austen Chamberlain, 227. See also, Sandars to Balfour, 11 Mar. 1910, B.P. 49766, ff. 176–7: 'I, of course, put the point about the revenue which would be sacrificed and his answer was that he did not think we should lose anything because we should have to give it back . . .'
24 Sandars to Balfour, 15 Mar. 1910, B.P. 49766, f. 183.
25 Sandars to Balfour, 18 Mar. 1910, B.P. 49766, ff. 186–95.
26 G. L. Courthope to Austen Chamberlain, 6 Feb. 1910, A.C.P. 8/5/9.
27 Memorandum by H. C(haplin), Jan. 1910, B.P. 49797, ff. 96–103.
28 N. Blewett, *The General Elections of 1910*, 160.
29 Sandars to Maxse, 24 May 1910, M.P. 461.
30 Willoughby de Broke to Maxse, 19 June 1910, M.P. 461. See also, Lord Hugh Cecil to Maxse, 10 June 1910, M.P. 461: 'I see no objection to a Conference: as long as we enter it without our hands being tied. The more the matter is discussed the weaker the Government's position will appear and the larger opportunity there will be of dividing the Reformers from the Vetoists.'
31 Willoughby de Broke to Maxse, 4 June 1910, M.P. 461.
32 Collings to Maxse, 11 Aug. 1910, Willoughby de Broke to Maxse, 17 and 20 Aug. 1910, M.P. 462.
33 *Morning Post*, 10 Sept. 1910.
34 Collings to Maxse, 11 Aug. 1910, M.P. 462. See also, Collings to Maxse, 2 Sept. 1910, M.P. 462.
35 Copy, Austen Chamberlain to Balfour, 23 Sept. 1910, A.C.P. 8/6/16.
36 Sandars to Balfour, 13 Sept. 1910, B.P. 49766, ff. 242–6.
37 See Lansdowne to Balfour, 24 Sept. 1910, B.P. 49730, f. 121; Sandars to Balfour, 14 Sept. 1910, B.P. 49766, ff. 247–9.
38 Long to Balfour, 3 Oct. 1910, B.P. 49777, ff. 68–9.
39 Copy, Balfour to Derby, 6 Oct. 1910, B.P. 49743, f. 18.
40 Goulding to Law, 4 Aug. (1910), B.L.P. 21/3/10.
41 Garvin to Maxse, 10 Oct. 1910, M.P. 462.
42 Copy, Law to Balfour, 19 Oct. 1910, B.L.P. 22/4/1.
43 Sandars to Balfour, 2 Oct. 1910, B.P. 49767, ff. 1–4. See also, Sandars to Short, 3 Oct. 1910, ibid., ff. 5–6.
44 Copy, Balfour to Austen Chamberlain, 21 Sept. 1910, B.P. 49736, ff. 85–7.
45 Lansdowne to Balfour, 24 Sept. 1910, B.P. 49730, f. 122, enclosing Ampthill to Lansdowne, 20 Sept. 1910.
46 Long to Balfour, 3 Oct. 1910, B.P. 49777, ff. 68–9; Wyndham to his father, 17 Sept. 1910, Guy Wyndham (ed.), *Letters of George Wyndham*, ii. 406.
47 Austen Chamberlain to Balfour, 23 Sept. 1910, B.P. 49736, ff. 91–6. See also, Austen Chamberlain to Law, 29 Sept. 1910, B.L.P. 18/6/125.
48 Maxse to Law, 29 Sept. 1910, B.L.P. 18/6/24. See also, Maxse to Goulding, 29 Sept. 1910, Wargrave Papers, A/3/2.
49 Willoughby de Broke to Croft, 29 Sept. 1910, Croft Papers, WI/3; Willoughby de Broke to Maxse, 30 Sept. 1910, M.P. 462.
50 Austen Chamberlain to Law, 29 Sept. 1910, B.L.P. 18/6/125.
51 Ibid.
52 Memorandum by H. A. G(wynne), 29 Sept. 1910, B.L.P. 20/19.
53 Copy, Law to Austen Chamberlain, 1 Oct. 1910, B.L.P. 18/8/12. See also, Law to Maxse, 4 Oct. 1910, M.P. 462: 'I think it would be a fatal thing if a salary were

paid to M.P.s large enough to make political life a career for the clever adven-
turers of the middle classes which would mean that we should have a House
composed almost entirely of lawyers . . . On this question I have a pretty open
mind, but I would not be satisfied simply to support the Osborne Judgement
without being prepared with some alternative plan to make working class representation feasible; and personally, I should much prefer payment of members
even to a voluntary levy by the Trades Unions, if carried on by the Trade Union
organisation. That would still mean Trade Unionism would be a political force
and to whatever extent the present tendency in that direction succeeds, it simply
means political parties in the country are being driven into class divisions with
the working classes on one side and all others on the other.'

54 Copy, Law to Austen Chamberlain, 1 Oct. 1910, B.L.P. 18/8/12.
55 P. F. Clarke, *Lancashire and the New Liberalism* (1971), 332–4; Viscount Chilston,
   Chief Whip . . . Akers-Douglas, 174–8.
56 N. Blewett, *The General Elections of 1910*, 272.
57 For the T.U.T.R.A. see Kenneth D. Brown, 'The Trade Union Tariff Reform
   Association', *Journal of British Studies*, xx, 2 (1970), 141–53.
58 Hewins to Balfour, 14 Dec. 1908, ibid. 148.
59 L. S. Amery to Steel-Maitland, 5 Mar. 1909, Steel-Maitland Papers, G.D.
   193/141.
60 Hills was Unionist M.P. for Durham, not as Brown says, 'possibly a local
   leader'. K. Brown, 149–50.
61 L. S. Amery to Maxse, 12 Nov. 1909, M.P. 460. Maxse duly obliged. P. F.
   Clarke, 334.
62 Wolmer to Steel-Maitland, 29 Jan. 1910, Steel-Maitland Papers, G.D. 193/147.
63 Wolmer to Steel-Maitland, 6 July 1910, Steel-Maitland Papers, G.D. 193/149.
64 Wolmer to Steel-Maitland, 3 Aug. 1910, Steel-Maitland Papers, G.D. 193/149.
65 Salisbury to Balfour, 1 Oct. 1910, B.P. 49758, ff. 245–6.
66 Willoughby de Broke to Maxse, 30 Sept. 1910, M.P. 462; copy, Law to Austen
   Chamberlain, 1 Oct. 1910, B.L.P. 18/8/12.
67 Garvin to Maxse, 6 Oct. 1910, M.P. 462.
68 Austen Chamberlain to Law, 29 Sept. 1910, B.L.P. 18/6/125.
69 N. Blewett, *The General Elections of 1910*, 163.
70 Ibid. 272.
71 Pretyman to Austen Chamberlain, 26 Sept. 1910, A.C.P. 8/6/19.
72 Copy, Austen Chamberlain to Pretyman, 30 Sept. 1910, A.C.P. 8/6/26.
73 Copy, Austen Chamberlain to Balfour, 30 Sept. 1910, A.C.P. 8/6/27.
74 Balfour to Croft, 6 June 1910, Croft Papers, BA/19.
75 Pretyman to Austen Chamberlain, 5 Oct. 1910, A.C.P. 8/6/30.
76 Pretyman to Austen Chamberlain, 28 Oct. 1910, A.C.P. 8/6/35.
77 Ibid.
78 Balfour to Austen Chamberlain, 7 Oct. 1910, A.C.P. 8/6/32.
79 Sandars to Short, 24 Oct. 1910, B.P. 49767, ff. 13–17; Sandars, 'Note sent to me
   by Sir A. Acland-Hood', 2 Nov. 1910, B.P. 49767, ff. 21–2.
80 Sandars to Short, 24 Oct. 1910, B.P. 49767, ff. 13–17.
81 Sandars, 'Note sent to me by Sir A. Acland-Hood', 2 Nov. 1910, B.P. 49767,
   ff. 21–2.
82 *Morning Post*, 23 Sept. 1910.
83 Ibid. 6 Oct. 1910.
84 Ibid. 5 Oct. 1910.
85 Ibid. 8 Oct. 1910.
86 e.g. Maxse to Croft, 19 and 22 Oct. 1910, Croft Papers, MA/20 and MA/25.

87 *Morning Post,* 8 Oct. 1910.
88 Ibid. 19 Oct. 1910.
89 Garvin to Maxse, 6 Nov. 1910, M.P. 462. Strachey on the other hand was delighted with the Reveille manifesto because of its line on Ireland: 'so enchanted with it that I read most of it aloud to Amy . . . it cheered me up more than anything I had read for a long time because I was really getting very much alarmed about the dry rot which seems to have been setting in as regards Federalism. I shall certainly back up the Reveille people in the " Spectator" '. Strachey to Maxse, 7 Nov. 1910, M.P. 462.
90 F. S. Oliver to Maxse, 9 Nov. 1910, M.P. 462.
91 Lloyd George's memorandum of 17 Aug. 1910 is printed in Sir Charles Petrie, *The Life and Letters of the Right Hon. Sir Austen Chamberlain* (1939), i. 381–8.
92 G. R. Searle, *The Quest for National Efficiency,* 185. The narrative of events here is based on Searle's account, although the conclusions differ.
93 Austen Chamberlain to F. E. Smith, 21 Oct. 1910, Sir Austen Chamberlain, 283–4.
94 Austen Chamberlain to Cawdor, 21 Oct. 1910, ibid. 286–7.
95 Balfour to Austen Chamberlain, 22 Oct. 1910, ibid. 287–9.
96 Ibid.
97 F. E. Smith to Law, 19 Oct. 1910, B.L.P. 18/6/126.
98 A. Gollin, *The Observer and J. L. Garvin,* 205.
99 H. A. Gwynne to Sandars, 20 Sept. 1910, B.P. 49767, f. 111.
100 G. R. Searle, 182.
101 Crewe to Asquith, 22 Oct. 1910, Asquith Papers, Box 12, ff. 197–8.
102 Grey to Asquith, 26 Oct. 1910, Roy Jenkins, *Asquith,* 217.
103 G. R. Searle, 189.
104 Ibid. 191.
105 Ibid. 188.
106 Ibid. 191.
107 Garvin, A. Gollin, 209, which gives details of Garvin's role in the coalition negotiations, and of the proposals for federal Home Rule for Ireland mooted within the Unionist party at this time.
108 F. E. Smith to Law, 19 Oct. 1910, B.L.P. 18/6/126.
109 See A. Gollin, 215–19.
110 *Morning Post,* 18 Nov. 1910; *National Review,* Dec. 1910.
111 Sandars to Balfour, 18 Oct. 1910, B.P. 49767, ff. 9–10.
112 Copy, Balfour to Mr. Turner, 11 Oct. 1910, B.P. 49861, ff. 52–4.
113 Copy, Law to Balfour, 19 Oct. 1910, B.L.P. 22/4/1. Derby was reassuring. Derby to Law, 21 Oct. 1910, B.L.P. 18/6/128.
114 Sandars to Garvin, 11 Nov. 1910, A. Gollin, 240. Cf. Sir Austen Chamberlain, 298.
115 Sir Austen Chamberlain, 298–9.
116 Ibid. 300. See also, Austen Chamberlain to Balfour, 15 Nov. 1910, B.P. 49736 ff. 111–12.
117 Sandars to Garvin, 21 Nov. 1910, A. Gollin, 255–6.
118 Sandars to Garvin, 26 Nov. 1910, ibid. 257.
119 Ibid. 260.
120 Copy, Law to Balfour, 26 Nov. 1910, B.L.P. 18/8/14.
121 Balfour to Austen Chamberlain, 28 Nov. 1910, Sir Austen Chamberlain, 303–4.
122 Austen Chamberlain to Balfour, 28 Nov. 1910, B.P. 49736, ff. 113–15.
123 Sandars to Law, telegram, 28 Nov. 1910, B.L.P. 18/6/137.
124 Law to Sandars, telegram, 29 Nov. 1910, B.P. 49693, ff. 6–8.

125 Balfour to Austen Chamberlain, 30 Nov. 1910, Sir Austen Chamberlain, 306.
126 See N. Blewett, *The General Elections of 1910*, 187. Blewett quotes the objections of 'a still indignant Walter Long'. Long was in favour of a limited use of the referendum. See Long to Balfour, 29 Nov. 1910, B.P. 49777, ff. 75–6.
127 Garvin to Sandars, A. Gollin, 260.

CHAPTER II. BALFOUR'S RESIGNATION

1 Austen Chamberlain to Balfour, 1 Dec. 1910, B.P. 49736, ff. 128–9.
2 Sir Austen Chamberlain, *Politics from Inside*, 302; Austen Chamberlain to Balfour, 2 Dec. 1910, B.P. 49736, ff. 129–31.
3 Rowland Hunt to Austen Chamberlain, n.d., A.C.P. 8/7/16.
4 R. Jebb to Austen Chamberlain, 6 and 8 Dec. 1910, A.C.P. 8/7/17 and 18.
5 Lawrence to Austen Chamberlain, 9 and 13 Dec. 1910, A.C.P. 8/7/21 and 22.
6 Maxse to Goulding, 10 Dec. 1910, Wargrave Papers, WA/3/2.
7 Maxse to Law, 14 Dec. 1910, B.L.P. 18/6/145.
8 Sir Austen Chamberlain, 307–12.
9 Balfour to Austen Chamberlain, 13 Dec. 1910, ibid. 306–7.
10 Lansdowne to Sandars, 17 Dec. 1910, B.P. 49730, ff. 149–50.
11 Sandars to Short, 15 Dec. 1910, B.P. 49767, ff. 38–41; Derby to Sandars, 15 Dec. 1910, B.P. 49743, f. 19. Derby also complained to Law. Derby to Law, 17 Dec. 1910, B.L.P. 18/6/147.
12 Maurice Woods to Steel-Maitland, 18 Dec. 1910, Steel-Maitland Papers, G.D. 193/149
13 Sandars to Garvin, 19 Dec. 1910, A. Gollin, *The Observer and J. L. Garvin*, 275.
14 Blumenfeld to Sandars, 17 Dec. 1910, B.P. 49861, ff. 99–102.
15 Garvin to Sandars, 15 Dec. 1910, Garvin to Northcliffe, 15 Dec. 1910, A. Gollin, 274–5.
16 Garvin to Goulding, 16 Dec. 1910, Wargrave Papers, WA/3/2.
17 A. Gollin, 287.
18 *Observer*, 8 Jan. 1911, ibid. 288.
19 Garvin to Northcliffe, 1 Feb. 1911, ibid. 288.
20 F. E. Smith to Law, 3 Jan. (1911), B.L.P. 18/7/151.
21 Sandars to Balfour, 1 Jan. 1911, B.P. 49767, ff. 76–7.
22 Sandars to Balfour, 5 Jan. 1911, B.P. 49767, ff. 78–9.
23 Copy, Steel-Maitland to Sandars, 20 Jan. 1911, Steel-Maitland Papers, G.D. 193/152.
24 Sandars to Steel-Maitland, 22 Jan. 1911, Steel-Maitland Papers, G.D. 193/152.
25 Charles Bathurst to Steel-Maitland, 19 Jan. 1911, Steel-Maitland Papers, G.D. 193/149.
26 G. Locker-Lampson to Steel-Maitland, 25 Jan. 1911, Steel-Maitland Papers, G.D. 193/151.
27 Milner to Steel-Maitland, 23 Jan. 1911, Steel-Maitland Papers, G.D. 193/151.
28 Lansdowne to Sandars, 19 Mar. 1911, B.P. 49730, ff. 203–4.
29 Lansdowne to Balfour, 19 Mar. 1911, B.P. 49730, f. 196.
30 Sandars, Note of March 1911, B.P. 49767, f. 115.
31 Willoughby de Broke to Maxse, 29 Jan. 1911, M.P. 463.
32 Copy, Steel-Maitland to Northcliffe, 7 Feb. 1911, Steel-Maitland Papers, G.D. 193/151. See also, Steel-Maitland to Northcliffe, 18 Feb. 1911: 'I think the

Archangel Gabriel would be a failure as Chief Agent unless he had a policy for which to organise.'

33 Willoughby de Broke to Steel-Maitland, 8 June 1911, Steel-Maitland Papers, G. D. 193/152/3.
34 Sandars to Balfour, 30 June 1911, B.P. 49767, ff. 132–3.
35 Maxse to Steel-Maitland, 15 June 1911, Steel-Maitland Papers, G.D. 193/151.
36 W. Ormsby-Gore to Maxse, 19 June (1911), M.P. 463.
37 Willoughby de Broke to Maxse, 19 June 1911, M.P. 463.
38 F. E. Smith to Balfour, 14 July 1911, B.P. 49861, ff. 271–2.
39 Willoughby de Broke to Maxse, 19 July 1911, M.P. 463.
40 Sandars to Balfour, 11 Aug. 1911, B.P. 49767, f. 152.
41 Balcarres to Balfour, 11 Aug. 1911, B.P. 49861, ff. 309–10.
42 Sandars to Balfour, 14 Aug. 1911, B.P. 49767, ff. 155–61.
43 Maxse to Sandars, 24 July 1911, B.P. 49861, f. 278. Austen Chamberlain was equally despairing. See Sir Austen Chamberlain, 352.
44 Collings to Joseph Chamberlain, 3 Aug. 1911, J.C.P. 22/52.
45 Sir Austen Chamberlain, 349.
46 B. E. C. Dugdale, *Balfour*, ii. 70.
47 Wyndham to Milner, 15 Aug. 1911, Milner Papers, Box 194.
48 Sir Austen Chamberlain, 358.
49 Ibid. 371.
50 Ibid. 372.
51 Steel-Maitland to Balfour, 17 Oct. 1911, B.P. 49861, ff. 351–6.
52 Peter Fraser, 'The Unionist Debacle of 1911 and Balfour's Retirement', *Journal of Modern History*, 35, 4 (1963), 362.
53 Sir Austen Chamberlain, 361.
54 B. E. C. Dugdale, ii. 83.
55 Maxse to Steel-Maitland, 29 June 1911, Steel-Maitland Papers, G.D. 193/154/4.
56 Sandars to Balfour, 10 Sept. 1911, B.P. 49767, ff. 168–9; and n.d. (c. 17 Sept. 1911), B.P. 49767, ff. 177–88.
57 Malmesbury to Austen Chamberlain, 11 Oct. 1911, A.C.P. 9/3/40.
58 R. E. Prothero to Maxse, 23 Oct. 1911, M.P. 464.
59 Copy, Balfour to Sandars, 22 Feb. 1904, B.P. 49762, ff. 84–5.
60 *National Review*, Sept. 1911, 16.
61 Ibid. Nov. 1911, 354–64.
62 Midleton to Balcarres, 1 Sept. 1911, Balcarres Papers.
63 Midleton to Balcarres, 6 Sept. 1911, Balcarres Papers.
64 Steel-Maitland Memorandum, 20 Sept. 1911, B.P. 49861, ff. 329–33.
65 Ibid.
66 Alice Balfour to Steel-Maitland, 18 Sept. 1911, Steel-Maitland Papers, G.D. 193/153/3.
67 Steel-Maitland Memorandum, 20 Sept. 1911, B.P. 49861, ff. 329–33.
68 Copy, Steel-Maitland to Balcarres, 12 Sept. 1911, Steel-Maitland Papers, G.D. 193/152/2.
69 Balcarres to Steel-Maitland, 3 Oct. 1911, Steel-Maitland Papers, G.D. 193/153/2.
70 (?) C. A. Vince to J. T. Middlemore, 26 Oct. 1911, M.P. 464.
71 Maxse to Croft, 18 Oct. 1911, Croft Papers, MA/28/1–2.
72 Maxse, circular letter, 2 Nov. 1911, M.P. 464.
73 P. A. Clive to Maxse, 7 Nov. 1911, M.P. 464.
74 Mark Sykes to Maxse, 4 Oct. 1911, M.P. 464.
75 W. Astor to Maxse, 27 Oct. 1911, M.P. 464.
76 Mark Sykes to Maxse, 4 Oct. 1911, M.P. 464.

77 Leconfield to Maxse, 22 Oct. 1911, M.P. 464.
78 Collings to Maxse, 2 Nov. 1911, M.P. 464.
79 J. T. Middlemore to Maxse, 24 Oct. 1911, M.P. 464.
80 (?) C. A. Vince to J. T. Middlemore, 26 Oct. 1911, M.P. 464.
81 R. E. Prothero to Maxse, 30 Oct. 1911, M.P. 464.
82 Charles Craig to Maxse, 24 Oct. 1911, M.P. 464.
83 (?) C. A. Vince to J. T. Middlemore, 26 Oct. 1911, M.P. 464.
84 H. A. Gwynne to Maxse, 23 Oct. 1911, M.P. 464.
85 Long to G. E. Buckle, 25 Oct. 1911, Sir Charles Petrie, *Walter Long and His Times* (1936), 170.
86 Sir Austen Chamberlain, 371.
87 Sandars, 'A Note on the Events leading to Mr. Balfour's Resignation', B.P. 49767, ff. 291–310.
88 *The Times*, 9 Nov. 1911.
89 Maxse to Law, 17 Nov. 1911, B.L.P. 24/3/47.
90 Copy, Law to (George) Balfour, 18 Dec. 1911, B.L.P. 33/3/34.
91 Sir Austen Chamberlain, 408.
92 T. Comyn Platt to Steel-Maitland, 21 Dec. 1911, Steel-Maitland Papers, G.D. 193/154/5.
93 Croft to Law, 30 Nov. (1911), B.L.P. 24/4/92.
94 Sir Austen Chamberlain, 392. See also, Austen Chamberlain to Law, 11 Nov. 1911, B.L.P. 24/3/11.
95 Derby to Law, 13 Nov. 1911, B.L.P. 24/3/30.
96 Sir Austen Chamberlain, 408.
97 Copy, Law to Derby, 14 Nov. 1911, B.L.P. 33/3/4.
98 Sir Austen Chamberlain, 415–16.
99 Lansdowne to Law, 19 Feb. 1912, B.L.P. 25/2/74. Cf. Sir Austen Chamberlain, 421.
100 Copy, Law to Lady Primrose, 26 Feb. 1912, B.L.P. 33/4/17.
101 Sir Austen Chamberlain, 432–6.
102 Copy, Law to Lady Primrose, 26 Feb. 1912, B.L.P. 33/4/17.
103 Lord Hugh Cecil to Austen Chamberlain, 3 Oct. 1911, A.C.P. 9/3/10.
104 Sir Austen Chamberlain, 360.
105 Amery to Law, 22 May 1912, B.L.P. 26/3/35.
106 Willoughby de Broke to Law, 5 May 1912, B.L.P. 26/3/11.

CHAPTER 12. REACTION

1 Lord Hugh Cecil to Maxse, 12 Nov. 1910, M.P. 462.
2 Sir Austen Chamberlain, *Politics from Inside*, 370.
3 Ibid. 362.
4 Maurice Woods to Maxse, 9 Mar. (1912), M.P. 466.
5 Tullibardine to Law, 19 Mar. 1912, B.L.P. 25/1/47. See also, R. and T. Moore to Law, 9 Mar. 1912, B.L.P. 25/3/20.
6 Charles Bathurst to Law, 16 Mar. 1912, B.L.P. 25/3/40.
7 Collings to Joseph Chamberlain, 17 Mar. 1912, J.C.P. 22/39. Collings was more thoughtful than most, proposing 'Compulsory Arbitration and the setting up of an independent judicial tribunal for the settlement of all trade disputes—a Tribunal invested with powers to enforce its decisions on employers and employees alike, and for this purpose to have powers over Trade Union funds.

There is no other way out. Without these safeguards the granting of a minimum wage would surely lead railwaymen and other working-men to follow in the footsteps of the miners to whom the Government have completely surrendered.'

8 Copy, E. Micklem to H. Praed, 6 Jan. 1912, B.L.P. 25/1/31.

9 John Baird kept Law posted on the government's negotiations with the miners from the owners' point of view. See Baird to Law, 12 and 15 Mar. 1912, B.L.P. 25/3/22 and 34.

10 G. R. Askwith to Law, 15 and 17 Mar. 1912, B.L.P. 25/3/37 and 41; H. H. Asquith to Law, 15 Mar. 1912, B.L.P. 25/3/38.

11 G. R. Askwith to Law, 15 Mar. 1912, B.L.P. 33/3/37.

12 Copy, Law to Carson, 20 Mar. 1912, B.L.P. 33/4/24.

13 Copy, Law to F. C. Gardiner, 8 Mar. 1912, B.L.P. 33/4/21.

14 Selborne to Law, 8 June 1912, B.L.P. 26/4/13.

15 Copy, Law to Carson, 20 Mar. 1912, B.L.P. 33/4/24.

16 Collings to Joseph Chamberlain, 14 Apr. 1911, J.C.P. 22/50. Collings 'declined to join on the grounds that though I think payment of members a questionable step, I cannot see any other alternative to the reversal of the Osborne Judgement and to oppose both is simply a policy of negations . . .'

17 Balfour to Law, 29 Sept. 1911, B.L.P. 19/9/193.

18 Maurice Woods to Steel-Maitland, 27 Oct. 1911; copy, Steel-Maitland to Maurice Woods, 30 Oct. 1911, Steel-Maitland Papers, G.D. 193/155/4.

19 Copy, Law to Mr. Cockerell, 26 July 1913, B.L.P. 35/5/47.

20 Steel-Maitland to Law, 12 Nov. 1913, B.L.P. 30/4/27.

21 Copy, Law to Collings, 6 Aug. 1913, B.L.P. 33/5/51. This was in reply to a letter from Collings arguing that repeal should not become party policy. Collings to Law, 5 Aug. 1913, B.L.P. 30/1/7.

22 Copy, Law to W. Latey, (?) 24 Apr. 1914, B.L.P. 34/2/66. Also S. Rosenbaum to Law, 11 Nov. 1913: 'You indicated that it was your intention to say that payment of members would be repealed.' B.L.P. 30/4/23, and, copy, Law to F. E. Smith, 2 July 1914, B.L.P. 34/2/82.

23 Willoughby de Broke to Maxse, 20 Mar. and 16 June 1912, M.P. 466.

24 For Lloyd George's Land Campaign see H. V. Emy, 'The Land Campaign: Lloyd George as a Social Reformer', in A. J. P. Taylor (ed.), *Lloyd George. Twelve Essays* (1971), 35–68.

25 Collings to Law, 17 May 1912, B.L.P. 26/3/28.

26 e.g. J. L. Green to Malmesbury, 29 June 1912, B.L.P. 26/5/1. Malmesbury wrote to Law in support of the League and its policies, as did Selborne. Malmesbury to Law, 1 July 1912, B.L.P. 26/5/1; Selborne to Law, 2 July 1912, B.L.P. 26/5/4.

27 Malmesbury to Law, 5 July 1912, B.L.P. 26/5/9.

28 *Rural World*, XXIV, No. 784, Aug. 1912. See also, Willoughby de Broke to Maxse, 11 June 1912, M.P. 466: 'land purchase can never be a success without a tariff'. He was sceptical of the success of small ownerships, but 'I shall not cold water this idea as I believe it is our best chance of getting people to vote for the much needed Tariff on Agricultural Produce.'

29 Copy, Steel-Maitland to A. Glazebrook, 28 Aug. 1913, Steel-Maitland Papers, G.D. 193/157/6. This action temporarily alienated Collings who feared the question would be shelved. Milner reassured him. Collings to Milner, 9 and 10 July 1912; copy, Milner to Collings, 12 July 1912, Milner Papers, Box 104.

30 Balcarres to Steel-Maitland, 20 Aug. 1912, Steel-Maitland Papers, G.D. 193/156/2. See also, Balcarres to Law, 14 Aug. 1912, B.L.P. 27/1/38.

31 Milner's Diary, 28 Dec. 1912, Milner Papers, Box 275.

32 Steel-Maitland to Law, 27 Jan. 1913, B.L.P. 28/2/86.
33 James F. Hope to Law, 27 Feb. 1912, B.L.P. 25/2/60.
34 e.g. Salisbury to Law, 1 May 1912, B.L.P. 26/2/2.
35 Lord Hugh and Lord Robert Cecil to Joseph Chamberlain, 6 Mar. 1912, J.C.P. 22/23.
36 Lord Robert Cecil to Law, 9 Mar. 1912, B.L.P. 25/3/19.
37 Derby to Law, 14 Mar. 1912, Randolph S. Churchill, *Lord Derby, 'King of Lancashire'* (1959), 162.
38 Copy, Joseph Chamberlain to Lord Hugh Cecil, 14 Mar. 1912, J.C.P. 22/22.
39 Lord Hugh Cecil to Law, 16 July 1912, B.L.P. 26/5/29.
40 R. A. Yerburgh to Law, 6 Aug. 1912, B.L.P. 27/1/25.
41 J. S. Randles to Law, 10 Aug. 1912, B.L.P. 27/1/33.
42 Balcarres to Law, 5 Sept. 1912, R. Churchill, 163.
43 S. F. Firth to Law, 15 Apr. 1912, B.L.P. 26/2/28.
44 Lawrence to Law, 1 May 1912, B.L.P. 26/3/3.
45 Sir Austen Chamberlain, 366.
46 Lawrence to Maxse, 14 June 1912, M.P. 466.
47 T. W. A. Bagley to Law, 12 June 1912, B.L.P. 26/4/19.
48 (?) F. F. Lics to Austen Chamberlain, 20 July 1912, A.C.P. 10/3/3/
49 Lansdowne to Law, 10 Oct. 1912, B.L.P. 27/3/28.
50 Strachey to Law, 15 Nov. 1912, B.L.P. 27/4/33.
51 A. Cluttall to W. Boyd Carpenter, 11 Dec. 1912, B.L.P. 28/1/40.
52 Long to Law, 9 Dec. 1912, B.L.P. 28/1/11.
53 Lansdowne to Law, 15 Dec. 1912, B.L.P. 28/1/43.
54 Sandars to Short, 22 Dec. 1912, B.P. 49768, ff. 38–9.
55 Strachey to Law, 12 Dec. 1912, B.L.P. 28/1/26: 'all I want to do', Strachey wrote, 'is to help the Unionist party win ... My difficulty is that I am over-whelmed with evidence that the biggest crowd is not the anti-referendum crowd, but the pro-referendum crowd ... What I go by is the astonishing evidence of despair ... shown by Tariff Reformers ... I imagined that they and their newspapers would all be declaring that everything was now well and victory certain. Instead of that they seem as depressed as I am ... I am quite prepared to sacrifice not only my Free Trade views but also my views about Food Taxes in order that we may save the Union. What I do not want is that the making of that sacrifice may be the very thing which will lead to the de-struction of the Union.' Strachey took heart from the Ashton speech, seeing it, as Sandars did, as the end of the food duties. 'I early realised,' he wrote to Law, 'that what would embarrass you would be if I were to throw up my hat over the speech. I have therefore avoided that, though I felt bound to point out, that if in subdued terms, that the ultimate result of the policy set forth must be that Food Taxes will not be proposed by the Unionist party.' Strachey to Law, 19 Dec. 1912, B.L.P. 28/1/63.
56 F. E. Smith to Law, 19 Dec. 1912, R. Churchill, 164.
57 P. Wodehouse to Law, 19 Dec. 1912, B.L.P. 28/1/62.
58 Balcarres to Law, 5 Sept. 1912, R. Churchill, 163.
59 Derby to Law, 20 Dec. 1912, B.L.P. 28/1/65.
60 Derby to Law, 21 Dec. 1912, R. Churchill, 171–2.
61 Balcarres to Law, 26 Dec. 1912, B.L.P. 28/1/92.
62 P. Wodehouse to Law, 22 Dec. 1912, B.L.P. 28/1/75.
63 Copy, Law to Selborne, 20 Dec. 1912, B.L.P. 33/4/78.
64 E. L. Oliver to Derby, 18 Dec. 1912, R. Churchill, 168.
65 Derby to the King, 16 Nov. 1911, ibid. 155–6.

66 Derby to Balfour, 22 Dec. 1912, ibid. 172.
67 Law to Balcarres, 24 Dec. 1912, ibid. 174.
68 Law to Derby, 24 Dec. 1912, ibid. 173.
69 Law to Balcarres, 24 Dec. 1912, ibid. 174.
70 Derby to Long, 25 Dec. 1912, ibid. 176.
71 Copy, Law to J.P. Croal, 1 Jan. 1913, B.L.P. 33/5/1.
72 Balfour to Derby, 20 Dec. 1912, R. Churchill, 169–70.
73 Derby to Lord Hugh Cecil, 1 Jan. 1913, ibid. 179.
74 Balcarres to Law, n.d., ibid. 174. The letter in the Bonar Law Papers is dated 28 Dec. 1912, B.L.P. 28/1/98.
75 e.g. Strachey to Law, 12 Dec. 1912, B.L.P. 28/1/26; Lord Hugh Cecil to Derby, 20 Dec. 1912, R. Churchill, 165–6; Lord Robert Cecil to Law, 4 Jan. 1913, B.L.P. 28/2/19.
76 G. R. Lane Fox to Law, 11 Dec. 1912, B.L.P. 28/1/15; Mark Sykes to Law, 17 Dec. 1912, B.L.P. 28/1/48; Evelyn Cecil to Law, 4 Jan. 1913, B.L.P. 28/2/20.
77 Goulding to Law, 20 Dec. (1912), A.C.P. 10/3/33.
78 Ridley to Austen Chamberlain, 29 Dec. 1912, A.C.P. 10/3/48.
79 Lord Robert Cecil to Law, 4 Jan. 1913, B.L.P. 28/2/19.
80 W. Astor to Austen Chamberlain, 20 Dec. 1912, A.C.P. 10/3/6.
81 Law to Chaplin, 31 Dec. 1912, R. Blake, *The Unknown Prime Minister. The Life and Times of Andrew Bonar Law 1858–1923* (1955), 114–15.
82 Printed in Sir Austen Chamberlain, 510–13.
83 Sir Charles Petrie, *Austen Chamberlain*, i. 330–2.
84 Austen Chamberlain to Law, 24 Dec. 1912, Sir Austen Chamberlain, 495–7.
85 Ibid. 509.
86 Ridley to Austen Chamberlain, 3 Jan. 1913, A.C.P. 9/5/72; F. S. Oliver to Milner, 17 Dec. 1912, Milner Papers, Box 194.
87 Milner's Diary, 1 and 2 Jan. 1913, Milner Papers, Box 276.
88 Lawrence to Austen Chamberlain, 5 Jan. 1913, A.C.P. 9/5/49.
89 Jebb to Austen Chamberlain, 4 Jan. 1913, A.C.P. 9/5/42.
90 H. G. Williams to Law, 18 Dec. 1912, B.L.P. 28/1/60.
91 Garvin to Astor, 19 Dec. 1912, A. Gollin, *The Observer and J. L. Garvin*, 374.
92 Law's memorandum, 7 Jan. 1913, Sir Austen Chamberlain, 510–13.
93 Amery to Austen Chamberlain, 27 Dec. 1912, A.C.P. 10/3/1.
94 Amery to Austen Chamberlain, 5 Jan. 1913, A.C.P. 9/5/1.
95 Lawrence to Austen Chamberlain, 5 Jan. 1913, A.C.P. 9/5/49.
96 Lawrence to Austen Chamberlain, 8 Jan. 1913, A.C.P. 9/5/52.
97 G. A. Williamson to Lawrence, 6 Jan. (1913) (dated 1912), A.C.P. 9/5/54.
98 F. Leverton Harris to Austen Chamberlain, 6 Jan. (1913), A.C.P. 9/5/34.
99 Lawrence to Austen Chamberlain, 5 Jan. 1913, A.C.P. 9/5/49.
100 Chaplin to Austen Chamberlain, 16 Jan. 1913, Sir Austen Chamberlain, 516–17.
101 Ridley to Austen Chamberlain, 14 Feb. (1913), A.C.P. 9/5/74. Internal evidence indicates that this letter was written in January.
102 Sir Austen Chamberlain, 519–20.
103 A. Colefax to Austen Chamberlain, 14 Jan. 1913, A.C.P. 9/5/14.
104 Ridley to Austen Chamberlain, 21 Jan. 1913, A.C.P. 9/5/73.
105 Milner's Land Memorandum and the comments of various Unionist leaders are in Milner Papers, Boxes 101 and 104.
106 Lansdowne's comments on Milner's Land Memorandum, Milner Papers, Box 101.
107 *Rural World*, XXV, 795, July, 1913.
108 Prothero to Steel-Maitland, 4 Feb. 1913, Milner Papers, Box 104.
109 Selborne to Law, 10 Feb. 1913, B.L.P. 29/1/24.

110 Peto *et al.* to Long, 1 Aug. 1912, B.L.P. 27/1/17. The signatures to the letter and report are missing, but Petos' participation, and the nature of the proposals, which included not only import duties on both foreign and colonial wheat, but bounties on home grown wheat if the price fell below 35*s.* a quarter, suggests that the committee was composed largely of tariff reform radicals.

111 Report of the Committee on Unionist Agricultural Policy, 12 Aug. 1913, Milner Papers, Box 101. It was indicative of the difficulties the Unionist party faced in devising a land policy that it suffered from a superfluity of committees on the subject, both unofficial and official. 'We have', Lord Edmund Talbot told Milner in July 1913, 'two Unionist (private) Committees which consider questions on (1) agricultural land, (2) social reform . . . both know they overlap on questions such as housing, agricultural wages etc. They have eventually agreed that five members from each should form a committee to confer and report for the consideration of the leaders of the party on a line of Unionist policy on the land question.' Talbot to Milner, 15 July 1913, Milner Papers, Box 101.

112 Alexander Thynne to Talbot, 22 Aug. 1913, B.L.P. 30/1/13. Lansdowne, who was one of the landowners named, considered the idea impractical.

113 Copy, Law to Lansdowne, 2 Sept. 1913, B.L.P. 35/5/53.

114 Lansdowne to Law, 4 Sept. 1913, B.L.P. 30/2/7.

115 Pretyman to Law, 28 Oct. 1913, B.L.P. 30/3/64.

116 A Unionist Agricultural Policy: By a Group of Unionists, 1913.

117 Pretyman to Law, 29 Oct. 1913, B.L.P. 30/3/66.

118 Pretyman to Law, 28 Oct. 1913, B.L.P. 30/3/64.

119 W. Astor *et al.* to Law, 8 Nov. 1913, B.L.P. 30/4/12.

120 Hills to Law, 28 Nov. 1913, B.L.P. 30/4/40. See also, G. Terrell to Law, 2 Jan. 1914, B.L.P. 31/2/6.

121 e.g. James F. Hope to Steel-Maitland, 28 Nov. 1913, B.L.P. 30/4/40.

122 Salisbury to Law, 18 Feb. 1914, B.L.P. 31/3/33.

123 Long's Memorandum, 6 May 1914, B.L.P. 32/3/13.

124 Long to Law, 31 Oct. 1913, B.L.P. 30/3/77.

125 Long's Memorandum, 6 May 1914, B.L.P. 32/3/13. For Eve's hostility to the minimum wage see H. V. Emy, 'The Land Campaign', 60, and a report of a meeting between Law and a deputation from the Farmers' Union of Cornwall, B.L.P. 40/5/6.

126 H. W. Palmer to Law, 16 Jan. 1913, B.L.P. 28/2/66.

127 Chaplin to Law, 11 Jan. 1913, B.L.P. 28/2/52.

128 J. Foster Fraser to Law, 28 Mar. 1913, B.L.P. 29/2/44.

129 *M.N.T.R.* Oct. 1913; G. A. Bellwood to Law, 11 Nov. 1913, B.L.P. 30/4/24.

130 C. Turnor to Baird, 4 Sept. 1913, B.L.P. 30/2/23.

131 C. Turnor to Baird, 28 Sept. 1913, B.L.P. 30/2/32; Lansdowne to Law, 4 Oct. 1913, B.L.P. 30/3/4.

132 Hewins to Steel-Maitland, 17 Nov. 1913, Hewins Papers.

133 Steel-Maitland to Law, 28 Oct. 1913, B.L.P. 30/3/62.

134 C. Campbell and G. A. Bellwood to Law, 24 Oct. 1913, B.L.P. 30/3/51. Law also promised to take up the question of freight rates with the railway companies, and to assist the N.F.U. in contesting an agricultural constituency, and reiterated existing Unionist policy that tenants should be able to purchase their holdings on the breaking up of an estate. G. A. Bellwood to Law, 11 Nov. 1913, B.L.P. 30/4/24. More controversially, Law also promised to impose duties on flour, hops, and possibly barley. Law had always considered hops a special case, but the promises with regard to flour and barley, which Bellwood under-

stood him to make, represented a considerable shift in his position in his attempts to placate the farmers. In November he took Page Croft to task for suggesting that 'food' in the Edinburgh policy referred only to wheat and meat and that the party still proposed a duty on flour and 'non-essential foodstuffs such as barley, oats and hops.' Croft to Law, 8 Nov. 1913, B.L.P. 30/4/17; Law to Croft, 10 Nov. 1913, Croft Papers, BO/4; Croft to Law, 11 Nov. 1913, B.L.P. 30/4/24. Law saw another deputation from the N.F.U. on 6 Feb. 1914, which revealed that Unionist policy, as it stood, went a long way towards meeting the farmers' demands on security and rating relief. Boraston to Law, 9 Feb. 1914, enclosing a transcript of the interview of 6 Feb. B.L.P. 31/3/32.

135 C. Turnor to Baird, 4 Sept. 1913, B.L.P. 30/2/23; A. Colefax to Law, 15 Jan. 1913, B.L.P. 28/2/62.

136 Hewins to Steel-Maitland, 17 Nov. 1913, Hewins Papers.

137 Sir Austen Chamberlain, 300.

138 Copy, Law to T. A. Kell, 17 Mar. 1914, B.L.P. 34/2/42.

139 In his Land Memorandum Milner proposed that 'the state should put a bounty on agricultural produce . . . A bounty would, without raising prices, put the agricultural employer into the same position as if they had been raised, and so enable him to pay better wages.' But despite the numerous times bounties were proposed, e.g. by Long's unofficial committee, by Bathurst, they were apparently never considered as the basis of a Unionist land policy because they would incur, even more than the promise of rating relief, the accusation of doles to landowners. Milner also suggested profit-sharing.

140 Copy, Law to T. A. Kell, 17 Mar. 1914, B.L.P. 34/2/42.

141 Sir Austen Chamberlain, 527.

142 Duncannon to Law, 5 Nov. 1913, B.L.P. 30/4/7; H. Pike Pease to Law, 12 Nov. 1913, B.L.P. 30/4/29; Duncannon to Law, 11 and 18 Nov. 1913, B.L.P. 30/4/25 and 43; Copy, Law to Austen Chamberlain, 2 Dec. 1913, B.L.P. 33/6/104.

143 Chaplin to Law, 30 Jan. 1914, B.L.P. 31/2/72; James F. Hope to Steel-Maitland, 28 Nov. 1913, B.L.P. 30/4/40.

144 Milner to F. S. Oliver, 23 Oct. 1913, Milner Papers, Box 211.

CHAPTER 13. RADICAL UNIONISM

1 Balcarres, Political Notes, 3 Jan. 1913, Balcarres Papers.

2 Jebb to Austen Chamberlain, 4 Jan. 1913, A.C.P. 9/5/42.

3 Austen Chamberlain to Steel-Maitland, 3 July 1913, Steel-Maitland Papers, G.D. 193/152/2.

4 See Neal Blewett, 'Free Fooders, Balfourites, Wholehoggers. Factionalism within the Unionist Party, 1906–1910', *Historical Journal*, xi. 1 (1968), 97–8.

5 Copy, Steel-Maitland to A. Glazebrook, 24 Dec. 1913, Steel-Maitland Papers, G.D. 193/159/6.

6 M.N.T.R. 20, 2 Feb. 1914, 79.

7 Ibid. 19, 6 Dec. 1913, 336–7.

8 W. Astor to Law, 8 Nov. 1913, B.L.P. 30/4/12. See also, Milner to Law, 24 Oct. 1913, B.L.P. 30/3/50.

9 Rowland Hunt to Law, 2 Jan. 1914, B.L.P. 31/2/8.

10 Selborne to Law, 19 Dec. 1912, B.L.P. 28/1/64.

11 Amery to Maxse, 10 Jan. 1913, M.P. 468. See also Astor to Maxse, 15 Mar. 1913, F. S. Oliver to Maxse, 30 Dec. 1913, Willoughby de Broke to Maxse, 11 Jan. 1913, M.P. 468.

12 Willoughby de Broke to Law, 19 Nov. 1912, B.L.P. 27/4/44.
13 Willoughby de Broke to Maxse, 24 Apr. (1911?), M.P. 464. He thought this doctrine 'went down like hot cakes' at Jarrow.
14 Selborne to Law, 19 Dec. 1912, B.L.P. 28/1/64. See also, J. F. Hope to Steel-Maitland, 1 Jan. 1914, B.L.P. 31/2/3.
15 For a discussion of the traditions of Tory Democracy and Liberal Toryism in the nineteenth century, see Paul Smith, *Disraelian Conservatism and Social Reform* (1967).
16 Copy, Maxse to Tryon, n.d., M.P. 469.
17 Wyndham to W. S. Blunt, 12 Sept. 1912, J. W. Mackail and Guy Wyndham, *Life and Letters of George Wyndham*, ii. 729.
18 Wyndham to his mother, 19 Jan. 1913, ibid. 732.
19 Wyndham to Hilaire Belloc, 29 Jan. 1912, ibid. 717: 'I found that working-men in Lancashire, weavers, spinners and a miner (one) quite understand that Rural England must be restored.'
20 Winterton to Maxse, 20 July 1911, M.P. 463.
21 Amery to Law, 18 Jan. 1913, B.L.P. 28/2/30.
22 Milner's Land Memorandum, Milner Papers, Box. 101.
23 M.N.T.R. 17, 3 Sept. 1912, 155.
24 Copy, Law to Selborne, 20 Dec. 1912, B.L.P. 33/4/78.
25 Lord Hugh Cecil to Balfour, 4 May 1907, N. Blewett, 'Free Fooders, Balfourites, Wholehoggers', 95.
26 G. R. Lane Fox to Maxse, 30 Oct. 1912, M.P. 467.
27 Copy, Jebb to Croft, 1 Nov. 1912, Jebb Papers.
28 Copy, Jebb to Ware, 30 July 1912, Jebb Papers.

Selected Bibliography

A. MANUSCRIPT COLLECTIONS

Birmingham University Library
   Sir Austen Chamberlain Papers
   Joseph Chamberlain Papers
   Letters Additional (for W. Allard)

Bodleian Library
   Asquith Papers
   Milner Papers
   Monkbretton Papers
   J. S. Sandars Papers
   Selborne Papers

British Library
   Avebury Papers
   Balfour Papers
   Campbell-Bannerman Papers
   Lord Robert Cecil Papers
   Viscount Gladstone Papers
   Ritchie Papers
   Ripon Papers
   J. A. Spender Papers

Cambridge University Library
   Crewe Papers

Churchill College, Cambridge
   Chandos Papers
   Croft Papers
   McKenna Papers

Guildford Muniments Room
   Onslow Papers

House of Lords Record Office
   R. D. Blumenfeld Papers

Bonar Law Papers
Lee Papers
Lloyd George Papers
Strachey Papers
Wargrave Papers

Institute of Commonwealth Studies
Richard Jebb Papers

National Library of Scotland
Elibank Papers
Elliot Papers
Haldane Papers
Rosebery Papers

Newcastle University Library
Runciman Papers

Public Record Office
Cromer Papers (typed transcript)

Scottish Record Office
A. J. Balfour Papers
Gerald Balfour Papers
Balfour of Burleigh Papers
Novar Papers
Steel-Maitland Papers

Sheffield University Library
Hewins Papers

Strathclyde Regional Archives
J. Parker Smith Papers

West Sussex County Record Office
Maxse Papers

The late Earl of Crawford kindly allowed me to consult the papers of
Lord Balcarres for parts of this study.

B. NEWSPAPERS AND PERIODICALS
Constitutional Year Book
Contemporary Review
Daily Telegraph

Fortnightly Review
Liberal Magazine
Monthly Notes on Tariff Reform
Morning Post
National Review
National Union Gleanings
Outlook
Rural World
Spectator
Standard
Tariff Reform League: Leaflets; Handbook for Speakers
The Times
Parliamentary Debates

C. BIOGRAPHIES, MEMOIRS, ETC.

(Arranged by subject. Place of publication, London, except where indicated.)

Amery, L. S., *My Political Life. Vol. 1. England Before the Storm 1896–1914*
    (1953)

Asquith, H. H.
Jenkins, Roy, *Asquith* (1964)
Spender, J. A. and Asquith, Cyril, *The Life of Henry Herbert Asquith, Lord
    Oxford and Asquith,* 2v. (1932)
Koss, S., *Asquith* (1976)

Balfour, A. J.
Dugdale, B. E. C., *Arthur James Balfour, First Earl of Balfour,* 2v. (1936)
Young, Kenneth, *Arthur James Balfour* (1963)
Zebel, S. H., *Arthur James Balfour* (1973)

Balfour of Burleigh
Balfour, Lady Frances, *A Memoir of Lord Balfour of Burleigh* (1925)

Campbell-Bannerman, Sir Henry
Spender, J. A., *The Life of the Rt. Hon. Sir Henry Campbell-Bannerman,* 2v.
    (1923)
Wilson, J., *The Life of Campbell-Bannerman* (1972)

Lord Robert Cecil
Chelwood, Viscount Cecil of, *All The Way* (1949)

Chamberlain, Sir Austen
Chamberlain, Sir Austen, *Politics from Inside* (1936)
Petrie, Sir Charles, *The Life and Letters of Sir Austen Chamberlain,* 2v. (1939)

Chamberlain, Joseph
Garvin, J. L. and Amery, Julian, *The Life of Joseph Chamberlain*, 6v. (1935–69)
Boyd, C. W. (ed.), *Mr. Chamberlain's Speeches*, 2v. (1914)
Fraser, P., *Joseph Chamberlain. Radicalism and Empire, 1868–1914* (1966)
Gulley, E. E., *Joseph Chamberlain and English Social Politics* (New York, 1926)

Chilston, Viscount
Chilston, Viscount, *Chief Whip. The Political Life and Times of Aretas Akers-Douglas, Viscount Chilston* (1961)

Churchill, Lord Randolph
Churchill, W. S., *Lord Randolph Churchill*, 2v. (1906)
James, R. R., *Lord Randolph Churchill* (1959)

Churchill, Sir Winston
Churchill, Randolph S., *Winston S. Churchill. 1874–1965. Vol. 2. Young Statesman* (1967)
James, R. R., *Churchill, A Study in Failure. 1900–1939* (1970)
Pelling, H., *Winston Churchill* (1974)

Clarke, Sir Edward, *The Story of My Life* (1918)

Collings, Jesse
Collings, J. and Green, J. L., *The Life of the Rt. Hon. Jesse Collings* (1920)

Croft, Henry Page, *My Life of Strife* (1949)

Cromer, Earl of
Zetland, Marquess of, *Lord Cromer* (1932)

Derby, Earl of
Churchill, Randolph S., *Lord Derby, 'King of Lancashire'* (1959)

Devonshire, Duke of
Holland, Bernard, *The Life of Spencer Compton, Eighth Duke of Devonshire*, 2v. (1911)

Esher, Viscount
Brett, M. V. and Esher, Viscount (eds.), *The Journals and Letters of Reginald, Viscount Esher*, 4v. (1934–8)

Fitzroy, Sir Almeric, *Memoirs*, 2v. (1923)

Garvin, J. L.
Gollin, A. M., *The Observer and J. L. Garvin. 1908–14* (1960)

Gladstone, Herbert
Mallet, C., *Herbert Gladstone. A Memoir* (1932)
Gladstone, Viscount, *After Thirty Years* (1929)

Goschen, Viscount
Elliot, A. R. D., *The Life of G. J. Goschen, First Viscount Goschen. 1831–1907*, 2v. (1911)

Spinner, T. J. Jnr., *George Joachim Goschen. The Transformation of a Victorian Liberal* (1973)

Grey, Sir Edward
Trevelyan, G. M., *Grey of Fallodon* (1937)
Robbins, Keith, *Sir Edward Grey. A biography of Lord Grey of Fallodon* (1971)

Griffiths-Boscawen, A. S. T., *Fourteen Years in Parliament* (1907)

Haldane, Viscount
Maurice, Sir Frederick, *Haldane, 1865–1928*, 2v. (1937)
Sommer, D., *Haldane of Cloan* (1960)
Koss, S., *Lord Haldane. Scapegoat for Liberalism* (1969)

Hamilton, Lord George, *Parliamentary Reminiscences and Reflections*, 2v. (1916, 1922)

Harcourt, Sir W. V.
Gardiner, A. G., *The Life of Sir William Harcourt*, 2v. (1923)

James of Hereford, Lord
Askwith, Lord, *Lord James of Hereford* (1930)

Hewins, W. A. S., *The Apologia of an Imperialist*, 2v. (1929)

Hicks Beach, Sir Michael
Hicks Beach, Lady Victoria, *The Life of Sir Michael Hicks Beach*, 2v. (1932)

Lansdowne, Marquess of
Newton, Lord, *Lord Lansdowne, A Biography* (1929)

Law, Andrew Bonar
Blake, R., *The Unknown Prime Minister. The Life and Times of Andrew Bonar Law 1858–1923* (1955)

Long, Walter
Petrie, Sir Charles, *Walter Long and His Times* (1936)

Milner, Viscount
Gollin, A. M., *Proconsul in Politics. A Study of Lord Milner in Opposition and in Power* (1966)

Morley, Viscount
Hamer, D. A., *John Morley. Liberal Intellectual in Politics* (1968)

Northcliffe
Pound, Reginald, and Harmsworth, Geoffrey, *Northcliffe* (1959)

Ripon, Marquess of
Wolf, L., *The Life of the First Marquess of Ripon*, 2v. (1921)

Rosebery, Marquess of
Crewe, Marquess of, *Lord Rosebery*, 2v. (1931)
James, R. R., *Rosebery* (1963)

Salisbury, Third Marquess of
Cecil, Lady Gwendolyn, *The Life of Robert, Third Marquess of Salisbury*, 4v.
   1931–)
Taylor, Robert, *Lord Salisbury* (1975)

Smith, F. E.
Birkenhead, Earl of, *F. E. The Life of F. E. Smith, First Earl of Birkenhead*
   (1960)

Smith, W. H.
Chilston, Viscount, *W. H. Smith* (1965)

Sykes, Sir Mark
Leslie, Shane, *Sir Mark Sykes. His Life and Letters* (1923)

Willoughby de Broke, Baron, *The Passing Years* (1924)
Winterton, Earl, *Pre-War* (1932)
——, *Orders of the Day* (1953)

Wyndham, George
Mackail, J. W., and Wyndham, Guy, *The Life and Letters of George Wyndham*,
   2v.
Wyndham, Guy (ed.), *The Letters of George Wyndham*, 2v. (1915)

D. OTHER PRINTED BOOKS

Amery, L. S., *The Fundamental Fallacies of Free Trade* (1906)
Balfour, A. J., *Economic Notes on Insular Free Trade* (1903)
Blake, R., *The Conservative Party from Peel to Churchill* (1972)
Blewett, Neal, *The Peers, the Parties and the People. The General Elections of 1910*
   (1972)
Brown, B. H., *The Tariff Reform Movement in Great Britain 1881–98* (Columbia,
   1943)
Brown, K. D. (ed.), *Essays in Anti-Labour History* (1974)
Cecil, Lord Hugh, *Conservatism* (1912)
Chamberlain, J., *Imperial Union and Tariff Reform. Speeches delivered from May
   15th to November 4th, 1903 by the Rt. Hon. Joseph Chamberlain, M.P.* (1903)
Clarke, P. F., *Lancashire and the New Liberalism* (1971)
Craton, Michael, and McCready, H. W., *The Great Liberal Revival 1903–6*
   (1966)
Croft, Henry Page, *The Path of Empire* (1912)
Emy, H. V., *Liberals, Radicals and Social Politics. 1892–1914* (1973)
Garvin, J. L., *Tariff or Budget* (1910)
Gilbert, B. B., *The Evolution of National Insurance in Britain* (1966)
Goldie, M. H. G., *Trade and the National Ideal* (1911)
Group of Unionists, A, *A Unionist Agricultural Policy* (1913)
Hamer, D. A., *Liberal Politics in the Age of Gladstone and Rosebery* (1972)

Hynes, S., *The Edwardian Turn of Mind* (1968)

Jenkins, Roy, *Mr. Balfour's Poodle* (1954)

Judd, D., *Balfour and the British Empire* (1968)

Langer, W., *The Diplomacy of Imperialism* (2nd edn., New York, 1960)

Lawrence, Elwood P., *Henry George in the British Isles* (Michigan, 1957)

Lyons, F. S. L., *The Irish Parliamentary Party 1890–1910* (1951)

McBriar, A. M., *Fabian Socialism and English Politics 1884–1918* (1962)

Malmesbury, Earl of (ed.), *The New Order. Studies in Unionist Policy* (1908)

Matthew, H. C. G., *The Liberal Imperialists. The Ideas and Politics of a post-Gladstonian Elite* (1973)

Matthews, A. H., *Fifty Years of Agricultural Politics, being the History of the Central Chambers of Agriculture* (1915)

Milner, Viscount, *The Nation and the Empire* (1913)

Nowell-Smith, S. (ed.), *Edwardian England. 1901–14* (1964)

Peel, Hon. George, *The Tariff Reformers* (1913)

Pelling, H., *The Origins of the Labour Party* (1965)

——, *Popular Politics and Society in Late Victorian Britain* (1968)

——, *Social Geography of British Elections* (1967)

Porter, B., *Critics of Empire* (1968)

Rempel, R. A., *Unionists Divided. Arthur Balfour, Joseph Chamberlain and the Unionist Free Traders* (Newton Abbot, 1972)

Rowland, Peter, *The Last Liberal Governments*, 2v. (1968, 1972)

Russell, A. K., *Liberal Landslide. The General Election of 1906* (Newton Abbot, 1973)

Scally, R. J., *The Origins of the Lloyd George Coalition* (Princeton, 1975)

Searle, G. R., *The Quest for National Efficiency* (Oxford, 1971)

Semmel, B., *Imperialism and Social Reform. English Social and Imperial Thought 1895–1914* (1960)

Smith, P., *Disraelian Conservatism and Social Reform* (1967)

Southgate, D., *The Passing of the Whigs 1832–86* (1962)

Stansky, P., *Ambitions and Strategies. The Struggle for the Leadership of the Liberal Party in the 1890s* (1964)

Strachey, J. St. Loe, *The Manufacture of Paupers* (1907)

——, *The Problems and Perils of Socialism* (1908)

Taylor, A. J. P. (ed.), *Lloyd George. Twelve Essays* (1971)

Thornton, A. P., *The Imperial Idea and its Enemies* (1959)

Tyler, J. E., *The Stuggle for Imperial Unity 1868–1895* (1938)

Wyndham, G., *The Development of the State* (1904)

E. ARTICLES

Blewett, Neal, 'Free Fooders, Balfourites, Wholehoggers. Factionalism within the Unionist Party, 1906–10' *Historical Journal*, xi, 1 (1968), 95–124

Boyle, T., 'The Formation of Campbell-Bannerman's Government in December 1905. A Memorandum by J. A. Spender', *Bulletin of the Institute of Historical Research*, xlv, 112 (1972), 283–302

Bristow, E., 'The Liberty and Property Defence League and Individualism', *Historical Journal*, xviii, 4 (1975) 761–89

Brown, K. D., 'The Trade Union Tariff Reform Association' *Journal of British Studies*, ix, 2 (1970), 141–53

——, 'The Labour Party and the Unemployment Question, 1906–10', *Historical Journal*, xiv, 3 (1971), 599–616

Clarke, P. F., 'British Politics and Blackburn Politics, 1900–1910', *Historical Journal*, xii, 2 (1969), 302–27

——, 'Electoral Sociology of Modern Britain', *History*, 57, 189 (1972), 31–55

Collins, D., 'The Introduction of Old Age Pensions into Great Britain', *Historical Journal*, viii, 2 (1965), 246–59

Cornford, J., 'The Transformation of Conservatism in the late Nineteenth Century', *Victorian Studies*, vii (1963), 35–66

Fanning, Ronan, 'The Unionist Party and Ireland', *Irish Historical Studies*, xv, 57 (1966–7), 147–71

Fraser, Peter, 'The Liberal Unionist Alliance. Chamberlain, Hartington and the Conservatives 1886–1904', *English Historical Review*, 77 (1962), 53–78

——, 'Unionism and Tariff Reform. The Crisis of 1906', *Historical Journal*, v, 2 (1962), 149–66

——, 'The Unionist debacle of 1911 and Balfour's Retirement', *Journal of Modern History*, xxxv, 4 (1963), 354–65

Hamer, D. A., 'The Irish Question and Liberal Politics 1886–94', *Historical Journal*, xii, 3 (1969), 511–32

Jacobson, P. D., 'Rosebery and Liberal Imperialism 1899–1903', *Journal of British Studies*, xiii, i (1973), 83–107

Jones, R. B., 'Balfour's Reform of Party Organisation', *Bulletin of the Institute of Historical Research*, xxxviii, 97 (1965), 94–101

McCready, H. W., 'Home Rule and the Liberal Party 1899–1906', *Irish Historical Studies*, xiii, 51 (1962–3), 316–48

——, 'The Revolt of the Unionist Free Traders', *Parliamentary Affairs*, 16 (1963), 188–206

Rempel, R. A., 'The Abortive Negotiations for a Free Trade Coalition to defeat Tariff Reform. October 1903 to February 1904,' *Proceedings of the South Carolina Historical Association* (1966), 5–17

——, 'Tariff Reform and the Resurgence of the Liberal Party. May 1903 to February 1904', *Proceedings of the Canadian Historical Association* (1967), 156–66

——, 'Lord Hugh Cecil's Parliamentary Career, 1900–1914. Promise Unfulfilled', *Journal of British Studies*, xi, 2 (1972), 104–30

Sykes, A., 'The Confederacy and the Purge of the Unionist Free Traders 1906–1910', *Historical Journal*, xviii, 2 (1975), 349–66

Weston, C. C., 'The Liberal Leadership and the Lords Veto 1907–1910', *Historical Journal*, xi, 3 (1968), 508–37

Zebel, S. H., 'Joseph Chamberlain and the Genesis of Tariff Reform', *Journal of British Studies*, vii, i (1967), 131–57

Index